BRITISH POPULAR FILMS 1929–1939

In a field generally neglected by film scholarship, *British Popular Films 1929–1939* makes a valuable contribution to the social and British film history of the period. Stephen Shafer's study of the role of cinema in 1930s British society uses research on the early cinema to offer original answers to questions such as why the British public was not more critical and disruptive during the economic hardship and unemployment of the Great Depression.

Shafer's study challenges the conventional historical assumption that British feature films during the thirties were mostly orientated toward the middle classes. Instead, he makes the critical distinction between films intended for West-End and international circulation and those intended primarily for domestic, working-class audiences. Far from being alienated by a "middle-class institution," working men and women flocked to see pictures featuring music-hall luminaries such as Gracie Fields and George Formby.

This contention is supported by an impressive amount of new research into unexplored source material, from statistics of working-class cinema-going to letters in fan magazines. From these fascinating letters, cinema itself emerges as the only solace that made life bearable during the Depression (it was listed by one Leeds shop girl, along with food and shelter, as one of the necessities of life). Significantly, escapist films such as *High Society*, *Pygmalion*, and *The Lambeth Walk* were box-office hits in the impoverished industrial north.

Shafer's detailed analysis of individual films helps to build up our understanding of contemporary attitudes, perceptions, and values, and offers a partial answer to why British society survived the strain of the slump and Depression.

A major study of British cinema during the thirties, *British Popular Films* will also prove indispensable for historians of modern Britain and all those concerned with popular culture.

Stephen C. Shafer has created and taught courses in film and history at the University of Illinois over the past twenty years. He currently serves as Assistant Dean in the University's College of Liberal Arts and Sciences. He is a member of the British Film Institute, the American Historical Association, the Society for Cinema Studies, and the Popular Culture Association.

STUDIES IN FILM, TELEVISION AND THE MEDIA

General Editor: Dr Anthony Aldgate
The Open University

THE AMERICANIZATION OF GERMANY, 1945–1949
Ralph Willett

FILM AND POLITICS IN AMERICA: A SOCIAL TRADITION
Brian Neve

EUROPEAN CINEMAS, EUROPEAN SOCIETIES, 1939–1990
Pierre Sorlin

BRITISH POPULAR FILMS 1929–1939

The cinema of reassurance

Stephen C. Shafer

London and New York

For Sue and Karen and Mom and Dad

First published 1997
by Routledge
2 Park Square, Milton Park, Abingdon, Oxon, OX14 4RN

Simultaneously published in the USA and Canada
by Routledge
270 Madison Ave, New York NY 10016

Transferred to Digital Printing 2007

Typeset in Times by
RefineCatch Limited, Bungay, Suffolk

Brtitish Library Cataloguing in Publication Data
A catalogue record for this book is available from the British Library

Library of Congress Cataloging in Publication Data
A catalogue record for this book has been requested

ISBN 0–415–00282–6

Publisher's Note
The publisher has gone to great lengths to ensure the quality
of this reprint but points out that some imperfections in the
original may be apparent

CONTENTS

ACKNOWLEDGMENTS

This book is a product of a longstanding interest in the history of motion pictures and specifically in the relationship between film and the history of this century. My college and graduate work centered on an interdisciplinary approach to history; during my graduate studies in modern British history, my focus began to shift to a growing fascination with the products of the British film industry, which seemed to me remarkably unappreciated both critically and academically, as a possible resource in examining the country's social history. The result was a doctoral dissertation some years ago from which this work has evolved with the benefit of years of additional research and of teaching film and history.

In the preparation of this study, I have had the assistance and support of a substantial number of individuals who have provided me with suggestions and encouragement. First and foremost, I am especially grateful to Professor Walter Arnstein of the University of Illinois whose calm, reasoned, and sensible advice enabled me to initiate my study in the first place and who has been a source of continuing inspiration both professionally as a scholar and teacher and personally as a friend. The earliest drafts of this material additionally had the benefit of the observations and comments of Professors John Frayne, Caroline Hibbard, and J. Alden Nichols, all of the University of Illinois. I also cherish many lengthy conversations on film and British history early in my work with Professor Randall McGowen of the University of Oregon, with Professor Jim Huston of Oklahoma State University, and with Dr Esther Simon Shkolnik. In particular, I want to thank Mr Gary Steller of Burlington College who read an early version of this work and provided me with excellent stylistic suggestions. Also, a portion of this material was presented to the Midwest Conference on British Studies and to the British History Association of the University of Illinois, and I am grateful for the comments and suggestions I received at that time.

Although my primary duties at the University of Illinois center on my responsibilities as an Assistant Dean in the College of Liberal Arts and Sciences, for over twenty years I periodically have taught courses in the History Department here, and I am grateful for the encouragement I have received from many individuals in the department who have been supportive. In particular, I wish to express my gratitude to my friend and colleague, Professor John Dahl, now retired from the University of Illinois with whom I first began teaching Film and History in the 1970s. In recent years, I have had the benefit of the insights and encouragement from my teaching colleague, Professor Fred Jaher, also of the University of Illinois. In addition, I value and appreciate my association with the excellent faculty members of the university's Unit for Cinema Studies; I especially wish to express my thanks to the Assistant Director of the Unit, Dr Richard Leskosky, whose expertise and friendship I have enjoyed for years. I also want to thank Associate Dean Robert Copeland of the College of Liberal Arts and Sciences who has been supportive of my completion of this project. I also am grateful to the many students I have encountered in the classes I have taught over the past twenty years; they have proven to be a continuing source of inspiration to me, and I have delighted in the insights and enthusiasm I have derived from them.

I also would like to thank the staff of the British Film Institute's Library in London which provided continuous assistance in finding the treasures in their outstanding collections during the two summers of research I spent in London some years ago. The staff of the University of Illinois Library also has provided invaluable help in enabling me to make use of the outstanding collection of film materials that have been assembled in Urbana. Since British films from this period are so difficult to find and screen, particularly in the Midwest of the United States, I have depended heavily on the resources in these libraries to locate information about the making of the films themselves and about their plots, in periodicals, screenplays, and other sources. The assistance I have received in tracking down many hard-to-find materials, and in the case of the University of Illinois Library, in acquiring some very obscure items, has been invaluable. I also want to extend my appreciation to Ms Sandy Fitzgerald who has done an excellent job in typing the various manuscript revisions of this book and in transferring the text into disk form.

A special note of appreciation must be expressed to three individuals without whose help this project never would have been realized. I owe an immense debt of gratitude to Professor Tony Aldgate who first noticed this study in its earlier form as a doctoral dissertation and who subsequently suggested that it be revised for publication. I have long admired Professor Aldgate's work, and I was honored by the fact that he regarded my efforts as worthy not only of his attention but also of revision for publication. His suggestions and advice were especially helpful at a late stage in the preparation of this manuscript. Likewise, I wish to thank Ms Rebecca Barden of Routledge for her continuing interest in seeing this project through to publication in spite of the fact that completion was delayed on a variety of occasions. In the course of the years since I began work on this book I have experienced numerous setbacks caused by an almost incredible string of misfortunes and personal grief, from a devastating flood which resulted in the loss of some research materials, to the deaths of both of my parents. Ms Barden's patience and encouragement enabled me to complete this project at a point when it otherwise might have been abandoned. I also wish to thank Katherine Hodkinson for all her help in the editing stage of this project.

Over the years, I have been blessed with the insights I have gained from a number of very dear friends who have enriched me not only with their interest in my work but also with their encouragement. In that regard I want to thank Keith Peterson, Barry Birnbaum, and, especially, Richard Harris of the Chicago *Sun Times*, with whom I have exchanged a number of ideas and comments about my research in the course of our friendship. John Jackanicz, whose knowledge of film and social history is exceptional, read an earlier version of this study and has offered helpful comments and suggestions over the years; he also alerted me to rare film showings from this period in the Chicago metropolitan area and kindly tolerated my presence as an extended houseguest when the Chicago Film Festival ran a series of British musicals from the thirties a number of years ago. I also want to thank my friend, Larry Goldenberg, whose judgments about films are invariably on target and whose knowledge of the film industry is encyclopedic, for his insight about motion picture history and for his supportive comments over the many years of our friendship; Mr Goldenberg also kept me informed on important related film events in and around Chicago.

I also want to express special thanks to three individuals who have been especially helpful to me. Jeff Moll provided an inestimable degree of help in the early stages of this project with his assistance on the statistical aspect of this study. Aside from introducing me to the joys of word processing, my loyal friend George M. Kwain read through an earlier version of this study and made several worthwhile suggestions; he also helped me locate several obscure films, and with his wonderful sense of humor, helped me retain my perspective at various difficult moments. Also Donald Jackanicz of the United States National Archives has made numerous helpful and supportive suggestions to me about my research over the many years of our friendship; on a number of occasions, Don has taken time out of busy trips to places like London, New York, or Los Angeles to track down in obscure bookshops volumes and research materials I have needed.

Finally, I would like to express my appreciation to my late grandparents, Matthew and Eleanor Koch, and to my late parents, Edison H. and Shirley Shafer, for their continual support for my scholarly efforts. In particular, I want to recognize the importance of my parents' contribution. Although they did not live to see this book published, they had a great deal to do with the fact that it came to be written in the first place; because of their careers in music and show business, I developed an early and continuing fascination with the entertainment industry and its relationship to modern life, and accordingly their spirit lives on in every single page of this book. I also cannot express deeply enough my gratitude to my wonderful wife Sue, who typed the very first version of this work, and to my daughter Karen for the sacrifices they both endured in making this book a reality. No one could have better encouragement and support than I have had from my wife and daughter, and I am eternally grateful to them. In concluding, I also would like to thank three wonderful British performers whose work I came to love and admire – Miss Jessie Matthews, Mr Jack Buchanan, and Miss Gracie Fields – for making my exploration of British films such an enjoyable and delightful research project. Of course, I am responsible for any and all errors.

Dr Stephen C. Shafer
June, 1996

1

INTRODUCTION

For the historian, the examination of films has provided a useful means of exploring the taste and values of different periods of the twentieth century. Numerous studies have assessed the relationships of the various national film industries to the societies in which they operated. Among the most interesting of these works are several that have dealt with American society during the ordeal of the Great Depression in the 1930s; for instance, Andrew Bergman's *We're in the Money* utilized effectively the content of the films themselves to show certain preoccupations in Hollywood's response to the economic crisis in the United States. Other studies have examined the response of the film industries in other nations to the Great Depression, particularly in France, Germany, and Italy.[1]

But, amazingly, while attention in film scholarship has been focused on this general issue, one of the most significant of the national film industries until recently has been uniformly neglected. In fact, the British film industry in the 1930s, at the time one of the largest in the world, has been mostly forgotten. The common perception of the contribution of Britain to world cinema is that it helped pioneer the documentary film, and less significantly, that it provided a genuine, if only temporary, challenge to Hollywood in the period after the Second World War. The usual conclusion about British movies of the 1930s, however, is that they are not really worth studying, and if discussed at all, they usually are dismissed aesthetically with a contemptuous reference to the "quota quickies" and with adjectives like "amateurish" and "stodgy." Another conclusion frequently reached about British films during the thirties is that they were "stage-bound" and, accordingly, not popular with the working class. For instance, George Perry, in his survey of British film, referred to the "glut of stage adaptations" and the plotlines reflecting the "*mores* of the country drawing room" that predominated during this period; citing the "stilted delivery," the "cinematic inexperience," and the "cultured West End accent" of screen actors as an annoyance to popular audiences, Perry asserted that good British cinema had evolved into a middle-class institution at a time of "misery, poverty, and unemployment for the working classes," and he

1

determined that "most British films failed absolutely to sense the mood of the audience."[2]

This conclusion, hastily arrived at, commonly shared and repeated, from survey to survey, is contrary to fact. An exploration of the films themselves shows a remarkable diversity and range; in many cases, neglected or forgotten features from this period hold up incredibly well and demonstrate a quality that utterly surprises one, after reading the usually disparaging comments in most general surveys. Undoubtedly this poor reputation was a product of a general impression of the low-budget movies made to satisfy provisions of the "Quota Act." The quota was a product of the Cinematograph Films Act passed by Parliament in 1927 which established the percentage of British films that an exhibitor was required to rent in any one year. Because of block booking, in which exhibitors were required to show a package of films sight unseen, a condition demanded by American distributors, the British film industry had slumped alarmingly by the mid 1920s. Discussions had continued since the war years on ways to deal with the problem of facilitating British production. After extended debate, Parliament approved a requirement that beginning in 1928, a quota of British films, initially only 5 percent of the features shown, but rising by statute to 20 percent by 1935, had to be exhibited. All films would have to be registered with the Board of Trade, and a time limit for booking was imposed. Although the result was to generate new films and new companies, an unfortunate by-product was the emergence of cheaply made "quota quickies" which could then be booked inexpensively to meet the requirement. American distributors then acquired these often poorly crafted British features for release in the UK in order to meet the government's quota requirement and legally circulate Hollywood films; other companies met the requirement by setting up their own production facilities and releasing their own low budget offerings. In this manner, the letter of the law could be met.

Although some of these low-budget films – like many "Poverty Row" productions in Hollywood that were sometimes shot in as little as four to seven days – were undeniably of poor quality because of the inexperience of many of the people involved, others proved surprisingly worthwhile and even good. The rapid expansion and the looser standards of the companies that supplied quota films gave many prominent movie figures their start in the industry. Unfortunately, the reputation of the poorer movies made under this system caused the general term "quota film" to become, unfairly, synonymous with the term "bad film"; as Charles Davy noted in 1937, this arrangement "helped Hollywood further by serving as a usefully bad advertisement for British production."[3]

When the Cinematograph Act was renewed after the first ten years, following recommendations by a Parliamentary investigative committee under the direction of Lord Moyne, revisions were made to discourage the "quota quickies"; specifically, a minimum budget was required for a film to qualify, and the percentage of required films was dropped temporarily to twelve and a half percent for renters and fifteen percent for exhibitors, later to rise to thirty and twenty-five percent respectively. As a result, in the late thirties, MGM and other Hollywood units began to make higher quality films in England. But the basic conclusion that "quota films" were all necessarily bad or that all British films were somehow tainted by the quota structure is fundamentally wrong.[4]

Similarly, the conclusion that all British films were "stage-bound" drawing-room dramas is also fallacious; while it was true that in the first years of the sound era producers searching around desperately for properties naturally relied on stage vehicles, the great majority of films were created from original stories or were based on novels and stories already published. As the decade went on the reliance on plays was substantially reduced so that by the last three years of the decade, as Table 1.1 demonstrates, fewer than one in five films were taken from stage plays.

Table 1.1 Films based on plays

Year	Proportion of the films released	%
1929	25 of 86	29.1
1930	38 of 99	38.4
1931	64 of 134	47.8
1932	53 of 150	35.3
1933	53 of 181	29.3
1934	66 of 183	36.1
1935	50 of 185	27.0
1936	54 of 219	24.7
1937	35 of 211	16.6
1938	30 of 158	19.0
1939	18 of 98	18.4

Calculated from: Denis Gifford, *The British Film Catalogue, 1895–1970: A Guide to Entertainment Films*, Newton Abbot, Redwood Press for David and Charles, 1973.

Additionally, to assume that all plays were necessarily "middle-class" in nature is to ignore the tradition of provincial and working-class dramas and music-hall sketches (these were not automatically distinguished from legitimate West-End stage plays in credits).

Correspondingly, the number of films based on novels and stories increased as the decade went on, as Table 1.2 reveals.

Presumably, the films based on novels or radio plays (as listed in Table 1.3) removed any temptation to depend on a "proscenium arch" filming approach to the dramatic property.

In fact, until very recently, the primary inspiration for most British films and the source of most film performers in the thirties have seldom been

Table 1.2 Films based on novels or stories

Year	Proportion of the films released	%
1929	25 of 86	29.1
1930	12 of 99	12.1
1931	15 of 134	11.2
1932	25 of 150	16.7
1933	26 of 181	14.4
1934	27 of 183	14.8
1935	46 of 185	24.9
1936	42 of 219	19.2
1937	43 of 211	20.4
1938	29 of 158	18.4
1939	34 of 98	34.7

Compiled from: Gifford, *op. cit.*

Table 1.3 Films based on radio productions

Year	Proportion of the films released	%
1929	0 of 86	0.0
1930	0 of 99	0.0
1931	0 of 134	0.0
1932	1 of 150	0.7
1933	0 of 181	0.0
1934	1 of 183	0.5
1935	4 of 185	2.2
1936	1 of 219	0.5
1937	3 of 211	1.4
1938	2 of 158	1.3
1939	4 of 98	4.1

Compiled from: Gifford, *op. cit.*

discussed in the literature; that source was the music hall, which was only fitting, since the "halls" had been the primary purveyor of entertainment for the English working classes prior to the age of motion pictures. Ironically, these exiles from the music hall, who were not completely committed to the artificial conventions of stage tradition, gave the most realistic portrayals on the screen. Film-maker Alberto Cavalcanti called attention to the versatility of music hall performers, who were attracted to a medium in which they could personify a wide variety of types because they were "unfettered by the rigid dignity of the drama" and, accordingly could "turn themselves to any subject"; he refers to the "almost documentary aspect" of the films in which music hall performers appeared, and observed that the stories, settings, and backgrounds "were those of everyday life" which made them appealing "to all classes of the public" and gave them more "social importance" because they were "closer to contemporary problems."[5]

In another context, John Fisher reminisced about the extraordinary personal popularity of the great music hall comedians who were revered "not merely for the laughter they raised" but also "because of the basic social identity they shared with the bulk of their audiences"; Fisher added that "with their origins [and] their attitudes often firmly rooted in the working class" the screen images of these variety stars were "fixed in this world" so that they "could at the same time be identified as ordinary people and as stars in spite of themselves."[6] With the onset of sound, these performers could project not only the visual characteristics but also the aural qualities of everyday life, endearing themselves to the movie-going public. Individuals like Ernie Lotinga, and his character Jimmy Josser, Will Hay, and his befuddled Narkover educational authority figure, Max Miller and his cheeky "chappie," the Lupino family (Wallace, Barry, and Stanley), George Robey, Violet Loraine, and dozens of other headliners came to the screen in the thirties and promptly created highly memorable characters.

One of the most prominent of these music hall performers was Arthur Lucan, whose "Old Mother Riley" washer-woman character not only made a successful shift to the screen, but also became the central figure in one of the longest lasting movie series in British film history. Though admittedly a farce caricature, "Old Mother Riley" is a good case study of this type of portrayal and helps to show the appeal of such music hall performers' work. Lucan's make-up and costume evoked a realistic impression of the harshness of life for the working classes; regardless of whether the situations being portrayed were farcical in nature, his rubbery, bony features when garbed in a long dress, shabby shawl, and tattered bonnet provided a remarkably authentic vision of real life existence to which working-class audiences responded. Fisher describes Lucan's "legendary" characterization in spite of its "absurdity" as being "subtle" and "humane" with a "definite credibility, a strict, even if zany fidelity to working class life"; he adds that her gossipy character and her "reliance upon the lesser creature comforts, namely her chair, her fire, and her gin" along with her "determination and strength in shortened circumstances" all worked together to evoke, in spite of her vulgarity, the "touching portrayal of someone who was only too true a figure . . . of the British social structure."[7] Fisher noted that the character, also, in a humorous way, touched upon the problems of poverty in old age by concentrating on "unwantedness . . . loneliness, and ill-health."[8] What is significant about this popular character was "the neglect of Old Mother Riley by the West End" which, Fisher pointed out, was "characteristic of the attitude which existed towards the . . . unsophisticated provinces"; Lucan's films found their "readiest audience" in the "North country market" in Lancashire and Yorkshire, though the character itself "represent[ed] a unique hotch-potch of provincial traits" including the "quaint illogicality and endearing blarney" that was the "unmistakably Irish" persona "of the Liverpool dockside and neighboring industrial towns."[9] Because the movies of these transplanted music hall stars like Arthur Lucan rarely played the influential West End, critics rarely wrote about them, except in terms of ridicule. Consequently, they have been largely ignored by social historians and forgotten by students of film. And yet, throughout the decade of the 1930s, British moviegoers flocked to see pictures by music hall luminaries from the industrial North of England such as the legendary Gracie Fields and the popular singer-comedian George Formby, who was often praised as the "male Gracie Fields."[10]

These music hall performers often accompanied their screen portrayals with popular songs. Formby, the "gormless" comic son of the famous music hall veteran George Formby, senior, for instance, was best known for the humorous, slightly naughty, but invariably cheery tunes that he sang in his films in the late thirties. The songs which he performed while accompanying himself on a ukulele became extremely popular records, and as Formby became Britain's box office leader in the latter part of the decade, his discs sold millions. The words of the songs invariably conveyed a sense of optimism and wishfulness. For example, the tune "Feather Your Nest," from the film of the same name, (lyrics by Formby and veteran song writers Harry Gifford and Fred E. Cliffe), imagines what a couple would do when they finally get rich, and their speculations center on the fun they might have in a "lovely bathroom all new." The rather mundane idea that riches might bring a real bathroom reminds us of the assorted luxuries, such as bathrooms, that were not taken for granted in the thirties. Similarly, in "Hitting the High Spots Now," written by the same trio, from *Trouble Brewing*, with lyrics that are vaguely reminiscent of the American Depression tune "We're in the Money," Formby reminds his audience that optimism is often the key to success. The song is suffused with notions such as "grey skies are turning blue" and that "troubles over – I'm in clover. Everything's OK." The character adds that all his "frowns have turned to smiles" and that there are "no wrinkles" on his brow.

> I feel like a millionaire, I'm all deluxe, and how!
> I'm in the money, tasting the money.
> Hitting the high spots now.

The main philosophy of the song is a conclusion that all of this good fortune emerges from a fairly simple attitude:

> Life is what you make it, so make it worthwhile.
> Whatever comes, just take it.
> You've got to swing along and get in rhythm.

In so doing, the singer is "on top of the world" and is "making good, and how!" Indeed, he is "living like a lord," although in a musical aside, he adds "the Lord knows who, or how." The emphasis, then, is on forbearance, with the clear conclusion that in keeping an optimistic viewpoint, one can be "Hitting the high spots now!"

Even in unashamedly "escapist" features, certain messages implicit in the film's content could be suggested to the audiences troubled by the economic woes they encountered each day. Because these films were "escapist" in nature, they have not been regarded seriously. Yet the very fact that these features were "escapist," that is, movies designed to take a viewer out of reality, can often make them more valuable to the social historian than so-called "serious films," for in this "escapism" can be found the dreams and aspirations of people whose lives are troubled and pain-filled.

The assumption that British films did not address the needs of the working classes, and that they were not appealing to them, therefore must be re-evaluated. In many cases, far from ignoring the laboring poor, the movies were directed toward them, focusing in a light-hearted way on their problems, preoccupations, and day-to-day concerns. But such involvement with the working classes ordinarily did not occur in films employing theatrical per-formers. The proximity of the West End to the British studios meant that many performers in the theaters in the evening could be in films for extra money during the day. The attitude of these stage actors toward the films they were making was at best condescending, and often contemptuous. In his memoirs, George Arliss, for one, openly admitted this elitist attitude: he said that the stage actors were decidedly "snobbish" and felt that they were "superior" to screen actors who had been tempted by the availability of "vulgar money" to appear in the movies. He observed that the London actors were "particularly uppish" because they "appeared before the Best People" and were upholding "the honor of our profession"; indeed, they feared that if they "stepped down into movies," they would "lose prestige" and never again be regarded as "superior actors." Not until economic necessity and theatrical unemployment required some income would a stage actor be likely to lower himself to appear in films. This attitude provided opportunities for many non-featured performers. As Arliss put it, "small part" actors "whose 'profes-sion' was in the habit of neglecting them for periods of six to nine months at a stretch" often "came to the conclusion that honor was likely to get a trifle tarnished if it wasn't polished up with a little butcher's meat now and then." By taking the film roles that the more distinguished stage luminaries dis-dained, those actors who traditionally "all their lives had had to fight for a living" now "found themselves actually in demand . . . receiving salaries such as they could not have believed possible"; but Arliss concludes, they could never have reached such success "if the superior class had been a little closer at their heels." [11]

With this kind of contempt for movie work and for the film public, the fact that some of the features playing the West End were unappealing to the working classes would not seem surprising and accounts for some of the negative criticism of movies. A sense of vitality was more prevalent in the lower budgeted, but more widely appreciated movies starring music hall trained performers.

In the British cinema, then, two major trends (one deriving from legitimate stage plays and the other from the music halls) arose following the introduction of sound; these trends were paralleled by the distribution patterns of the movies themselves, with the features starring music hall performers playing in the provinces but never playing in the West End, and with prestige productions with legitimate stage actors having trouble at the box-office outside London. The effect of this division in British film production has tended to create a misconception about the themes and approaches in the films produced during this decade.

Certainly, the cinema had become a continuous, vital, meaningful influence in the lives of British citizens, particularly those in the laboring classes, for whom it had taken on the quality almost of a necessity. As an institution, moviegoing had become in the thirties a permanent fact of life. For instance, the Gallup poll in January, 1938, showed that only 3 percent of the population attended the cinema less than once a month; 38 percent went to the movies at least once or twice a month, 47 percent attended every week or ten days, and 12 percent saw movies more than once a week.[12] Surveys conducted by the film industry showed that in terms of popularity British films and British performers more than held their own against the pervasive American films; for instance, in 1934, three of the four most popular directors were British: Alexander Korda, Tom Walls, and Victor Saville.[13] Similarly, film-goers in one fan magazine that conducted an admittedly unscientific but much publicized popularity contest for actors and actresses (in which as many as thirty thousand "votes" would be cast), usually listed just as many British as American performers in their "Top Ten."[14]

But surveys and statistical evidence of this kind do not tell the full story. Much more impressive and emphatic as social documents were the comments made in the "Letters to the Editor" sections of such inexpensive fan magazines as *Film Weekly*, *Picturegoer Weekly*, and *Film Pictorial*, which were very popular among the working class; these forums for public opinion reveal in a dramatic way how audiences reacted to what they saw on the screen. Often the contributors would reveal their occupation, or lack of occupation, so that a researcher would have a perception of what the individual's status was. These comments invariably were valuable in demonstrating whether British films were being ignored by the working classes.

The experiences, then, of the working classes in England in regularly attending the movies during a decade of painful economic conditions takes on some importance. As a regular activity, film-going clearly must have satisfied various needs; the fact that people in such dire monetary straits that they often did not know how they would feed themselves, wanted to spend what little they had for this kind of amusement, suggests how powerful these needs apparently were.

This study will attempt to explore the product of the British studios in the 1930s; in so doing it will endeavor to show what filmgoers, especially those from the working classes, found at the neighborhood cinema and why they wanted to attend. The question of the popularity of British movies also will be addressed. Efforts will be made to show in what ways the film industry and its products responded to the public, especially in a time of trouble. The specific content of British popular films will be examined, both statistically and on an individual film basis. Possible implicit messages and themes in these movies will be explored, and evidence will be offered to suggest how these ideas were shaped, how films portrayed the class structure, and in what ways societal values were reinforced by the British features of the Depression era.

2

MYTHS AND UNSUPPORTED ASSUMPTIONS

A statistical overview of the content of British popular movies in the thirties

THE NEGLECT OF THE BRITISH CINEMA OF THE 1930s

Of the major developed film industries in the world since the sound era began, the British popular cinema of the 1930s is possibly the least known and least studied and is certainly, for its size, the least respected. Though the British film industry was, at the time, "the largest outside America," its output has been continually castigated and ridiculed as being artistically inconsequential.[1] For instance, film historian Arthur Knight, describing British features of the period as "muddled . . . cheap, [and] artless," has observed in his survey of international film that "until the very end of the thirties," the British production companies "remained notoriously devoid of either inspiration or vitality"; he speculated that as a consequence "disenchanted young men who might have contributed their vigor and talents to the entertainment film abandoned it in favor of the explored realms of documentary" and what was produced by the "harried commercial studios" was "little more than shabby imitations of Hollywood's poorest offerings."[2] Another film historian dismissed "the basic content" of feature films in Britain, at least during the first eight or nine years of the talkie era "as trivial and without contemporary emphasis," and spent less than four pages of a 709-page survey of motion picture history on the decade, in spite of the fact that the author was himself British.[3] Gerald Mast devoted even less time to the topic, with no more than a few sentences out of 575 pages of his widely respected volume on what he called the "artless, craftless cheapies" produced in Britain between the wars.[4]

Even publications specifically surveying British film history have displayed a similar contempt for features from the thirties, with the lack of attention paid to the period sometimes almost ironic in its proportions. For instance, George Perry's popular one-volume history of the British cinema had a cover design with the names of twenty-three great British film personalities, no fewer than sixteen of whom were either best known in the 1930s or achieved their fame or success during this decade; yet Perry covered the entire period with a scant 26 pages out of 367.[5] A 1978 publication attempting to identify the so-called "great British films" of the sound era discussed merely twelve films from the thirties.[6] Film scholarship in general has for the most part neglected the output of this period, and to a large extent, the content of British features from the thirties remains a mystery. Aside from a few well known titles and the names of a handful of personalities and directors working in British film who subsequently became internationally prominent, even the specialist in cinema studies is hard-pressed to remember details about British motion pictures in this period.[7]

Several reasons can be cited for this neglect. Certainly the reputation of these films has contributed significantly to the lack of interest in them. For years, what little material was written about British features in the thirties merely echoed the general assumptions and comments that others had made. Film analysts had no real need to challenge the prevailing view because there appeared no diversity of opinion on the subject and because other periods in other countries which had aroused controversy and which had better reputations remained to be studied. Even if British features from the thirties were not being studied extensively, commentators continued to observe the detrimental aesthetic effect of the Quota Act and wrote contemptuously and with confidence about the "quota quickies," as if all British productions were infected by these movies. Most writers agreed with Arthur Knight's description of English studios being in a "quota-protected rut," producing films that were unimportant and unworthy of any critical attention.[8]

In part, this attitude was fostered in the early 1930s by the American film industry which feared the potential damage to its domestic and foreign markets should the British film industry develop to any great prominence.[9] Not only might English language films from Great Britain have found audiences in the United States among independent theater owners, but also, and perhaps more importantly, they might have interfered severely with the distribution of American films to very important markets for Hollywood productions in the British Empire and Commonwealth, on which American studios had come to depend.[10] Trade publications early in the sound era, when Hollywood was already in a distressed state about the changeover from silent film production, reflected this virtual paranoia. Articles in *Variety*, for example, characterized critical comments on American talkies in the British press as anti-American propaganda designed to "de-popularize" Hollywood productions.[11] Attacks on the Quota Act and suggestions that the British Board of Film Censors were being particularly tough on American productions repeatedly appeared among the pages of trade periodicals in the United States.[12]

Accordingly, Hollywood made it difficult for British films to be shown in America, often buying films and then preventing their exhibition. Those rare British films that were exhibited in America usually received limited distribution at best. Even though one producer, Alexander Korda, did manage to arrange for distribution of his films through an American company, United Artists, this particular company had only a tiny share of the American market. In fact, United Artists, unlike the other major Hollywood producers, owned no theaters in America. Only the small, independent exhibitors who could not obtain or afford the major Hollywood features ran the output of the studios at Denham, Elstree, and Shepherd's Bush, and the audiences who came to these small cinemas were limited to slumdwellers in the city and the farmers and townsmen in small, rural communities. As Griffith and Rotha have observed, even if this kind of an American audience could comprehend the West End accents "which was more than doubtful," they certainly "could not understand the films"; with British productions "shown to the basic, primitive cinema audience – children and very simple people" who were only accustomed to genre like "the Western, the melodrama, and the slapstick comedy of Hollywood . . . [h]ow could the products of the Denham rose-garden be expected to flourish?"[13] Even with Korda's arrangement with United Artists, one British periodical in the late 1930s reported that "less than thirty percent" of British productions were ever released in any fashion in America; the author reported that this limited distribution also helped account for the American belief that all British films tended to be "serious and ponderous" since comedies, which comprised the majority of British features, were almost never shown in the United States.[14] In specific instances, high quality British productions were prevented from American distribution because of censorship problems; various reasons were given, but the usual suspicion was that Hollywood was simply fearful of any potentially popular British film and had exerted its influence with censorship boards as a form of revenge against American films that had been banned in England.[15] Additionally, American film producers were quick to latch onto any criticism of a British production for whatever reason. Trade papers were filled with comments about the unintelligibility of British accents or the shoddiness of production values in contrast to those of American films. Performances were ridiculed, though the same performers were then welcomed into Hollywood productions. British producers also complained that American distributors in England encouraged the making of cheap, low quality, inferior features and forced them upon exhibitors to fulfill quota requirements in order to make the impression in the public that it was "impossible to make a good picture in England."[16]

Naturally, then, with such a reputation to overcome, unqualified international successes among British films from the thirties were few. While budgets for American movies were ordinarily larger, and while productions may have been more lavish and accomplished, by comparison with British features, the intensity of the anti-British criticism encouraged by American film-makers undoubtedly has led to the mostly uniform reputation of the entire English motion picture output during the decade of the thirties. The more one views and studies British films from the 1930s, the more one realizes that these blanket condemnations, though historically understandable, are unfair, inappropriate, and inaccurate. The production values of a large portion of the several hundred films viewed for this study usually were comparable and sometimes virtually indistinguishable from those of contemporary Hollywood features. Certainly budgets were low for the "quota quickies," but these films, often produced for distribution in England only by the British subsidiaries of Hollywood companies, consisted of only a fraction of all British films made during the period; and some of these films triumphed over their budgets.[17] More importantly, the "quota" films often provided a necessary training ground for performers and film-makers who were later to become very successful and to earn international reputations in movies; actors, like James Mason; actresses, like Margaret Lockwood; and directors, like Michael Powell and Adrian Brunel started in the so-called "quota quickies."[18]

Another reason why British commercial motion pictures from the thirties have been neglected is a simple logistical problem: they are not widely available for viewing or analysis. Like virtually all motion pictures made in the thirties, the British features were filmed on nitrate stock which decomposes after a period of time. Preservation of films accordingly has been a major concern for film archives throughout the world. But with limited budgets and with the high cost of transferring films to safety stock, priorities have had to be established; the low regard in which British films of the thirties have been held has caused them to be somewhat under-represented in film collections, as other more prominent features had to be saved.[19] The apparent loss of much of the output of the Warner Brothers' Teddington studio some years ago is particularly regrettable. Since most of the British film companies of the 1930s no longer exist, the studio archives are not reliable sources. Some – but not by any means all – British features were sold to television and are occasionally revived on British or even American television. Revivals of British films at the National Film Theatre of the British Film Institute in London and at other second-run theaters are infrequent, but they invariably are received enthusiastically by the public.

For Americans, though, the problem of finding and screening such films is more pronounced. As recently as the early 1980s, of the more than 1700 British productions running thirty minutes or longer made between 1929 and 1939, only approximately 165 titles were listed in the United States as being available for rental or for sale from distributors (many of whom have relatively tiny, irregular, somewhat undependable operations).[20] Counting titles available for television exhibition in North America a total of 146 additional movies could be added to the list: this total excludes the 135 features which are not listed as available both on television and for rental and sale, and a large proportion of these are ordinarily inaccessible for private screenings.[21] Thus, even if scholars had been more interested, research on the British popular film of the 1930s would have proved difficult to conduct; accordingly, other, more popular subjects have received far greater attention, and British films prior to the Second World War have remained in relative obscurity. The situation has improved slightly in the last decade with the video revolution; a number of companies specializing in obscure, out-of-copyright films have increased the options to view these productions since a good many British films from this decade have not had their copyrights renewed. However, often the prints transferred to video are poor, with incomplete and grainy transfers from second generation dupes; it is rare to obtain a video from a complete print of high quality. Making evaluations from such poor examples is risky. But it is true that the availability question has improved a bit over the years.

In the process of preparing this study, over two hundred of these features have been located for viewing over a fifteen-year period. Spending time in London on different occasions during special National Film Theatre career retrospectives of the films of Gracie Fields, Jessie Matthews, George Formby, and Will Hay proved to be a matter of lucky timing for an American otherwise unable to take advantage of all of the tempting offerings from the British Film Institute collection listed in the monthly NFT booklets he received here in the States; although any visit to London usually resulted in being able to see one or two rarities from this period, the possibility of examining an entire collection of films during one of these NFT tributes was especially helpful.

Outside the United Kingdom, all endeavors to locate these motion pictures have proved to be far more problematic. Television programmers unfamiliar with movies from this period occasionally schedule British films that feature recognizable American performers who travelled to England to make a film or two; likewise, productions from this era that starred British actors and actresses who were later to emigrate to Hollywood also sometimes are shown on American television. By carefully scrutinizing television listings, the diligent enthusiast of films from this decade sometimes can catch such features in the United States, especially on cable or on independent broadcast channels. Occasionally, if one is alert to the schedules of specialized film societies, one also might find these films revived at archival screenings.

Still, the goal of tracking down as many as possible of these hard-to-locate productions in the United States more often than not requires extraordinary effort, and frequently the endeavor assumes almost comical proportions. Patient and understanding friends in other cities have become accustomed to frantic, long distance phone calls from the author of this study alerting them to late night television showings, noticed in newspaper listings, of otherwise forgotten British films and beseeching them to set their videotape machines to record the items for research purposes. Whenever special showings of British films are announced in places like New York or Chicago, efforts must be made to try to attend as many of the screenings as possible. Especially memorable in this regard was one twelve hour, overnight marathon in a freezing

Chicago auditorium, during which beautiful 35mm prints of seven 1930s British musicals (on loan from the British Film Institute) were projected at the Chicago International Film Festival in the mid 1980s; one's enjoyment of the delightful films inevitably was tempered by the sheer physical difficulty of trying to keep fingers warm enough to continue writing detailed notes about productions one was not likely to be able to see again.

Fortunately, in the last few years, with the growth of mail order video companies specializing in out-of-copyright productions, a number of features from this period previously seldom seen in the United States have been made available for home viewing. While the quality of prints being used for the videos varies drastically, and while the ordering of the films proves quite expensive, nonetheless, dozens of titles that have never been available before can now be examined in detail for the first time.

Still, for someone interested in this period, it remains very frustrating to consider the sizable number of these movies that continue to be elusive and unavailable for viewing. To obtain a more thorough overview of British films, then, other sources of information must be examined to permit some analysis of a wider cross section of the British cinematic output. Screenplays at the British Film Institute Library have been helpful in this regard, as are reviews and criticism from contemporary newspapers and film commentators. But especially useful are plot synopses and feature articles in contemporary fan magazines and industry publications; for the most part, these accounts have been neglected or at least under used in research on this period. These written accounts of the movies that appeared at the time of the release of the films often include revealing production details and provide remarkably detailed and informative background information. Comparisons of plot evaluations from the magazines with the films themselves suggest that the accounts in these fan periodicals and trade publications were generally quite accurate and reliable. While first hand examination of the films themselves would always be preferable, given the lack of availability of British films of this era, and the likelihood that a significant number of these features are now lost, this material at least provides help in reconstructing the cinematic output of the period.

Another reason why British features in the 1930s have remained less well known involves Britain's greatest contribution to the development of world cinema. As Walter Allen has observed when one contemplates the role British film has played in the general history of cinema, it is, indeed, to the British motion picture of the thirties that one's thoughts turn. But it is not the popular features that are considered significant; rather "one's mind turns . . . to the superb documentaries that John Grierson fathered and Sir Stephen Tallents fostered, first at the Empire Marketing Board and then at the Post Office." [22] To say that these films critically have overshadowed the popular British cinema of the decade would be a vast understatement. Film historians generally concede that it was the British under Grierson that gave the impetus to the documentary movement, and many, like Arthur Knight, feel that the documentary movement, more than any other factor, shaped the most memorable period of British commercial cinema, the years immediately following the Second World War.[23] Thus, the lack of attention to the British popular film industry is fairly easy to understand, given its reputation, its traditional rivalry with Hollywood, the unavailability of its output, and the contrast with the truly significant documentary movement taking place at the same time.

THE PEOPLE'S CINEMA

That the British cinema during this period generally has been dismissed as meaningless, stuffy, and stage bound, regarded in the words of one writer as a "middle-class institution," with its origins in the kind of "drawing-room" drama seen from " a stall seat in Shaftsbury Avenue" presents a remarkable irony.[24] The fact is that, for a "middle-class institution," the British film was remarkably popular among the working classes. Certainly movie-going had become a national pastime, with almost nineteen million people attending their cinemas weekly.[25] As historian C. L. Mowat has observed, "to the large majority [of the] unemployed . . . the main problem was to keep warm, and to conserve low energy"; cinema-going fulfilled these goals and at the same time enabled audience members to obtain a "passing distraction" from the "boredom" of their day-to-day existence. Indeed, Mowat goes on to cite statistics showing that in Cardiff, for instance, 52 percent of the unemployed young people interviewed visited the movie theaters once a week, and "almost half of these twice a week"; similarly in the cities of Liverpool and Glasgow, as many as 80 percent of those polled attended at least once weekly.[26]

George Orwell, who spent months studying and living with the working classes during the worst years of the Depression, was also aware of the importance of movies for these people. In his moving study of the Depression era working classes, Orwell remarked that in a decade "of unparalleled depression," the "consumption of all cheap luxuries" had risen, and the two examples that had "probably made the greatest difference of all" were "the movies and the mass-production of cheap smart clothes"; an individual might have only a half-penny in his pocket, "not a prospect in the world, and only the corner of a leaky bedroom to go home to," but in his "new clothes" he could "stand on the street corner, indulging in a private daydream" of himself as Clark Gable, and such a fantasy "compensates . . . for a great deal."[27] Orwell went on to comment that this "development of cheap luxuries [such as] . . . the movies" had proven in the midst of a potentially explosive economic crisis to be "a very fortunate thing for our rulers,", because it was "quite likely that . . . [such pleasure had] averted revolution."[28]

Whether Orwell's contention was correct or not, the working classes themselves provided ample testimony of their devotion to the movies and to the escape the cinema provided. The importance the working classes attached to the films they saw and to their regular visits to the movie-houses can be seen in some of the contemporary British fan magazines they purchased so avidly. Such publications as *Film Weekly*, *Picturegoer Weekly*, and *Film Pictorial* provided detailed information for the cinemagoer on all aspects of the film experience each week for the minimal cost of around threepence.

Although exact circulation figures on these publications are difficult to obtain, the profusion of fan magazines and the variety from which to choose at the newsstand suggests their great success in the public marketplace; when other popular enterprises were failing in 1931, the monthly *Picturegoer* was so successful that it changed to a weekly.

In the letters sent to these periodicals, movie fans related their love for films and told what the cinema meant to them in an increasingly chaotic, frustrating, and troubled world. One shopgirl from Leeds went so far as to outline her entire weekly budget and included movies with such other necessities as food and shelter.

> I wonder whether people realize how very strong is . . . [the] effect [of movies] on the lives of hundreds of girls in similar positions to myself. Here is my weekly budget: Wages 32s – Board and lodging 25s – Saturday visit to cinema 1s – Monday visit 7d – Thursday visit 7d – That makes 27s 2d. Then there is threepence for *Film Weekly* and 3 shillings for dress allowance. That means I have 1s 7d left. People consider me smartly dressed, but that is undoubtedly because I copy the clothes I have seen in films. Powders, soap and odds and ends are those used by my favorite film stars. When I get a rise in salary, I shall be able to afford another night at the pictures.[29]

Another letter-writer who identified himself as a member of the working classes concurred that the movies were vital for survival.

> Plain men and women are turning with almost a sign of thankfulness to the cinema, which has become now a stark necessity, taking their minds off the continual struggle for existence during these days of stress and strain. Looking forward to an enjoying two or three hours at the "pictures" definitely lightens the load and tends to free the mind of petty worries so easily magnified. It is the pause enabling us to get our "second wind," so to speak before "tackling the morrow's problems" . . . For it is entertainment which takes our minds out of the rut, so apt to end in a slough.[30]

Still another letter-writer commented that he could not "imagine what the world would be like . . . without cinemas," and acknowledged that the very "thought" of it sent "a feeling of panic . . . through my mind."[31]

Whether such hyperbole was shared by all members of the working classes is not certain, but many letter-writers observed that, if anything, the movies had even greater meaning for the countless unemployed. A letter-writer in

August, 1935, pointed out his sympathy for "the vast numbers of unemployed in my district whose only entertainment consists of going in the evening, once or twice a week to one of the local cinemas." [32] Another letter attacked those who criticized the proliferation of movie entertainments, observing that those who were against the spread of motion pictures were precisely "those who can afford to pay well for their relaxation, boxes at the opera, seats for the best concerts, etc."; the writer added,

> I wonder if they have ever given a thought to what the "pictures" mean to the working people and especially to the very poor? Their lives are a constant grind to make ends meet, with the fear of unemployment hanging over them all the time. Not for them theatres or concerts; their Mecca is the "pictures" . . . here for a few pence tired men and harassed women can leave their cares behind and for a few hours live a life that otherwise would never be theirs. Music and singing, love and laughter, all are there . . . . [O]ur best singers – all the famous bands, the pick of the world's actors, all are there to do service for them, and no singer or actor has a finer critic or a firmer friend than the workingman or woman . . . . After the show they go home rested and refreshed, better for the brief hours' respite from their ordinary life; and the rest of the week will be brightened by snatches of a song, a lilting melody, or a chuckle at a remembered wisecrack by one of the comedians. [33]

The letter concluded with the author relating what working-class people had told her of their regard for the movies.

> Women have told me frankly that they would rather go without their dinner than their visit to the pictures. "What folly!" I can hear the highbrows say . . . but have *they* ever known what it is to go on, week in, week out, planning, contriving, working, to keep a home and family on totally inadequate means, without a break, without hope of anything better? One woman told me in deadly earnest: "Ma'am, if it wasn't for a visit to the pictures I should go as mad as a hatter," and I believe her. I have seen, and I *know*. . . . More power to the singers, actors, and actresses, for they are doing a wonderful work. . . . [T]hey brighten the lives of poor people. [34]

One unemployed man from Gateshead-on-Tyne wrote to *Film Pictorial* in late 1932 to explain the therapeutic effect films had for him psychologically; signing himself "Cheery," he noted,

> I am a "dockyard matey," out of work on the dole. But I manage to save an occasional ninepence for the cinema and am never happier than when I see a film with gorgeous scenes of song, dance, and merriment. Why does it make me happy? Because it fills a gap in my life. I do not hanker after luxury or wealth; these I know I can never gain; but such

films take me out of myself, out of gloomy Tyneside, and provide the escape from reality without which I should grow dull and despairing.[35]

Another letter-writer went so far as to personify the movies as the perfect companion.

> In this modern age, we have an ideal friend – the cinema; a friend who is ever willing to stretch forth welcoming arms to all, to give entertainment to suit every taste . . . . Is there anyone who can relieve the monotony of drab existence so successfully and renew lost courage? The cinema – our ideal friend – is being clamored for by every civilized human being as a means of relaxation from a monotonous life; some to forget their sorrows and some to study humanity. No other place could afford such a complete survey of mankind as cinema, our ideal friend.[36]

The same sentiment was expressed in a remarkably similar eulogy from an anonymous letter-writer in the pages of a different publication, the *Picturegoer Weekly* in 1931. With the heading "to the Movies," the note began:

> You are my best friend. You give me everything, though you ask of me nothing. You never fail to cheer and though you sometimes make me weep, you always comfort me. You make me laugh and forget all cares. I am a globe-trotter, though I never leave my native town. I am well informed, I am an authority on drama, current events, fashions, etiquette, and music. I believe in God, miracles, love, and just folk. I know there is a pot of gold at the end of the rainbow, for I have been there. I seldom leave my neighborhood, but you will find me in every city, town, village, and hamlet in the world. And so because of you, I am a very remarkable fellow. My age? I am all ages. My name? It is legion. I am a movie-fan.[37]

Of course, not all films shown in British cinemas were made in Britain, and it is customary to assume that American films were favored consistently by audiences. But contemporary sources demonstrate a far less certain preference. An item in *Film Weekly* in early 1933 noted that contemporary filmgoers knew "that they . . . [could] depend on a good-quality British film" and that they were "glad to pay good money to see it"; the commentary added that this was proven "by the recent admission of an American film distributor that a British film can make three to four times as much money in this country as a Hollywood picture of equal quality."[38]

In fact, to a notable degree, letter-writers often stated an open dislike of American films in comparison to features produced in Great Britain. A woman from Birmingham complained in one letter that too many Hollywood features were being shown, saying "it is only my sense of humor that keeps me suffering in my seat through those eternal 'backstage,' racketeering, collegiate American films without having to be taken away, foaming at the mouth"; though she claimed that her tastes were not "aggressively British and proud of it," nevertheless she found English films:

> *clean* wholesome and above all REAL. They take me into a familiar atmosphere, among places and people I *know* even if they are sordid and prosy . . .. These American "cuties" and "gunmen" mean little or nothing to us; their far-fetched, impossible doings leave us cold; I would rather see one *Rookery Nook* than twenty American "stupendous epics" . . . . Elstree, your pictures are good enough for me.[39]

While certainly not all filmgoers shared this view, the popularity of British films was undeniable and has been overlooked to a significant extent. Even the much maligned "quota quickies" had their devotees. One "letter to the editor" of *Film Pictorial* in that section of the magazine which was known significantly as "the Screen Parliament" observed that quota pictures were far more enjoyable and meaningful than American short films.

> These little productions, some of them only forty or fifty minutes long, may well take the place of the miserable drivel from America purporting to be comedy which we have had to endure far too long. Surely the average English audience would prefer the robust but wholesome humour of . . . [British quota films] . . . to the nonsensical antics of most American two-reeler comedians.[40]

Perry's contention that the British cinema was unresponsive to the working classes would seem to be difficult to understand or justify, then, given the popularity of these movies among the poor and unemployed. If British films during the Depression years appealed to largely working-class audiences, the question of what the content consisted becomes important. A variety of studies on Hollywood films of the thirties already have attempted to relate American movies to social concerns in the United States during the Depression.[41] But such content analysis has not hitherto been endeavored with regard to British films. How, then, could such an effort be undertaken?

AN OVERVIEW OF CONTENT

An overview of the content of the British cinema was greatly facilitated with the publication in the mid 1970s of the massive volume compiled by Denis Gifford which catalogued all entertainment films made in Britain from 1895 to 1970. Gifford's work took sixteen years to compile, and it listed cast, credits, and plot synopses of well over fourteen thousand films; it quickly became the most reliable source of information of its kind. Reviewers subsequently praised it as being "dependable and monumental," and film historian Roy Armes referred to it as being "indispensable."[42]

Gifford described twenty-three basic categories or "subjects" into which he

Table 2.1 Classification of feature films from 1920 to 1939

Year	Total	Adventure	Comedy	Crime	Drama	History	Musical	Romance	War	Children	Sport	Horror	Fantasy	Revue
1929	86	5	11	29	19	1	2	14	1	—	1	1	1	1
1930	99	4	31	20	11	—	18	4	4	1	2	—	1	2
1931	134	1	47	40	12	1	11	20	1	—	1	—	—	—
1932	150	4	59	32	16	—	21	15	1	—	1	1	—	—
1933	181	3	82	31	15	1	20	15	3	—	4	1	3	2
1934	183	4	59	41	19	3	33	14	1	—	3	2	2	2
1935	185	9	68	37	15	5	29	11	2	—	3	—	4	2
1936	219	6	74	45	16	7	48	4	2	—	1	1	4	10
1937	211	13	61	47	17	4	36	10	8	—	3	—	—	12
1938	158	4	58	37	14	3	23	7	4	—	—	—	—	6
1939	98	2	29	34	12	—	5	2	5	—	3	1	—	3

Assorted Religion (2 – 1933) Compilation (2 – 1938) Animal (1 – 1930; 1 – 1936) Unclassified (1 – 1933)

Compiled from: Denis Gifford, The British Film Catalogue, 1875 1970: A guide to Entertainment Films, Newton Abbot, Redwood Press for David and Charles, 1973.

grouped all British films from 1895 to 1970. Of the twenty-three subdivisions he used, sixteen classifications were applied to the just-over seventeen hundred British productions running thirty minutes or longer produced in the thirties.[43] Of necessity, these categories are relatively terse and sketchy, and Gifford himself indicated in his introduction the problems and limitations of these single-word categorizations; but despite the difficulty of generalizing from these groupings, at least all of his evaluations were based on published descriptions and have the unprecedented virtue of being consistently applied to the total output of presumably every British studio. Therefore, using Gifford's data, a general, comprehensive though admittedly limited overview of the content of British films in this decade could be ascertained for the first time. Unfortunately, no such statistical information accompanied Gifford's published listing. So a first step toward understanding just what comprised the content of British cinema during this period might be obtained by a close survey of Gifford's material.

The rough statistical overview represented in Table 2.1 which was obtained by carefully counting all of the various films over thirty minutes in length and using Gifford's classifications revealed some very interesting patterns.[44] The steady increase in comedy films through 1933, and the subsequently high numbers of comedy productions throughout the remainder of the decade in relation to other categories suggest the popularity of "escapist" film fare.[45]

Table 2.2 Films described as comedy films

Year	Proportion of the films released	%
1929	11 of 86	12.80
1930	31 of 99	31.00
1931	47 of 134	35.00
1932	59 of 150	39.33
1933	82 of 181	45.30
1934	59 of 183	32.25
1935	68 of 185	36.75
1936	74 of 219	33.80
1937	61 of 211	28.90
1938	58 of 158	36.70
1939	29 of 98	29.60

Compiled from: Gifford, *op. cit.*

After the tumultuous transition year of 1929, when British studios were converting to sound and therefore were in flux, comedy films comprised roughly between 30 and 35 percent of the total number of features released each year by British production companies. In 1933, at the low point of the slump, close to one-half of all films made in Britain were "comedies." Only near the end of the decade, in 1937 and 1939, when the worst of the economic crisis had passed, did the figure ever slip below 30 percent, and the difference in these two years from the 30 percent figure is negligible.

The equivalent numbers for musicals, usually considered equally escapist, are also revealing, though perhaps not as telling as those for comedies.

Table 2.3 Films described as musical films

Year	Proportion of the films released	%
1929	2 of 86	2.30
1930	18 of 99	18.00
1931	11 of 134	8.20
1932	21 of 150	14.00
1933	20 of 181	11.00
1934	33 of 183	18.00
1935	29 of 185	15.67
1936	48 of 219	21.90
1937	36 of 211	17.06
1938	23 of 158	14.56
1939	5 of 98	5.10

Compiled from: Gifford, *op. cit.*

The percentages of musicals produced throughout the thirties were usually in the mid-teens, with the high point being 1936 when the forty-eight British musicals constituted about 22 percent of all releases. Though 1931 would seem to be aberrant, it should be remembered that 1931 is generally considered to be a year in which the musical film genre was being re-evaluated in the film industry both in Britain and in other countries.[46]

The figures become somewhat more impressive when revues, which were typically musically orientated, are incorporated. Although Gifford differentiates between revues and musicals, revues would include almost invariably a large proportion of songs, sing-alongs, and musical numbers. In many cases, the revues would be assemblages of the most prominent and well-known music hall acts.

When these two categories are lumped together, the proportion of "musical-type" films is shown to be somewhat more significant, particularly in the latter years of the decade. In five of the eleven years, totals of around 20 percent or higher of the output of British studios were musically orientated. In 1936, perhaps significantly, also the year in which the most comedies were released, almost sixty musicals and revues were produced in Britain, a figure that represents more than one of every four films released that year.

The increasing number of revues that appeared is, in itself, a noteworthy phenomenon. With the beginning of the gradual decline of the music halls, it was perhaps inevitable that the cinema, traditionally regarded as heir to the

Table 2.4 Films described as musical films and films
described as revues

Year	Proportion of the films released	%
1929	3 of 86	3.50
1930	20 of 99	20.20
1931	11 of 134	8.20
1932	21 of 150	14.00
1933	22 of 181	12.15
1934	35 of 183	19.12
1935	31 of 185	16.75
1936	58 of 219	26.50
1937	48 of 211	22.75
1938	28 of 158	18.35
1939	8 of 98	8.20

Compiled from: Gifford, *op. cit.*

halls in that it was the primary source of entertainment for the working classes, would adopt some of their performers. The introduction of sound was a necessary prerequisite to this development, but once sound was pervasive in British cinema, revues featuring music hall acts gradually became more common and more popular. By booking such films, cinema managers also presumably could reduce the costs of hiring live acts, to which audiences in some of the bigger cinemas had become accustomed as part of the programs. With the same kinds of acts that previously had performed live now available on the screen, these movies could provide entertainment more efficiently and more inexpensively than live performances.

The films kept some of these entertainers employed and active, and also served as a means by which these performers could work their way into the motion picture industry; for example, before the long running "Old Mother Riley" series about a comic washer-woman began, its protagonists, the team of Arthur Lucan and Kitty McShane, who had created the characters in a successful music hall act, had made an appearance in a revue. Thus, the emergence of revue films is a significant development in itself, though the percentages may seem negligible.

These three categories represented a large proportion of all British releases in the thirties. When musicals, revues, and comedy films are totalled together, they are shown to be the majority of British releases almost every year of the decade; in 1936, three of every five features were in one of these three categories.

These three categories make clear the highly "escapist" nature of British cinema during this decade.

The largest of the remaining categories is the crime film which seems to have been exceedingly common among British productions.

Table 2.5 Films described as revues

Year	Proportion of the films released	%
1929	1 of 86	1.50
1930	2 of 97	2.00
1931	–	–
1932	–	–
1933	2 of 181	1.10
1934	2 of 183	1.10
1935	2 of 185	1.00
1936	10 of 219	4.56
1937	12 of 211	5.70
1938	6 of 158	3.80
1939	3 of 98	3.10

Compiled from: Gifford, *op. cit.*

Table 2.6 Films described as comedies, musicals and revues totalled together

Year	Proportion of the films released	%
1929	14 of 86	16.28
1930	51 of 99	51.50
1931	58 of 134	43.28
1932	80 of 150	53.33
1933	104 of 181	57.46
1934	94 of 183	51.36
1935	99 of 185	53.51
1936	132 of 219	60.27
1937	109 of 211	51.66
1938	87 of 158	55.06
1939	37 of 98	37.75

Compiled from: Gifford, *op. cit.*

During most years of the decade, between two and three of every ten British films were crime features. But here the figures may be slightly deceptive in that this particular category covers perhaps the widest range of possibilities. Because of the all-inclusive nature of the way in which this category is defined, it is somewhat ambiguous. No differentiation is made, for example, between detective movies, gangster and street-crime thrillers, caper features about gentleman jewel thiefs, and mad-killer films, cops-and-robber epics, or simply old-fashioned, drawing-room murder mysteries. In other words as a genre, the crime film can take on many different forms; as Carlos Clarens observes in his study of the genre, "the crime film is . . . difficult to isolate, lacking as it does the readable iconography of the Western and the clarity of intent of the horror films."[47] Thus, the number of "crime films" may have

Table 2.7 Films described as crime films

Year	Proportion of the films released	%
1929	29 of 86	33.70
1930	20 of 99	20.20
1931	40 of 134	29.85
1932	32 of 150	21.33
1933	31 of 181	17.10
1934	41 of 183	22.40
1935	37 of 185	20.00
1936	45 of 219	20.55
1937	47 of 211	22.27
1938	37 of 158	23.42
1939	34 of 98	34.70

Compiled from: Gifford, *op. cit.*

been swollen unduly by the loose definition of the category, and it might be wrong to presume any sociologically abnormal fascination with crime among the film-going public.

One small surprise in these figures is the relatively insignificant proportion of "history" films, since this genre is one of the few areas in which British commercial cinema of the thirties was able to develop any lasting international reputation. The success of Alexander Korda's *Private Life of Henry VIII* seems to have inspired a brief, though surprisingly small, trend toward history films.

These movies had greater success abroad, perhaps because so many of them were made by Korda whose distribution agreement insured access to American markets; accordingly, the films became better known and have retained a lasting prestige.

Table 2.8 Films described as history films

Year	Proportion of the films released	%
1929	1 of 86	1.5
1930	– of 99	–
1931	1 of 134	0.75
1932	– of 150	–
1933	1 of 181	0.55
1934	3 of 183	1.64
1935	5 of 185	2.70
1936	7 of 219	3.20
1937	4 of 211	1.90
1938	3 of 158	1.90
1939	– of 98	–

Compiled from: Gifford, *op. cit.*

Table 2.9 Films described as dramatic films

Year	Proportion of the films released	%
1929	19 of 86	22.10
1930	11 of 99	11.11
1931	12 of 134	9.00
1932	16 of 150	10.67
1933	15 of 181	8.30
1934	19 of 183	10.40
1935	15 of 185	8.10
1936	16 of 219	7.30
1937	17 of 211	8.00
1938	14 of 158	8.86
1939	12 of 98	12.25

Compiled from: Gifford, *op. cit.*

Straight dramatic films seem to have remained fairly constant in proportion to other British releases, but the percentages are still low throughout the thirties.

In most years dramatic films represented only between 8 and 10 percent of the output of British studios. One would expect to find most films dealing with any social messages in this category; thus, the small percentages are again suggestive of a highly escapist cinema industry.

But other kinds of dramatic films are listed under other categories. For example, each year at least a few released are characterized as war films.

The number of war films during the decade rose, particularly in the later years, just before the Second World War, although a mini-trend in 1930 had resulted in several features with anti-war messages.

Table 2.10 Films described as war films

Year	Proportion of the films released	%
1929	1 of 86	1.15
1930	4 of 99	4.04
1931	1 of 134	0.75
1932	1 of 150	0.67
1933	3 of 181	1.67
1934	1 of 183	0.55
1935	2 of 185	1.00
1936	2 of 219	0.90
1937	8 of 211	3.80
1938	4 of 158	2.53
1939	5 of 98	5.10

Compiled from: Gifford, *op. cit.*

Table 2.11 Films described as romances

Year	Proportion of the films released	%
1929	14 of 86	16.28
1930	4 of 99	4.04
1931	20 of 134	14.90
1932	15 of 150	10.00
1933	15 of 181	8.30
1934	14 of 183	7.65
1935	11 of 185	6.00
1936	4 of 219	1.80
1937	10 of 211	4.74
1938	7 of 158	4.43
1939	2 of 98	2.04

Compiled from: Gifford, *op. cit.*

By contrast, romances seem to have declined in popularity. In the early thirties, romance films were a substantial fraction of each year's production totals. But by the late years of the decade, the number of romances had declined to less than 5 percent a year.

Adventure movies do not seem to have been as widely produced as might have been expected; but again, the vague notion of what constitutes an "adventure" film may make these figures less meaningful than they might otherwise have been. As a rule, though, adventure films rarely accounted for as much as 5 percent of a year's releases.

One category that is deceptively insignificant is that which Gifford calls sport films. Although the listings are proportionally very small, in fact, when one examines the short synopses Gifford includes, one discovers that a large number of films in other categories (such as comedy, crime, musicals, and

Table 2.12 Films described as adventure films

Year	Proportion of the films released	%
1929	4 of 86	5.80
1930	4 of 99	4.04
1931	1 of 134	0.75
1932	4 of 150	2.67
1933	3 of 181	1.67
1934	4 of 183	2.20
1935	9 of 185	4.86
1936	6 of 219	2.74
1937	13 of 211	6.16
1938	4 of 158	2.80
1939	2 of 98	2.04

Compiled from: Gifford, *op. cit.*

Table 2.13 Films described as sports films

Year	Proportion of the films released	%
1929	1 of 86	1.15
1930	2 of 99	2.00
1931	1 of 134	0.75
1932	1 of 150	0.67
1933	4 of 181	2.20
1934	3 of 183	1.64
1935	3 of 185	1.62
1936	1 of 219	0.45
1937	3 of 211	1.40
1938	– of 158	–
1939	3 of 98	3.10

Compiled from: Gifford, *op. cit.*

adventures) also deal with various sports such as English football or racing or at least with aspects of sports such as gambling. If such films were included, this category would have been substantially larger.

The other categories were not highly represented each year, although a brief flurry of fantasy and horror films in the mid thirties can be detected. Table 2.14 lists the percentages for all films and categories by year.

Of course, British studios released in addition to these features and featurettes, hundreds of short entertainment films. An analysis of these extremely rare films cannot be undertaken in this study, though Gifford's data again provide a rough overview of what these movies consisted. [See Table 2.15.] Several of the categories were unique to short films.[48] As in the case of the features, musicals and comedies made up the majority of the releases. The remarkable total of 130 musical shorts in 1929 represents early sound experimentation, but even in subsequent years, when sound films were firmly established, the totals remained comparatively high for this category. Escapism, then, can be seen prominently in the short films produced, as well as in the features.[49]

These figures are revealing, yet their utility in assessing the cinematic tastes of the British working classes in the thirties is limited at best. The categorization of these films does provide at least a rough grouping of the product of British film studios and demonstrates in what proportions the various types of features were being produced; but beyond that, few specific assumptions can be made without more information. After all, the decision to make a movie can be determined by a variety of factors such as cost effectiveness; public acceptability is not always the most important concern for producers. In Britain, with the quota system such an important consideration in the thirties, several studios specialized in making the low-budget "quickies" that were used to balance American releases and fulfill legal obligations. With

Table 2.14 Percentages of categories for features

Year	Adventure	Comedy	Crime	Drama	History	Musical	Romance	War	Children	Sport	Horror	Fantasy	Revue
1929	5.80	12.80	33.70	22.10	1.15	2.30	16.28	1.15	–	1.15	1.15	1.15	1.15
1930	4.00	31.00	20.00	10.00	–	18.00	4.00	4.00	1.00	2.00	–	1.00	2.00
1931	0.08	35.00	29.85	9.00	0.08	8.20	14.90	0.08	–	0.08	–	–	–
1932	2.67	39.33	21.33	10.67	–	14.00	10.00	0.07	–	0.07	0.07	–	–
1933	1.66	45.30	17.10	8.30	0.55	11.00	8.30	1.66	–	2.20	0.55	1.66	1.10
1934	2.20	32.25	22.40	10.40	1.64	18.00	7.65	0.55	–	1.64	1.10	1.10	1.10
1935	4.86	36.75	20.00	8.10	2.70	15.66	6.00	1.0	–	1.62	–	2.10	1.00
1936	2.74	33.80	20.55	7.30	3.20	21.90	1.80	0.90	–	0.45	0.45	1.80	4.56
1937	6.16	28.90	22.275	8.00	1.90	17.06	4.74	3.80	–	1.40	–	–	5.70
1938	2.53	36.70	23.42	8.86	1.90	14.56	4.43	2.53	–	–	–	–	3.80
1939	2.04	29.60	34.70	12.25	–	5.10	2.04	5.10	–	3.10	1.0	–	3.10

Assorted Religion (1939 – 2%) Compilation (1938 – 1.25%) Animal (1930 – 1%; 1936 – 0.45%) Unclassified (1933 – 0.55%)

Compiled from: Gifford, *op. cit.*

Table 2.15 Categories of entertainment short films produced in Britain in the thirties

Year	Total short film releases	Comedy	Crime	Drama	Musical	Act	Fantasy	Religion	Misc.
1929	163	26	1	–	130	–	1	–	5
1930	47	20	1	4	22	–	–	–	–
1931	18	5	2	–	10	–	–	–	1
1932	28	6	1	–	14	6	–	–	1
1933	28	10	–	1	5	10	1	1	–
1934	28	3	5	15	2	2	–	1	–
1935	27	5	4	1	5	10	–	–	2
1936	35	5	–	1	9	20	–	–	–
1937	6	–	1	–	4	1	–	–	–
1938	36	9	6	1	11	–	6	–	3
1939	15	4	3	1	4	–	–	1	2

Assorted: Adventure (2 – 1929) Romance (1 – 1932; 2 – 1938) War (1 – 1929) Sport (1 – 1929) Compilation (1 – 1931; 1 – 1938) Animal (1 – 1935; 1 – 1939) Chase (1 – 1929) Trick (1 – 1939; 1 – 1935)

Compiled from: Gifford, *op. cit.*

their often poor production values and the noticeable haste with which they were concocted, these features were not usually popular with the public, and yet they figure just as prominently in totals of films produced. In addition, some films are routinely more expensive to make than others, and the lower return on the investment may encourage a producer to select a cheaper, less risky property and thereby to ignore other types of films. War, fantasy, adventure, horror, and historical/costume films are usually more expensive, so this fact may account for the relative insignificance of these categories.

The inability, then, to differentiate between successful features and films rejected by the public and the difficulty in assessing the motivations of producers makes the raw numbers and percentages imperfect as barometers of public taste and acceptance. Without accurate box office data on specific films, more definitive judgments would be speculative; however, such information is rarely available and is always difficult, if not impossible, to obtain. However, public acceptance can be measured or inferred in a variety of other ways.

The reissue of a film usually signifies its acceptance by the public, since ordinarily, only films that are successful or appreciated are ever reissued (although it is undeniable that some films may have been re-released because of a shortage of movies available for circulation). Nonetheless, if the first run of a film was not successful or if a producer did not have reason to expect that a reissue would be profitable, a movie would not be circulated a second time. Gifford supplies information about reissues. By totalling the numbers of

Table 2.16 Feature films subsequently reissued

Year	Total	Adventure	Comedy	Crime	Drama	History	Musical	Romance	War	Children	Sport	Horror	Fantasy	Revue
1929	15	–	2	3	5	–	–	4	–	–	–	–	–	1
1930	11	1	6	2	–	–	1	–	1	–	–	–	–	–
1931	16	–	10	3	1	–	2	1	1	–	–	–	–	–
1932	16	–	6	2	2	–	4	2	1	–	–	–	1	–
1933	31	1	16	1	4	1	5	1	1	–	–	–	1	–
1934	30	1	7	3	2	2	13	1	2	–	–	–	–	2
1935	39	3	13	7	–	2	7	2	–	–	–	–	1	2
1936	56	1	12	12	4	3	16	2	–	–	–	1	3	2
1937	75	8	23	14	6	2	10	4	4	–	1	–	–	3
1938	60	3	22	14	8	1	8	2	2	–	2	–	–	–
1939	42	1	15	11	4	–	3	1	3	–	–	1	–	1

Compiled from: Gifford, *op. cit.*

Table 2.17 Percentages of feature films that were
subsequently reissued

Year	Proportion of the films released	%
1929	15 of 86	17.44
1930	11 of 99	11.11
1931	16 of 134	11.94
1932	16 of 150	10.66
1933	31 of 181	17.13
1934	30 of 183	16.39
1935	39 of 185	21.08
1936	56 of 219	25.57
1937	75 of 211	35.55
1938	60 of 158	37.97
1939	42 of 98	42.86

Compiled from: Gifford, *op. cit.*

British films from this period identified by Gifford as being subsequently reissued, the movies with the presumably greater public acceptance can be discerned, and any correspondence to the raw totals and percentages previously examined can be highlighted. Table 2.16 shows these reissues by year and by category; it should be noted that many of these films were reissued more than once and that most of the reissues listed for 1929 were silent films that were re-released in 1930 with complete or partial soundtracks added.

Perhaps the first and most notable revelation of this table is that so many British films from the period were reissued. If one accepts re-releases as a fair judgment of approval, then, these percentages provide further evidence to

Table 2.18 Percentages of reissued films represented
by reissued comedies and musicals (with revues)

Year	Proportion of the films released	%
1929	3 of 15	20.00
1930	7 of 11	63.64
1931	12 of 16	75.00
1932	10 of 16	62.50
1933	21 of 31	67.74
1934	20 of 30	66.67
1935	22 of 39	56.41
1936	30 of 56	53.57
1937	36 of 75	48.00
1938	30 of 60	50.00
1939	19 of 42	45.24

Compiled from: Gifford, *op. cit.*

Table 2.19 Percentages films identified as reissues

Year	Adventure	Comedy	Crime	Drama	History	Musical	Romance	War	Sport	Horror	Fantasy	Revue
1929	–	13.33	20.00	33.33	–	–	26.66	–	–	–	–	6.66
1930	9.09	54.54	18.18	–	–	9.09	–	9.09	–	–	–	–
1931	–	62.50	18.75	6.28	–	12.50	–	–	–	–	–	–
1932	–	37.50	12.50	12.50	–	25.00	6.25	6.25	–	–	–	–
1933	3.33	51.61	3.22	12.90	3.22	16.13	6.45	3.22	–	–	3.22	–
1934	7.69	23.33	10.00	6.66	6.66	43.33	3.33	3.33	–	–	–	–
1935	1.78	33.33	17.95	–	5.13	17.95	5.13	5.13	–	–	2.56	5.60
1936	10.68	21.43	21.43	7.14	5.36	28.57	3.57	–	–	1.78	5.36	3.50
1937	5.00	30.66	18.66	8.00	2.66	13.33	5.33	5.33	1.33	–	–	4.00
1938	2.28	36.66	23.33	13.33	1.66	13.33	3.33	3.33	–	–	–	–
1939	–	35.71	25.23	9.52	–	7.14	2.28	7.14	4.78	2.28	–	2.28

Compiled from: Gifford, op. cit.

dispel the notion that British films of the decade were either unpopular or ignored.

Over two in every five films were being re-released by the end of the thirties in contrast to one in ten in the early thirties and one in four or five midway through the decade. Among the reissued films, comedies and musicals again predominate, and, if anything, the statistics demonstrating this preponderance are even more dramatic, particularly in the early years of the decade.

In all but the years 1936–1938, the percentages in Table 2.18 are higher than those in Table 2.6. Table 2.19 shows the percentages of all reissued films per year. A few minor differences from Table 2.14 can be observed. War films, adventures, and histories seem slightly higher proportionally among the reissued films which may be a result of heightened interest in these films during the war years later; crime films and dramas, however, involve about the same or slightly lower percentages. But, in general, the proportions of the re-released films seem to reflect fairly accurately the patterns established by the categories of all releases. From this data, laughter and songs would seem to have been the main characteristics of not only most British films but also presumably those films which British audiences wanted to see again.

While the information derived from this implicit assumption of popularity has been instructive, for the purpose of this study, several major questions remain untouched by all of this analysis. Though Gifford's broad categorizations are useful, the content of British popular cinema remains largely a mystery even after such a close inspection of what can be gathered from his data. Though the categories of films that were produced by the studios and their proportionate significance has been presented, the nature of neither characters nor plots has been considered. Without further investigation, Perry's assertion that British cinema was, by nature, "middle class," thus remains unchallenged, though the devotion of the working-class patrons to their movies is suggestive. For this reason, a more detailed examination of these features is necessary before an attempt can be made to assess their general appeal or their specific appeal to the working classes.

3

DEPICTING THE WORKING CLASSES IN BRITISH FILM IN THE THIRTIES

Escapist versus realistic portrayals

If the British public, and especially the working classes, were so fond of the cinema, what accounts for this popularity? One possible explanation may have something to do with the fact that in these productions, the working classes could see themselves being portrayed even if that depiction was not particularly true to life. Certainly, the undeniable appeal of the British film for the working-class audiences that frequented the cinema in part may have been conditioned by the prevalence of working-class characters, environments, and situations in the movies being produced.

In spite of the generally held belief that British films avoided the working classes, a close examination of the content of British features during the decade shows that working-class characters and situations appeared with considerable regularity in British movies. Working-class characters were mentioned in many of the plot synopses, listings of credits, and reviews, as indicated in Table 3.1.

Table 3.1 Features in which members of the working classes are mentioned in the plot synopses, credits, and reviews

Year	Proportion of the films released	%
1929	31 of 86	36.0
1930	37 of 99	37.4
1931	47 of 134	35.1
1932	66 of 150	44.0
1933	76 of 181	42.0
1934	89 of 183	48.6
1935	94 of 185	50.8
1936	83 of 219	37.9
1937	93 of 211	44.1
1938	55 of 158	34.8
1939	26 of 98	26.5

In five of the eleven years, the working classes figured significantly enough to be mentioned in more than two of every five films produced in Britain, and in 1935 and 1936, they were prominent in almost one of every two films made; in every other year of the decade, except somewhat surprisingly the last year prior to the war, working-class characters figured in more than one of every three features that were released.

The evidence is similar for those films in which working-class characters were actually the protagonists or central figures in the plot. As indicated in Table 3.2, the percentages, which could hardly be described as negligible, in most years, hover rather consistently between 35 and 45 percent.

In addition and far more frequently, a recognizable working-class character could be found in the cast at least in a minor or supporting role. As Table 3.3 reveals, in five of the eleven years, a working-class character was

Table 3.2 Features in which members of the working classes are protagonists

Year	Proportion of the films released	%
1929	33 of 86	38.4
1930	27 of 99	27.3
1931	51 of 134	38.1
1932	65 of 150	43.3
1933	62 of 181	34.3
1934	75 of 183	41.0
1935	82 of 185	44.3
1936	74 of 219	33.8
1937	76 of 211	36.0
1938	62 of 158	39.2
1939	27 of 98	27.6

Table 3.3 Films in which at least one supporting role involves a working-class character

Year	Proportion of the films released	%
1929	38 of 86	44.2
1930	50 of 99	50.5
1931	61 of 134	45.5
1932	70 of 150	46.7
1933	95 of 181	52.5
1934	92 of 183	50.3
1935	82 of 185	44.3
1936	112 of 219	51.1
1937	100 of 211	47.4
1938	59 of 158	37.3
1939	49 of 98	50.0

somehow involved in more than half of the films produced by British studios, and in all but one of the remaining years, at least nine of every twenty features had working-class characters in at least some minor part.

Additionally, a fairly significant minority of the films produced every year were set in a working-class environment of some kind, such as in mines, in factories, in shipyards, in neighborhood pubs, or in slums. Table 3.4 demonstrates that usually one out of every three films had a working-class setting and that in 1934 and in 1935, the proportion was approximately two of every five English films.

Table 3.4 Features with working-class settings

Year	Proportion of the films released	%
1929	30 of 86	34.9
1930	32 of 99	32.3
1931	42 of 134	31.3
1932	53 of 150	35.3
1933	42 of 181	23.2
1934	73 of 183	39.9
1935	80 of 185	43.2
1936	74 of 219	33.8
1937	67 of 211	31.8
1938	52 of 158	32.9
1939	27 of 98	27.6

But again, these raw figures are far more interesting than significant. The mere presence of a working-class character does not mean that he or she is an appealing figure; nor does it provide any sense of how the audience reacted to that presence or of how the character was portrayed. In fact, considerable evidence suggests that at least among some audience members, the portrayals of the working classes were regarded as inaccurate and shallow.

Writing in a 1938 issue of *Film Weekly*, movie commentator Glyn Roberts issued a stunning indictment of the way the British film industry had caricatured the laboring people of Great Britain. This critique is worth reviewing. Roberts observed that the "picture of contemporary Britain presented in our cinemas" depicted a "working population" that was "remorselessly good humoured" and that seemed to be "clowning about every damn thing that ever comes along"; Roberts contrasted that image with the reality of the "small clerks, factory hands, transport workers, waitresses ... [and other] wage earners" who were "friendly, normal, quiet, and chronically tired human beings." While they may "know a joke when they see one," Roberts emphasized their concerns were "more serious" such as "a relative in hospital, a son out of work, grim money shortages, undernourishment, family travels," and they know such things "are *not* funny."[1]

Moreover, Roberts went on, when these ordinary working people go to the movies, the screen counterparts they see, include farcical stereotypes with chauffeurs "wallowing in servility," "moronic" servant girls, gardeners "falling over buckets and rakes," fake bus conductors "with the RADA accents and weak, twisted mouths of Shaftesbury Avenue juveniles," and caricatured mothers "who look like burlesques of burlesques of burlesques of something Cicely Courtneidge did when the world was young." Roberts further charged that "the biggest stars" in Britain "connive at this insolent treatment of the population"; by contrast, a performer in other countries "can specialize in working class . . . characteristics and remain dignified . . . and as many sided as life itself" rather than being "a mere buffoon." Roberts then pointedly asks whether British and others must be "molly-coddled and fed with this sugared skim milk" with "every real emotion stunted, every reasoned conviction forgotten." [2]

This overemphasis on comedy, Roberts felt, was paralleled by a generally unrealistic sense of drama in British productions; and what drama there was rarely involved the British working classes. Whenever serious drama is attempted, Roberts contended, "nine times out of ten it is phony, bogus, trivial, and genuinely laughable"; typically, such films involved principal characters "in 'immaculate' evening dress" showing "how the rich live" and centering on the "*smart* people." [3] Roberts added that among the world's more developed film industries, the British seemed backward in their depiction of the "comparatively poor," by which was meant "the people who not only have to work to live," but who "have to put their minds on things that matter." Roberts reminded that these people comprise "an overwhelming majority" of the population, and "no national film industry ignores these people." For instance, in Russia, "they are the only people who matter," and in France, "a mirror is held up to them as the rest of the people"; in America, Roberts observed the wealthy are "ruthlessly caricatured in films" and "excepting them alone, there are no class distinctions in the country, no ludicrous layers and castes . . . one language, not two." But in Britain, Roberts only saw the working classes portrayed in comedy.[4]

Roberts concluded that the film industry's dependence on the British stage stifled any reasonable portrayal of the working classes, and that a realistic depiction of the lives of ordinary people would never be possible without a substantial change in the way British movie production was conducted. Calling for an end to the "disastrous . . . practice of drawing on the West End theatre" for actors "to depict the ordinary people in films," Roberts urged the film industry to "organise its own school for acting, recruiting its players from all classes" and giving them a nationalistic technique, not the current artificial style which combines "nauseating affectation with wearied disdain"; clearly, the film industry "at present . . . insults the nation with the distorting mirror of its productions." [5]

The editors of *Film Weekly* apparently concurred with Roberts' assessment and expressed amazement that British audiences tolerated this outrage; in a commentary about the article, they wondered,

> Why have the people who work for their living, eat tinned salmon, and occasionally drop an aspirate always to be made ridiculous in British films? Why do British audiences, consisting of at least 95% of these very people, stand for it . . .? [T]he very people upon whom the film industry here as everywhere else depends . . . are apparently content . . . to sit through film after film in which trading on some falacious analogy of "traditional British humour," the whole working class population of these islands is presented as a fawning, tedious, pinheaded rabble of flunkeys and cretins.[6]

The overall validity of Roberts' indictment is difficult to assess, but the evidence for this view was limited at best, and the evidence against it was, in some ways, more persuasive. The question of what is a genuine portrayal and what is artificial is highly debatable and is largely a matter of perception. However, some of the qualities in features to which Roberts objected can be surveyed. Table 3.5 is a listing of all features in which working-class

Table 3.5 Films depicting working-class characters comically

Year	Proportion of the films released	%
1929	23 of 86	26.7
1930	32 of 99	32.3
1931	37 of 134	27.6
1932	49 of 150	32.7
1933	46 of 181	25.5
1934	52 of 183	28.4
1935	73 of 185	39.5
1936	79 of 219	36.1
1937	57 of 211	27.0
1938	47 of 158	29.7
1939	29 of 98	29.6

characters could be considered to be humorous caricatures; that is, films tallied in Table 3.5 include features considered to be comedies with working-class characters providing at least some of the humor, movies categorized as dramas or other non-comedies in which working-class characters provide comic relief for the plot, and productions in which the working-class figures are seen as essentially incompetent or bumbling.

The criticism of working-class characterizations made by Glyn Roberts was one with which other writers and commentators agreed; but an amazingly consistent disparity always has existed between the observations of scholars and critics on the one hand and members of the public on the other. Often the people have had more charitable points of view toward specific films. If the numerous films listed in Table 3.5 were nevertheless regarded with contentment by British film patrons, then the validity of Roberts' criticism for the audiences of ordinary people is questionable.

The extent to which Roberts' views were shared by the public, thus becomes a major question, assuming their contentment was genuine. Letter-writers to the fan magazines often took similar stands in their notes, sometimes criticizing the portrayal of the working classes in recent films they had seen, or calling for realistic depictions of laboring people. Specifically responding to Roberts' comments, several people writing to *Film Weekly* in the issues that followed agreed with his criticism. A lady from Wellington wrote, "Thanks a million to Glyn Roberts for the truest criticism of British film snobbery I have read in many years"; she added her belief that "the people who run our picture industry are too class-ridden, too old-school-tie conscious ever to make or to want to make an honest and sincere working man's film."[7] A London filmgoer, who identified herself as "a working woman who visits the local cinema regularly" observed that she "writhed at the mental deficients portrayed as workers in British films."[8] Another London woman suggested that "ordinary men and women" were just as "annoyed" at the British film industry for its treatment of the working classes as Mr Roberts; the writer, possibly a charwoman, added, "we don't mind having fun poked at us, but it should be fun, and it should be at *us*, not at . . . mythical [working class types] . . . especially phony charwomen."[9]

Similar comments from time to time had been made throughout the decade. About five years earlier, a letter-writer from Southsea, in a note to *Picturegoer Weekly*, observed that a recent article he had read had suggested "the possibility of a film with the slums forming the background, throwing a ghastly sidelight on social conditions in modern England." The correspondent said:

> The need for such a film cannot be emphasized far enough. England does not boast of a Dickens in the present generation who could waken us to the evils of slumdom. But she does possess the kinematograph, brought nearer and nearer to perfection by science and invention. The kinema can be used with advantage to present a manifesto of life in slums to the general public. British producers will not have to look for a scenario and setting. Why not grasp the opportunity while it is still ours.[10]

In 1937, a letter was published attacking "the general standard of English screen comedy"; the writer argued, "we are still too fond, for instance, of jeering at the discomfiture of working class types when placed in unfamiliar social surroundings, thereby revealing British upper class snobbery for the world to note."[11] A writer in a 1932 letter to *Picturegoer Weekly* resented what she felt were the "grossly exaggerated" portraits of East-End life in some current films, adding "people are not public house mad these days."[12] Several letters resented the traditional method of depicting working-class characters through accent, clothing, and other short-hand devices that instantly suggested one of the "lower orders." A 1933 letter to *Film Pictorial* complained about the necessity of depicting working-class characters in the broad, farcical style of the music hall; the correspondent wrote that this "inability to drop the 'music hall' complex when introducing such characters as landladies, servants, and British women" was the "chief weakness" of "British film production," and while "these exaggerated characters are very humorous when placed in the music hall, . . . in the atmosphere of the cinema, they arouse only disgust in the mind of any Briton." [13] Another filmgoer complained that a "real life" Cockney had yet to be seen on film, because all Cockney impersonations were merely standard "types." [14] A shopgirl similarly berated the style of speaking used by actresses in roles representing her occupation; in a 1937 letter, she bitterly commented with regard to a particular film:

> I feel I must protest against the exaggerated and out of date characterisation which spoils so many British films . . . The average shop-girl speaks probably as well as . . . [the actress] does in private life. I know several shop-girls who also resented this picture. All too frequently we get these caricatures of ordinary people . . . and it won't do. [15]

Another criticism of working-class characterizations suggested that British films portrayed the conditions in which they lived and the nature of their lifestyles in an unduly favorable manner. A 1933 letter to *Film Weekly* observed that the actors playing these roles are "too smartly dressed"; the writer noted that an actor in one film he had seen appeared "in a check suit with his trousers creased better than mine ever are," and "yet he is supposed to be a distributor of handbills." [16] A 1938 film fan from Folkestone echoed these thoughts.

> Many filmgoers have expressed the wish that they would like to see more films dealing with ordinary persons, but unless some stars are willing to sacrifice their personal vanity in such parts, I can only view such films with apprehension. Most past portrayals of the working girl heroine, for instance, have left me cold. We are asked to sympathise with a poor girl who hasn't a cent to pay a heartless landlady her room rent. Yet, generally, this same poor girl is garbed in clothing the cost of which would keep any real life working girl for a year, and who has make-up that, in spite of her struggles against the hard world, is a perfect example of Max Factor's art. All this gives us no excuse to forget that our "poor working girl" actually earns a colossal salary and has a private bathing-pool and a . . . mansion. Are we asking too much of our "idols" to expect them to play ordinary mortals like ourselves. [17]

Complaints were also registered about the seemingly endless succession of impersonations of English police as comic Cockneys; one filmgoer wrote that such portrayals of a policeman as "an ill-spoken clumsy piece of officialdom ... always with a broad Cockney accent ('Ere, 'Erb, catch 'old of 'im; come on, nah, me lad, we've got her)" were an outright "misrepresentation." [18] Even the leading British film expert on the portrayal of the Cockney, Gordon Harker, at least once was subject to a filmgoer's wrath; one angry London movie fan wrote from Bermondsey:

> Who is this bloke Gordon Harker? We read of his fine Cockney charac-
> terizations. I think they are very poor. Why people in London visit
> kinemas and roar with laughter at Harker rendering a burlesque of a
> Cockney, I cannot understand. This is 1934, yet the leading English
> exponent of Cockney wit gives us impressions of people of fifty years
> ago. A person I know is continually ragged for referring to his "Old
> Dutch." I am 28, have lived amongst the Cockneys all my life, and I can
> honestly say that if any of my work mates, whose ages range from
> twenty to seventy, spoke and acted like Gordon Harker, we would give
> him a raspberry . . . . It is time that Gordon Harker came out of the past
> and gave us an impression of the present. Let him go to Billingsgate
> again, and this time take stock of any intelligent workers there – not
> their grandfathers. [19]

One writer from London seemed to sum up this point of view that British films too often took the easy way out in their stereotypical, Cockney characterizations of the working classes; in a 1933 letter to *Picturegoer Weekly*, complaining about the "use of the Cockney dialect in British films," he wrote:

> This type of speech in its proper place and time is highly effective . . .
> but I see no reason why every metropolitan policeman, barmaid, or
> shop assistant who has to appear should be made to speak this way.
> I have lived in the East End all my life and know that the average shop
> girl, for example, is an intelligent and well-spoken person. Besides
> giving the impression . . . that the working class Englishman is an
> uneducated half-wit, the Cockney tongue jars on our own nerves, when
> put in the mouth of an obviously unskilled exponent. [20]

But these negative reactions to the portrayal of the working classes were hardly uniform; in fact, the absence of more such critical responses, along with the presence of at least as many comments defending British films and the continuing popularity of these movies among the working classes suggests that there was no consensus about working-class characterizations among filmgoers. For example, the last of the above mentioned letter-writers may have been generally critical of the film industry, but unlike the Bermondsey film fan he found no fault with Gordon Harker's Cockney performances, calling them "highly effective . . . [and] admirably [performed]." [21] A gentleman from Brighton who identified himself as a Cockney, in a subsequent issue of *Picturegoer Weekly*, quickly defended screen Cockney portrayals, and particularly those of Gordon Harker; replying to the letter of the Bermondsey filmgoer, and after asking who the "bloke" thought he was in criticizing Harker as a Cockney, the correspondent wrote indignantly:

> [W]ho dares suggest that Gordon Harker does not give a perfect portrayal of the London Cockney? As a Cockney myself, wot I will say, an' wot I does say is, "Blimey!" Harker "Cockneys" are absolutely true to life; he avoids even the slightest exaggeration . . . I meet "dyed in the wool" Cockneys that are as like our screen Harker as two peas, and "Old Dutch" is a term in constant and everyday use. As one "bloke" to "annuver" . . . have you not been toying with the facts to make your letter read better? Nark it.[22]

And other stereotyped screen Cockneys received similar praise for their authenticity. A London moviegoer in a 1937 letter to *Film Weekly* praised comic Max Miller's portrayal of the Edgar Wallace Cockney character "Educated Evans," saying the characterization was "amusing, human and plausible."[23] Another letter-writer suggested veteran character actor Hal Gordon who appeared in countless features in minor roles was an authentic and believable Cockney.[24] Whether the depiction was comic or serious did not seem to matter to some filmgoers who were satisfied and impressed with the realism of British features, in spite of what others may have thought. In fact, at least one letter-writer felt that British films were especially truthful in their depiction of poverty:

> British films are unique in one way . . . . For in our films when a heroine is supposed to be poor she really looks poor . . . Gracie Fields, for instance, in *This Week of Grace*, Florence Desmond in *Sally in Our Alley*, and the stars in *Britannia of Billingsgate*, to mention but three examples, all looked "hard up." Every one of these actresses looked real and natural .[25]

In addition, believability and harshly realistic portrayals of the working classes were not necessarily attractive to all working-class moviegoers. One letter-writer in 1937 contended that British features were too realistic, and that this accuracy was unpleasant to filmgoers; the writer observed that "I have seen many English films dealing all too faithfully with poverty and working class life," and, he concluded, "while such verisimilitude may be admirable in theory it seems in practice to make bad cinema."[26] Another correspondent defended the broad, farcical depictions of the working classes, observing that in such film roles, "exaggeration" was necessary "for the simple reason that the . . . kinema-goer is seeking *entertainment* and likes the characters laid out clearly before him"; the filmgoer "has no desire to worry his brain with the effort of puzzling out what type or class of individual the actor is trying to portray!"[27]

In general, a sizable portion of the letters that addressed the question of how true-to-life British films should be in depicting working-class existence argued for less realism and more escapist presentations. One 1934 letter in *Film Pictorial* responded to another reader's earlier suggestion calling for movies "dealing with slum life" by arguing, "when will some people realize that the screen is to provide *entertainment*"; the filmgoer added, "We all . . . are fully aware of [slum existence and] its horrors, but we do not want it thrust before us when we seek pleasure."[28] A typist stated the point eloquently in a letter to *Picturegoer Weekly* in 1932 in which she wrote, "it does not follow that because I am a typist I want to see films about typists"; "on the contrary," she maintained, "I like my heroine to be . . . one of the thousand things I am not."[29] She concluded that while others may have been critical of British film escapism, she preferred to see "roles" that were "quite unlike the one I play for 35 bob a week."[30] A similar sentiment was expressed by another writer who felt depressed after seeing films that were too realistic; he observed:

> Instead of coming out of the kinemas in a happy frame of mind, care and worry at least temporarily banished, far too many pictures are making us leave with the tragic theme of the story we have just watched still haunting us . . . . Perhaps life is not always cheerful, but when we go to the kinema we want romance – we want to get away from [the] harsh realities . . . [of our lives].[31]

One filmgoer, in a July, 1933 letter to *Film Pictorial*, seemed to sum up this point of view most effectively, as she rhetorically asked, "Why do we spend our pocket money and our leisure hours at the cinema?":

> To see our ordinary everyday lives portrayed on the screen over and over again? Emphatically not! What we want is to be carried right away from our own sphere of life – we see and hear enough about *that*! – and be taken to realms which have hitherto existed only in our imagination.[32]

This debate, in one form or another, raged in the letter sections of the fan magazines throughout the thirties, one group calling for realism, social commentary, and unexaggerated films of everyday life, and the other calling for escapism, comedy, and fantasy. Admittedly, many of those among the working classes who were encouraging realistic portraits of ordinary people seemed preoccupied with a nationalistic fear that farcical characterizations of common people might create a low opinion of British citizens abroad. A good portion of letters cited earlier included passages such as this one, from a letter by a filmgoer who called herself a "working woman"; after criticizing the humorous, farcical caricatures of the working classes in British films, she added, " I wonder what reaction Continental and American audiences have when they see an average British film, and what they must think of the average Britisher," and concluded, "It can't be at all . . . complimentary."[33]

But clearly other writers were not motivated by this vague, almost paranoid, nationalistic pride. One well reasoned and well argued letter appeared in a late 1938 issue of *Film Weekly*:

> Now that family films are so popular, I would like to mention one serious fault which is tending to make them quite artificial. Real life is made up of sordidness, troubles which comprise sickness, unemployment and the continual fight to exist. These facts suggest dramatic material if properly treated. The family films contain very little drama, and always concern themselves with middle class family life. Surely there is enough material in a lower class family to make one really first rate film? The mother and father, bringing up a family, fighting against poverty and sickness, the different members of the family, if well characterised, would provide drama and studies of real people. So far, in family films, the mother and father have been too good to be true; the children are more real, but need modifying to some extent. Here's hoping that some producer will be enterprising enough to see the need for a realistic film.[34]

These sincere objections from obviously regular and serious moviegoers must have troubled the film producers, just as they were troubled by those who insisted on only escapist films.

This dilemma, then, posed a massive problem for the film industry in its attempts to respond to the wants and needs of its audiences, and more importantly, in its efforts to make a profit. Determining exactly what the public was seeking always has been a problem for the purveyor of public entertainment. When opinions about one aspect of this entertainment are diametrically opposed, judgments become expensive guesses about public taste. That the British film industry, or at least segments of it, did make efforts to depict the working classes more accurately cannot be denied.

Throughout the decade, evidence shows that attempts were being made for more accurate depictions of the working people on every level of production from the performers to the studio executives. Some of the actors told the fan magazines that they had "researched" their roles by spending time among the "ordinary people" whom they were attempting to impersonate. Veteran character actor Edmund Gwenn in a September, 1933 article in *Film Pictorial* entitled "Edmund Gwenn's Men are – Real Men" told of the pains he took in depicting a working-class man.[35] Gordon Harker told *Picturegoer Weekly* of his detailed research about the different types of Cockneys in a 1935 article, emphasizing the authenticity of his characterizations.[36] This technique was beautifully summarized in the same publication several years later, as George Carney, another specialist at portraying working-class characters, discussed his technique of researching the type of person he was to play; in so doing, he perhaps inadvertently, revealed just how difficult it was to divorce such characterization from a native, earthy sense of humor. Carney observed that whenever he was cast in a character part, he would "make a point of spending as much of my time as possible with the type of man I am to play"; he would "go to the places in which [such] . . . characters live and work and play" and would "quietly study them at first hand." For instance, when Carney played a fish and chip "specialist" in *Say It With Flowers*, he "spent nearly a month haunting the little eating shops in the neighborhood of Shoreditch and Hackney," studying "the way the people spoke and moved," getting "their viewpoint on life . . . [and their] special interests in work and play," and understanding "their attitudes to things in general." He then described "making careful mental notes" of people he was watching in a fish and chip shop in the East End and over-hearing two "road-sweeps" describe, in all seriousness, professional tech-nique; concluded Carney, such professional analysis of menial labors might seem "funny to us no doubt," but, he added, "unless one can sympathise with and understand the attitude of the man to whom a piece of clever sweeping means everything," one cannot "hope to give a true picture of him" when making a film.[37]

Whether other ex-music hall performers studied the people they were depicting in films or ever felt the need for such research is not clear. But others laboring in the film industry indicated they too were striving for authenticity and honest views of ordinary people. While working as a screen-writer in the early thirties, before his long directing career had begun, Robert Stevenson observed in an article that working-class characters, and Cockneys in particular, were ideal for the talking picture, and predicted that inevitably, the overwhelming majority of all English pictures would involve working-class roles; he noted, additionally, that "wise producers" already were researching such lifestyles for inclusion in their films.[38] Some directors also were seeking authenticity in their productions. Basil Dean, Michael Powell, John Baxter, Carol Reed, and even Alfred Hitchcock, among others, were cited in various articles throughout the decade as having made at one point or another extraordinary efforts to guarantee that their films had realistic char-acterizations, settings, and situations.[39] Similarly, from time to time, these same directors would indicate their general intentions of being as realistic as possible.[40]

Even the producers would sometimes offer opinions as to the necessity of responding to the public outcry for honesty and authenticity in the portrayal of real people. For example, in discussing producer Victor Saville's plans for *The Citadel*, author A. J. Cronin observed to interviewer, J. Danvers Williams, that "drama must have its roots in the life of the people" and commented that in making *The Citadel*, Saville would endeavor "to get out of the studio as much as possible" by "going to South Wales to get authentic shots of the coal-mine sequence." Cronin said, "the incessantly-moving colliery wheel, the cage, the men covered in dirt, the contrast between the bright sun and the deep pit . . . should all make first-class dramatic – or . . . cinematic . . . material." He concluded by expressing the hope that the film would provide a "fairly comprehensive picture of the varying grades of English social life" and would show "the evils of the present system" where "wealth accumulates in the pockets of the few while labourers and miners bring up families on 37s 6d a week."[41] The article, obviously planted as a promotional piece, nevertheless clearly showed the producer's intention of appealing to that segment of *Film Weekly*'s readership that had so vocally sought realistic portraits of the working classes.

Another example was an article that appeared in the May 6, 1933 issue of *Picturegoer Weekly*, written by the Chairman and Managing Director of Sound City Studios, Norman Loudon; in the essay, Loudon urged "that our studios . . . get down to the business of portraying the activities of our every-day life."[42] Since "film is a vivid and vital medium," Loudon felt it should show "vivid and vital subjects" instead of remaining "content to play with light and flimsy dramatics"; he urged producers to "get out and beyond" the studio walls and to "pry into the recesses and the secrets of the drama of mankind." Loudon, noting that there was "no lack of material" and "no lack of public support for such films as these," claimed that "subjects of our national life" were "crying out for filming." His decision a year and a half earlier to form Sound City Studios had been influenced by those beliefs. He had also been impressed by his observation at the picture houses he attended of "American films that flashed with brilliance the activities of American everyday life." Since "too often the British counterpart was a flirtatious farce or a cocktail effervescence," Loudon was convinced he could put into effect his convictions and "Let Films Live!"[43] Loudon then discussed and promoted several of Sound City's latest productions which involved "Labourers earning . . . weekly wages, itinerant vendors, shoeblades, 'butt end' collectors, and rogues," and finally enthused "What a chance for real characterisation!"[44]

While Loudon undoubtedly expected such discussions would also attract working-class filmgoers, or at least those who wanted to see such films, the more direct method of appealing to audiences was through advertisements. Here again, the approach often was an emphasis on realism of the character-ization of working people. For example, the publicity for the 1934 film, *Say It With Flowers*, about a group of Cockney flower vendors centered on the phrase "A real story of *real* people."[45] An advertisement for the 1935 film, *Turn of the Tide*, about two Yorkshire fishing families, similarly emphasized its accurate national characterizations, calling it a "thoroughly British film."[46]

Throughout the pages of the *Gaumont–British News*, a publication distributed not only to the employees of the studios making the films for the company but also to the employees of the theaters in the Gaumont–British chain, suggestions continually were being made on how to gear publicity about certain films to the working classes. For example, a 1931 drama about mill workers, *Hindle Wakes*, inspired one Birmingham cinema manager to have his ushers and attendants "decorated . . . with the insignia of the mill towns of the north, namely in clogs and shawls" to demonstrate the genuine working-class environment of the film.[47] The advertising campaign for *The Fire Raisers*, a 1933 feature dealing with arsonists which had been widely praised as an honest attempt at realism, made reference to some of the requests for accuracy in depicting the working classes, as street displays in working-class neighborhoods referred to it as "The Film the Public Demanded."[48] For the Betty Balfour 1934 vehicle, *My Old Dutch*, about the lives of a Cockney family, costers were used on the street to publicize the film.[49]

Sometimes the publicity for a film would emphasize the working-class characters even if they played only a small part in the plot, or if their function in the films was essentially minor. For example, upon the release of the internationally praised 1930 feature, *Journey's End*, (an early anti-war production based on R. C. Sheriff's famous play), a house publication distributed to the patrons of one English cinema, the *Stoll Herald*, told of the featured roles in the film played by two English comedians who specialized in working-class characters. With customary publicity exaggeration, readers were told of the accuracy of these portrayals.

> They are typical of England, they crystallise and personify those very attributes we worship and admire . . . . [They] possess that certain something we are glad to call British. It is marvellous to see these men, through the medium of the screen living out their lives in one of the most difficult and dangerous periods of history, living it with supreme courage and superb heroism.[50]

Yet the roles of the two characters are so small that they are almost nonexistent; as a matter of fact, one of the chief criticisms of the film is that it was essentially concerned with the officers and not the enlisted men and that it portrayed the enlisted men in the stereotypical way. Clearly, the minor working-class characters were emphasized in the publicity strictly to respond to those who wanted to see accurate characterizations of the working classes.

The fact that the studios were paying direct attention to these calls for realistic characterizations was shown by an item that appeared in a fan magazine and was subsequently discussed in the *Gaumont–British News*. In October, 1932, a secretary wrote to *Film Weekly*, complaining of the artificial portrayal of typists in British films.[51] In the next month's issue of the *Gaumont–British News*, the critical letter was reprinted with the admonition, "Surely there must be a live-wire typist concealed somewhere in studios who could give the stars a lesson before the film is taken."[52]

But if the studios were paying attention to the cries for realism, they were also responding to the appeals for escapism. For example, a 1932 article in *Picturegoer Weekly* entitled "Should Films Stick to Fantasy" written by the popular former music hall comedian Lupino Lane, summed up the point of view that the cinema was only doing the public a service if it provided the audience with escapist fare. Lane wrote that "surely the greatest art of all lies in making your fellow creatures happy," and in that sense, "the kinema ... because of its unique ability to 'take you out of yourself' ... can be the most joyful make-believe in the world"; accordingly, the "business of the film" should be to make audiences "forget their own drab lives." Lane observed that if a laborer "who has toiled all day in a workshop" or a woman "whose household drudgery is sapping her imagination" can attend a cinema and "enter a world of colour and romance for a couple of hours then the film has achieved something very nearly great." Noting that audiences "expect the kinema to give them something which they cannot get anywhere else," Lane observed that "the luxurious seats, the spectacular entrances, the soft music" all provide some qualities of life that many in the audience "cannot get anywhere else," and it is this element of being "transported to another realm [that] they know ... doesn't exist" that is the primary reason why filmgoers "pay their shillings for the privilege of entering it." [53]

Few of the letter-writers favoring the escapist film would have been likely to have disagreed with Lane's forceful defense of this approach to moviemaking. Nor would they have been likely to have disagreed with his rebuke of the more realistic portrayals of the lives of ordinary people and their problems by those film-makers with a more serious orientation. Lane contended that as soon as "a director attempts to become intellectual" his approach is "liable to become laboured and heavy"; he added that when a film-maker concentrates on a "social problem" or a "moral," it invariably "spoils or holds up that action which is the very life blood of the screen," because the cinema should be "a land of fantasy far from the solid earth and the harsh realism of ordinary life." Such "concrete ... analysis" and "realism," in the view of Lupino Lane, is better suited to other media like the stage or literature, and he predicted that "the craze for stark realism [in films] is [not] likely to last very long." [54]

Other performers and film-makers expressed similar sentiments in various publications throughout the decade. Director Walter Forde in a 1932 article called "The Films I Should Like to Make" told interviewer Clifford Eccles that the present crisis period was comparable to the war period with "the difficulty of living and enjoying life ... seldom ... greater for masses of people all over the world"; with "everyone ... feeling poor" and with many going hungry, the world is regarded "with disgust and fear" which means "that people in search of entertainment no longer want to see ... pictures which either in subject or treatment remind them of their own lives." In words strikingly similar to those attributed to Lupino Lane, Forde contended the audiences wanted "escape into a lighter gayer world" where they could "forget for a few hours their troubles and forebodings"; he concluded that "of that famous trio, they want more of love and laughter, and less of life." [55] Forde went on to predict that future "big box office successes ... will be mainly, if not entirely, romantic in character"; he argued that since music provides one of the "best aids" to romance, British film producers "should have as much music ... in pictures" as possible. Noting that since the "two things a man can do and be happy without a penny in his pocket" are to "sing and make love," if British films "show people singing and making love . . . our . . . penniless audiences will be able to identify themselves with the characters on the screen, and they, too, will be happy"; consequently, Forde concluded that the movies he wanted to film were "cheerful musical pictures with a strong love interest" because his ambition was to have his audiences departing the cinema "smiling and oblivious for a time" to "income tax collection, . . . unemployment and all the other bogies of 1932." [56]

Other directors and producers may have been paying attention to concerns over realism and films about the toils and difficulties of everyday life, but the word that was coming from the exhibitors themselves who knew their audiences intimately was largely in favor of light, escapist entertainment. A note in a late December 1930 issue of *Film Weekly* observed that "At the present time, there is a preference for laughter-making films of all types." [57] Such observations continued throughout the decade. For example, the story was told in 1938 of a mild-mannered elderly lady who became almost violently upset, complaining to the manager "at a little back street cinema . . . in Bristol" because he had been putting on such "rotten entertainment"; she argued that the social dramas that had been playing there were too "grim" and "a little too near life to be attractive." [58]

Veteran film exhibitor and trader Willf Anderson actually worked in British cinemas during the decade and subsequently sold home movies from his business in California; for years he regularly wrote a fascinating series of columns in his bi-monthly catalogue about his experiences working as a cinema operator and manager in the small cinemas known as "dumps" in the Northern industrial areas of England during the thirties. In one of his columns, he reflected on the appeal of escapist films at the depth of the Depression; he noted that in industrial areas "where life was somewhat grim at the best of times," during the thirties. . . "the real MAGIC of motion pictures . . . was the BIG attraction." He confirmed that "especially in England" the public "flocked to the movies . . . for an escape from the everyday routine," and for the audiences, "it didn't matter much what was showing" because "the movie-going public wasn't all that critical"; in fact, Anderson contended, "in the North of England," no matter what the portrayal was, whether realistic or not, "the movies were the greatest thing since the New Testament!" [59]

According to Anderson, the patrons of these "dumps" attended so regularly that even the most uncomfortable of cinemas "did a land-office business." He characterized the "clientele" as consisting largely of "coal-miners and ship-builders" who were "rough, tough, dirty individuals" taking life as it came and not "stand[ing] on ceremony when it came to expressing an opinion"; with that in mind, Anderson reiterated that to this audience, movies were supposed to be "entertaining . . . affording an 'escape' from the humdrum lives that were the lot of these simple people." Echoing the more traditional responses to music hall entertainment, the filmgoers to which Anderson referred "reacted as one to the action on the screen"; they "laughed . . . hissed . . . cheered and sometimes got a little 'carried away' when a particular screen hero faced terrible danger!"[60] From his experiences, Anderson has developed something of a philosophy of film-showing, based on his knowledge of what people wanted to see during those difficult years, which he expressed eloquently in another of his columns; "basically," he concluded, "the object of motion pictures is to entertain, to offer an 'escape' from reality and become part of a new exciting world of wonder."[61] This point of view evidently was shared by others who were employed in these working-class districts.

A sense of what working-class audiences specifically favored was occasionally reported by managers to film publications. For example, the manager of a cinema in one of the small Scottish industrial towns reported in a December, 1933 letter to *Film Weekly* that the "most popular films" that were exhibited at his theater were unquestionably "British musicals," and the manager then went further and provided some specific titles of films that were particularly well appreciated.[62] These titles provide a fascinating glimpse of what satisfied audiences, and a remarkable pattern emerges from the features especially cited by the manager as being the most favored movies his patrons identified.

In virtually every feature, the principal characters were individuals with working-class occupations who had contacts and ultimately successes with middle- and upper-class characters. Among the films he identified, *Sunshine Susie* was an immensely popular Renate Muller musical released in late 1931 about a secretary being romanced by a banker who was posing as a clerk to win her hand. Another Renate Muller vehicle cited by the cinema manager was *Marry Me*, a late 1932 musical about a recordist (that is one who works in a record studio) who wins a social climber by becoming a housekeeper. Two Jack Buchanan musicals were mentioned, and both have similar themes. *Yes, Mr Brown* was an early 1933 musical in which the secretary to a factory manager played by Jack Buchanan poses as his absent wife so that he can impress his American boss. The classic *Goodnight Vienna*, released in the spring of 1932, is another Buchanan vehicle, this time about a general's son who is engaged to a countess but who falls in love with a shop girl in a flower store. The manager also referred to *Maid of the Mountains*, a fall, 1932 musical release directed by Lupino Lane in which a bandit poses as the governor of an Italian province, and *King of the Ritz*, a Stanley Lupino musical circulated in the spring of 1933 about a porter who saves a widow's jewels and is made a duke. All of these films, along with the Jack Hulbert–Cicely Courtneidge comedy, *Jack's the Boy*, released in the summer of 1932 about a police commissioner's son who wants to start out at the bottom as a policeman, "played to phenomenal houses," according to the Scottish cinema manager.[63] This popularity of these specific films was not an isolated phenomenon limited to one Scottish industrial town, a point attested to by the fact that virtually all of the films cited, except for the two Renate Muller musicals, were reissued later in the 1930s.[64] Among the other films cited by the manager as "successes" included *Smilin' Along*, a short 1932 comedy featurette released late in the year starring Rene Ray as a flowergirl who impersonates a maid at her beloved's engagement party.[65] Clearly, the depictions of the working classes in these films were largely fanciful and were far less realistic and accurate than some critics would have desired, yet their widespread popularity, an appeal that extended to working-class audiences, showed that these movies were appreciated and desirable.

The publicity designed for these escapist films advertised and promoted their fantasy and wish-fulfillment qualities. *Sunshine Susie*, for example, was portrayed in advertisements as "A Cure for the Deepest Depression" or as "An Excellent Cure for the Blues."[66] Gracie Fields' 1933 vehicle, *This Week of Grace*, in which Miss Fields plays a fired factory worker whose family, by an odd set of circumstances, is called upon to manage a duchess's castle, was characterized in some of its publicity as a "Cinderella in Modern Dress."[67]

The reasons for these conflicting signals to the film industry from the moviegoers are complex and not easily identifiable, but part of the solution probably lies in the heterogeneity of the different regions of the United Kingdom and its society. Numerous sociologists have observed and identified substantial differences among the multiple levels of the working classes, and the responses of these various levels of cinema patrons likewise may have differed according to their status in society. More importantly, however, attitudes varied by region, as some contemporary analysts suggested. For example, one performer observed that "the brand of humour which has been acclaimed by ... audiences in Manchester, Liverpool, Leeds, Birmingham, Glasgow, Belfast, and the hundred and one other towns in Britain is a comparatively safe gamble for the screen" because it was appreciated by a wide-ranging provincial audience; by contrast, "the traditional West End [comedy] is in many instances an almost certain flop when transferred to a wider and more general audience." He added that "only occasionally does the picture which breaks records in the West End do likewise in the country at large, and many films which London appears not to notice go from one success to another in the provinces," and he cited as a classic example Gracie Fields' pictures which "have not for the most part had great West End receptions, but ... have proved immense successes in the provinces." At the same time, "some ... satires, hailed in London as masterpieces, have failed to please in certain industrial centres."[68] As a result of these distinctly different markets, many British films intended essentially for provincial audiences would never play the London West End. For example, at the time that George Formby was Britain's leading film box office attraction, in the late 1930s, as Alan Randall and Ray Seaton pointed out in their biography of the singer–comedian, "West End cinemas did not want Formby films"; yet, in the North, "the public would be hanging from the rafters," and the movies often would be so popular that "in certain areas the films were booked and re-booked over and over again."[69]

This pattern of noticeable differences in regional tastes was observable in the variation in popularity of numerous other performers who were especially well received in industrial areas and the provinces, but not in London. But even this regional popularity varied from one area to another. A 1933 article by film commentator Oliver Baldwin entitled "What Films Do the Public Like?" in *Picturegoer Weekly* acknowledged these inconsistencies and the impact they had on the public's film-going tastes; Baldwin noted that while "the general opinion is that British filmgoers are only interested in comedy of the orthodox stage type," the form that "appreciation" of comedy takes "is by no means universal."[70] That is, Baldwin argued, "Lancashire may like slapstick comedy, whilst Birmingham may appreciate pure farce"; in addition, Baldwin felt that there was a place for a film that would examine "not . . . the foibles of society and the incredible stupidity of 'below stairs,'" but rather a movie "showing real people as they are, their difficulties in these uncertain times and the great struggle for economic security that is the personal battle for so many millions of our fellows." Baldwin acknowledged that producers "fear there would be no interest in such an idea and that the expense would not justify the project" because "films that have a message are also looked upon with disfavour"; but he expressed a strong conviction that film-makers do not have to "[play] down to" the "untutored public."[71] Thus, Baldwin's conclusion was that with the nation's diversity, the film industry should be encouraged to make movies dealing with a wide variety of subjects and with a wide range of viewpoints, in order to respond to the differing needs of the various audiences it served. Said Baldwin, since "it is incredibly difficult to know what the British people like" because "what is called 'entertainment' in the West End is often merely boring in Newcastle, [and vice versa]" he regarded it essential that British film companies "vary their types of entertainment in order to give the public" a choice at the cinema.[72]

The response of the British film industry to these two contrasting and confusingly opposite approaches to characterizing the working classes was, perhaps predictably, inconsistent, as the dilemma about how to portray ordinary people in movies persisted throughout the thirties. The assumption often made that the film-makers were unresponsive to the request for more honest characterizations must be dismissed because, as has been shown, people in the movie industry were aware of the complaint and at least some of them were making efforts along these lines. But the survey of the features released during the decade shows that, in spite of lip service to the contrary, the overall pattern, of films with humorous caricatures of working-class characters, did not really change. Table 3.5 discloses the fact that the percentages of films in which working-class characters were either comic relief or were portrayed comically remained consistently high. In most years at least one in every four features released portrayed the working classes comically; in 1930 and 1932, the figure was approximately one out of every three releases, and in 1935 and 1936, the number approached two of every five features.

These statistics again reinforce the implication that the escapist cinema retained its enormous popularity with the public. True, some working-class filmgoers were troubled by the comic portrayals of ordinary people. But those who objected were apparently in the minority; the seeming willingness of at least segments of the film industry to respond to the criticism was offset by the fact that other patrons did not seek and in fact avoided realistic social drama. Escapist cinema remained profitable.

4

MISTAKEN IDENTITIES
The *Pygmalion* motif

In the darkest days of the slump in England, film-going audiences were likely to emerge from British cinemas humming the catchy melody from one of the era's most popular tunes. If they remembered the simple, yet lively words, they might have found themselves uttering the optimistic theme of the song in which the lyrics announce

> I'm looking on the bright side, though I'm walking in the shade,
> Sticking out my chest, hoping for the best,
> Looking on the bright side of life.

The song continues this hopeful sentiment, noting that though

> Today I'm in the shadow; tomorrow, maybe,
> The clouds will lift, and let the sun shift over to me.

The tune concludes with a reaffirmation that

> I'm looking on the bright side, though today's all care and strife,
> I can wear a grin, sticking up my chin
> looking on the bright side of life.

So sang the immensely popular Gracie Fields in her second film, the 1932 musical comedy feature entitled, appropriately enough, *Looking on the Bright Side*; in many ways, this cheery verse, which became a successful recording in the thirties can be said to have summed up the content of a substantial portion of all British films made during the period from 1929 to 1939. With a majority of movies during most years consisting of comedies, musicals, and other escapist film fare, the emphasis on the movie screen throughout the difficult decade of the thirties was on "looking on the bright side," helping the audience to forget its troubles and cares.

Accordingly, certain themes and plot lines reappeared consistently in the films. For the working classes, the movies contained subtle messages encouraging forbearance, optimism, patience, complacency, and faith. At the same time, however, some British films portrayed the middle and upper classes as objects of derision and ridicule, often suggesting that the simple life of the working classes was superior to the more complicated, more artificial existence of the elites. Similarly, success and wealth frequently were depicted as bringing more misfortune than happiness. At the same time, however, wish fulfillment stories and rags-to-riches tales in the movies gave audiences the opportunity to imagine and to experience vicariously what it would be like to be made a millionaire or to become a member of the aristocracy; such features continued to be released year after year. The content and themes of all of these various types of films made in Britain have been never surveyed extensively. Yet, their success and continuing popularity throughout the decade suggests that these movies can reveal an interesting and perhaps significant insight into the dreams and concerns of ordinary people, and specifically the working classes in Depression England; at the least, they disclose the attitudes of British film-makers about the fantasies and dreams of their audiences.

While such escapist productions comprised the majority of the film output of the various studios, more serious movies also must be considered. The more realistic portrayals of ordinary people that figured in at least some features and the limited social commentary that occasionally was suggested in others reveal a different side of British film production, existing in a minor but nevertheless identifiable contrasting counterpoint to the other, more common styles. The question of what political topics and points of view, if any, can be observed in these features is another subject worthy of investigation, especially since the potency of the cinema as a medium and communicator of ideas and as a highly effective device for propaganda has been acknowledged since the earliest days of film-making.

IMPERSONATIONS OF THE UPPER CLASS

Whether realistic or unrealistic in nature, the cinematic depiction of the working classes and the social structure in Britain often followed various recognizable patterns among several traditional and typical plots. In these films certain predictable story "formulae" can be identified which were reused in screenplays regularly. Each of these plot formats also offered possibilities for several variations which also can be distinguished readily.

Perhaps appropriately, British films during the decade often seemed preoccupied with some aspect of the class structure of English society. This theme, if not overtly, then at least indirectly, functioned in numerous features throughout the Depression years. Britain's movie-makers not unexpectedly focused repeatedly in their productions on the parallels and contrasts between the middle and upper classes on the one hand and the working classes on the other; while these comparisons were often artificial, and though inter-relationships among the classes were not always the central object of the movies, their presence continually suggested the interdependence of the traditional levels of British society, whether the films concentrated on the humorous or on the tragic implications of the class structure. This depiction of the relationship of the working classes to other divisions of British society took a variety of forms.

One of the most prevalent examples of this theme was what might be termed the "mistaken identity" format, a plot device that in its basic form is perhaps as old as comedy and drama are themselves. In British films of the thirties, the confusion would develop, for example, from a pseudo-'Pygmalion" motif in which a working-class individual might pose as or be mistaken for a member of the upper or middle class. Almost equally popular and nearly as frequently employed was the converse plot situation, that is, the story in which the upper- or middle-class character, for whatever reason, would pose as or be mistaken for someone from the working classes. In either case, typically, the drama or, more frequently, the comedy in the story would arise from the situational contrast of the individual and his surroundings; in the process, the character invariably would gain some new wisdom or insight from his or her experiences.

Numerous examples of these two similar types of film plot involving inverted class position and identity can be cited from this period. Sometimes the plot would center around individuals who resemble one another but who are of different social strata or positions. This exchange of identities often loosely approximated the story-line of Mark Twain's *The Prince and the Pauper*. For example, an early feature entitled *The Vagabond Queen* originally made as a silent in 1929, but subsequently released in 1930 with a sound track, exemplified this format. In this comedy, Betty Balfour, who had starred earlier in the twenties as the Cockney waif, "Squibs," in a series of very popular silent British features, had a dual role as a Ruritanian Princess named Xonia and as a Cockney girl named Sally. As might be expected, Princess Xonia and Sally are look-alikes. For that reason, in an effort to frustrate and block a rebellion, Sally is substituted for the Princess and takes her place on the throne, where she finds that being a princess is not an easy task.

The same basic format was used in other films such as the 1932 production *It's A King* starring veteran stage and screen comic Syd Howard as a Ruritanian King Albert and as his double, a commoner named Albert King, with whom he changes places to avoid an anarchist plot, and the 1937 Seymour Hicks feature, *Change for a Sovereign*, about a similar exchange involving a Ruritanian King named Hugo who yearns for the "simple life of the country cottage."[1] In the latter film, the monarch tires of the formalities of his position; bored with court responsibilities and ceremonial duties like laying cornerstones, King Hugo tells his government he will go on strike unless he and his wife, Queen Agatha, played by Violet Farebrother, are allowed to take a vacation. The movie concentrates on demonstrating how restricted the life of a monarch is, and it is perhaps not a coincidence that it was released only a year after the abdication crisis in Britain had demonstrated to the public that Edward VIII was not even free to marry whomever he chose. The monarchical life is also shown to be somewhat detrimental to family well-being as Hugo's son, Prince William, played by Bruce Lister, is portrayed as a spoiled, sulky, undisciplined young man who always gets what he wants; the implication is that being a ruler makes it difficult to raise a family responsibly. So when the King demands an opportunity to live simply for a while, although his government feels it would not be healthy for such an absence to be known to the people, they are forced to grant him the sabatical. To prevent any problems, a double for the monarch, also played by Seymour Hicks, is located; but the substitute turns out to be an alcoholic incompetent, disgracing the monarchy with his riotous behavior.

Hugo's ambitious rivals, the evil Archduke Paul and his wife, the Countess Rita, played by Ralph Truman and Chili Bouchier respectively, use the opportunity for a conspiracy to challenge the King politically. Meanwhile, the monarch and his family, who have been smuggled out of the palace, are enjoying their sojourn in the country. But gradually they learn that even the simplest lifestyle of the most ordinary people can be complicated in some ways, as they find themselves unprepared to cope with some difficulties and inconveniences; for example, their cottage is stocked with canned food, but the royal family does not possess a can-opener. They decide to return to the castle, in the end, just in time; as the Archduke is about to have himself proclaimed King before a public throng, the King appears, recovers his position, and thwarts the conspiracy.

But the swapping of identities did not always involve monarchs; for example, a 1933 feature entitled *Gentleman's Agreement*, one of the much maligned, so called "quota quickies," had a different kind of exchange. In this film directed by veteran film-making pioneer George Pearson, the central figure is a wealthy, spendthrift youth who has had the advantage of a good education but has chosen not to do anything with it. For the sake of his own self respect, the idler decides to change his lifestyle and finds a tramp who agrees to trade places with him. In the process, the "down and out" discovers business skills while the wastrel falls in love with an out-of-work typist, played by Vivien Leigh, at this time still an unknown in only her third screen role.[2] Not unexpectedly, the young man's experiences among common people with everyday problems change his frivolous outlook on life in due course. Another variation was the Claude Hulbert comedy, *Big Business*, released in October, 1934, in which Hulbert plays a dual role as a businessman and his out-of-work look-a-like; when the unemployed double takes the place of the businessman, he manages to save the company from ruin.

Obviously, to suggest that such story situations were rarely believable would be an understatement of vast proportions; but more importantly, the concept, however fancifully presented, that a person exalted as a monarch or a highly educated, wealthy young man would find desirable the thought of exchanging positions for the "simple life" of a person from the working classes is a powerful suggestion that perhaps instead of envying and hating the upper classes, one should count one's blessings about not having their cares and should even pity them. The comically troubled situations that sometimes arose from such exchanges also suggested the desirability of people staying in the "natural" positions in which they would seem to belong; this implication, which appeared continually in the films of the thirties, was another potent, though unstated argument for the *status quo* in society.

In several of these "mistaken identity" films the working-class characters would take on the guise of a wealthier or more socially respectable person for the deliberate purpose of some specific deception. Often this purpose was derived from economic necessity. For example, *A Sister to Assist 'Er*, while essentially a broad farce, dealt with the necessity of preserving a place in which to live, in spite of not being able to pay the rent, an experience and difficulty with which many working-class audience members were probably painfully familiar. For that reason, while moviegoers could laugh at the elaborate ruse by which the principal character preserves her lodgings, the desperation and resourcefulness of her effort were not very far from being believable to them.

Understandably, then, this classic plot derived from an old music hall sketch, which had been filmed on six separate occasions by British studios, was so popular that twice it was produced in feature-length versions during the Depression, once in 1930 and again in 1938, the latter of which was re-released later presumably because of its popularity. The story concerned a penniless old woman, appropriately characterized by *Film Weekly* as a "slum-widow" who is about to be evicted from her lodgings by her mean-spirited landlady.[3] Rather than be thrown out, she imaginatively impersonates a non-existent, supposedly long lost rich sister. Of the 1938 version of this often-filmed tale, the *Monthly Film Bulletin* wrote that its "humour is of the ... typical Cockney kind [with, as usual] ... much drinking both before and, of course, during the famous impersonation scene" and with "the settings ... appropriately dingy." The ruse is so successful for the impoverished old woman that not only does she dupe the landlady, but when the heroine decides to marry the local fishmonger, she receives "a handsome wedding present," as a result.[4]

Ambition sometimes figured as a motivation in these films for this deceptive behavior. For example, a 1933 feature called *My Old Duchess*, directed by comic Lupino Lane and written by veteran music hall impresario Fred Karno, dealt with an impersonation intended to help a vocational aspiration; the movie was a tale of a lowly stage manager who pretends to be a duchess in order to make an impression on a movie executive.

A more energetic example is the early 1936 Jack Hulbert vehicle, *Jack of All Trades*. The irrepressible Hulbert played Jack Warrender who is "unemployed and responsible for an aged mother"; to make ends meet he "takes a temporary job as a waiter," and circumstances quickly lead to a series of adventures in which he "lets himself be mistaken for a guest, falls in love with an heiress and goes home in a taxi with a drunk Robertson Hare" who portrays a bank employee named Lionel Fitch.[5] The following day, Warrender connives his way into the bank where Fitch works, and "in his efforts to make his personality felt," Hulbert's character is responsible for involving several big business men in the creation of a new company designed to promote "a scheme of his own invention." But when "Jack's imposture is discovered," the "promoters of the company" are too committed to be able to withdraw, and the result is a new shoe factory where Jack gets a job as nightwatchman. Ultimately, he helps extinguish a fire "started by a gang of crooks," in the process rescuing the heiress; in the end "Jack lives up to the title by being master of no trade, but only a bluff, at which he shows himself a past master."[6] That the film was intended as nothing more than light, frothy escapism is undeniable; the advertising for the movie emphasized this quality with publicity slogans reading "From Bank Director to Night Watchman – Jack Sings and Dances His Merry Way," in spite of the fact that the progression suggested is one of failure.[7] But, with the characteristic vigor that typified Hulbert's style of comedy, the feature hardly projected a spirit of negativism, demonstrating instead how one man in his desperation to avoid unemployment and to find success was willing to try an improbable bluff. While Hulbert's persona was not really working-class in nature, the situation of unemployment was surely one with which many working-class audience members could identify, and the implied message, which could have been applied to almost all Hulbert films, of being indomitable and resourceful in the face of overpowering odds and incredible difficulties, was unquenchably optimistic. In fact, Hulbert convinces the bankers to adopt his plan by reciting Henry V's speech before Agincourt to rally the financiers as if he were a military leader.

One of Jessie Matthews' starring vehicles, a 1936 musical comedy entitled *It's Love Again*, involved a similarly positive point of view and an equally audacious bluff on the part of the protagonist. In this Victor Saville directed feature, Jessie Matthews plays lowly chorus-girl Elaine Bradford. When newspaper gossip columnist Peter Carlton, played by Robert Young, attempts to fabricate a scoop by inventing in his column a society lady named Mrs Smythe-Smythe who supposedly has just returned from big game hunting in India, Elaine sees an opportunity to gain notoriety for her hoped for song and dance career; thus, she poses as the imaginary socialite, gains a successful show business career, reveals publicly her deception, and ultimately wins Peter Carlton. Though in real life Jessie Matthews' publicity did not hide her own working-class origins, her screen image, like Hulbert's character, was not typically working class; but at least in this film, her humble status as a chorus girl and her dreams of rising above that level made her character one with which working-class moviegoers easily could identify. Certainly, the publicity for the film emphasized the movie as "the sparkling, daring romance of an out-of work chorus girl who cannot land a job"; though not really inaccurate the emphasis in the slogan on the unemployment aspect is most revealing, in terms of what facet of the films the studio felt was most exploitable.[8]

While ambition such as that exemplified by Elaine Bradford, Jessie Matthews' daring chorus girl, bordered on illegality, occasionally in features of this type, that border would be crossed; that is, sometimes crime could be the intended purpose of the impersonation. For example, *Silver Top*, described at the time of its release in January, 1938 as a "crook melodrama" set in an "idyllic village ... [of] model cottages with lattice windows and bowers of roses," though criticized by at least one contemporary reviewer as "naive, sentimental and ... unconvincing," nevertheless had another such willful deception.[9] The story told of an elderly woman named Mrs Deeping, played by Marie Wright, who is the proprietress of the sweet shop in the village and who has inherited a fortune. Meanwhile a pair of crooks named Dashka Vernon and "Flash" Gerald (Betty Ann Davies and Brian Buchel) are involved in a bad auto accident on the road outside Mrs Deeping's store. The kindly old woman takes care of the girl, Dashka, to nurse her back to health; but while Dashka is recovering, she learns that Mrs Deeping has a long lost son named Ronnie. Dashka then schemes to have a member of her gang impersonate Mrs Deeping's son in order to bilk the old woman of her wealth. The gang member chosen for the assignment is an ex-convict named Babe (David Farrar); Babe had been released only recently from prison and quickly begins his part of the ruse. But complications in the scheme arise; the *Monthly Film Bulletin*'s review summarized the resolution of the deception which kept the working-class deceiver from having to be arrested. Babe finds himself receptive to the village life which he comes to enjoy; at the same time, he becomes fond of the Vicar's daughter. His adjustment to his new community gradually becomes so complete that when threatened with exposure by Dashka and Flash, he defies them. They then reveal the deception to Mrs Deeping, but they are then surprised "when she tells them that their story is no news to her" because she long has known "the Babe" is not her Ronnie. But she indicates "she believes his repentance to be genuine," and she tells them she intends to adopt him anyway "trusting to the salutary influence of the Vicar's daughter to do the rest" in the way of completing his reform.[10]

But impersonations of wealthier people by working-class characters also were used in some features to avert a crime or to apprehend its perpetrators. For example, the 1936 comedy, *My Partner, Mr Davis*, was the story of an out-of-work individual who fabricates an imaginary business partner in order to hinder a fraudulent financier. In Alfred Hitchcock's memorable 1936 mystery *Young and Innocent*, the young heroine, Erica Burgoyne, played by Nova Pilbeam, and the innocent hero Robert Tisdall (Derrick de Marney), who has been falsely accused of murder, enlist the aid of an aged tramp and china-mender named Old Will, played by Edward Rigby, to help them find the real murderer in order to clear the hero's name. Only Old Will can recognize the real criminal, a tormented musician who works as a drummer in a hotel band. The endeavor proves successful in spite of great adversity and unlikely odds when the china-mender accompanies the girl into the crowded ballroom of the fashionable hotel at which they know the murderer with his characteristic twitching eye will be playing. The sequence opens with the tramp trying to behave in a manner appropriate to that of an upper-class gentleman and predictably not succeeding. Rigby's astute and gently humorous performance and especially his character's uneasiness and social discomfort almost steal the audience's attention from the inherent suspense in the scene. For example, when Old Will orders from the dubious waiter two cups of tea, one for himself and one for the girl, he demonstrates his inexperience in such social situations; when the waiter asks "India or China?", the exasperated old china-mender reveals that he is unaware of such fine distinctions, and uncertain about the appropriate response, he replies, as if in answer, "Tea."[11]

While this impersonation was not necessarily a successful one, the characterization of Old Will was highly effective, and at least one letter-writer to *Film Weekly* wrote that the primary reason he liked the film was because of its portrait of the tramp and the other "real people" among whom the hero must search when trying to find and identify Old Will.[12] Critics agreed that Rigby's caricature of a working-class character and particularly his performance in the scene in which he searches for the murderer in the society ballroom were outstanding.[13] Perhaps because Old Will was so clumsy in his attempted deception, his believability as a realistic character was enhanced; and at least one reviewer felt that despite the improbable plot, the success of the film was precisely due to its believable characterization. Noting that one of the film's "great charms" is its focus on "normal everyday people living a normal everyday life in a typically English country setting," the critic in the *Monthly Film Bulletin* observed that there were "no superfluous characters" in the movie, each one fitting into "his or her appointed place" and contributing "to the total effect." Citing Hitchcock's "admirable [use of] . . . varied settings," his effective portrayal of a common lodging house, his "keen and penetrating observation," his "innumerable small touches," and his exceptional "knowledge of human nature," the review especially praised the "brilliant work . . . put in by the supporting players" calling attention especially to Edward Rigby's Old Will which is referred to as a "little gem of character acting."[14]

Occasionally, *both* an escape from a crime and the need to apprehend a criminal would be the purpose of a working-class character's impersonation of a more exalted station. In *Strictly Illegal*, a comedy released in February, 1935 starring veteran comedian Leslie Fuller, a bookie poses as a churchman to escape a presumed crime, but the impersonation ultimately leads to the prevention of a jewel theft. In this feature, based on the Con West – Herb Sargent play *The Naughty Age*, Fuller portrays Bill the Bookie, a street-corner gambler who thinks he inadvertently has killed a policeman. To escape arrest, he assumes the apparel and identity of a parson, and as a consequence discovers he is the honored guest at a country manor-house; there, while continuing his masquerade as a cleric, he uncovers an attempt to steal the jewels of Lady Percival, played by Cissie Fitzgerald, and after predictable slapstick by-play he saves her valued possessions.

More often, however, in these films of the thirties, a working-class character would misrepresent his wealth, status, or background for romantic reasons. One of Gracie Fields's popular features was a 1936 musical comedy directed by Monty Banks called *Queen of Hearts* in which she plays Grace Perkins, a poor but lively seamstress who lives in Brixton with her working-class family from Wigan and who dreams of a show business career. Working in a shop opposite a theater, Grace becomes fascinated with a nearby theater and particularly with her idol, Derek Cooper, played by John Loder, who happens to be appearing currently. One night, while awaiting an opportunity to get his autograph, Grace inadvertently becomes a passenger in Derek Cooper's auto after he has been drinking following a quarrel with his leading lady. Grace helps the almost unconscious actor escape any difficulties with the law, gets him safely to his home, and takes his coat to mend. When she brings it to the theater the next day, she is mistaken for a wealthy society woman named Mrs Van Leur who is willing to back a production if she is given the lead in it. Grace decides to take advantage of the misunderstanding to further her chances for a relationship with her idol (who does not recognize her) and also to reveal her performing talents, so she continues to impersonate the wealthy society woman; ultimately she is successful, both in cultivating her romance and in escaping her working-class origins for a show business career.

A similar deception was to be found in the plot of the 1932 filmed version of Aimee and Philip Stuart's play, *Nine Till Six*, directed by Basil Dean and with a cast including Elizabeth Allen and Florence Desmond. The movie was a romance involving a dressmaker who makes use of a gown in order to attend a dance with an aristocrat. However, the impersonation and the little indiscretion needed to carry out the deception backfire in this film, and the heroine is accused of theft; it is important to note that working-class characters posing as upper- or middle-class characters were not always successful in these plots.

Another motivation inducing working-class characters to pose as individuals from the upper or middle classes in these movies was often a desire to help a member of the elite. For example, a 1932 comedy, *High Society*, released during the summer of that year also featured Florence Desmond, this time as a Cockney maid named Florrie who attempts to help her mistress out of a troublesome situation by impersonating a society lady. Another helping hand was extended by a secretary in one of Jack Buchanan's popular musicals; the film was *Yes, Mr Brown*, released in January, 1933 and was jointly directed by Buchanan and Herbert Wilcox. In this feature, based on the play *Geschaft Mit Amerika*, Buchanan played a factory manager named Nicholas Baumann who lives in Vienna. Following an argument over her pet dog, his wife Clary (Margot Grahame) decides to leave him; this separation occurs at just the wrong moment because Nicholas' boss from America, Mr Brown, played by Harley Powers, is coming to visit the factory. To prevent his supervisor from developing a low opinion of him, Nicholas' secretary, Anne Webber, Buchanan's perennial co-star Elsie Randolph, agrees to pose as his wife, and the usual comic complications result.

A virtually identical basic plot line can be found in *Too Many Wives*, a comedy released a few months later. In this movie, Jack Hobbs is John Wildeley, whose wife Hilary, played by Nora Swinburne, is away when he must entertain an important foreign aristocrat, Baron van Schlossen, portrayed by Claud Fleming, with whom he hopes to do business. Desperate, Hobbs approaches the maid Sally (Viola Keats) and persuades her to act as his wife. The deception and the mistaken identities provided the humor in this otherwise forgettable feature.

In some films the confusion was not the result of a willful deception. In such instances, the working-class individual was usually more passive and somewhat bewildered as others, usually from the middle or upper classes, made the mistake of assuming the character was from a higher station and was simply incompetent; but at other times the working-class protagonist would rise to the occasion. One example of the format was *Bargain Basement* (also known as *Departmental Store*) a May, 1935 comedy directed by Leslie Hiscott, in which a shady department store manager confuses an ex-convict former safe-cracker with the protagonist, the disguised heir and nephew of his employer. The reviewer in the *Monthly Film Bulletin*, who found the film "amusing" with "exceedingly funny . . . dialogue," noted that "all ends well with the exposure of the manager who has been cooking the accounts for some years and with the union of the hero and the lady detective." [15] An earlier comedy, *The Wrong Mr Perkins*, released in January, 1931, starred Herbert Mundin as Jimmy Perkins, a poor man whom a banker confuses with wealthy namesake Arnold Perkins. The banker's efforts to make Jimmy Perkins his partner bewilder the fellow, leading to comic situations.

But a more competent kind of protagonist appeared in *Almost a Gentleman*, a 1938 comedy starring music hall favorite Billy Bennett. The story concerns a night watchman named Bill Barker who is troubled by noisy neighbors; when he attempts to complain to the hostess of a dance party in a neighboring house that festivities are keeping him awake, he is mistaken for a wealthy glue manufacturer who has the same name. Two "share-pushers," one of them played by veteran film villain Gibb McLaughlin, talk him into purchasing shares in a phony gold mine. The following morning, assuming that the erstwhile "glue king" must know a good investment when he sees it, the society people begin putting their money in the mine. Learning of Bill's identity, the share-pushers appoint him Chairman of the Company, but Bill proves to be cleverer than they assume him to be. Becoming suspicious, Bill "destroys every paper he can lay his hands on"; he faces the angry shareholders of the company and steels himself for an angrier response when word "comes that there is gold in the mine after all." Said the *Monthly Film Bulletin*, the "whole thing" projects "a naivete, and a homely vulgarity which disarm criticism"; Kathleen Harrison especially was praised for her "clever study of a bewildered but not helpless Cockney wife." [16] Bill thus turns out to be competent and successful in his transformed identity.

Another competent working-class substitute was the protagonist of the late 1935 Gaumont–British comedy release, *The Guv'nor*; in this major production, George Arliss portrayed a whimsical tramp named François Rothschild, but nicknamed "the Guv'nor." Though set in France, the presence of Arliss, perhaps the essential and typical Englishman, in the title role and what one reviewer described as the "obviously English surroundings" of the film meant that the movie hardly seemed Gallic in nature. [17] The plot centered on the coincidence between the tramp's name and that of the great French banking family Rothschild.

In the feature, the "Guv'nor" is a philosophical tramp who enjoys his freedom as a vagabond with his comic sidekick, Flit, played in Cockney style by Gene Gerrard. However, his wanderings are cut short when he is arrested for the crime of poaching; while being tried before a magistrate, the tramp's real name is revealed. A series of unusual flukes result in his being appointed president of a major financial institution that is on the verge of failure; executives of the firm hope that by naming a "Rothschild" to the Board of Directors, the public's shaken confidence in the firm will be restored. At the same time, with the directorship in such inexperienced hands, the retiring President, M. Barsac (Frank Cellier), who turns out to be a villainous schemer, hopes to be able to use "the Guv'nor" to carry on his swindling activities until he has enriched himself enough to abscond with the company's funds; in particular, he is endeavoring to deprive a virtuous young lady named Madeleine (Viola Keats) of her rightful claim to a lucrative mining operation.

Meanwhile, the "Guv'nor," in his simplicity and also as a result of the misidentification, has a startling effect on the financial world; at one point, for example, the old tramp telephones for a little corn to be used in feeding the city pigeons, and the effect of his name results in a commotion at the Stock Exchange. Similarly, the swindler, Barsac, underestimates the newly prosperous tramp who, through luck and cunning, uncovers Barsac's villainy, thwarts all his schemes, restoring the mine to its proper owner, and saves the failing banking institution. At the moment of his greatest success, he then chooses to leave his position to continue his carefree life as a tramp, as the movie concludes.

Again, a story-line such as this one contained potent, unstated implications that were orientated toward the *status quo*. The suggestion that financial difficulties were attributable to specific, identifiable villains was often used as a plot device, particularly during the difficult years of the thirties. Although more complex explanations for financial problems such as bank failures would have been far more difficult to portray and perhaps far less satisfying dramatically, the fact that characters with malicious intent were invariably responsible for the problems in such plots meant that the economic system was never questioned. Certainly, the depiction of a remedy in the form of someone as humble as a tramp with common sense who could set the troubles right did reinforce a positive impression of both the working classes and the social system. Additionally, the tramp's decision to return to his humble background upon completing his task of setting everything right again, like a latter-day Cincinnatus, also underscored the superiority of the "simple life"; the film implied that even if a working-class character had the chance to remain a financier or bank president, after a while, he would yearn for his working-class lifestyle and want to return to it.

The advertising for *The Guv'nor* also was noteworthy. Publicity slogans described the film, saying "[George Arliss is a] . . . whimsical old tramp, the Guv'nor . . . just out of a doss house . . . who deserts the highway and becomes a financier"; the emphasis of the publicity appeal here is on the active case, as if "the Guv'nor" himself was responsible for the transformation of his situation.[18] By contrast, in the movie, only chance misidentification resulted in his becoming a financier. Thus, the publicity subtly suggested, without a mention of fate, a much more fluid social situation where tramps indeed could become financiers, and, in this way, such an approach lent itself more readily to a moviegoer's fantasies and wish fulfillment.

But in some features, working-class characters were not just mistaken for one of the elite, they actually were transformed through some plot device into wealthy members of the upper or middle classes. Usually in the story-line this conversion was accomplished by some unexpected inheritance, and the fortune often had mixed blessings. For example, in the drama *Windfall* an August, 1935 release based on an R.C. Sheriff play, Edward Rigby is an old ironmonger named Sam Spooner who inherits fifty thousand pounds. For a while, Sam and his wife Maggie, played by Marie Ault, use the opportunity to live in a more lavish style than they ever have experienced before. But the effect this luxury has on Sam's son, Tom Spooner (Derrick de Marney), who quickly becomes a society wastrel and loafer, creates a doubt about the advantages of the inheritance. To teach Tom proper values and to set an example, the old ironmonger returns to work, in spite of his fortune. But the job proves to be far too strenuous, and a mishap results that proves to be almost fatal. Clearly, the inheritance has been shown to be a disrupting influence and not an altogether carefree legacy.

In several of the films, the inheritance actually included a title. In one of Michael Powell's earliest directorial assignments, the 1932 musical,

His Lordship, based on Oliver Heuffer's novel, *The Right Honorable*, comedian Jerry Verno played Bert Gibbs, a Cockney plumber who becomes a peer. Ultimately, though, his transformation also brings troubles; his comic difficulties include an engagement to a persistent, anxious, Russian film star.

Similarly, the Syd Howard comedy *Chick* released in late 1936 based on an Edgar Wallace story involved another aristocrat who rose from the working classes; Howard is Chick Beane, a porter working at a college, who inherits a dukedom, but who ultimately rejects it. After receiving his inheritance, Chick is troubled with swindlers supposedly representing an oil company, who pretend to find oil on his estate; in the film, he successfully thwarts their plans while solving the romantic problems of others. Critics had praise for Howard's portrait of "an amusing and human character study of [a] downtrodden Yorkshireman"; wrote one reviewer on the subject of Howard's character, "he doesn't have much success while he is a member of the peerage, but when an unsuspected claimant appears, he comes into his own, and makes a success of life on a less exalted plane." [19]

A slight variation of this story-line was the plot of the 1936 romantic comedy, *King of the Castle*. Released in February of that year, the feature concentrated on the struggles to establish the aristocratic identity of a character previously thought to be of the working classes; in this case, the disputed recognition of the aristocratic heritage of the character was the central focus of the plot. In the movie, Billy Milton portrays Monty King, a lowly clerk working for Trellis and Company who is in love with a rich American girl, Marilyn Bean (June Clyde); Marilyn is the daughter of Henry Bean, portrayed by Arthur Finn, who turns out to be the United States representative of Trellis and Company. Monty had met Marilyn while rescuing her from the river after inadvertently capsizing her boat. The publicity from the mishap and rescue results in the clerk's picture appearing in the newspapers; the photo is then noticed by a loyal family butler named Pullen. Pullen, played by character actor Claude Dampier, instantly recognizes Monty and identifies him as the missing heir, Lord Drone. Pullen immediately seeks Monty and with him attempts to establish the identity legally. Along with Marilyn, whom Monty has been romancing, the butler and clerk encounter numerous complications. Among the obstacles is Monty's employer Sir Percival Trellis (Paul Balke), who is infatuated with Marilyn and who attempts to thwart the clerk in various ways. Trellis is aided by Marilyn's father who opposes his daughter's love affair with a lowly clerk; together, they conspire to have Monty transferred away, but he is unwilling to give up his love and sacrifices his job rather than be separated from the object of his romance. Other complications are provided by the presence of bailiffs (among them veteran comedian Jimmy Godden) and by the prospective sale of the valuables and contents at Drone Castle, Monty's ancestral home, which the bailiffs arrange. In the nick of time, however, the necessary proof is obtained in a desk discovered among the auctioned items from Drone Castle; Monty's identity is authenticated,

Marilyn's suitor is thwarted, her father endorses his daughter's engagement to the newly restored aristocrat, and all ends happily.

One of the most popular films to exhibit this format variation was a 1939 musical release which was based on a late thirties legendary London stage production that has been called, perhaps without exaggeration, "probably the most successful comedy in the history of the British theatre."[20] The stage version, which was presented at the Victoria Palace for an astonishing several thousand performances and which had had at the time of its West End closing after more than fifteen hundred performances, the second longest run in London theatrical chronicles, was known as *Me and My Girl*; successfully revived in a Broadway run in the 1980s, it was written by Arthur Rose, Douglas Furber, and Noel Gay with considerable inspiration and assistance from the play's star, veteran screen and stage comic Lupino Lane. But when the play was filmed, the resulting movie which appeared in April, 1939 was renamed *The Lambeth Walk* from the title of the widely acclaimed, world-wide hit dance tune (described by the performer who created it as a "slow, cocky sort of march, a Cockney walk") which it originated.[21] As the ensemble sang "Any time you're Lambeth Way, any evening, any day/You'll find them all doing the Lambeth Walk," audiences felt compelled to join in.

In the feature, Lane recreated his immortal stage performance as the cocky little Cockney, Bill Snibson. Snibson had been a comic character in an earlier stage success, a racing comedy called *Twenty to One*, and the part, that of "a bookie who had joined the Anti-Gambling League in a fit of remorse" as performed by the irrepressible Lane, had become so popular that it gradually was built up to become the principal role.[22] *Twenty to One* ran for over four hundred performances at Oswald Stoll's lavish and huge Coliseum in the mid thirties, and with the subsequent provincial tour, Lane had played the role 1025 times.[23]

The immense response to the character necessitated another Snibson story, and *Me and My Girl* was the result. The plot of the film and the stage version concerned the little Cockney's inheritance of a title; but when Snibson becomes a duke, much to the chagrin of his new-found aristocratic relatives, he encounters class consciousness, elitism, and numerous difficulties. As the improbable story progresses, however, the effervescent Snibson gradually "humanises" the other upper-class characters and resists becoming stuffy and aristocratic himself, remaining loyal to his common girl friend, Sally, played in the film by Sally Gray. Again, in this film, the values and attitudes of the common, working people were contrasted, however artificially, with those of the elite and were found to be superior. In such features, when the protagonist remained true to his nature, he invariably was happier at the end of the movie.

This contrast was precisely the design of the original production according to Lane's biographer James Dillon White. The idea, discussed at a brainstorming session among the original writers (and attributed to Lane himself) of placing Snibson in an aristocratic environment full of "tradition and stuffed shirts" playing a "long-lost heir . . . in a real ducal home with suits of armour, a lot of flunkeys, and a real snooty dowager" where nothing much has "changed in the last two, three hundred years" was intended as a dramatic device to upset the stereotyped theatrical upper class, to "shake them up a bit," and to serve as "a breath of modern times blowing away the stale air of centuries." [24] When one writer was said to have asked, "I don't know, *are* there such places?", Lane was reported to have replied, "Of course there are – anyway, what the hell, if we can make the audience believe it"; in this sense, Lane was suggesting that the reality of the situation was essentially unimportant to audience members, and that artificial depictions did not matter as long as they were understandable within the confines of the story. [25] Lane's confidence that the story line would appeal to the public was hardly misplaced.

The Lambeth Walk, as a film, was critically well received in spite of its somewhat hackneyed, fanciful, contrived plot; reviewers praised Lane's performance when the film was released, calling it a "personal success" and observing that Lane "reveals a talent for the comedy-pathos of the 'little man' reminiscent of Chaplin." [26] More importantly, though, the film, like the play, was incredibly popular, in spite of the fact that the theatrical version had been performed not only all over England but also had been heard on British radio and even on early television. Although the stage version had languished somewhat in the weeks of the pre-West End tour prior to the London opening, the play became so popular that Lane was ultimately to depict Bill Snibson in *Me and My Girl* for over five thousand performances; specifically, among these appearances had been a slightly abbreviated version on BBC Radio in January, 1938, and a complete presentation performed at the Victoria Theatre before their Majesties King George VI and Queen Elizabeth, which was broadcast live over BBC television service, the first time in history that a musical comedy was televised from the stage of theater. [27] While the theme of the plot had been regarded as so questionable and so unlikely to be successful that the Stoll organization, in spite of its longstanding relationship with Lane, had rejected any thought of financing the original show, its lasting popularity, even at the risk of radio and television over-exposure, suggests that, as Lane had predicted, British audiences never tired of the production or got their fill of the story. In fact, the film also turned out to be so popular that it also had to be reissued in time.

PYGMALION AS A CASE STUDY

Probably the most celebrated feature to employ the theme of mistaken identity in the thirties, and certainly one of the most popular British motion pictures ever released, was the 1938 filmed version of George Bernard Shaw's classic comedy *Pygmalion*. The well known plot dealing with Professor Henry Higgins's efforts, to teach proper English to the flower girl, Eliza Doolittle, in order for her to impersonate a lady at a Society gathering at which she is mistaken for a princess, was translated effectively into a film by the brilliant Anthony Asquith's solid direction and by the memorable performances of Leslie Howard as Higgins and Wendy Hiller as Eliza. Often regarded by critics as one of the few feature films from Britain during this decade to be worthy of lasting praise and recognition, *Pygmalion* has even been included by at least one critic among the seventy-five best movies ever made outside America.[28] More interestingly, though, *Pygmalion* provided yet another example, and certainly the best known and perhaps most complex illustration of the transformation of a working-class movie character into a member of the upper or middle class; of course, in this case, the metamorphosis is accomplished through the social engineering of Shaw's phonetics professor, who believes he can dissolve social distinctions linguistically.

The details of the plot of Pygmalion by now have become familiar, particularly after the thousands of performances of the Lerner and Loewe musical, *My Fair Lady*, which it inspired, and they need not be recounted in minute detail here, since the film was a very close adaptation of Shaw's original play. Professor Henry Higgins wagers with Colonel Pickering, an expert on dialects, played by Scott Sunderland, that he can take a lowly flower girl from Covent Garden and, using elocution and grammar lessons, can convince anyone that she is a lady. The girl he uses, Eliza Doolittle, agrees to the intensive instruction in the hope of improving her social status to the point where she might someday open her own flower-shop, and she moves into Professor Higgins's home for her instruction. When her dustman father Alfred Doolittle, veteran character actor Wilfrid Lawson, comes to try to extort money from Higgins, the Professor and the Colonel are taken with his seemingly amoral philosophy of life, and as a joke, after he departs, they submit his name to an American philanthropist, in the process describing him as "the most original moralist at present in England."

In the meantime, Eliza's vigorous training is successful. For her first public appearance, Eliza attends a tea party given by Professor Higgins's mother, played by Marie Lohr, and her shaky triumph prompts Higgins to take her to an Ambassador's Reception. A disreputable Hungarian linguist named Karpathy (Esme Percy), who is trying to determine her identity, declares that she is a princess, and Higgins's experiment is declared a success. But with the effort concluded, Eliza is unhappy for she must now return to her earlier circumstances; she has also fallen in love with Higgins, and when she leaves him after rebuking him for his egoism and insensitivity to her, Higgins begins to realize she has become something more than the guttersnipe with which he began his experiment. Meanwhile, equally unhappy, Alfred Doolittle, who has been given a lucrative lecturing job by the American philanthropist, also upbraids Higgins for making him a success and thereby shackling him to a middle-class morality. When Eliza seeks advice from Higgins's mother, the

Professor comes to realize that he has become fond of the "lady" he has created.

The movie's similarity to the original play derives in part from Shaw's insistence on keeping his works unchanged when they were filmed. Shaw had resisted motion picture luminaries such as the Warner Brothers, Alexander Korda, Louis B. Mayer, and Samuel Goldwyn, all of whom approached him about the adaptation of some of his plays to the screen, before settling on the obscure, essentially penniless Gabriel Pascal, who solemnly had promised the playwright that if he were allowed to produce filmed versions of his work not a word of dialogue would be altered.[29]

Although Pascal guaranteed there would be no tampering with the play by allowing Shaw to oversee the production, for which reason Shaw publicly stated "the man is a genius" comparing him as an art impresario with Diaghileff, a few significant changes did take place. Pascal's widow Valerie summarized the changes in her book on Shaw's relationship with her husband. New scenes included the efforts of the housekeeper Mrs Pearce giving the wailing Eliza her initial bath; the sequences with the love-smitten Freddy continually waiting for Eliza in front of the house; the exchange between Freddy and Eliza on the street; and the sequence when Eliza understands she cannot go back to her origins at Covent Garden. Shaw also had provided a reception scene which Pascal "elaborated" into the Embassy Ball "where the film reached its crescendo . . . as Eliza was literally transformed into a princess in front of the audience." The Hungarian Pascal provided the touch that identified the Queen and Crown Prince in the scene as being from his own native Transylvania, and he saw to it that Eliza "at the height of her female charm . . . be suspected of *Hungarian* royal origin." Shaw, apparently amused at the concept, "was only too glad to oblige his magyar friend" and was willing to change the name of Higgins's "hairy and bombastic" ex-pupil, from Nepomuck "to the more Hungarian-sounding Karpathy." Because the essence of the play and film and the basis for the story of Pygmalian was precisely the "miracle of metamorphosis," in this case "performed by phonetics," Pascal believed the "most important scenes in the movie should be the ones where Higgins teaches Eliza"; accordingly, Shaw "worked out these scenes in great detail." [30]

These changes, which were to enhance the film, nonetheless were not easy to suggest to the great playwright. Anthony Asquith, the son of former British Prime Minister H.H. Asquith, was chosen, perhaps because of his own social prominence, as the person who initially requested that Shaw allow the insertion of the additional scenes; he has described the "splendid . . . interview" at which Shaw consented to the changes. After being "delegated to go and see Shaw," in order "to sell him the idea so that he'd write the scenes," Asquith met Shaw and his wife for luncheon. With Shaw "in splendid form" discoursing on music throughout the luncheon, Asquith found himself nowhere near the point of accomplishing his objective. When he finally "broached the subject," Shaw "thought the idea was out of the question"; fortunately, Mrs Shaw "came to [the] . . . rescue" and "commanded him to listen to what [Asquith] . . . had to say." Although he "was trembling with nerves" at the very notion of presuming to make suggestions to the great playwright, Asquith nonetheless asked Shaw to let him "read to him the kind of thing [he] . . . had in mind," adding that the expectation was that Shaw would compose the actual material; "very reluctantly and impatiently" Shaw agreed to hear the proposals, and Asquith began reading. At one point, apparently, Asquith recited a phrase in which he referred to Eliza coming "up the stairs with the frozen calm of the sleepwalker," and the expression apparently "pleased him" to the extent that "he kept repeating [it] . . . and from that moment on he was settled, hooked"; as a consequence, Asquith observed "I will take that much credit for the extra scenes."[31]

However, the most significant change, the film's ending, was one to which Shaw was unalterably opposed, and yet the change made its way into the movie. In the play, Higgins was left laughing ironically and uncontrollably, in his mother's parlor at the apparently likely prospect that Eliza, whom he has come to admire, will marry Freddie Eynsford-Hill and open a modest flower-shop. In the film, however, the distraught Higgins returns home, realizing his fondness for Eliza. But instead of marrying Freddie and opening a flower-shop as Shaw had wanted, Eliza would enter Professor Higgins's study and have, what Valerie Pascal would describe as "a moment of complete victory," seeing "her tormentor in the loneliness of his room, head bowed, listening to her recorded voice from the Cockney past"; with the "sight [stirring] . . . the eternal female" in her, Eliza would turn off the recording device and "finish the recorded sentence softly" uttering the line "I washed my face and hands before I came in, I did." Now triumphant, with his creation having returned and "subdued . . . to her master," and knowing "that their future relationship depended on his behavior at that moment," Higgins would lean back, stretch his legs, "and then, as if it were the crown of a newly anointed king" he would push up his hat "triumphantly" and ask her for his slippers, "leaving the public assured that Eliza would be running for those slippers to the end of her days."[32]

Shaw had been concerned with the casting of Leslie Howard as Higgins preferring someone like Charles Laughton or character actor Cecil Trauncer for precisely the reason that he feared a matinee idol like Howard would necessitate a "Hollywoodish" ending in which, as he put it, "the public will like him and probably want him to marry Eliza, which is just what I don't want."[33] Yet, Shaw was curiously quiet about this "perversion" of his ending, though he had gone to great pains in elaborating an ending in the flower-shop.

The reasons for his silence were unclear, though perhaps they were related to the film's phenomenal success. In contrast to two earlier British filmed adaptations of the plays of Shaw, the January, 1931 release, *How He Lied to*

Her Husband and the September, 1932 release, *Arms and the Man*, both supervised by BBC radio producer Cecil Lewis, both of which were dismal flops, *Pygmalion* was an extraordinary triumph, both critically and with the public. Shaw was lionized by the public after a number of years of relative critical decline, and because of his supervision of the script, Hollywood awarded the elderly playwright the 1938 Oscar for best screenplay, though the actual credit for the script lists W.P. Lipscomb, Cecil Lewis, and Ian Dalrymple along with Asquith and Shaw.[34] The film also garnered numerous other citations including Oscar nominations for Best Picture, Best Actor, and Best Actress, and won the Volpi Cup at the Venice Film Festival.[35] Shaw was told "You are a greater box-office star [in Hollywood] . . . than Greta Garbo," and newspapers reported that "a man with a long white beard is writing a new chapter in motion-picture history," becoming known, in the process, "among millions of people who had never heard of him before."[36] Pascal, himself, was included among *Time Magazine*'s list of the ten most famous men of 1938, along with Hitler and the Pope.[37]

Reviewers in England were extravagant with their praise, most agreeing with the critic in the *Monthly Film Bulletin* who commented that the movie was "brilliantly amusing and remarkably undated" with "flawless . . . intelligent and witty performances," especially by Wilfrid Lawson whose personification of "Eliza's father must be just about the cleverest piece of character acting ever seen in a British film."[38] And the public also loved the movie and its Cinderella story. *Film Weekly*'s fan poll of June, 1939 for the preceding year was a measure of this popularity, rating *Pygmalion* as the best film of the year, Wendy Hiller's Eliza as the best performance by an actress for the year, and Leslie Howard's Higgins as the second best performance by an actor for the year (losing only to Ralph Richardson in Victor Saville's *South Riding*).[39] The film was so popular it was reissued at least four times.

The changes in the plot were interesting in that they enhanced the social transformation aspect of the film. Shaw, himself, observed in his epilogue to the text of the original play, that a romantic ending for such a presentation was too implausible because too great a social gap would exist between Higgins and Eliza, no matter how extensive her transfiguration into a creature of the upper class; as the playwright expressed it, "Galatea never does quite like Pygmalion" because "his relation to her is too godlike to be altogether agreeable."[40] Without allowing the audience to see Eliza function as a lady, perhaps Shaw was correct.

But with the inclusion of the reception scene, in which the audience could share the experience of her transformation into a lady, suddenly this elevation became a credible fantasy; the moviegoer could witness the spectacle of Eliza personifying a lady, along with Higgins, and for Higgins to reject her or for her to reject Higgins no longer would be unsatisfying in a simply dramatic way, but also would be inconsistent with the success of Higgins' experiment. In this sense, the implied alliance at the end of the film completed the transformation; she was acceptable to him as an equal. Yet, paradoxically, in the process, she acknowledged his mastery, but only willingly as an equal, as a signal of her love. "I washed my face and hands 'afore I came, I did," she says, resuming her working-class identity, and Higgins requests his slippers with confidence; but the audience and Eliza know by then what Higgins also has said to her at the end of the argument in his mother's parlor, to the effect that "By George, Eliza, I said I'd make a woman of you; and I have." Telling her that he approves of her "like this," he adds that "Five minutes ago you were like a millstone round my neck. Now you're a tower of strength; a consort battleship."[41] He regards Eliza, then as an equal. The tub scene in which she is bathed and in which her clothes are ordered to be burned also emphasizes the transformation, with Eliza physically shedding her working-class identity. Where Higgins worked on her speech habits, altering them to those of a duchess, Mrs Pearce accepts her responsibility for transforming her appearance, as she expressed it, from that of "a frowzy slut to a clean, respectable girl fit to sit with the gentlemen in the study," adding "you can't be a nice girl inside if you're a dirty slut outside."[42]

The film, as well as the play, was a curious mixture of mild social commentary and Cinderella wish-fulfillment fantasy, and the complexities are not easily distinguished. The implication that the plot suggested was a potentially revolutionary one: all that separated classes were manners and speech patterns. This almost subversive concept, as mildly as it was expressed in *Pygmalion*, may have been actually enough to have prevented the film from being made in the early thirties when Cecil Lewis was attempting his feeble adaptations of Shavian works; producers in 1932 were fearful with *Pygmalion* of intervention by the censors, also, in part, perhaps because of the eyebrow-raising circumstances of a young woman living in the same house as a confirmed bachelor.[43]

Yet, in spite of the fact that Higgins proved his "revolutionary" theory, he himself displayed no social consciousness or concern about the fact that a person's "kerbstone" speech habits could confine that person to the gutter; he seemed only interested in Eliza's transformation as an academic exercise. In one scene, Mrs Pearce reproached Higgins for this insensitivity: "I know you don't mean her any harm; but when you get what you call interested in people's accents, you never think or care what may happen to them."[44] Higgins believed himself to be a fair person, insisting that he "treat[s] a duchess as if she was a flower-girl" and adding that "the great secret" is not possessing "bad manners or good manners or any other particular sort of manners, but having the same manners for all human souls"; he concludes that "the question is not whether I treat you rudely, but whether you ever heard me treat anyone else better."[45] But in fact Higgins does show contempt for the lower classes. He refers to her variously as a "squashed cabbage leaf, . . . [and a] disgrace to the noble architecture of these columns," as "baggage," as a "draggletailed guttersnipe," and as

75

"insect". He suggests that anyone "who utters such depressing and disgust-ing sounds has no right to be anywhere – no right to live," and observes that Eliza and her kind are "incapable of understanding anything," having "not any feelings that we need bother about."[46] Higgins tells Mrs Pearce that "when I've done with her, we can throw her back into the gutter" because "the girl . . . is no use to anybody," and he has no answer to the question of what is to become of her other than to say "what does it matter what becomes of you."[47] One would be hard pressed to characterize this attitude in any way other than as elitist.

The "revolutionary" perspective of the work was further undercut by the suggestion, also made in numerous other less distinguished features, that those who were transformed from the working classes were not as happy as they were before they were able to experience an upper- or middle-class life-style. Eliza says as much when she bitterly asks Higgins "Why didn't you leave me where you picked me out of – in the gutter? . . . Now you've made a lady of me I'm not fit to sell anything else [but myself]. I wish you'd left me where you found me."[48]

But Eliza was not the only working-class character in the film to be trans-formed, and Alfred Doolittle's unhappiness was even more profoundly expressed. His good fortune in receiving a share in the philanthropist's "Pre-Digested Cheese Trust" worth four thousand pounds a year, has, in the dustman's opinion, "ruined" him and "destroyed [his] . . . happiness"; as Doolittle observes to Higgins, "[you have] tied me up and delivered me into the hands of middle-class morality." Reminding Higgins that as a dustman he was "happy" and "free," Doolittle bemoans his present condition with its worries and conventions. With relatives requesting his help, Doolittle laments that they do not earn " a decent week's wages among the lot of them," and accordingly, he has "to live for others and not for myself," a condition he condemns as "middle-class morality." Unable to relinquish this newly imposed mentality by giving up the money because he doesn't have "the nerve," Doolittle concludes that the "deserving poor might as well be millionaires for all the happiness they ever has," but he "as one of the undeserving poor" has "nothing between me and the pauper's uniform but middle class."[49]

Doolittle's unhappiness at finding himself victimized by relatives and acquaintances seeking charity and his frustration at feeling himself con-strained by middle-class values were amusingly ironic; his yearning for his simpler dustman existence was a reminder to audiences that social improve-ment did not necessarily bring peace of mind. His adoption of some of the milder prejudices of those who were more prosperous intimated that a laborer should not hold such biases against his social betters since he too might hold them if he was part of the middle- or upper-class Establishment.

Similarly, Eliza's displeasure at having been made dissatisfied with her existence suggested that wishing to improve one's social position was fruitless because such transformations could only bring turmoil. These ideas provided additional dimensions to the characters of the flower girl and her father. Deftly formed by the satirical genius of Shaw who crafted his characters' arguments and viewpoints with a strong sense of social irony, Eliza and Alfred were classical working-class creations, both of the English comic stage and the British cinema. But the charm of the film nevertheless was the Cinderella quality which the movie version emphasized. As Roy Armes has observed "*Pygmalion* is a culminating point of British 1930s cinema because it deals consciously and explicitly with the underlying but often concealed themes of the decade – class, morality, accent." [50]

Clearly film stories like that of *Pygmalion*, by nature, appeared to moviegoers interested in wish-fulfillment. Even the titles of a few films directly indicated the basis of such an attraction; titles like *If I Were Rich* or *If I Were Boss* reflected this interest, even if the plot subsequently undercut the appeal, with the working-class characters regretting their transformations just as Eliza and Alfred had in these films. In fact the improvement in a person's situation (of which a moviegoer might dream) frequently brought trouble to the protagonist in the feature, or it changed his personality in an undesirable way. Although rarely written by writers as clever as Shaw, such movies often suggested that a working-class character would not be able to handle the concerns of someone in a better social circumstance; therefore, such people were better off not having their fantasies come true.

A good example of this theme was the May 1936 comedy release, *If I Were Rich*, which had curious, though not unexpected, political overtones. In this feature based on Horace Annesley Vachell's play *Humpty-Dumpty*, the aged, wealthy Earl of Mottisfont dies while on a hunting excursion. His brother, General de la Mothe, played by Clifford Heatherley, and his daughter Chrissie, portrayed by Kay Walsh, travel to the aristocrat's castle; they are accompanied by the young man who is expected to be the new Earl, Jack de la Mothe (Frederick Bradshaw), who must attend the official reading of the old Earl's will. All three characters are shocked to learn that thirty years earlier a secret marriage unknown to anyone else had resulted in an unexpected heir; the legal inheritor turns out to be the village barber, Albert Mott, comic Jack Melford. Ironically, Albert is an outspoken and adamant socialist; his tirades against the rich and against the aristocracy are known to all. However, when Albert, who had no knowledge of his ancestry, learns that he is to be the new Earl, he quickly changes his political stance and eagerly adopts family traditions and a far more conservative attitude. Unfortunately, when he and his "missus," played by Minnie Rayner, move into the castle, despite their attempts to adjust to their improved circumstances and their new environment, they find themselves uncomfortably out of place; their discomfort and unhappiness is underscored by typical comic scenes of societal inexperience, awkwardness, and confusion. Gradually, Albert and his wife come to yearn for their earlier, simple, working-class lifestyle. Ultimately, Albert's inheritance turns out to be an error, much to the barber's relief, and Jack de la Mothe, as originally expected, becomes the new Earl; the disclosure enables Albert to return to his former circumstances, where he can once again comfortably, espouse a socialist view.

The suggestion, not only that Albert was happier as a barber than as an Earl, but also that a socialist would give up his principles quickly if he were made a wealthy man, was one that a conservative might share. At least one critic found the film distasteful for that reason; the reviewer in the *Monthly Film Bulletin* wrote that *If I Were Rich* was a "comedy . . . with well-tried situations" but added that it was "lacking in fundamental good taste." Conceding that the movie "will amuse those who take it at its surface value" and that it possesses "some obvious fun," the reviewer nonetheless was troubled with the notion "that relatives are glad when a rich old man dies"; although such plotlines are "not unknown" in comedy vehicles or in real life, that fact notwithstanding, "jokes can grate even if they are based on truth." As for *If I Were Rich*, the critic noted, the situations "erred on the cheap side"; in fact, "one questions if it is really so funny to treat a poor man as a buffoon, incapable of rising to a new situation and only longing to return to his shop." Indeed, "Bert is 'put through it' as if he were an untouchable aspiring to Brahmin rank." [51] Therefore, in a sense such a feature enticed a moviegoer with dreams of what it might be like to be rich and then reassured him that he really would not want to be wealthy; this film thus preached the *status quo* and suggested that anyone who really wanted to be better off was misguided.

But films with this theme were not always light, frothy comedies. Another example, similarly titled *If I Were Boss*, released early in the spring of 1938 with a parallel theme, was a drama; the story revealed what happened to a rather self-centered store clerk in an egg company who constantly bragged about what he would do if he ran the company.

In the somewhat complicated plot, Bruce Seton is a lowly, but ambitious clerk, Steve Brook of the Biltmore Egg company. Brook is in love with Pat, a typist portrayed by Googie Withers; Pat works for the owner of the company, Mr Biltmore, played by Ian Fleming, as his secretary. When Steve receives an unexpected inheritance of fifteen thousand pounds, he takes the money and invests it in the egg company; with the company somewhat weakened, Steve finds that if he demands repayment of the loan, the business will collapse. To prevent the bankruptcy, he is allowed to take over from Mr Biltmore who, now broke, is offered a low-level job at six pounds per week. Unfortunately, Steve quickly proves he is illequipped to run the business effectively. In spite of warnings from Mr Biltmore and from Pat against any such transactions, the swell-headed former clerk consummates a deal with a crafty competitor named Owen Reeves (Charles Olivier); Reeves plans to divest himself of a shipment that has gone rotten by getting Steve to take the eggs. Reeves is helped in his plot by his beautiful confederate, Irma, played by Julie Suedo, who attracts Steve and convinces him to complete the deal, whereby he will take the eggs and store them until their market value rises. Even though Pat points out to Steve his payment for the amount Reeves wanted will deprive the firm of its ready cash reserves, when Irma comes for the money, the infatuated Steve gives her the cheque. In the meantime, attempting to investigate the quality of the produce, Mr Biltmore is trapped in a new gas storage chamber. Pat rescues him in an unconscious state just in time, and as a result Steve discovers that the eggs are bad and that he has made a mistake; he saves the company in the nick of time by stopping payment of the cheque at the bank.

Although reviewers found the film to be "absurd, and unreal . . . [lacking] originality," its story was revealing in that it undermined the desirability of a working-class character's ever aspiring to a somewhat modest supervisory position; it implied that an individual who ponders what would happen "if he were boss," would find that, given the chance, he would not really know what to do or to expect, and therefore would probably find himself a failure.[52] The implication here was that the working person should stay in his proper place, and let the "bosses," who at least know what they are doing, be the "supervisors."

Another working of this particular theme was found in the remarkably grim, September, 1932 release, *Men of Steel*, based on a now forgotten novel by Douglas Newton. Apparently the film has also been forgotten, but at a time in the early thirties when so many reviewers and articles in Britain were calling for more movies in an industrial or working-class setting, it was remarkable that this movie as described largely escaped attention. In this atypical feature, the working-class character was something of an anti-hero; when he was placed in a management position, he turned out to be as callous and ruthless as the type of boss whom he had previously criticized.

Set in the industrial Midlands in Sheffield, the story concerns a young steel-worker named James "Iron" Harg, played by John Stuart, who works as a foreman in the Paxton Steel Foundry. A bright and inventive character, Harg is troubled by the unsafe nature of the old equipment with which he and his men must work. Insisting that something must be done about the hazardous situation, Harg forces his way into the office of the factory owner, Charles Paxton (Franklin Dyall), on behalf of his men and in a scene of violent confrontation, the grease-covered foreman demands that replacements must be found for the outdated and unsafe machinery in the factory on which Paxton has economized and with which the lives of hundred are risked. Indignant and outraged at the imposition, Paxton advances on the steelworker to throw him out of the office, bellowing "How dare you!"; but Harg responds, in part out of desperation at the callousness he perceives in Paxton's management, and knocks him down before leaving. Later, with the help of Heather Angel as a factory girl named Ann Ford, who loves him, Harg perfects a new steel-making process which the company quickly adopts; his ingenuity earns him a seat on the company's Board of Directors, where he rapidly gains additional power. Abandoning his sweetheart, Ann, Harg has a love affair with Paxton's daughter Audrey, played by Benita Hume; Audrey is trying to act as a control over Harg's business actions. But when she breaks the romance, and he realizes that she has been deceiving him in part as a response to get revenge for his treatment of her father, he attempts a power takeover and finally gains control of the entire plant through a series of clever maneuvers.

In his new position, Harg's egoism and selfishness bring out his own ruthless qualities. When the workers address their requests for new machinery to him, Harg flatly rejects them; this denial causes an immediate and irreconcilable breach with Ann who can no longer excuse his behavior or his managerial coldness. His neglect of the very reforms he had been seeking leads to a terrible disaster in which one of the big outdated boilers in the plant bursts, with molten metal spreading throughout the factory. In the confusion, Ann's brother "Snuffy," played by Alexander Field as comic relief, is trapped in the mishap; only heroic measures by Harg, who finally realizes his own inconsistency, prevent further tragedies. His conversion and ultimate marriage to Ann puts a rather unrealistic happy ending to an otherwise cynical and seemingly hard-bitten movie. Although reviewers characterized the ending of the film as "too predictable," they generally agreed with the suggestion of one critic who said "there is a certain interest in the grim industrial setting." [53] Another critic observed with regard to *Men of Steel* that since "English industrial backgrounds have been badly neglected" on the screen, "it is refreshing to see one used in this straightforward, workmanlike, if rather obvious story"; the reviewer found "interesting" the "background of steel works" and "the relations of master and man." [54]

One unusual and especially evocative instance involving a working-class character posing as a member of the elite occurred in Alexander Korda's critically acclaimed screen biography, *Rembrandt*, with Charles Laughton as the Dutch painter. The film, which was generally regarded as one of the finest to be produced in England in the thirties, and as perhaps Korda's best production, centered on Rembrandt's loves and on his personal tragedies in the latter part of his life. The use of impersonation in this film was unusual in that it was not really central to the plot, not did it involve one of the major characters; yet, it was meaningful within the context of the movie's theme.

Throughout the feature, passing references were made to Rembrandt's practice of having painted beggars and common people rather than men of substance. But specifically in one sequence, the audience was shown Rembrandt's method of employing such individuals, with a tattered beggar near the wharves of Amsterdam whom he came to use as a model for his depiction of the Biblical King Saul. In the scene, as he is painting the cynical, bearded pauper, in order to put his subject in the proper mood and in order to get the expression from him that he is seeking, Rembrandt movingly describes Saul as a "great king, and a great hero of his people" who was "mighty and strong." Rembrandt reminded his model that "the Spirit of the Lord was not upon him" and "he that hath not the Spirit of the Lord within him, all the power of the world and the riches of the earth shall not avail for his heart will be troubled." The suggestion that wealth and material well-being are really unimportant so strongly affects the beggar that tears well in his eyes. When Rembrandt concludes by reciting the twenty-third psalm, the painter invests his model, played effectively by Roger Livesey, with an aristocratic melancholy. The implication was that a nobility existed in all men, no matter what their circumstances; the sequence also suggested that a working-class individual might find consolation in the realization that even a king like Saul with power and riches at his command could be far less happy and far more distressed than a poor man.

This suggestion paralleled the general theme of the film, which was concerned with adversity and how an individual could deal with it and ultimately could overcome it. This motif was made apparent in the introductory titles to the feature which observed that while Holland was a world power in the seventeenth century with trade throughout the world, her "proudest glory" ironically was "the son of a miller from Leyden", who proved to be "the greatest painter that has ever lived"; though "he died in obscurity" with "belongings worth no more than a few shillings," in the contemporary world, "no millionaire is worth the money the works of Rembrandt would realize, if ever offered for sale." A protagonist emerging from modest beginnings to gain success, whose life ended in failure and poverty, and who ultimately became one of his country's most famous figures, posed the implied question of how that character was able to deal with his hardships. The plot of the feature, though seemingly unrelated in any way to Britain in the thirties, nevertheless contained interesting contemporary overtones.

At the beginning of the film, Rembrandt is seen as a fairly successful if somewhat iconoclastic portrait artist; but soon his distinctive painting style proves to be insulting to prospective patrons among the bourgeoisie and nobility, and this leads to his ultimate bankruptcy. Uncaring town burghers and public officials place liens on his works, ending his prosperity and preventing him from being able to sell any additional paintings; in this way, they guarantee his impoverishment. At the same time, he endures the personal tragedy of the death of his beloved wife Saskia. His lack of success drives away his apprentices. But Rembrandt, though troubled by his financial setbacks and his personal problems is philosophical and seemingly undisturbed. When one of his most loyal apprentices bitterly reflects that Rembrandt's financial problems and failures are undeserved, the painter calmly reassures him, saying, "Every man has a destined path; if it leads him into the wilderness he's got to follow it with his head held high and a smile on his lips"; he adds that material success really means little to him, asking "What is success? . . . My world is insubstantial."

The film implied that his phlegmatic response to adversity came from Rembrandt's own modest background; though the family of Rembrandt was known to have been a fairly prosperous one, the movie eliminated any hint of his relatives having been wealthy. In the film, Rembrandt at one point observes that he was from a "family of peasants." When his problems are at their worst and his career seems ruined, he visits his home for a rest; during dinner in one scene, he delights in "black bread – *peasant's bread*," adding that, with it, he now feels he is at last "home" again. Clearly, the audience was being asked to believe that Rembrandt was one of the people. Later in the film, the kitchen maid whom he comes to love learns of a method of solving his financial difficulties from the example of a crude, obviously working-class, fishmonger's wife. The suggestion obviously was that strength and wisdom were to be derived from the common people. In this way, the movie sought to have the audience identify with an otherwise remote era and with a person whose profession and reputation were likely to be alien to the experience of ordinary filmgoers; not only did Rembrandt proudly assert his peasant ancestry, but he also returned to his origins when he was troubled and when he needed inspiration, symbolically even deriving a spiritual sustenance from a peasant meal. Thus, the protagonist of the film was himself also something of a working-class character posing as a person of a higher station; he found himself at odds with the nobles and bourgeoisie with whom he had to deal and more comfortable among his fellow peasants. He renewed himself and his creativity during visits with his peasant family.

While spending time with his strongly religious relatives, Rembrandt finds in the Scriptures a passage which helps sustain him through his difficulties. Laughton movingly recites the Biblical passage which echoes his own despair and his lost prosperity:

> I considered the days of old, the ancient times; will the Lord cast off forever? Will He be favorable no more? Hath His mercy clean gone forever? Doth His promise fail forevermore? Hath God forgotten to be gracious? Hath He in anger shut up his tender mercies? And I said this in my infirmity. That I will remember the years of the right hand of the Most High. I will remember the works of the Lord. Surely I will remember Thy wonders of old.

The passage marked both his resignation to his problems and his reconciliation with whatever difficult future he had to face.

Ultimately Rembrandt falls in love with the simple young kitchen maid named Hendrikje Stoffels, played by Elsa Lanchester, and in spite of their modest income, she makes him happy. As she tells him, at a point of further unhappiness when their house is being sold to pay off creditors, she needs for her happiness only a little "warm soup, a cloak," and her Rembrandt; and he, in reply, answers her, saying in admiration, "I've come into a fortune." This idea, that one could be wealthy without being rich, and that even the poorest person could possess the greatest "fortune" if he had someone to love, was a scarcely concealed recommendation for a philosophy enabling one to deal with troubles and adversity. Rembrandt, with his demonstration of patience and strength in accepting his own problems, was apparently intended to be suggestive of a role model for any audience member who was suffering from the economic hardships of the Depression years. If Rembrandt bore no animosity toward government officials and burghers who seemed cold and unfair to him, the implicit message was that the moviegoer should not be disturbed by a British government or ruling order that had been criticized for having done so little to ease the pains of Britain's Depression. Again, the essential message was one of forbearance and patience; such a theme encouraged the *status quo* and discouraged efforts to change.

What consolation was left for the common man amidst all the pain he was expected to endure was implied in a Biblical passage quoted by Rembrandt near the end of the film. In the scene, Rembrandt has been invited by a group of wealthy young men and women to join them in a tavern for a drink. The boisterous young people toast a variety of ephemeral, materialistic items, as the amused Rembrandt observes their folly; "to beauty," "to women," "to youth," "to love," "to money," and "to success," they offer in rapid succession. Finally, Rembrandt mutters his own philosophy, quoting directly from Ecclesiastes.

> Vanity of vanities, all is vanity. I have seen all the works that are under the sun, and, behold, all is vanity and fixation of spirit. For in much wisdom is much grief, and he that increaseth knowledge, increaseth sorrow. Perceive that there is nothing better than that a man shall rejoice in his own works. For that is his portion.

Thus, an answer to hardship could be found in a man's own work, the old artist and presumably the Bible were suggesting. The contrast between the apparently prosperous laughing, carefree, young ladies and gentlemen, and the wise old impoverished painter was graphically illustrated. The subtle suggestion that a workman should overcome his own problems by just working harder and taking pride in his labors was really a rather reactionary theme. Thus, the film in its own way commented on misery and suffering; and such misfortunes, perhaps not coincidentally, were by-products of the Depression that England's moviegoers were experiencing once they left their cinemas. The implicit theme of this film, that an individual should be strong in the face of hardship and should take pride in whatever was his life's endeavor or vocation, certainly could be applied to British society at the time of the film's release as a possible, though admittedly conservative, approach to dealing with social crisis and economic breakdown. Although some critics, like Graham Greene, objected to the Biblical recitations in the movie, primarily because "they . . . have nothing to do with the story," in fact, they were central to the film's implied ideology.[55] The Biblical readings had the effect of underscoring the need for faith in God during the worst misfortune; they also lent a kind of spiritual authority to the method by which this seventeenth-century artistic Job chose to manage his own problems.

The film's concern for this basic message and for the difficulties of class structure in society were apparently intentional; evidence has shown that these matters were being discussed by the film-makers throughout the production. A biographer of Charles Laughton has written that Korda had sold the idea of making the movie to the actor by promising that "he intended to emphasize" the great painter's "intense sympathy for the poor" and his suffering at the "hands of the pompous and stupid aristocracy and bourgeoisie of seventeenth-century Holland which had failed to appreciate Rembrandt's genius, stripped him of his possessions, and reduced him to begging in the streets"; this approach appealed to Laughton, who himself held a "contempt for class distinctions." [56]

Korda's biographer Karol Kulik has observed that both Laughton and his director intended to interpret Rembrandt as a "peasant philosopher who refused to let financial adversity, his too early success, and society's . . . short-sightedness hinder [him]"; Korda wanted to depict Rembrandt's perseverance by "describing his last years: his depression . . ., his disinterested attitude toward his increasing poverty and eventual bankruptcy, his . . . attempt to return to the peasant life of his family." [57] Kulik noted that the director who was concerned with the "audience identification of Laughton with Rembrandt" sought to convey the idea that like a tattered street beggar, "the artist [was] . . . 'beggar' to his patrons." [58] The movie may have been artistically a great triumph, but if Alexander Korda was seeking to have moviegoers "identify" with Rembrandt and his philosophy, his efforts were largely unsuccessful; for whatever reason, whether or not filmgoers perceived the subtle "suffer and be still" message of the movie, as Charles Higham has observed, "the public of the time rejected the film . . . decisively," and the feature proved to be a major financial failure for Korda. [59] Yet, ironically, Charles Laughton's performance was voted by movie fans in *Film Weekly* as the third best achievement by a British actor for 1936, and enough people liked the feature to vote it the ninth best production of the year. [60]

FREQUENCY OF THE MOTIF

This plot structure in which working-class characters impersonated, became, or were mistaken for an upper- or middle-class character was extensively used in British films in the thirties. Table 4.1 shows just how frequently this device was employed by scenario writers in Depression- era features. In all but the turbulent first two years of the decade, when the transition to sound was taking place, no fewer than one in ten movies released had some kind of mistaken-identity format similar to the type of plot discussed in the preceding pages; this story device appeared in some form in as many as one in six

Table 4.1 Films in which working-class characters become, impersonate, or are mistaken for upper- or middle-class characters

Year	Proportion of the films released	%
1929	6 of 86	7.0
1930	7 of 99	7.1
1931	16 of 134	11.9
1932	25 of 150	16.7
1933	26 of 181	14.4
1934	18 of 183	9.8
1935	25 of 185	13.5
1936	25 of 219	11.4
1937	24 of 211	11.4
1938	22 of 158	13.9
1939	14 of 98	14.3

movies released in 1932 and in approximately one in seven features made in 1933, 1935, 1938, and 1939.

Table 4.2 demonstrates a general evaluation of these portrayals. Obviously, in some films the working-class character's impersonation was successful, with results in the story that benefitted both the protagonist and others. In other features, the personification led to confusion and problems that were only resolved when the character returned to his normal, original status.

The plot outcomes suggest that these impersonations more often than

Table 4.2 Evaluation of plot outcome in films in which working-class characters become, impersonate, or are mistaken for upper- or middle-class characters

	Successful results			Unsuccessful results	
Year		%			%
1929	3 of 86 released	3.5		3 of 86 released	3.5
1930	4 or 99 released	4.0		3 of 99 released	3.0
1931	12 of 134 released	9.0		4 of 134 released	3.0
1932	16 of 150 released	10.7		9 of 150 released	6.0
1933	21 of 181 released	11.6		5 of 181 released	2.8
1934	11 of 183 released	6.0		7 of 183 released	3.8
1935	11 of 185 released	5.9		14 of 185 released	7.6
1936	15 of 219 released	6.0		10 of 219 released	4.6
1937	10 of 211 released	4.7		14 of 211 released	6.6
1938	14 of 158 released	8.9		8 of 158 released	5.1
1939	9 of 98 released	9.2		5 of 98 released	5.1

not had a beneficial effect on the characters and situations, but the action in a good many features did imply the opposite, that is, that these deceptions and alterations of social strata only brought unhappiness and complications for those involved.

5

MISTAKEN IDENTITIES
Posing poverty

DETECTIVES, DISGUISES, AND HITCHCOCKIAN DECEPTIONS

In the last chapter, the type of film in which a working-class character posed as an upper-class person was considered. The "mistaken identity" format, however, also worked in the other direction, with characters from the elites posing as working-class individuals. The motives and circumstances differed in the various films, but this plot device was as common in the thirties as its opposite.

In certain movies, impersonations were almost to be expected, simply by the nature of the film genre itself. For example, in detective movies, one mechanism that seemed pervasive, no matter what the specifics of the story, was that the hero or detective at some point in the plot would have to disguise himself as a bargee, dockworker, vegetable vendor, or some other working-class character to gather evidence in the East End of London or in some other working-class district. For example, in the rarely seen seven British screen incarnations of Sherlock Holmes in the thirties, the great detective (personified once each by Raymond Massey and Robert Rendel and five times by the memorable Arthur Wontner) several times disguises himself as a laborer or workman (as he did frequently in Conan Doyle's stories). In Herbert Wilcox's 1931 production of *The Speckled Band*, Raymond Massey, as the legendary sleuth, masquerades as a workman to obtain evidence to protect the heroine, played by Angela Baddeley, from her murderous stepfather, the evil Dr Grimesby Rylott, depicted in grand fashion by Lyn Harding. Though Arthur Wontner was in his late fifties and early sixties when he essayed the role in the 1930s, his Sherlock Holmes also posed as characters such as a peddler woman and as a tar in an atmospheric East End pub.

Other cinema detectives undertook similar impersonations in numerous British productions of the period. In the summer, 1929 release, *Downstream*, a detective takes a job as a bargee to prevent a girl's suicide and to apprehend her villainous lover; similarly in the May, 1934 feature, *Warn London*, John Loder plays Inspector Yorke, a detective who disguises himself as a tramp

87

named Barraclough in an effort to hinder a German adversary named Dr Herman Krauss, played by Edmund Gwenn.

Often the detective would pose as an ex-convict either to infiltrate a gang or to gather evidence. For example, an April, 1931 adventure release titled *Contraband Love* had a detective impersonating an ex-convict in Cornwall trying to catch a band of smugglers. One popular illustration of this plot was the February, 1938 thriller, *Mr Reeder in Room 13*. Directed by Norman Lee, the film, which was based on the Edgar Wallace novel *Room 13*, centered on a detective for the Bank of England named J.G. Reeder, played by Gibb McLaughlin. In the movie, Reeder is searching for a band of counterfeiters and obtains the help of the well-to-do Johnny Gray from the Foreign Office (Peter Murray Hill). Assisting Reeder, Johnny agrees to a scheme to gather evidence which requires that he obtain information from men in prison; thus, he is arrested for passing counterfeit notes, and after being convicted, he is sentenced to a term in prison, where he hopes to be able to learn about the identity of the counterfeiters from other convicts. On the day Johnny is released, he discovers that his girlfriend, Claire Kane (Sally Gray) has that morning married his prime suspect, Major Floyd. The Major is really a man named Jeff Legge (Leslie Perrins) and he and his elderly ex-convict father Emmanuel (D.J. Williams), have been printing the forged notes. Emmanuel had been the business partner of Claire's father Peter (Malcolm Keen) and he is seeking revenge for having had to serve a twelve-year prison sentence, while Kane had been free. Ultimately, Johnny finds an old jail being used by the counterfeiters, and after being captured by the villains, he is rescued at the film's conclusion by Mr Reeder, just before the gang attempts to hang him. The movie was so popular that additional J.G. Reeder stories had to be produced to meet public demand.

Interestingly, in many such detective thrillers, the leader of the evil-doers turns out to be a respected member of the upper class, taking advantage of his working-class subordinates and leading them astray. In the May, 1936 release, *Wednesday's Luck*, a detective masquerades as a former prison inmate to try to obtain evidence about the criminal activities of the head of a supposed benevolent society. One very popular rendering of this plot was the August, 1937 release, *The Squeaker*, directed by the American, William K. Howard, and based on a novel by Edgar Wallace. In this Alexander Korda production, Edmund Lowe plays Inspector Barrabel, whom film historian William K. Everson has characterized as a "formerly respected detective, down and out through drunkenness, [who is] given a chance to redeem himself by posing as an ex-con and joining the organization of a philanthropist who employs ex-crooks for, as the Yard suspects, further criminal activities."[1] The villain, played by Sebastian Shaw, is a man named Frank Sutton, the head of a shipping company who used his respectable business dealings to conceal his illegal activities as "The Squeaker," a notorious stolen jewel "fence." Ultimately, Inspector Barrabel redeems himself by capturing "the Squeaker."

One of the most interesting and more unusual features conforming to this general format was the June, 1933 release, *Doss House*, directed by the under-rated and largely neglected John Baxter.[2] A "doss house" was a term describing a kind of lodging for transients. The plot of the film was very pedestrian; Herbert Franklin plays a detective who disguises himself as a tramp in order to track down an escaped convict; a reporter, played by Arnold Bell, on the orders of his editor, portrayed by Frank Cellier, accompanies him. *Picture-goer Weekly* summarized the story-line of the film, noting that "John Baxter takes you to a doss house where London's down and outs, those who are lucky enough to pay the required ninepence for a night's lodging, exist." The characters who dwell at the doss house include a "discredited doctor," an aging "pianist whose downfall has been brought about by drink," and a "self-confessed murderer," and the film's reason for introducing the audience "to these poor wretches" is an investigation "conducted by a detective who is looking for an escaped convict"; the detective is "accompanied by a journalist who has been commissioned to get a human interest scoop," and the convict's "capture . . . supplies the dramatic climax" of the film.[3]

The interesting quality of *Doss House* was its starkly realistic setting and what one reviewer called "the little character studies" which emerge during the detective's investigations; at a time in the early thirties when such an environment was rarely used at all, for a feature to focus the bulk of its action on such a background was unusual.[4] The publicity for the feature emphasized this aspect of the movie. An article entitled "London's Underworld Filmed", in the May 12, 1933 issue of the fan-magazine, *Film Weekly*, focused on the movie's uncommon characteristics and its realism. Probably writing from publicity sheets provided by the studio, Sound City at Shepperton, the writer of the article noted that the "story [was] written by an author who is said to have lived in a doss house himself" and that Baxter also, in preparation for the film, had "visited . . . common lodging houses . . . in Bow, Kingsland Road, Seven Dials, and Hammersmith"; for that reason, the writer concluded the movie "gives an insight into the lives of the denizens of a typical 'down-and-out's' hotel" and "show[s] some of the wonderful human types" who live therein.[5] Commenting that the feature "promises to be . . . unusually interesting," the article demonstrated the degree of accuracy in the film by describing in detail the kind of lodgings the movie depicted and by showing a knowledge of the "rhyming slang" and expressions that were frequently heard in such lodgings. The article explains how Baxter sought authenticity in the film and was researching the doss houses with visits and tours; the film would show the activities, the language, the meals, and the sleeping quarters these men endured.[6]

But if the atmosphere of the film was authentic, the story and the characterizations may not have been so genuine. The men living in the doss house in the movie were portrayed as living in an environment that was "alert and animated". Noting that the "occupants are optimistic and cheerful," the article commented that even though some "have only just enough for their beds," they nonetheless are portrayed as "confident that the morrow will bring them more"; with references to what little money they actually have, the film demonstrates how a lodger endeavors to budget his meager coins and even to set aside "twopence for a rainy day – 'only,' he adds, 'there has been such a lot of rain lately.'" [7]

Reviewers praised the movie's "interestingly unusual 'slice of life' study" and its "imaginative direction". The critic in *Film Weekly*, wrote that this "definitely unusual . . . strange . . . [and somewhat] contradictory mixture" of a film "certainly breaks new ground in British pictures," though he added that the plot was "slender and unconvincing," and the contrast of "little vignettes of unreal sentimentality . . . played . . . against a background of grim realism" was not entirely successful.[8] Specifically, the inhabitants of the lodging-house on whom the story focused were probably not typical of the "down and out."

Picturegoer Weekly, though conceding that *Doss House* was "not a great feature" nevertheless observed that it was "an interesting one" and that it "shows that at least a British company has realised the potentialities and values of a thematic plot"; the review added, "the atmosphere is exceedingly good, and although the idea might have been explored more fully and more subtly, there is at least a feeling that one is in contact with something human and vital."[9]

Sound City in Shepperton, the young studio that made the film and subsequently re-released it, apparently because of its popularity, came to specialize somewhat in similar stories dealing with ordinary people; a number of their movies, which usually were released through MGM British, were directed by John Baxter, who developed something of a stock company of veteran theatrical and music hall actors and actresses whom he thereby kept in employment.

Probably the best known British film with a detective in disguise in a working-class position was Alfred Hitchcock's late 1936 release, *Sabotage*, which was distributed in America as *A Woman Alone*; like *Doss House*, *Sabotage* was of special interest because of the environment and setting of the story. Using Joseph Conrad's novel *The Secret Agent*, as its source, *Sabotage* on the surface concerned the undercover efforts of a detective named Ted Spense, played by matinee idol John Loder, who obtains a job as a greengrocer's clerk assistant in order to conduct surveillance against a suspected saboteur who runs a neighboring, small independent cinema or "fleapit" in London's East End. The cinema manager, a foreigner of unknown Eastern European origin named Carl Verloc, played effectively by Oscar Homolka, is married to a young American woman named Sylvia, portrayed by Sylvia Sidney, who knows nothing of her husband's contacts with a suspicious group of agents intent on disrupting London. Living with Verloc and his wife is her young, somewhat awkward little brother Stevie (Desmond Tester). Verloc, a somewhat pathetic, nervous villain, seems to be a kindly family man, genuinely caring for Sylvia and Stevie, but he is using his cinema as a front for terrorist activities.

As the film begins, Verloc has just completed an act of sabotage, having put sand in the electrical generators at Battersea, thereby throwing London into a blackout. But his act has failed to upset the people's morale or even to make an impact on the city, with Londoners shown cheerfully coping and cooperating in an almost festive, candlelit mood. Ironically only at Verloc's Bijou Cinema are there any problems, as customers who had been watching the film are demanding their money back from Mrs Verloc for having had their entertainment interrupted. The intervention of Spenser in his greengrocer's disguise prevents the situation from becoming more unruly.

At an aquarium the next day, the saboteur meets his superior to collect his payment, but he finds his efforts have brought him no reward; the superior is upset at the failure of the power cut to cause any major disruptions in the city. Showing Verloc a newspaper with headlines reading "Joking crowds carry on with oil lamps – comedy in the dark," the chief saboteur tells Verloc he will not be paid unless and until he commits a far more serious crime; specifically, he wants the cinema manager to have bombs explode at Piccadilly Circus on the following Saturday for the Lord Mayor's Show Day. Though Verloc at first refuses because of the danger to bystanders, protesting that he will not become "involved" in any venture in which "there will be a loss of human life," eventually he relents; from a pet shop run by the saboteur's chief supplier, a man known as the "Professor," played by William Dewhurst, Verloc obtains the necessary materials and the details of Saturday's plot.

Meanwhile, in an effort to ingratiate himself further and to obtain more information, Spenser takes Mrs Verloc and her brother to an elegant lunch at Simpson's on the Strand. At first the detective claims he has never been there before this splurge; but when Ted is identified as a regular customer by one of the waiters before he can be quieted, Mrs Verloc is left to puzzle out how a greengrocer's assistant possibly could have afforded meals there at any time. She eventually concludes that he must be a son of one of the owners of the grocery chain just learning the trade. In return for the meal, Ted is given a free pass to a movie matinee on Friday, which he uses as an opportunity to spy on Verloc and his hired co-conspirators. But Spenser is discovered in the act of snooping and is recognized by one of the terrorists, who promptly identifies him as a detective-sergeant from Scotland Yard. Verloc now finds himself under heavy surveillance; when he receives the timebomb concealed in a bird-cage and scheduled to detonate at 1.45 p.m., and yet finds he cannot depart from the building undetected, the saboteur realizes he must change his plan. He conceals the explosive in a film canister and tells the unknowing Stevie to deliver what he believes to be a film to a cloakroom in Piccadilly Circus, urging him to hurry. But Stevie, forever clumsy, is delayed, first by a street vendor in Petticoat Lane and then by the procession festivities; before he can deliver his deadly parcel, the bomb explodes aboard a bus, killing the young-ster and other passengers.

Back at the cinema, Mrs Verloc hears the news of the disaster and in a newspaper article recognizes the title of the film on the canister discovered in the rubble of the bus; in her grief, as if in a trance, she walks into the cinema during a children's matinee, begins watching a Walt Disney cartoon entitled "Who Killed Cock Robin?", and in spite of her gloom, begins laughing along with the children. Later Verloc confesses to her his complicity in Stevie's death and explains his own anguish; but at dinner, shortly thereafter, the troubled saboteur approaches his wife as she is carving a roast, and almost involuntarily, she stabs and kills him. The detective, who has by now fallen in love with her, offers to help her escape the country, but she insists on surren-dering herself to the police. But meanwhile the Professor has gone to the cinema to retrieve the birdcage in which he sent the timebomb to Verloc. Finding Verloc dead and hearing the approach of police sirens, the Professor detonates another bomb, blowing up himself, Verloc, and all incriminating evidence, thereby permitting the detective and Mrs Verloc a happy ending.

Film critics have suggested that the explication of a Hitchcock film often resembled the peeling of an onion; the deeper one went, the more layers of meaning one found. This metaphor was particularly appropriate for *Sabo-tage*. Generally regarded as one of Hitchcock's most complex works, the movie was distinctive in its portrayal of London life and in its authentic settings. *Sabotage* was also unique in its realistic depiction of the small neighborhood cinema in England and its importance in the community. Reviewers were especially impressed with this quality of the film. Said *Pic-turegoer Weekly*, "The London atmosphere is exceptionally good, and the scenes in the crowded streets, in the little Kinema, and elsewhere are pre-sented with a full share of realism." [10] *Film Weekly* praised Hitchcock's "glimpses of London life," and the *Monthly Film Bulletin* added "the London backgrounds are admirable [with] . . . the humour . . . typically Cockney." [11] In the *Spectator*, Graham Greene, who was finally won over to Hitchcock by the film, found the movie to be "convincingly realistic." [12]

Hitchcock's biographer, John Russell Taylor, has suggested that this rich-ness and accuracy in detail were due to Hitchcock's own knowledge "of the London he grew up in and knew like the back of his hand." Observing that "much of the detail is drawn from his own experience," Taylor cites as examples the greengrocer's shop, reminiscent of Hitchcock's "own childhood home," the little East End cinema "where he had his own experiences at the flicks," and the luncheon at Simpson's in the Strand, "Hitch's own favourite restaurant in his City days"; the whole environment of *Sabotage* including "the quirkily vivid scenes in the street markets, the back street shops, the cheery by-play of the peddlers, and the darker sense of crime behind closed doors in mean streets" all have parallels in Hitchcock's childhood and in "his early fascination with the domestic details of the murder cases he loved to read." [13] The film also seemed realistic because of its subject-matter, as Raymond Durgnat has noted. Not only does the feature remind one of the Sidney Street anarchists (though admittedly less than Hitchcock's earlier *The Man Who Knew Too Much*), but also Mr Verloc's "heavily Germanic style" reminds the audience of dangers of Nazi infiltration. Contemporary newspapers already were examining the questions of "the effect of aerial bombing on civilian morale," the need for air raid precautions, and blackouts. Durgnat concludes that in this way *Sabotage* "catches a dreamlike overlap between memories of the anarchists, depositing bombs, and the blackouts and terror which were later to materialize in the blitz." [14]

From the documentary-like opening (with a dictionary definition of the word and then images of machinery) to the closing shot (of Ted and Sylvia blending into the crowded street), *Sabotage* conveyed an unusual gritty realism in spite of its adventure/thriller structure; as Robert A. Harris and Michael Lasky wrote in their description of the production, "the film gains in realism as it continues," not only because Hitchcock interspersed it with a considerable amount of location material, but also, because of its complexity. [15]

Sabotage contained some apparently random bits of social commentary on the surface but at deeper levels of meaning, the film was a disturbing portrait of a troubled society, echoing with the anxieties of modern urban man. Maurice Yacowar, in his thoughtful study of Hitchcock's British films, observed that the "pessimistic premise at the heart of this film is that human life is a miserable and worsening lot." [16] The audience and the characters in the film they were watching were aware of urban misery in the form of mechanical breakdowns, family conflicts, destruction of property, crime and even espionage. Ordinarily, a person avoided these problems when going to the cinema; but in *Sabotage*, neither the movie's protagonists nor its viewers were insulated from these worldly concerns as they usually were at the movies. The setting of the film, in and around the comforting institution of the neighborhood cinema, where one regularly forgot such cares, thus held an especially unsettling significance. If the function of movies was simply to escape, that means of overcoming problems was shown to be hollow and unworthy (though at least, effective). When Sylvia begins laughing involuntarily at the cartoon, at a time of deep tragedy and personal grief, the generally held belief that films could temporarily provide a release from unhappiness is demonstrated; but the fact that in the next scene she murders her husband, leaves in doubt the question of whether her "escape" had been in any way therapeutic.

Hitchcock carried this disturbing, brutal treatment of reality further with one of his experiments in audience identification; as in the later and more celebrated *Psycho*, he killed off a leading character, Stevie, whom audience expectations would have considered to be invulnerable. In real life, a likeable child last observed playing with a puppy on a bus might die, but not in a movie. In this way Hitchcock shocked the audience into acknowledging that their world, their society, their London could not be considered a perfect, rational, structured, ordered place where events were predictable and would end happily. As Donald Spoto has observed, "Hitchcock examines the thin veneer of security which overlays the chaotic and destructive elements in ordinary life." [17] Nowhere was this better demonstrated than in *Sabotage*.

Additionally, in Hitchcock's world, a filmgoer could take little consolation in even the most harmonious and seemingly harmless appearances; this was demonstrated clearly just before Verloc was inadvertently to send his wife's little brother to his death on a terrorist mission. In the scene, Stevie tells him of a conversation he had with Ted in which the incognito detective had told the youngster that even the most dangerous "gangster" is likely to be "ordinary looking"; as he comments the camera tightens meaningfully on a shot of Verloc's face, that of just such a dangerous person with an ordinary appearance. Similarly, familiar objects take on a darker meaning. The Professor conceals his stored explosives in common kitchen containers such as a ketchup bottle and a jam jar, and the bomb Stevie carries is an innocent-looking film canister being returned to the movie company. With a delightful and typically perverse irony, Hitchcock suggested that even a filmgoer's beloved movies could be instruments of destruction.

The motives of the various characters contained both moral and political conflicts, and these endowed the feature with additional dimensions that a standard thriller could not contain. For example, the Professor was depicted as supporting a mean looking, grown up daughter, played by Martita Hunt, who lived in his shop, and who, in turn, had an illegitimate daughter whose father was unknown; the Professor described the situation coldly, saying, "it's her cross, and she has to bear it," and blaming her problems on lack of discipline in her upbringing.

But her corruption and moral guilt were shared and perhaps surpassed by the Professor who held contempt for the law and for order in society; in fact, the Professor's delight in terrorism was underscored when he commented to Verloc that he wished he were a "front-line fighter" again rather than having had to retire to the position of supplier to the other saboteurs. A darkly lit close-up of the Professor's hands as he talked suggested that many crimes, perhaps strangulations, had been committed by these soft, deceptively innocent-looking fingers. When he added to Verloc, "We all have our crosses to bear, hmmm?", he acknowledged his own corruption and guilt. Raymond Durgnat, in his analysis of the feature, implied that with this remark the Professor may have demonstrated an even greater, social guilt; that is, his methods of raising the girl may have led her to go astray, and these methods likely would echo through another generation to his grand-daughter. Describing the remark as "all the more meanly puritannical for the mother's bitterness and for the little girl's fresh, pert way," Durgnat argues that Hitchcock gives the audience a "glimpse" of the "impending and relentless incubation of shame which will crush her . . . for the vicarious sin of being alive . . . a transference, not of guilt, but of punishment, that is to say, an injustice".[18]

Ironically, by contrast, Verloc's family seemed to be warm and loving. Verloc appeared to care genuinely for both his wife and Stevie, and Mrs Verloc obviously respected him for having brought the youth into their family. Yacowar saw the Professor's family and its parallels to Verloc's family as a possibly political metaphor. Neither family has a father and "thus [they have] . . . no discipline." The "two fatherless families" might be seen accordingly as "images for a society that has been deprived of its traditional leadership"; therefore, they both are "struggling along the parallel roads of introjected despair (the Professor's family) and a broadening community spirit (Verloc's family, calling the cinema patrons family . . .)."[19]

But what often has been ignored in criticism of *Sabotage* has been the problem of Verloc's character. As noted before, Verloc was a sympathetic character who was well liked in the East-End neighborhood in which he ran this theater. Mrs Verloc characterized him to Spenser as "the quietest, most harmless, homeloving person" and referred to his kindness and gentle care for Stevie; his depiction by Oscar Homolka provided nothing to contradict this impression. In his book-length interview with Hitchcock, François Truffaut observed that Verloc's "personage" was endearing "probably because Oscar Homolka is plump," adding that in films, "generally speaking, chubby people are regarded as being kindly and rather loveable."[20] How, then, has a man so seemingly harmless and peace-loving become involved with a group of terrorists? Such complicity with men of violence seemed out of character for a man like Verloc. Certainly, his association with the saboteurs apparently had nothing to do with political affiliations or any overwhelming sense of dedication; he wanted to avoid involvement with any action that could result in loss of life, he regarded his superiors with contempt, referring to them as "swine," and he symbolically washed his hands after causing the blackout, as if trying to cleanse himself of his actions.

Few critics have bothered to speculate on Verloc's motivation, although Yacowar, in passing, observed that "Verloc is prompted to his espionage not so much by political conviction as by his wish to improve his family's financial lot."[21] But Yacowar's comment was not totally accurate in the sense that it failed to recognize the touch of desperation and financial necessity in the Verloc family situation. Though not impoverished, they clearly have been monetarily troubled. At the aquarium, the boss of the saboteurs responds to Verloc's initial refusal to carry out the bombing mission by observing that he must not need money; to this comment Verloc, quietly, almost ashamedly, mutters, "You know my situation." He then agrees to carry out the fatal mission. Mrs Verloc, almost panic-stricken during the blackout, maintains that she cannot give refunds to customers because "we can't afford it," and she explains to the detective at the luncheon that the family had emigrated from America to England because business had been so bad and their finances so disastrous. She adds that business now "was not terribly good," to which the detective observes "it's hard to make a one-man business work without a sideline." Thus, the danger of poverty had been a key factor, if not the single motivation, of Verloc's involvement with the terrorist group. Though the point was a subtle one, the movie thus suggested that the real source of social disruption was, in this sense, economic dislocation. The cinema manager's financial problems drove him to such desperation that he agreed to commit an act against his nature as a human being that would endanger hundreds of innocent bystanders. Here, then, was the root of the troubles in society with which modern man had to cope.

Hitchcock reinforced this point in the sales pitch of a toothpaste vendor. The vendor asks the crowd around him "What causes teeth to fall out?", and a heckler's voice cries out, "A punch in the jaw." The vendor answers his own question, commenting, "The process of decay, inevitable in all human organisms, but decay can be arrested – arrested instantaneously – by what?" Again, the heckler shouts out, "By a copper," and the vendor acknowledges the pun, replying in good humor, "Exactly, but if I may say so, just a little more than one . . . a few coppers." This humorous exchange, ostensibly just a sample of Cockney joking, actually summarized the film's implicit theme.

If the exchange was read as a metaphor for the "body politic" of society, the message became clear. When the vendor asked, "What causes teeth to fall out?", he essentially was pondering, "What creates a disruption of the system?" The heckler's response indicated, at least, that he interpreted the question in terms of society, and implied that violence, "A punch in the jaw," was the actual cause of a system's deterioration or collapse. The salesman's reference to this process as a natural one, calling it "decay, inevitable in all human organisms," suggested the universality of these disruptions; when he observed that "decay" could be "arrested" or stopped, the man in the crowd responded by elaborating on the double meaning of "arrest" and again emphasized the social rather than the medical meaning of the word. Hence, a disruption in society was "arrested" by authority in the person of police, that is, "by a copper." The vendor answered by echoing the pun with one of his own, which tended to merge the two meanings; he suggested that the "copper" used to arrest the cause of societal "decay," about which the heckler seemed to be talking, might require more help from other policemen, that is, "a few coppers." But the other implication of the word, that reminded the crowd that the toothpaste he was offering to remedy the medical problem of tooth decay cost more than just "a copper," emphasized the monetary meaning of the word. The exchange then offered two remedies for social disruption: "decay" could be prevented by authority in the form of police, or by cash.

Hitchcock demonstrated which solution was preferable. With money, there is an end to poverty, there would be no social disruptions, no "decay";

similarly, Mr Verloc would have been able to resist the deadly plans of the chief saboteur had he not been concerned with the potential dangers of his own financial problems.

By contrast, the prospect of police or authority as a solution was shown to be ineffective and, in some ways, objectionable. Hitchcock's own anxiety about police has been well documented; as he told Francois Truffaut, "I'm not *against* the police; I'm just afraid of them." [22] In *Sabotage*, the police and authority appeared largely unsuccessful and, in some ways, morally indistinguishable from the saboteurs. For example, the detective repeatedly made errors in his disguise as a greengrocer's assistant, allowing himself to be discovered listening to Verloc and his plans, being caught in a lie about his identity at the restaurant, and, most inexcusably, being a willing after-the-fact accomplice to Verloc's murder in encouraging Sylvia to escape.

In fact, Ted gave up his working-class impersonation not because he had discovered any information, but because his identity had been exposed. In a sense, Ted's impersonation was regarded in the working-class neighborhood as something of a crime itself. When Verloc, after learning Ted's identity, attempted to confront him, he found the detective had fled; but the green-grocer at whose vegetable stand Ted had been working then profusely apologized to the forgiving cinema manager, saying he had been forced to allow the deception to proceed. Ted also betrayed his contempt for the public and for the people he ostensibly was protecting, when in the midst of his defense of Mrs Verloc's ticket policy during the blackout, he muttered, "You're all ignorant, anyway."

Yacowar observed little difference between the detective and the saboteur. Ted allows Sylvia's guilt to be concealed by the Professor's death. As a detective, he "hounds" Verloc professionally, at the same time that he "undercuts him as a lover." Yacowar argues that the detective in this way "is presented as a parallel to Verloc," reaching Sylvia through his kindness to her little brother and "bringing in the cabbage like the provider Verloc was [intended] to be;" at the same time, like Verloc, Ted was "sabotaging justice by placing his personal desires ahead of social justice." Thus he concludes that "between Verloc and Ted there is [a] ... thin ... distinction." [23] Yacowar went on to note that "Hitchcock perhaps embellished this idea from Conrad's novel, citing the passage in which Conrad wrote, "The terrorist and the policeman both came from the same basket. Revolution, legality-counter moves in the same game; forms of idleness at bottom identical." [24] And political authority was seen in much the same way. Just as the saboteurs were willing to make sacrifices of innocent victims, so too did the political leadership. In the aquarium scene, the chief saboteur noted that three rare large turtles were to be sacrificed for the soup for the Lord Mayor's banquet; in what sense was this attitude, this willingness to sacrifice turtles, different from a political leadership that failed to respond to the welfare needs of its constituency in the midst of a devastating economic crisis?

But the responsibility for disaster was not traceable just to the saboteurs nor simply to negligent authority. *Sabotage* suggested a broader responsibility; in fact the central tragedy in the film, the explosion of the time bomb on the bus rather than in the building near Piccadilly Circus, was attributable in some ways to all of society. By showing Stevie being delayed in his errand by a policeman, by the toothpaste and hair tonic street vendor, by the Lord Mayor's Show, by a traffic jam, and by a mob of ordinary people, Hitchcock was insisting that civilization in general (authority, business, politicians, the urban environment, and all mankind) shared guilt for all events and all problems.

The argument that *Sabotage* was a film of profound social commentary may be considered somewhat unorthodox. Ordinarily Alfred Hitchcock was not thought of as a director whose films contained social or political messages, and, for the most part, with a few exceptions, his features were generally apolitical and devoid of any kind of social statement. But as Hitchcock admitted in a now forgotten interview with J. Danvers Williams in late 1938, "I have always wanted to make films with some sociological importance," but because of censorship, "in order to give utterance to the violent things which I want to express, I have been forced into fiction"; he added, "if you . . . make your villain a foreigner – officialdom raises no objections." [25] He concluded that "although circumstances have forced me into fiction, I have always sincerely tried to draw my characters and their behavior from genuine observations;" accordingly "given that the basic story is imaginary the characters, I think, always behave as real people should, in a similar set of circumstances." [26] Thus, in *Sabotage*, Hitchcock adapted the detective–thriller genre (and, incidentally, the type of film in which the detective impersonated a working-class character) to his own social vision.

UPPER-CLASS IMPERSONATIONS OF THE WORKING CLASSES

While impersonations were frequent in detective features, other types of movies showed aristocrats, businessmen, and others, attempting to pose as laborers and other working-class types. One of the most common plot formats in which this change occurred was a story in which an aristocrat for some reason would take a position as a butler or other service employee. Most of these films were comedies, and they can be found throughout the decade. For example, one of Britain's earliest feature-length sound releases was a comedy appearing in the summer of 1929 entitled *Taxi for Two* in which John Stuart plays Jack Devenish, the son of the aristocratic Lady Devenish, who obtains a job as a chauffeur in order to win the heart of a girl who has taken over a taxi business.

Another early example was *Lord Richard in the Pantry*, a farce comedy directed by Walter Forde and based on the 1919 play by Sydney Blow and

Douglas Hoare, adapted from Martin Swayne's novel. Released early in 1931, the story concerns Lord Richard Sandridge, a character described by one reviewer as "noodle aristocrat," played by Richard Cooper, "who, dreading arrest through the failure of a company, acts as a butler in his own mansion," and attempts to learn who is framing him; the trade periodical *Bioscope* said of the film, "though his misadventures are hardly to be viewed as possible, the acting by the star and supporting cast is so good, the incidents so delightfully absurd, and much of the dialogue so entertaining that there are no dull moments." [27]

A George Robey vehicle entitled *Birds of a Feather* directed by John Baxter in the mid thirties was another comedy which even more directly derived its humor from the contrast in the social classes inherent in an upper- or middle-class character posing as a servant. In this November, 1935 release, based on George Foster's play "A Rift in the Loot," Horace Hodges is the poverty stricken Lord Cheverton whose financial embarrassment necessitates his renting out his ancestral castle to a socially ambitious sausage magnate named Henry Wortle and his wife, portrayed by George Robey and Eva Lister. When the Wortles and their children move into the mansion, the aristocrat impersonates a butler in order to seek a hidden secret fortune. The *Monthly Film Bulletin*, in its review of the "domestic farce" noted the familiar nature of this plot, observing "there is nothing in the film to raise it above the average". Commenting on the remainder of the plot, the review notes that, "a burglary provides the necessary complications, and the story ends up traditionally with the financial rehabilitation of the earl, the retreat of the sausage king to suburbia, and the intermarriage of the two families through the son and daughter." [28] Even more extreme was an April, 1936 comedy release entitled *Servants All* which had a plot in which its impoverished aristocrat protagonists change places with their former servants.

Several major comedy stars, though not necessarily portraying aristocrats, took roles in films with this type of story-line. One of Jessie Matthews' non-singing roles was a light comedy released in January, 1933 entitled *The Man from Toronto*. In this feature, based on a popular Douglas Murray play, Jessie plays Leila Farrar, a widow who must pose as a maid to test and find out about the Canadian man she must marry in order to inherit a fortune. Directed by Sinclair Hill and co-starring Ian Hunter and Fred Kerr, the film helped establish Matthews as a star and was so well received that it was reissued as late as 1945.

Although comic Ralph Lynn was best known for the "Aldwych comedies" he made with Tom Walls and Robertson Hare, in one of his solo feature appearances, a 1936 comedy entitled *In the Soup*, the impersonation of a servant and the difficulties it created comprised a major portion of the film's humor. In this farce, Lynn is a solicitor named Horace Gillibrand; he and his wife Kitty, portrayed by Judy Gunn, find that they have leased an apartment simultaneously to two tenants. As a result, they are compelled to impersonate the servants who came with the flat but who have left without notice because they haven't been paid for months. The impersonation also is necessary because one of the tenants happens to be Horace's uncle, who must not be allowed to find out that Horace is married. As a consequence, Horace and Kitty endeavor to prepare an extensive dinner using only an electric iron, since the gas has been turned off. To extricate themselves from their problems, Kitty adds a sleeping mixture to the soup. As a result, those dining fall asleep in one another's arms; they then "are discovered in compromising attitudes by their various husbands, wives, and fiancés," and as one reviewer summarized the outcome, "the resulting tangles are ultimately straightened out" with everyone forgiving everyone else.[29]

While comedies predominated in films with this format, some exceptions, usually musicals, can be found with similar plots. A late 1932 feature entitled *Little Waitress* set in the Rhineland concerned Trudi, a waitress played by Elvi Keene, whose father, portrayed by character actor Moore Marriot, is really the impoverished Baron Halfsburg; in this musical, she is romanced by a tourist who pretends to be rich in order to impress her. In *Yes, Madam*, a musical feature based on a stage play adapted from K.R.G. Browne's novel, two cousins, Bill Quinton and Sally Gault (Bobby Howes and Diana Churchill), learn that they are to inherit a £160,000 legacy from an uncle if each spends one month in service without being fired. Never having been introduced to each other and not knowing each other's identity, they both take positions in the home of wealthy button manufacturer Albert Peabody, played by Wylie Watson, and his acerbic sister Emily, portrayed by Bertha Belmore. With Bill serving as valet-chauffeur and Sally serving as lady's maid, the two endeavor to earn their inheritance, but they are hindered by a third cousin, Tony Tolliver (Billy Milton), who stands to gain their shares if either of the two are unable to fulfill the conditions of the will. Although Tony is ultimately successful in getting them dismissed, in a slapstick climax, Bill and Sally gain the inheritance. A non-musical, comedy version of the film had been released in February, 1933, but the later musical interpretation released in November, 1938 was so popular it was reissued in subsequent years.

Another musical, *Ball at Savoy*, released in January, 1936 and set in Cannes, starred American actor Conrad Nagel as John Egan, a "diplomat who pretends to be a Baron who pretends to be a waiter who is suspected of being a thief, and who falls in love with a glamorous international singer"; actually, the reviewer in the *Monthly Film Bulletin* noted that the "vague sort of plot which starts the film and closes it [is] . . . slow, torturous, and almost entirely lacking in even superficial logic" but was really an excuse "to show off Lu Anne Meredith and Fred Conyngham as dancer-crooners, and Marta Labarr as a singer."[30]

One interesting musical variation was *Mr Cinders*, a late 1934 release with a plot loosely based on the story "Cinderella"; in this feature, Clifford Mollison plays Jim Lancaster, the impoverished nephew of Sir George Lancaster, played by Edmond Breon. Working in Sir George's household doing odd jobs, Jim rescues an American millionaire, Henry Kemp, portrayed by Finlay Currie, but his cousins Guy and Lumley (George Western and Kenneth Western) get the credit. When the millionaire's daughter, Jill (Zelma O'Neal), inadvertently bumps a policeman into a canal, she hides by posing as a new maid in the employ of Lady Agatha Lancaster, played by Esme Church. In this capacity, Jill serves as Jim's "fairy godmother" and arranges for him to be invited to her father's fancy dress ball; Jim is falsely accused of a robbery but, as in the fairy-tale, everything ends happily.

Perhaps the most popular musical example of this format was the Jack Buchanan feature, *Come Out of the Pantry*, which was released in November, 1935. In this film, the popular singer–dancer plays Lord Robert Brent, who travels to New York to sell some family pictures; but the money he obtains is lost when a bank in which he deposits the cash promptly folds, and Lord Robert finds himself impoverished and stranded in America, with an irate hotel manager demanding payment. When events seem to be at their worst, Lord Robert encounters an old family butler named Eccles (Ronald Squire), who agrees to help him by getting him a position as a footman for his current employers, Mr and Mrs Beach-Howard, portrayed by James Carew and Olive Blakeney. Their niece, Hilda Beach-Howard, played by Fay Wray, suspects Lord Robert's true identity; but when Lord Robert's older brother arrives to check up on his activities, and rumors circulate that he and Hilda are about to be engaged, the erstwhile footman decides to take charge of the matter. After learning that the bank in which his money was deposited has reopened, Lord Robert arranges to serve dinner; during the meal, he manages to propose to Hilda and is accepted. Although the plot was artificial, the film generally was well received and was reissued several years later. But at least one critic found the artificiality of the film's portrayal of the class system objectionable. In *The Spectator*, Graham Greene commented, "The snobbery of such a film as *Come Out of the Pantry*, in which a duke's son plays the part of a footman and shows himself so 'amusingly' sociable in the pantry, would be quite meaningless to any but an English audience"; Greene added that such "social snobbery . . . hampers the English cinema" because too much of "the material of English films . . . is . . . drawn from the leisured class, a class of which the director and his audience know really very little." [31]

Occasionally, romance films had characters posing as servants. One movie which Gifford classified as "romance" was the September, 1934 release entitled *Too Many Millions* in which a wealthy girl pretends to be a maid in order to aid and court an impoverished artist. Another romance which circulated about two years earlier, entitled *After the Ball*, involved the wife of a British diplomat at a world conference in Geneva. The heroine Elissa Strange, played by Esther Ralston, and the other treaty makers' wives have become weary at the interminable boring debates, so a grand masked ball is planned.

At the gala event, which Elissa attends accompanied by her maid because her husband Peter (George Curson) is attending a meeting, the diplomat's wife is mistaken for her servant. Eventually she encounters a friend of her husband, a diplomatic courier named Jack Harrowby, portrayed by Basil Rathbone, who does not know her true identity, and she becomes romantically involved, using the persona of the maid to carry on her flirtation. The deception results in typical confusion and a minor diplomatic crisis before the inevitable happy ending.

Judging by the frequency with which comedies of this sort were made, audiences seemed to delight in such films. Filmgoers apparently found it enjoyable to see on the screen movies in which members of the upper class were placed into an uncharacteristic position of subservience. The laughable predicaments in which the characters, now in some form of service, subsequently would find themselves seemed to answer an audience need. Not only could working-class filmgoers congratulate themselves that their "simple jobs" were so complex that their supposed betters would have problems performing similar tasks, but also the movies, in a way, vicariously provided audiences with an opportunity that otherwise never would exist in real life; that is, these features were a way for them subconsciously to say, "See, this is how it feels to be in servitude." But because the films were usually comedies, any bitterness in such feelings was removed; often, the proper social position of the characters was restored at the end of the movie and the *status quo* was preserved.

Impersonations of servants were not the only imitations upper- and middle-class characters attempted in films with this format; in numerous other features throughout the period, upper- or middle-class protagonists would personify all manner of laborers, peddlers and tramps for all sorts of reasons. For example, one 1929 release, a silent comedy entitled *Little Miss London* concerned a pickle magnate who, pretending to be broke, impersonates a laborer, while his daughter becomes infatuated with a salesman pretending to be a lord. A few years later, in a late 1936 comedy release called *Such is Life* (reissued later in the forties under the title *Music and Millions*), a millionaire attempts to pass himself off as a clerk in order to be in a position to aid a young typist's efforts to become a singer.

In *Strangers on a Honeymoon*, a comedy released in 1936 and based on Edgar Wallace's novel *The Northing Tramp*, Constance Cummings plays October Jones, an orphan living unhappily with unpleasant relatives on the border between Canada and the United States. A wealthy but stuffy would-be suitor seeks her hand in marriage, but she resists, telling him she would rather marry a tramp than live with him, in spite of his wealth. To make her point, she encounters a tramp named Quigley, played by Hugh Sinclair, whom she does, in fact, wed for spite; but Quigley turns out to be an English peer in disguise who is searching for two parts of a valuable deed to a piece of land containing oil, which has been held by his cousin and rival, Elfrida (Beatrix

Lehmann), and Sir Andrew Gregory (Edmund Breon). The remainder of the film is a standard comedy–adventure plot including a night in a deserted house, auto chases, improbable escapes, and an ultimately happy ending with the peer recovering the deed, defeating the villains, and also, of course, the heroine falling in love with the man she had married.

Frequently, the impersonation of a worker in films of this nature was accompanied by a subtle message or theme. For example, in *Mr Cohen Takes a Walk*, a drama released in December of 1935, the owner of a major department store leaves his position and disguises himself as a peddler. Directed by veteran American "B-movie" film-maker William Beaudine and based on a novel by Mary Roberts Rinehart, the story concerns Jacob Cohen, played by Paul Groetz. Mr Cohen is a self-made man who started as a peddler and eventually founded a large and successful department store. Mr Cohen's establishment is so efficiently arranged that he comes to feel unnecessary. His sons Sam and Jake, portrayed by Ralph Truman and Mickey Brantford, run the business without his aid or advice, and when his wife dies, Jacob flees from the unhappiness of his meaningless figurehead position. He abandons the store and, returning to his earlier life, poses as a wandering peddler, walking all over the countryside and enjoying himself again. But at his store, without his presence, relations between the employees and one of the brothers deteriorate into a serious problem. Learning of the difficulties, Jacob returns home in time to avert a devastating labor problem. The implication of the story is that the former peddler was the best manager because he knew more about the actual business of selling, and he knew more about his employees because he was from the working classes himself. His rejection of a luxurious but meaningless lifestyle in favor of returning to his modest, working-class background again conveyed the general theme that wealthier people were not necessarily happier people. The subtle message behind the plot did not go unnoticed by contemporary reviewers, one of whom objected to its presence, commenting "the propagandist conclusion is out of place." [32]

One of the best and most varied illustrations of this story-line was a Cary Grant film made in England and released in late 1936 called *The Amazing Quest of Ernest Bliss*; in this popular film which was reissued several times, a millionaire takes a variety of working-class jobs as therapy for a mental malaise. Based on a story by E. Phillips Oppenheim which had been filmed before as a silent serial, the plot concerns Ernest Bliss, a world-weary and unhappy millionaire, played by Cary Grant, who has just inherited over two million pounds. Trying to cope with his depression, he sees a Harley Street physician, Sir James Aldroyd, portrayed by Peter Gawthorne, who observes no illness, but diagnoses his problem as a boredom caused by underwork which will be remedied only if he abandons his current lifestyle and obtains a job for a year. But the doctor adds that he expects Bliss will not follow his advice; embarrassed by the doctor's comment, Bliss makes a wager with the doctor of fifty thousand pounds that he will earn his living for one entire year using none of his fortune.

But Bliss quickly finds that his efforts to obtain a job in times of unemployment meet with frustration. Reviewers noted the rather familiar pattern of the plot, with one commenting that the story was "not at all original" and observing that Bliss's efforts to find employment were "the usual struggle" in such features, "depicted by much the usual way – placards saying 'No hands wanted,' and footsteps plodding along pavements."[33] But Bliss is aided by a helpful elderly landlady, and he obtains a job as a gas-oven salesman, where he meets Frances, an attractive secretary, played by Mary Brian, who is struggling financially to help an invalid sister. A clever advertising ploy brings Bliss great success as a salesman, and he is offered a partnership which he declines because he wants to keep working. After quitting, he takes a job as an assistant clerk and porter to a woman greengrocer and later becomes a chauffeur, in which job he resists offers of easy riches from a gang of crooks. Amidst all of the hardships he experiences, he remains devoted to the kindly secretary, in spite of the charity of a soft-hearted former gold-digging mistress who, finding him apparently without any money and reduced to the position of a chauffeur, deliberately then leaves her diamond bracelet in his car in order to try to help him.

In the end, just a few days before Bliss is to win his wager, he learns that Frances has agreed to sacrifice her happiness, in spite of her love for him by marrying her employer in order to provide appropriate care for her sick sister; accordingly, Bliss sacrifices his bet to use his fortune in order to help her, which, in the words of one reviewer, "brings about a defeat which is no less glorious than a victory would have been."[34] His generosity leads to marriage with Frances, and at the wedding, the main guests are the numerous friends he has made in the working-class districts where he has been employed.

Obviously, the thrust of *The Amazing Quest of Ernest Bliss* implied that the "earnest bliss," suggested by the pun in the title, which the protagonist sought could be obtained by hard work, generosity, and self-sacrifice, all concepts with which working-class individuals in real life might well be familiar. Clearly, Bliss's happiness was to be derived from people rather than money which had created his isolation as a millionaire and left him depressed. As in so many other films, the subtle theme of the feature was that the ordinary moviegoer ought to be grateful in some respects for the simple pleasures in life which he could enjoy but which the wealthy ordinarily did not experience. *The Times* of London in its review commented on this inherent message, putting it in perspective when it observed it was "not really as amazing as all that" since "all ... Mr Bliss sets out to do is what millions of people are doing" everyday "without considering it [to be] anything out of the ordinary – that is, living on what they can earn." In mocking tones, *The Times* went on to note that Ernest Bliss "poor fellow, was one of those unfortunate young millionaires who appear to regard money with the same moroseness with which normal people regard bills;" accordingly, "once he is separated from his money," Grant's character turns out to be "a cheerful and likeable young man." *The Times* concludes "it is nice to feel that once the year is up" he will regard his fortune "with a kindlier eye, be able to marry Frances, and give a lovely party for the dear old landlady and all the other dear old people he comes across."[35]

The theme of self-sacrifice bringing "bliss" was underscored in the film by the kindly lodging-house keeper who allowed one tenant to remain in his room in spite of his inability to pay his rent and by the gesture of the gold-digger in aiding her former lover whom she thought had lost his fortune. Significantly, Ernest Bliss is taught to be happy by working-class characters. The cheery, calming assumption in the subsequently good-hearted behavior of the protagonist was a reminder to audiences that millionaires could enjoy the same simple pleasures that they did; given the opportunity to live like ordinary people, a wealthy person would turn out to be just as decent as any other working-class individual.

ROMANCE AS A MOTIVE FOR IMPERSONATIONS OF THE WORKING CLASSES

One of the conventions that reappeared frequently in films in which upper- or middle-class characters posed as working-class characters was the plot in which the impersonation was conducted for the purpose of one character carrying on a romance with another. For example, one of Jack Buchanan's more popular early sound features was the late 1931 release *Man of Mayfair* based on May Edginton's novel *A Child in their Midst*; in the film, Buchanan plays an aristocrat named Lord William who impersonates a workman in order to win the love of a dancer named Grace Irving, portrayed by Joan Barry, who is employed as a waitress in her mother's tea garden. A September, 1934 feature entitled *Too Many Millions* concerned a rich woman who pretends to be a maid in order to provide help and ultimately to romance a struggling artist. One of Carol Reed's earliest films, which he co-directed with Robert Wyler was a June, 1935 production entitled *It Happened in Paris* in which the situation was the same, but the genders were reversed; in this movie starring John Loder, a wealthy American impersonates a struggling artist in order to woo an impoverished young girl.

A slightly unusual, but rather interesting variation of the format was developed in *Side Street Angel*, a March, 1937 quota comedy directed by Ralph Ince at the Warner Brothers' Teddington Studios. In the movie, Peter, a wealthy young man portrayed by Hugh Williams hosts a party one evening, but during the festivities he discovers his fiancée in the arms of another man. Distraught, Peter departs from the gathering to walk through the streets of London. Down near the Embankment among the nightly collection of "down and outs," he encounters an ex-convict named "Soapy" McGill, played by Reginald Purdell, who encourages him to seek shelter from the night air. Escorting him to a hostel, "Soapy" introduces Peter to the efficient chief assistant, Anne (Leslie Brook). Peter quickly becomes infatuated with the welfare worker and tries to get any job which would keep him in contact with Anne. Confused and suspicious of the debonair lodger, Anne employs him to scrub the floors of the establishment. Meanwhile, "Soapy" assumes Peter to be a gentleman safe-cracker, and while bragging about his friend, he catches the attention of a gang of thieves who promptly kidnap Peter and force him to open a difficult safe. In the end, he is saved by Anne who then learns that he has purchased the hostel so that she can continue her efforts in aiding the poor. Again the film exhibited the theme of a wealthy individual "humanized" by his encounter with the working classes.

Probably the most celebrated and most highly praised example of this formula was the immensely popular, late 1931 musical release, *Sunshine Susie*. Directed by Victor Saville and based on Franz Schultz's play *Die Privatsekretarin* with future director Robert Stevenson participating in the adaptation, the story, like so many other English musicals and romances of the period, was set in Central Europe. In the plot, a Viennese banker, Herr Arvray, played by Owen Nares, pretends to be a clerk in order to romance a cheerful secretary with a positive outlook on life named Susie Surster, portrayed by the delightful Renate Muller. This attractive German actress whose character in the film seemed to be an early thirties exponent of the power of positive thinking gained a tremendous international triumph with the film, and even more successful was Jack Hulbert, whose "screen possibilities . . . as a light comedian . . . for the first time were developed to the full" in a role as "an endearing old janitor."[36]

Clearly the emphasis in *Sunshine Susie*, as in other such films with this plotline, was on the most extreme wish-fulfillment fantasy, and audiences seemed to love this approach. The reaction to this movie was described as nothing short of a "sensation" throughout Great Britain; one of the first successful musicals to be made by a British film company, *Sunshine Susie*, which was made for only about thirty thousand pounds, proved to be a tremendous financial success, running for as much as a year in some cinemas.[37] The *Film Weekly* fan poll for the best film of 1931 conducted in the spring of 1932 showed the film to be the most popular feature of the year.[38] The *Gaumont–British News* reported to its readers, the manager and employees of the Gaumont–British film chain, that the feature was "gladdening the hearts of . . . filmgoers at large"; it acknowledged that the film "seems to have captivated everybody, from the hard-boiled critic to the man-in-the-street." With repeat attendance and favorable word of mouth, "everybody is telling everybody else about it . . . and vowing that never in all their experience was there so certain a tonic." Such hyperbole aside, the *Gaumont–British News* summarized the film's appeal, noting that "it is a picture that grows on one . . . [radiating] geniality . . . [not] so much a picture as a rollicking page from real life." Audience members "do not seem to be looking *at* a picture" as much as "actually taking a part in it" because "it is so uncommonly natural, so vividly alive." [39]

The popularity of the film quickly reached the level where the expression "Sunshine Susie," according to one publication, had become "household words"; for example, in one area, a candy company issued a toffee confection named after the film character.[40] Newspapers began to explore the phenomenon; the *Daily Express*, for example, sought the comments of the public which it invited to criticize or praise the feature, and thousands responded, most acclaiming the movie in glowing terms.[41] One filmgoer wrote that while watching *Sunshine Susie*, "all around me, I could feel people enjoying themselves," and another noted, "It is pure, sweet and joyous – a picture of rare quality"; viewers apparently loved the film's positive point of view, one commenting, "its greatest recommendation is the golden thread of happiness running through the story."[42] But most contributors seemed to praise the escapist aspects of the story and the salutary value of such fantasy:

- "Sunshine Susie" throws a magic curtain between you and your trouble.
- It makes you come away feeling thoroughly happy and pleased with life.
- Sunshine is a magic tonic in these hard times . . .
- It is the necessary stimulant to the life of community . . .
- It is a mental tonic, wholesome and joyous.[43]

A letter-writer to *Film Weekly* noted the beneficial impact in a troubled society of a film like *Sunshine Susie*:

After seeing that happy and most delightful film, *Sunshine Susie*, it was forcibly impressed upon me, as I passed through a very poor and dreary part of London, that we should be very grateful to the cinema. Many cinemas in this district were showing the film, and I imagined the large numbers of hard-working mothers enjoying the entertainment for a few pence. If the films shows are not always as good as *Sunshine Susie* they generally provide just that escape from the hard facts of real life which is as good as a tonic to those who work hard and long for very little reward.[44]

The advertising for the film emphasized this escapism in the midst of economic gloom; advertisements billed the film as "A Cure for the Deepest Depression," with the double meaning of the last word more than clear.[45] In *Picturegoer Weekly*, the feature was described as "an excellent cure for the blues."[46]

Numerous publicity stunts were conducted in conjunction with the release of the film which emphasized its optimistic tone. Throughout England, in a number of communities, contests were held like the one conducted by the *Yorkshire Observer* and the New Victoria cinema in Bradford to find real-life

"Sunshine Susies" who had equally optimistic attitudes; for a week in April of 1932 the *Yorkshire Observer* published photos mainly of working-class girls fitting the description of how such "Susies" should appear. She might be "dark or fair," of "medium height and figure," and more typically "describe[d]. . . as pleasant and attractive rather than beautiful"; much more importantly, "her nature must be sunny," and she must have a "personality . . . that . . . seems to radiate happiness" to the extent that "you feel better for knowing her [because] . . . she seems to make the world a better place to live in."[47] Similar contests were held in Northampton, York, and elsewhere. Clearly, Susie was being promoted as a desirable role model in society. Apparently this contest to honor optimistic, cheery, working girls was thought important enough in Bradford for the committee to select the finalists to consist of such local dignitaries as "the Lady Mayoress of Bradford, the Deputy Lord Mayor, the School of Art Master, the Archdeacon of Bradford, and Stipendiary Magistrate."[48] Another promotion, in Newcastle, at the Queen's Cinema, involved a "sunshine lobby display consisting of three graduating suns, one directly behind the other," above which was placed the motto "Sunshine Susie will radiate happiness."[49]

But the most interesting aspect of the film's escapist quality was its famous musical number "Today I Feel So Happy" ("Ich bin ja heut so glucklich" in the original German version of the film) which quickly became one of the best known tunes in the world during the early thirties. In the feature, Susie sings the song out of the window of her flat until other residents in the apartment house, caught up in the infectious spirit of the optimistic refrain, join her as a chorus. Then, the melody is picked up elsewhere until finally, the song is performed by fifty secretaries in the typing pool who tap out the rhythm as they sing. The words of the tune, whose sense came by implication to be shared by all people in the sequence who heard the melody, were charged with a spirit of optimism that seemed somewhat out of place in the early thirties. The verse of the song observed that "there's a happy feeling everywhere, the world's a brighter place"; indeed, the singer's "load of care" has simply "vanished into space." She "can only see a sky of blue, where dark clouds used to be," so she wonders "is this happiness for others too, or only just for me?" The chorus of the song is an essentially repetitious, simple melody with the almost mindlessly optimistic thought "Today I feel so happy, so happy, so happy, I don't know why I'm happy, I only know I am."

Muller's recording in English of the tune by the song-writing team of Gilbert, Carter, Eyton, and Abraham sold a tremendous number of records, and the music was constantly "'plugged' by dance band and radio until everyone with a musical ear [knew] the melody."[50] Yet, as film historian Ivan Butler has observed in commenting about the "unrealized . . . hopes" that the tune's optimism engendered, while "Today I Feel So Happy" was "charmingly put over by Miss Muller," the song "has a somewhat forced gaiety at variance with the grim realities of life in an England where slumps and unemployment loom[ed]." [51]

The contrast, however, did not seem to have been noticed by contemporary filmgoers. An item in the in-house publication of the Gaumont–British film company noted that "everybody is humming the 'Happy' song." The author observed that the musical sequence in the film around the song had fascinated the public, commenting that the image of "that big array of typists in the bank, tapping away at their machines to a perfect rhythm . . . seems to have captured the popular imagination . . . and the imagination of typists, too" because "not one of them is out of step"; the piece reflects that as "their shoulders sway in unison, their fingers tap to the haunting lilt of the song" making the number "surely . . . one of the cleverest sequences ever caught by the celluloid reel." [52] The staging of this extremely popular number thus carried a subtle implication in addition to its unremitting optimism suggesting that in unified effort and compliant conformity was the promise of almost boundless happiness. The writer of the item seemed to be aware of the implicit message, almost of thought-control, of the scene when he pondered "what interesting possibilities are suggested by this film innovation"; indeed, he "wonder[s] if, one of these fine days, some big organization will really make the experiment; will arrange that its typists shall work to music." Although the concept "may appear in the light of a Utopian dream," nonetheless, "students of industrial psychology would no doubt agree that the idea has distinct possibilities," even for "the non-typing staff." [53]

Many of the promotions which advertised the film centered on "Today I Feel So Happy" and the typing chorus. Joint promotions with record stores and typewriters shops were common. [54] At one cinema which also still had a small house band, the tune was rehearsed in the lobby, and while pedestrian traffic stopped to identify the song, the manager reported that "the cleaners with the buckets and brooms, broke loose from their usual work and did a step dance in front of the theatre to the accompaniment of the orchestra," and finally, even "the usherettes, not to be out-done, joined in." [55] At another theater, the words of the tune were distributed to patrons, and at still another cinema, sing-alongs to the melody were part of the program. [56] In several cinemas, the song was played over the loud-speaker to passers-by, and in many of those larger cinemas that still had short stage shows, production numbers invariably centered on typists. [57]

Whether comic impersonations of servants or other laborers, whether detective stories, frivolous escapist musicals, romances, or message-orientated dramas, the frequency of movie plots with upper- or middle-class characters posing or being mistaken for working-class individuals is remarkably consistent with the frequency of converse plot situations, discussed earlier, as Table 5.1 reveals.

In all but one year, approximately one in ten movies made by British film companies exhibited this format; in three of the years, as many as one in six

Table 5.1 Films in which upper- or middle-class
characters impersonate or are mistaken for
working-class characters

Year	Proportion of the films released	%
1929	9 of 86	10.5
1930	6 of 99	6.1
1931	18 of 134	13.4
1932	27 of 150	18.0
1933	18 of 181	9.9
1934	21 of 183	11.5
1935	20 of 185	10.8
1936	36 of 219	16.4
1937	35 of 211	16.6
1938	15 of 158	9.5
1939	13 of 98	13.3

features had some kind of impersonation of this kind, and in one of those years, 1932, the ratio was closer to one in five pictures.

Again, in most of the films, the impersonations usually were successful or led to beneficial happenings for the protagonists as Table 5.2 demonstrates.

Table 5.2 Evaluations of plot outcome in films in which upper- or middle-class characters impersonate or are mistaken for working-class characters

Successful results			Unsuccessful results	
Year		%		%
1929	8 of 86 released	9.3	1 of 86 released	1.2
1930	5 or 99 released	5.1	1 of 99 released	1.0
1931	12 of 134 released	9.0	6 of 134 released	4.5
1932	19 of 150 released	12.7	8 of 150 released	5.3
1933	10 of 181 released	5.5	8 of 181 released	4.4
1934	15 of 183 released	8.2	6 of 183 released	3.3
1935	12 of 185 released	6.5	8 of 185 released	4.3
1936	23 of 219 released	10.5	13 of 219 released	5.9
1937	27 of 211 released	12.8	9 of 211 released	4.3
1938	9 of 158 released	5.7	6 of 158 released	3.8
1939	8 of 98 released	8.2	5 of 98 released	5.1

Although the differences are slight, a comparison between Tables 4.2 and 5.2 shows a minor variance that is perhaps worth noting; specifically, twice in the eleven years considered in Table 4.2 (1935 and 1937), the unsuccessful results in films of attempted working-class impersonations of upper- and middle-class characters outnumbered those of successful outcomes, and in one year, 1939, the results were even. In Table 5.2, the successful conclusions always outnumbered the unsuccessful effects of the impersonations. Thus, in these features, upper- and middle-class characters were slightly more successful in their attempts to masquerade as working-class individuals, than working-class protagonists were in their endeavors to be taken for upper- or middle-class characters.

6

INTER-CLASS ROMANCE
Social escapism

TRANSFORMATIONS INTO HARDSHIP

Just as some movies involved rags-to-riches stories in which working-class characters were made aristocrats or became wealthy, a motif involving upper- or middle-class protagonists that seems to have been prevalent in British features during the years of the Depression was the plot in which such a character somehow had become impoverished. Though no impersonation of the working class was involved, the films did have a transformation from luxury to hardship; often the main theme of these productions was adversity and a decline in status, and much of the plot would center on how a character reacted to these difficulties. The effect this setback had on the character and on the others in the film often provided a message or an example for dealing with adversity. In some features, the character would only pretend to be bankrupt for some purpose, but in most films conforming to this format, the poverty was real. In some instances, the character actually was bettered by his loss of wealth or position in some unexpected way, and in other cases, the protagonist was ennobled spiritually by the setback. But virtually all of the films with this kind of story-line dealt, if only superficially, with economic difficulties and the concept of failure, a day-to-day concern for many people during the thirties.

Some of these films suggested that the experience of poverty or bankruptcy was in some way valuable or useful. For example, in *The Happy Family*, a late summer comedy release in 1936 based on Max Cotto's play *French Salad*, the wealthy, hard-working head of the Hutt family, played by Dick Francis, decides that the members of his household have been behaving too irresponsibly and frivolously, and that they have become lazy; the mother, portrayed by Maidie Hope, is flighty and absent-minded, a daughter Robina (Glennis Lorimer) is scatter-brained, one son, Victor, depicted by Hugh Williams, has become involved with confidence men, and two of the sons, Noel and Leo, who have little talent, want nevertheless to go into show business as an actor and singer respectively. To cure them of their wastrel ways, the father resolves to pretend that his money is gone, and aided by his sensible daughter-in-law,

Barbara, Victor's wife, played by Leonora Corbett, he announces to the family that he is bankrupt. However, the family's attempts to earn money and their endeavor to economize are laughably unsuccessful. Through a plot twist, Mr Hutt does lose his money, but Barbara saves the day by revealing that she has established a successful business in selling bathroom fixtures which will provide employment for all family members. The implication in the film was that Mr Hutt's wealth had had a deleterious effect on the family. Vaguely reminiscent in its plot of some mid thirties American screwball comedies like *My Man Godfrey*, the movie suggested that success and wealth breed idleness and are therefore unhealthy. The prescription in such cases was hard work.

Other films suggested the same idea, though perhaps less directly; specifically, in several features, an individual who slipped into poverty rose, by the end of the film, to greater riches. In *Money Talks*, a November, 1932 comedy directed by Norman Lee, the prosperous protagonist must divest himself of all his fortune before he can obtain an inheritance that will make him even wealthier. In the December, 1935 release, *The Luck of the Irish*, based on Victor Haddick's novel, a financially troubled Irish country gentleman, Sir Barry O'Neill, played by Jimmy Mageean, with all of his possessions mortgaged, has only one hope of retaining his ancestral home; if his race horse, ridden by his son Derek (Niall MacGinnis), can win the Grand National, his financial troubles will be ended. Betting everything he owns, the squire at first appears to have won when the horse comes in first; but subsequently, the horse is disqualified, and all appears to be lost. Bailiffs take possession of the property, and a loyal servant is unsuccessful in his endeavors to regain some of the money. In the nick of time, however, an American unexpectedly agrees to buy the race horse at a generous price, enabling the squire to pay off all of his debts and to regain his prosperity. With a cast composed of actors from the Belfast Repertory Theatre, who were commended in at least one review as having "[made] up in sincerity for what they lack[ed] in experience of screen work," this forgotten little film, though regarded as "not original," nevertheless was praised for its "authentic backgrounds" and its "realistic atmosphere," as well as its "amusing picture" of people who can be "happy-go-lucky" in the face of hardship.[1]

Frequently in films involving impoverished upper- or middle-class characters, the effect of the decline in fortune was to lead to crimes of various types. For example, in the 1929 silent film *Lily of Killarney*, based on Dion Boucicault's play, *The Colleen Bawn*, an impoverished aristocrat in Ireland attempts to have his wife murdered in order to marry a wealthy heiress. The story was subsequently remade in a 1934 version directed by Maurice Elvey which was reissued periodically throughout the thirties. One of Michael Powell's earliest films, *Rynox*, a November, 1931 release based on a Philip Macdonald novel, concerns a bankrupt businessman who is so desperate that he commits fraud by faking his own murder in order to collect his insurance benefits. A May, 1933 quota release directed by Zoltan Korda entitled *Cash* has a bankrupt financier attempting to promote a company for his inventions by using counterfeit money; starring Edmund Gwenn as Edmund Gilbert, the needy protagonist who is working as a bank clerk, and featuring Wendy Barrie as his daughter Lillian, the film turns out to be a comedy with Gilbert being saved by the financial assistance of a helpful electricity inspector, played by Robert Donat, in one of his earliest roles. The somewhat cynical "moral of the film," according to Karol Kulik, "seemed to be that a superficial display of hard cash was all that one needed to win financial support from the big investors in the city of London"; this suggestion provided an explanation for the criminal desperation of the bankrupt leading character in the feature.[2]

But if poverty and loss of fortune could lead to crime, they also sometimes led essentially innocent characters to be suspected of criminal actions. For example, *The Brown Wallet*, another mystery directed by Michael Powell, and released in March, 1936 concerns John Gillespie, a publisher, played by Patrick Knowles, who has gone bankrupt because a partner has fled with his money. After vainly seeking financial aid from his wealthy Aunt Mary, portrayed by Henrietta Watson, he discovers in the taxi he is taking home a wallet containing bank notes worth two thousand pounds which someone apparently has left behind inadvertently; in desperation, he keeps the money. But when his aunt is found poisoned later in the evening and her safe is discovered with its contents removed, John is arrested for the murder. Although he ultimately is acquitted when the real murderer confesses, the suggestion is that someone who has lost his fortune may be desperate enough to commit a crime.

But in some features, impoverished aristocrats or formerly wealthy protagonists not only were able to cope with their fallen position but also were willing to sacrifice what little they had for the sake of others less fortunate than they. Some movies with this theme were remarkably socially orientated, and the messages were fairly overt. For example, in *Lest We Forget*, a July, 1934 drama released by Sound City and directed by John Baxter, Stewart Rome stars as Captain Rayner, a broke former officer who pretends to be wealthy in order to keep an agreement to hold a regimental reunion. Less than two years earlier, Rome had appeared in an almost identical plot in another Sound City dramatic production entitled *Reunion*; the earlier film concerns an impoverished former major named Tancred, played by Rome, who uses the occasion of a similar reunion to demonstrate his devotion and loyalty to his former subordinates. In the film, the nearly destitute officer donates the last of his money to help a struggling corporal.

The Chairman and Managing Director of the small but interesting Sound City operation, Norman Loudon, in a 1933 article in *Picturegoer Weekly* contended that *Reunion*, along with other Sound City productions like *Doss House*, were designed to deal with contemporary social concerns; Louden observed that "subjects of our national life are crying out for filming," and moreover, "there is no lack of material." For instance, he continued, in *Reunion*, the present social reality was depicted "through the eyes of an ex-army major reduced by ill fortune to the barest possible existence." He emphasizes that "the whole case is natural and colloquial," consisting of individuals "you have met" in real life "off the screen." Louden then describes the plot of the recent film release; having "fought for his country years before like thousands of others" the ex-major had found that "the vagaries of peace had baffled his honest purpose"; nonetheless, the former officer "instantly answers the call to attend his old regiment's reunion dinner" even though it requires "another visit to the pawnbroker and the accumulation of more unpaid bills," because "to his men he is still their leader and their hero" even though financially "none are probably in such sore straits." Because the major believes "he cannot confide in them his difficulties" he decides that his only option with his regiment "is to act with the same bravery and optimism that characterised their deeds together at the front" and to live his life with the knowledge "that a man is never deserted until he deserts himself." Characterizing the feature as an "unpretentious film ... made under difficult conditions," Loudon acknowledges that it "has received high praise," a fact that is "all the more striking in that the cast is composed entirely of men" in spite of the fact that "women today are such an essential element at the box office." The film's reception, Loudon suggests, provides "an indication of what I believe we should strive for at Sound City"; specifically, the movie's "predominant note" consists of "sincerity," "honesty," and "a firmness and resolve to purpose and action." If one cannot "believe in" a project, one "might just as well give up attempting to do it," because that person is "bound to fail." By contrast, Loudon's film *Reunion* "possesses a definite theme" reminding its audience that "you may grumble, but the man smiling next to you may be a sight worse off than you are"; and he concludes that "optimism does more for a man than a world of doubt and despair."[3]

Other features were a little more fanciful. For example, in *Tomorrow We Live*, a late 1936 dramatic release, a bankrupt financier decides to use the last of his money to give fifty pounds to each of twelve destitute men whom he finds all on the point of suicide. In the feature, which is somewhat similar to the 1932 American production *If I Had a Million* (though decidedly less whimsical), the financier Sir Charles Hendra, played by Godrey Tearle, who is himself contemplating suicide, attempts to discover what each of the twelve "down-and-outs" did with their new opportunities; after hearing their stories, he is inspired to make one last effort to restore his own fortune, and he succeeds. The optimistic "keep trying and never give up" attitude could hardly have been suggested more clearly.

Another sacrifice, this one of a slightly different nature is suggested in the August, 1933 production, *Head of the Family*. In this drama, a former financier has gone bankrupt, and to make ends meet, he must take a job working as a lowly night watchman for a rival magnate. In that position, he apprehends a young man who is attempting a robbery, who turns out to be his son. Here, the sacrifice and the main question of the film concerned a responsibility to law and justice in opposition to family loyalty. All of these films depicted the dignity with which even an impoverished character who seemingly had good reason for bitterness could exhibit in the face of economic hardship.

Far less meaningful but remarkably pervasive were the films in which the impoverishment of an aristocrat or formerly wealthy middle-class character led to romance. Usually these features were silly little escapist comedies, often involving only elite characters. For example, the July, 1938 Claude Hulbert comedy, *His Lordship Regrets* concerns Hulbert as the penniless young Lord Reggie Cavender whose finances are so desperate that he finds himself constantly being hounded by bill-collectors. Under the instructions of her father, a millionaire from South Africa, Mabel Van Morgan, played by Winifred Shotter, investigates Reggie's situation, and becoming interested in his problems, she adopts the name Mary Edwards and becomes his secretary. When a different, bogus Mabel Van Morgan shows up, Reggie's butler Dawkins (Aubrey Mallalien) sees an opportunity to help and attempts to play matchmaker; but at a house party Reggie falls in love with Mary rather than the phony heiress. The ending involves the exposure of the imposter, a revelation that Mabel's grandfather had duped Reggie's family and therefore owed him some money, and the marriage of the real Mabel to Reggie. Having little to do with reality, this artificial comedy with Hulbert's traditional portrayal of the "silly-ass" English aristocrat nevertheless was popular enough to be reissued.

Whether unrealistic or not, considering the frequency with which such a plot continually reappeared, films of this nature were remarkably common and presumably popular, especially as musicals. In the November, 1936 musical *Everything in Life*, for instance, a wealthy but temperamental opera star named Rita Bonya, played by Gitta Alpar, pretends to be impoverished in order to romance a struggling composer, Geoffrey Loring, portrayed by the former Hollywood silent film star Neil Hamilton; using the help of a sympathetic cotton magnate, Sir Algernon Spindle, the character actor H.F. Maltby, she sees to it that he is helped before ultimately winning his love. Future director Billy Wilder's screenplay for a 1932 German production *Es War Einmal Ein Walzer* served as the source for another musical released in late 1932, set in Vienna, called *Where Is This Lady?* which concerned a financially troubled banker and an equally insolvent heiress who fall in love and, together, try to convert a bank into a nightclub. One of Jack Buchanan's musicals, *That's a Good Girl*, which appeared in the autumn of 1933 and whose popularity dictated subsequent reissuances, concerned an easy-going, high-living heir who finds himself with money problems and attempts to solve his problems by playing matchmaker.

The appeal of these generally light-headed, frivolous features cannot be easily understood or explained except as simple escapism, or perhaps as an opportunity for moviegoers to see aristocrats and wealthy people in the uncomfortable and presumably unfamiliar position of being out of money and behaving irresponsibly. A rather off-beat comic variation of this plot can be found in the January, 1935 comedy *Lazybones* directed by Michael Powell; in the film, Ian Hunter plays Sir Reginald Ford, an unrepentantly lethargic baronet whose financially troubled family is trying to match him with a wealthy American heiress. Unhappy over such developments, the lazy lad surprises the family by taking their mansion and converting it into a "Work Centre for the Weary Wealthy."

The fantasy element was more understandable perhaps in features in which the impoverished, formerly wealthy protagonist romanced a working-class character; in such features could be found Cinderella escapism and an ideal dream world where social class and status were penetrable barriers between people. For example, in the spring, 1934 release *Rolling in Money*, based on R.C. Carton's play *Mr Hopkinson*, Isabel Jeans is the broke Duchess of Braceborough who intrigues to have her daughter marry a Cockney barber named Mr Hopkinson, played by Leslie Sarony, who has just come into a fortune.

One interesting example of such a format was the motion picture version of Ivor Novello's exceedingly successful stage play, *I Lived With You*, which circulated in the summer of 1933 about fifteen months after the play had been produced in the West End. In the film, Novello recreated his stage role as Felix Lenieff, a penniless, starving refugee who meets in the maze at Hampton Court a young typist named Gladys Wallis, played by Urusla Jeans; charmed by his manner and personality, the girl shares her sandwiches with the hungry young man who turns out to be an exiled White Russian Prince. Taking pity on him, the typist brings the Prince home to her Cockney family, and they take him into their household; but "with a naive disregard for conventions, no particular morals, and a pliable disposition," the Prince and his attitudes begin to disrupt the family.[4] They are influenced in such a way that Mr Wallis, portrayed by Eliot Makeham, takes a mistress; Mrs Wallis, played in "a grand, genial, rollicking performance" by Minnie Rayner, takes to vodka, and Gladys's shopgirl sister Ada, played by Ida Lupino, agrees to become the mistress of her employer.[5] In spite of a developing infatuation and romance, Gladys realizes the Prince's presence is unhealthy for the family. In the end, "he is persuaded to leave, and the family settles back to its comfortable and conventional rut."[6]

An advertisement for the movie in the house publication, the *Stoll Herald*, characterized the feature in such a way that prospective patrons were invited to imagine what the impact of such a visitor would be on their families.

A fascinating, entertaining comedy–drama full of amusing incidents, delightful cockney humour and a glimpse into real life incidents. A

117

dark-eyed, captivating, exiled Russian prince['s] . . . easy ways with life and the sale of valuable diamonds which were contained in a watch given by the Czar to his father soon undermine the morality of the hitherto happy and honest suburbia family until they are thoroughly demoralised. *What would you imagine would be the best solution to bring happiness to them?*[7]

Sir Edward Marsh in his introduction to the published edition of Novello's play observed that the "substantial theme" of *I Lived With You* was the "clash between two violently contrasted views of life," that is between the "aristocratic and autocratic." The "do-as-you-please" philosophy "impinges on the English lower-class responsibility" as an "attractive poison (for such it is to them) works through the veins," bringing the Wallis family "near to dissolution" before Gladys "takes charge and expels it from their system while there is still something to save."[8] Novello was said to have preferred the play and film to any of his other productions, and though the film was never reissued, the actor–playwright's repeated revivals and provincial tours testified to the lasting appeal of *I Lived With You.*[9]

The prevalence of movies made in Britain during the decade in which wealthy and socially elite characters suffer a major decline into an impoverished state is interesting; certainly, such a plot device can hardly be considered unique to the Depression era, but the figures which demonstrate the recurrence of this story-line feature are revealing. Table 6.1 shows the

Table 6.1 Films in which upper- or middle-class characters are bankrupt or impoverished

Year	Proportion of the films released	%
1929	7 of 86	8.1
1930	7 of 99	7.1
1931	9 of 134	6.7
1932	15 of 150	10.0
1933	9 of 181	5.0
1934	12 of 183	6.6
1935	16 of 185	8.6
1936	11 of 219	5.0
1937	6 of 211	2.8
1938	4 of 158	2.5
1939	1 of 98	1.0

frequency with which impoverished upper-class or middle-class characters were depicted in the plots of British features during the period from 1929 to 1939.

One striking aspect of this table is the consistency of the percentages of films reflecting the theme in the first two-thirds of the decade. Invariably from

1929 to 1936, from 5 to 10 percent of the films exhibited this characteristic. But in the remaining three years of the period, less than 3 percent of the films contained such events, and in 1939, the figure sank to 1 percent. The logical conclusion would be that audiences were finding such stories less meaningful and less amusing, and producers instead were searching for other more satisfying formulae. One also might assume that with more realistic, honest and true-to-life features being made, stories about irresponsible aristocrats and wealthy people who have lost their money were not as evocative as they once were. Perhaps, also, with improvements in the economy and general recovery from the slump, moviegoers did not want to be reminded of circumstances in which people had lost their money.

LOVE BETWEEN CLASSES

Closely related to the plot in which an impoverished upper- or middle-class character romances a working-class character was the extremely common story-line about a love affair between people of different social backgrounds where the essence of the story was the contrast in lifestyles; in film after film, most of them comedies and musicals, but a few of them, interestingly, dramas, the story of a working-class boy or girl in love with an aristocratic or wealthy lady or gentleman was told in various but basically similar movies. These features took on different surface characteristics, but the story usually came to one of two conclusions; either the characters found the romance painful, tragic, and essentially unsuccessful because they were from opposite social backgrounds or alternatively in true "happy-ever-after" fashion, they found the social distinctions to be minor and easily overcome. Both outcomes were fairly common as Tables 6.2 and 6.3 demonstrate. In most years, with a

Table 6.2 Films in which a romance takes place between working-class characters and upper- or middle-class characters with a successful resolution or "happy ending"

Year	Proportion of the films released	%
1929	7 of 86	8.1
1930	7 of 99	7.1
1931	15 of 134	11.2
1932	17 of 150	11.3
1933	24 of 181	13.3
1934	25 of 183	13.7
1935	18 of 185	9.7
1936	16 of 219	7.3
1937	24 of 211	11.4
1938	15 of 158	9.5
1939	1 of 98	1.0

Table 6.3 Films in which a romance takes place
between working-class characters and upper- or
middle-class characters with an unsuccessful
resolution, or "unhappy ending"

Year	Proportion of the films released	%
1929	14 of 86	16.3
1930	4 of 99	4.0
1931	7 of 134	5.2
1932	17 of 150	11.3
1933	11 of 181	6.1
1934	12 of 183	6.6
1935	14 of 185	7.6
1936	7 of 219	3.2
1937	16 of 211	7.6
1938	7 of 158	4.4
1939	11 of 98	11.2

few notable exceptions, the happy ending outnumbered the more troubled conclusions by a two-to-one margin. Of the few years, 1929, 1932, 1935, and 1939, the output in 1935 still saw a majority of the plots ending happily, and 1932 saw an approximately equal number of positive and negative outcomes. Only in 1929, still largely a year of silent features, and in 1939, when more realism seemed to be creeping into British film-making were there major variations.

Earlier in the decade, however, most of these features in no way could be perceived as depicting reality. A love affair between a nobleman and a shop girl, at least in film plots, seemed to be an almost everyday occurrence. For instance a spring, 1932 release entitled *Self-Made Lady* based on Douglas Newton's novel *Sookey* concerned a slum girl whose ambition leads her to become a dress designer; as she rises from her working-class origins, she is romanced by a medical student, by a boxer, and eventually, almost inevitably, by an aristocrat. A musical released about the same time called *Indiscretions of Eve* depicted a nobleman who becomes infatuated with a young girl who serves as a model for shop window dummies. In *Lancashire Luck*, a November, 1937 comedy, the daughter of a Lancashire carpenter and the son of an aristocrat fall in love and overcome a variety of problems. In the film, Wendy Barrie is Betty Lovejoy, whose carpenter father, George Lovejoy, played by comic George Carney, has just won the local football pools. With the winnings, George wants to open a teashop in the country, so he buys an old roadside cafe; unfortunately, his endeavors run into the opposition of the local aristocracy represented by Lady Maydew, portrayed by Margaret Damer, who resents the spread of commercialism in her area. But her attempts to ruin the business are complicated by the fact that her son Sir Gerald Maydew (George Galleon) has fallen in love with Betty. Ultimately the dispute is settled, and the relationship between Betty and her aristocratic beau progresses. Though criticizing the film for being "too sentimental," *Film Weekly* observed that the "little man against the local authority" theme provided "a few pleasantly authentic impressions of country life."[10]

Similarly, romance with the unemployed would seem to have been common for wealthy untitled millionaires or heiresses, if one were to judge by movie plots. In Michael Powell's *Something Always Happens*, for instance, Ian Hunter plays Peter Middleton, a "down and out" who, having lost his last few pounds at cards, nevertheless remains perpetually hopeful and confident that in the face of the worst misfortune, "something always happens." In the comic plot of this June, 1934 quota release, the poverty-stricken Peter must show his resourcefulness frequently, and initially he does so in obtaining a place to stay. He uses a street youngster named Billy, played by Johnny Singer, who is equally impoverished, to gain sympathy and ultimately room and board for them both with Mrs Badger (Muriel George) who is told that the youth had been granted to him in a custody decision. Such cleverness is also demonstrated in schemes to alleviate his poverty; although he is not above using trickery and outright deception, his quick wits bring success.

Learning of an opportunity, if he can obtain a Bentley to sell, he starts a conversation with a chauffeur of one of the vehicles he sees on the street and poses as a car salesman. The passenger in the car is a wealthy heiress named Cynthia Hatch, portrayed by Nancy O'Neil, whose father Ben (Peter Hawthorne) is the owner of a chain of petrol stations; Cynthia is amused by the fact that Peter is portraying himself as the owner of the car, and she responds to the deception by depicting herself as a "working girl." Inviting her to an exclusive restaurant where he knows from previous experience how to elude the bill, Peter romances the girl who is intrigued by his ingenuity; she, in turn, encourages him to explain some of his business ideas to Mr Hatch, though she does not disclose that he is her father. Unfortunately, Hatch is not impressed by new ideas, and Middleton is ejected from Hatch's office; in response, Peter takes his ideas to Hatch's competitors, the directors of the Blue Point Company, who are attracted to his idea to transform gas stations into more luxurious stopover places. The scheme turns out to be a tremendous success, and Middleton soon has worked himself up to the position of general manager of the Blue Point Company with Cynthia as his secretary. Obtaining inside information that a new bypass is to be constructed, Peter realizes he has an opportunity to obtain a measure of revenge against Hatch's company for humiliating him. But one of Peter's former associates, played by Barry Livesey, whom Peter had discharged previously for inefficiency, sells the news to Hatch, and Peter concludes that Cynthia with whom he was now in love had passed along the news. After a quarrel with the girl, Peter finds that the bypass is not to be built for fifteen years, and he uses the updated information to complete a favorable business deal with Hatch. He also learns of Cynthia's true identity, and in spite of their socially different backgrounds, the romance proceeds.[11] Naturally, in this production, the highly divergent backgrounds of the lovers prove to be no detriment to their romance and to the requisite happy ending.

Something Always Happens, according to reviewer Richard Combs, has a sub-text centering on "problems of industrial initiative and enterprise" and almost "might be subtitled 'How to Succeed in Business Without Really Trying'"; the hero who "finally turns the tables on his competitor (and potential father-in-law) by suppressing the news that a proposed bypass is not to be built for fifteen years" is a "young Turk" who mounts "attacks on fuddy-duddy ways."[12] Combs cited Powell's characterization of Peter Middleton as "a chap who never paid for anything," in characterizing him as "an opportunist and gambler, whose 'vision' amounts to the ad-man's ability to conjure something out of nothing." He observes that Middleton at one point says "it's money I get for selling something I haven't got to someone who doesn't want it," as he describes his way of making a living.[13] In this sense, Combs argued that *Something Always Happens*, like Powell's earlier industrial thriller *Red Ensign*, "can be read as a thinly disguised allegory for the plight of British film-making," which "cynically" suggested a quick "solution" to economic problems could be obtained from opportunistic gambling and even from deception in "adapt[ing] a readily convertible American model."[14]

But in another, wider sense, the film might also be seen as an allegory for British society in the Depression; if people are innovative, optimistic, and resourceful, "something always happens," and their depressed condition will be alleviated without disrupting the social order. In the fanciful plot of *Something Always Happens*, this improvement is represented by Peter's ultimate financial triumph and his successful relationship with Cynthia.

In a number of these films, the love affair occurs between a domestic employee and the aristocrat or wealthy person. For example in *His Grace Gives Notice*, a comedy which circulated during the summer of 1933, a butler keeps concealed the fact that he has inherited a title, so that he can romance the daughter of his employer. Similarly, in *Money Means Nothing*, a comedy which appeared in September, 1932, John Loder, as the financially troubled Earl Egbert, loves the daughter of his more solvent butler, even though he is engaged to another woman.

In *Full Speed Ahead*, an adventure released in November, 1936, the wealthy heroine Jean Hunter, portrayed by Moira Lynd, is the daughter of a director of a steamship company. When her father disapproves of her infatuation with the family chauffeur Tim Brent, played by Richard Norris, the headstrong girl decides to elope with the young man, and the couple sneak away, hiding on one of the company boats. The remainder of the plot is a fairly standard action tale, with, as the *Monthly Film Bulletin* noted, a "monotonous" degree of violence; the couple do not realize that the ship on which they have stowed

122

away has been purchased by a sinister South American politician for dubious, dishonest endeavors, and the officers and crewmen have been selected for their shady past. When Jean and Tim are discovered, the young man is forced to work aboard the ship, and in the process, he learns of a plot between the captain and his first mate to scuttle the vessel and collect insurance. But with the aid of the chief engineer and his donkeyman who had remained from the previous crew, the young couple regain control of the ship and return her to safety.[15] As improbable as the story may have seemed, the plot was no less unlikely than the ending in which the previously class-conscious father suddenly declares that "all is forgiven, and Brent is received into the family."[16] Presumably the father's change of heart never would have taken place without the chauffeur's heroics.

A significant proportion of these movies, though, were not set in English surroundings; often films in which upper- or middle-class characters wooed working-class protagonists had European, or more frequently Central European settings, as if perhaps to make the bridging of class boundaries more credible by placing it in another country. For example, one of Alexander Korda's early successes was the January, 1932 comedy *Service for Ladies*, based on Ernst Valda's novel, *The Head Waiter*. Filmed once before in a 1927 version, this comedy starred the young Leslie Howard as Max Tracey, a waiter in Austria who is helped in his efforts to romance a millionairess by a disguised monarch. In the process of his "rags-to-riches rise," he is mistaken for a prince before eventually winning the hand of his beloved.[17] Such highly improbable story-lines were fairly common throughout the decade.

Several of the films were made by British production companies under an agreement with UFA (the German film studio) and other continental producers to make English-language versions of films being made in German and other languages. One of the most famous examples of this type of production arrangement was the immensely popular 1931 musical release *Congress Dances* based on Erik Charell's German filmed operetta *Der Kongress Tanzt* starring the internationally known English singer Lillian Harvey, who had a tremendous popularity in Germany. In this case, the romantic relationship involves no less a figure than Tsar Alexander I of Russia (Willy Fritsch) and a young glove seller, Chrystel, portrayed by Miss Harvey; set against a backdrop of Vienna in 1814, the film concerns a visit by the Tsar to the city for the Congress. In the film, the crafty Prince Metternich, played by Conrad Veidt, conspires to have a Countess (Lil Dagover) distract and entertain the Tsar to keep him from attending important meetings. Finding a simple, good-natured substitute who resembles him to replace him for just such unusual circumstances and to fill in for him at public gatherings, the Tsar confounds Metternich by being in two places at once. But the Tsar also is bored with the meetings with Metternich and is tired with such scheming intrigues that are part of the nature of court life in general, so he decides to escape and to discover the joys of Viennese life. Infatuated with a shop girl who had been arrested for tossing him a bouquet of flowers, he personally has her rescued from the humiliation of a public flogging. She is telling the other shop girls and flowersellers about her adventure when one of the Tsar's assistants brings word that the Tsar wants to present her with her own country cottage, which turns out to be an enormous mansion.

The high point of the musical is a song attributed to song-writers Heymann and Leigh which became an international hit in 1931 and 1932 which she sings as she rides to her rendezvous with the flirtatious monarch; like "Today I Feel So Happy," the words of the song "Just Once For All Time" (known in German as "Das Gibt's Nur Einmal, Das Kommt Nicht Wieder") convey a sense of escape and lighthearted optimism. In the verse, amidst references to "laughing, singing, joy bells ringing," audiences are told that "life today is like a dream." Indeed, the song continues, people are seeking something and are trying to put unhappiness aside; that is, "Hearts are yearning, sorrow spurning," and the lyrics compare the unfolding story to a "fairy-tale" that happens to be "true." In the chorus that follows, lyrics celebrate that "just once for all time, does fortune treat you to happiness beyond all price"; if that is the case, and if "There's just one May-time" when "the whole wide world belongs to you," the song advises that one should seize that happiness, or "make that your May-time," and use that occasion "and start to live your life anew." Again, as in other popular songs from films of the period, the emphasis is on positive thoughts and avoiding unhappiness.

John Kobal, in his pictorial history of the musical, has observed that the sequence in which the song appeared "contain[ed] the essence of so much that is good about the film"; in the sequence, Chrystel is taking a ride in an open carriage passing through Vienna and into the countryside on the way to the castle which Tsar Alexander has presented to her. Kobal remarks that "her emotional state is expressed in the refrain of the song" which is "picked up" by the tradesmen in the markets, by the field-hands in the farms along the way, by parading soldiers, by washer-women, and by children to the extent that "the whole countryside seems to share her joy and express it in song."[18] Here again, as in *Sunshine Susie*, the staging of an essentially escapist musical number suggests that this optimistic message should be shared by all. Film critic James Agate, writing in the *Tatler*, at the time of the film's release, observed that the movie, and this sequence especially, was designed to appeal to the working classes. He observed that the "strength" of *Congress Dances* "is that there is no little typist or mannequin in London or Nuneaton or North Shields, or wherever this film may percolate, whose bosom will not throb tempestuously at the spectacle of Chrystel's rise to the position of uncrowned queen ." Agate added that as Chrystel climbs "into the carriage ... singing ... in the audience we may be sure that every little typist and mannequin is singing with her" just as "the whole population of Austria participates" seeming to have "learned the theme-song by divination."[19]

The enormous success of *Congress Dances*, particularly in the industrial

North where it played to record crowds, especially in Manchester and Liverpool, made it one of the biggest attractions of the year; the *Gaumont–British News* reported that "the film has completely captured Lancashire's not easily excited imagination," and publicity suggested that the feature's reputation may not have been hurt by the fact that it was especially well-liked among the members of the royal family and by other dignitaries.[20]

Numerous other such features were released in ensuing years, perhaps trying to capitalize on the success of *Congress Dances*. One example was *The Only Girl*, a May, 1933 musical release again starring Lillian Harvey; this time, she is Julietta, a singing hairdresser and lady's maid, whose voice is so beautiful that it causes a French duke at the court of Napoleon III, played by Charles Boyer, who thinks that it belongs to the Empress, to fall in love with it. Similarly, Hungarian soprano Gitta Alpar starred as the little milliner, Jeanne, in a late 1935 British release called *I Give My Heart* based on Carl Millocker's 1879 operetta, *The Dubarry*. Set in the court of Louis XV, who in the film is depicted by Owen Nares, the story of the film concerns Jeanne who at first is infatuated with Rene, a young man from her own station, played by Patrick Waddington. But, then, Jeanne is persuaded to marry Count DuBarry, portrayed by Arthur Margetson, and subsequently she is projected into the royal court as part of an intrigue to use her as a bait for the king. At the same time, she finds that she has opponents who also intrigue against her and those who support her, especially the Marechale de Luxem Luxembourg (Margaret Bannerman). One of her enemies, Choiseul, "makes the mistake of rousing the Paris mob against her" only to discover that as a "child of the people" she is able to go out "to meet them with her old friends of the milliner's shop" who "join forces in praise of Jeanne"; she is then able to "return triumphant to the court."[21]

One of Jack Buchanan's greatest triumphs, *Goodnight Vienna*, was a film that conformed to this plot structure; in this March, 1932 release produced and directed by Herbert Wilcox, Buchanan portrays the son of an Austrian General, Captain Max Schlettoff, who is engaged to the niece of the Emperor in pre World War I Vienna. But he soon finds himself infatuated with Viki, a shop girl in a flower store, played by Anna Neagle in her first major role, who is, of course, unsuitable for Max's family; but while Captain Max goes off to fight in the Great War, Viki becomes an international opera star, which inevitably makes her acceptable to the snobbish family. Kobal has observed that "Snobbish caricatures were a popular ingredient" of English musicals, "especially with the audiences who might have been thought to resent this stereotype," and he noted that in many of Anna Neagle's subsequent features, the plots "were riddled with caricatures"; Kobal explains that the predictable pattern had her "usually the servant girl who married the son of the noble household against family opposition." She would abandon her spouse "for his sake under pressure from his social and snobbish family" and then would become a successful performer on stage in London while her husband in his unhappiness at her departure joins the regiment to further "family tradition." The plot, Kobal continues, usually has him being promoted through the ranks and her becoming a theatrical star without the two of them encountering one another for the next fifty years "until he discovers her, old but unchanged, entertaining his troops." In some cases, Neagle is the daughter about whom he has been unaware, and "a dramatic reunion" with a "flashback into the good old days" when he first met her mother ensues.[22] Obviously, many of the features of this format originally had been present in the more continentally orientated *Goodnight Vienna*; it was hardly surprising that some of the plot characteristics of the Buchanan–Neagle feature would be copied since this production was a tremendous success. The film ran for over thirteen weeks at the Capitol Cinema in London and was re-released time after time throughout the thirties and forties; costing £23,000, the feature earned over £15,000 in Australia alone and broke records throughout England.[23]

Like other musicals, *Goodnight Vienna* contained one of the cheerful, optimistic tunes that seem to have been omnipresent in the thirties; in this case, the song "Living in Clover", written by George Posford again proved to be a success, after being recorded by Buchanan. In the lyrics of the tune, Buchanan relates that he is "done with blue days" because "just one or two days" in the company of his love has "changed the world for me"; now the "sun is shining, the skies are blue – life's just wonderful," and he concludes that he is "living in clover, brimming all over, with love." Here the implicit message of the song, independent of the plot, again was clear; the singer has had unhappy days, but with his beloved, no matter what the circumstances (or in the case of the film's plot, no matter what her social background was) the "sun [will be] shining" and "life [will be] just wonderful."

But the big, international hit from the movie, and one of Jack Buchanan's best-selling records was Posford's title song "Goodnight Vienna" which to a certain degree summed up the charm of these continental musical screen romances. When Buchanan sings "Goodnight, Vienna, you city of a million melodies," he is addressing both the locale and the features of these musical romances. The words of the song evoke images of "moonlight" filling the "air with mystery," of flowers and "gypsy guitars that sing to the starry skies," of "new lovers" embracing "beneath your linden trees"; in general, the city is seen as a "haven of hearts that seek romance." Thus, the lyrics of "Goodnight Vienna" characterize many of these plots. As the song suggests, the setting of the story is, in some respects, the real hero of the film, because it is the instrument that enables the unusual events to take place; "of our romances, you're the hero," the song maintains, and it is the "enchantment" and the "magic" that permits "hearts" to be "brimming" and that enables the violation of the social order in which a General's son rejects the Emperor's niece for a common shop girl.

The plot device used in *Goodnight Vienna* to bridge the social gap between the participants in the romance and to resolve the differences in their social ranking, namely a career in show business, was frequently used in other films involving love affairs between working-class and upper- or middle-class protagonists. For instance, a 1936 Gene Gerrard comedy entitled *Such is Life*, which was reissued to audiences in subsequent years, concerned a millionaire helping a typist become a singer. In another similar example, the March, 1937 musical comedy, *Mayfair Melody*, British baritone Keith Falkner played Mark Adams, a singing mechanic in an auto factory. Adams' habit of optimistically singing while he works in the factory brings him to the attention of Brenda, the spoiled and impulsive daughter of the magnate who owns the factory. Brenda, played by Joyce Kirby, after hearing Adams sing, decides to help him with a singing career; she obtains lessons for him with an Italian voice teacher named Collecchi, portrayed by Ian McLean, and, in time, the former mechanic is given the lead in a musical comedy. Naturally, by the end of this undistinguished feature, the working-class hero's romance with the heiress is a success.

The depiction of the working-class characters in such fantasies were hardly authentic; as one reviewer observed about the singing mechanic in *Mayfair Melody*, his "faultless speech never suggests the faintest impression of a mechanic." [24] But reality hardly mattered in fanciful plots of this nature; the show business settings and the fairy-tale story-lines were the primary appeals of these features, and the commonness of this type of plot was testimony to its popularity.

One interesting variation which, significantly, was released in June, 1936 was *Everything is Rhythm* starring bandleader Harry Roy and his orchestra. Roy had a veteran London hotel band, and in 1936, he was "right at the peak of his fame, the darling of society and general public alike [with] . . . regular broadcasts, variety tours and recordings [that] had made . . . his Band a household name throughout Britain." [25] In this escapist fantasy, Roy and his band portray Harry Wade and his Crusaders, who are "auditioning for a job at a plush West End Hotel" as the movie begins. When the booking agent turns them down, "they are preparing to give up and disband" until Harry's resourceful brother and manager, Bill Currie, playing himself, rushes in at the last minute to give them the news that "by a bit of skullduggery," he has arranged a chance for them to try out before "the actual owner of the hotel." [26] The owner instantly recognizes their talent and hires them; in this way, in the opening, the feature instantly characterized the bandleader as an underdog kind of character, thus making it easy for the audience to sympathize with him.

The romance in the plot quickly developed from that point; after opening at the hotel, Harry notices in the hallway a beautiful girl, played by his real-life wife, the former society personality Elizabeth Brooke who was known as "Princess Pearl." The girl turns out to be Princess Paula of the Ruritanian country of Monrovia who is taking a vacation at the hotel; mistaking Harry for a waiter, she tells the bandleader to bring coffee to her room. Harry finds the real waiter and bribes him so that he can take the coffee to her; while serving her, Harry finds himself falling in love with the beautiful woman, and "the pair are obviously attracted to one another." [27] Later that night, the Princess goes to the ballroom, and there she finds that her waiter is really a bandleader. The cheery tune that the band plays, "Make Some Music," written by song-writers, Meskill and Ray, one of the many typically optimistic anthems that could be heard in Depression era British musicals, reflected the positive, carefree point of view that troubles could be overcome with a sunny disposition. In the verse of the tune, the singer claims to "know a perfect recipe for everything that worries me," and commenting that "it's simple," he offers to "pass it along" to those who listen; the profound secret he elucidates is that "if you want to wear a smile" then the lyrics suggest:

> When you are blue, and you would be jolly,
> Here's what to do, if you're melancholy:
> Shuffle and shake, get happy, and make some music.

No matter what form this music-making takes, whether whistling or humming a tune, "never delay it, just sing it or play it, and good times will follow soon." The suggestion that by simply wearing a smile, problems could be overcome was a reassuring if naive notion for Depression era movie audiences. [28]

Though charmed by the tune, the Princess is nevertheless disturbed by the deception, thinking the bandleader has been making fun of her. To retaliate, the next morning when he attempts to carry on the masquerade by bringing her breakfast, the Princess imperiously "orders him about outrageously until eventually she reveals that she knows his true identity"; when he learns her true identity, the two reveal their love to one another in a song entitled "Life is Empty Without Love" which they sing together on a private recording to be kept as a souvenir. [29]

The recording, however, soon causes the two lovers major problems as one disk is stolen by Miss Mimms (Clarissa Selwyn), who serves as Paula's "dragon-like maid and companion," to be dispatched to Monrovia along with the details of this unacceptable romance. Since Paula's father, the Duke, played by Robert English, had sought to arrange Paula's marriage to Count Rudolph (Gerald Barry), her report is not viewed favorably, and the Duke immediately demands her return. Regretfully, Paula writes a love-letter to explain her quick departure which she asks Miss Mimms to deliver to Harry, but the treacherous servant destroys it, replacing it with a fake letter informing Harry that his encounter with Paula had been "only a . . . game" and ordering him to have no further communication with Paula. Sadly, Harry abandons the relationship and concentrates his efforts on a world tour with his band. [30]

Eventually, Harry Wade and his Crusaders are booked into Monrovia, predictably on the eve of the marriage Paula is being forced to undertake. Count Rudolph, knowing of the previous romance, forbids her to attend the band's opening performance, but she defies him, and when Harry sees her, he sings to her the song they recorded together. Returning to the castle, Paula finally has realized the effect of the schemes and treachery of Miss Mimms, and she now plots to meet Harry so that she can offer an explanation of what happened. Her plan is to order the band to perform at a Royal Command performance; however Harry is still angry, and he defies the command, which in turn outrages the Duke. He dispatches "the Royal Troops to escort the band to the Palace." When one of Paula's ladies-in-waiting carries a communication from the Princess to the bandleader with the message that she still loves him, he responds by sneaking into her room by ascending "a rope made of bed sheets." The scandal of their meeting is reported by Miss Mimms to the Duke, but Harry and the Princess board an airplane with the band and fly away to a presumed happy ending.[31]

Peter Orchard observed that the "story line [of *Everything is Rhythm*] was little more than an excuse for Harry and his boys to show off their skills as a great bunch of entertainers" and concluded that the plot "had obviously been suggested by Harry's recent much publicized marriage to the so-called 'Princess Pearl,' a society beauty who was actually Miss Elizabeth Brooke, daughter of Sir Charles Vyner Brooke, the 'White Rajah of Sarawak.' "[32] Orchard's analysis may have been partly correct, but the timing of the film's release, at a point when Britain was in the midst of a national crisis over the King's romance with Mrs Simpson and the possibility of abdication, seemed more than coincidental. The theme of the movie, that a royal figure would be willing to sacrifice her position for the love of someone who was socially unacceptable, was, with the sexes reversed, a topic of genuine concern to British citizens at this time. The concept that wealth and position did not necessarily bring happiness was the corollary of this theme, and the song that the bandleader and the Princess sang to one another in the movie, "Life is Empty Without Love," which is reprised several times through the feature and which was written by Roy and his wife, demonstrated this idea which runs through many other similar film romances. In the song's verse, Harry asserts that:

> I've tasted fame, and seen what money buys
> Yet all the same, I always realize
> That sweet content was meant for two, dear.
> And one alone, upon his own, is blue.

The chorus considers variations of the notion that "Life is empty, without love, not worth living, without love" culminating in the thought "Your kiss I've known, now I'm alone, life is empty without love." The assumption in the song again contained a subtly *status quo* message; that is, the most impoverished individual could be more fortunate than a princess if he or she had love. Hence, romance did not depend on logic which might argue against an inter-class love affair; love was an emotion that even the poorest person could experience as happily as the wealthiest. Though the bandleader was not a working-class character, the fact that he was mistaken for a waiter and the fact that he was victimized by the family of the Princess who regarded him as a social inferior made him a character with whom audiences easily could identify.

Audiences came to expect this plot structure; ultimately if the story did not conform to these conventions, that is, if the character's rise in status due to show business success did not produce happiness, moviegoers, or at least the critics, sometimes were disappointed. For example, one of Gracie Fields's musicals, the spring 1937 feature, *The Show Goes On* had a comparable narrative; in this unusually serious, faintly autobiographical Gracie Fields vehicle, the heroine is Sally Scowcroft, a Lancashire mill girl who wants to go on the stage in spite of parental objections. When a consumptive composer named Martin Fraser, played by veteran stage actor Owen Nares, overhears her singing, he decides to help her career, writing songs for her. The difference in this film was that the songwriter dies before a happy ending can take place between him and the socially inferior mill girl he helps; following a dispute between the two, Sally learns that her patron is very ill and gives up a major opportunity in order to be with him while he recuperates. But, partly to encourage her to pursue her career, the composer treats her in an unfriendly manner; Sally leaves him and instead marries a young man from home, moving away in the process. Meanwhile, the composer's illness inevitably results in his death.

As historian Jeffrey Richards has observed in a perceptive analytical career article on Gracie Fields, director Basil Dean's "approach" to both the theme and the portrayal of the Gracie Fields character "is markedly and characteristically different" in *The Show Goes On*. Richards notes that in the film, Sally's "stardom is achieved at the cost of personal unhappiness," specifically her "relationship with and later death of Martin"; in the scene when she learns of his death while she is preparing for a new show, she gets the sad news "in long shot with her back to the rest of the company" and then as the rest of the cast leaves, she "brokenly sings" his tune "A Song in Your Heart" as a "last tribute."[33]

Interestingly enough, though this production did achieve enough of a success to earn subsequent reissues, the film was generally thought to be one of the least memorable of the Gracie Fields features of the thirties. As Basil Dean observed in his autobiography, "the popular newspapers condemned *The Show Goes On* out of hand, one of them concluding its article with . . . 'It is enough to satisfy her fans.'"[34] Said the reviewer in the *Monthly Film Bulletin*, "it is no injustice to suggest that it is the least satisfactory film that Gracie Fields has made," in part attributing its inability to please to the film's less conventional ending and its "astonishing lack of comedy."[35]

But the reviewers were not alone in being troubled by such unconventional unhappy conclusions; even letters to fan magazines from moviegoers complained about Gracie's character losing the man she loved.[36] The fact that the film did manage to be successful was perhaps more a testimony to the star's popularity and to the much publicized fact that the movie was to be her last production for a British company before the start of her newly signed contract with the American based Twentieth Century Fox. The opportunity to see "Our Gracie" in a British feature one last time before the American studios attempted their inevitable glamorization of her persona may have outweighed a widely held perception of the film as being unsatisfying, attracting her fans in spite of the film's content.

In a few films, the rise of an entertainer from a lowly street performer to stardom was accompanied by a failure by the protagonist to recognize a true love from a working-class background; in such features, the newly successful entertainer's relationship with a wealthy or elite character often is depicted as being shallow and generally unsuccessful. In *Limelight*, an early 1936 release directed by Herbert Wilcox and starring his wife, Anna Neagle, and the legendary performer, Arthur Tracy, the "Street Singer," Tracy portrays Bob Grant, an impoverished busker who is aided on his way to stardom by chorus-girl Marjorie Kaye, played by Miss Neagle. But when the busker becomes a success, he begins romancing a rich socialite, to the disappointment of the heart-broken chorus-girl, before ultimately coming to his senses and returning to the dancing chorine who loves him.

An almost identical plot occurred in Tim Whelan's far better known July, 1938 release, *St Martin's Lane*. In this "romantic drama of London's theatreland" written by Clemence Dane, Charles Laughton plays Charlie Saggers, characterized in one review as "a middle-aged, kind-hearted Cockney who entertains theatre queues [with] . . . his big turn . . . a dramatic recital entitled 'The Green Eye of the Little Yellow God'"; the review in the *Monthly Film Bulletin*, in summarizing the plot, noted that Charlie "is happy and contented in his precarious way of living and in his two friends Arthur and Gentry, fellow buskers," played by Gus McNaughton and Tyrone Guthrie.[37] But problems enter Charlie's life when he encounters an unreliable but vivacious young woman named Liberty, the beautiful Vivien Leigh.

Charles Higham, in his biography of Charles Laughton, argued that the actor gave one of his "most memorable" performances in the film. Charlie Saggers is performing his recitation before a queue outside the Holborn Empire when he is shoved aside by a group of fans seeking the autograph of one of the show's performers. In the confusion, a coin is stolen from Charlie's cup by the unrepentant but beautiful "Libby." Charlie chases after the street girl and learns that she is a professional thief who proceeds to steal a silver cigarette case from journalist Rex Harrison, in front of a sandwich stand.

Charlie follows her and catches up with her in "an empty mansion" into which she has broken, where, "in an exquisite sequence, he sees her dance on the dusty floor in the moonlight"; captivated by her charm, beauty and talent, Charlie falls in love with her "but he is too shy to reveal this to her." [38] Eventually, Charlie discovers that "Libby ... is down on her luck and has been driven to petty stealing," so to help reform her, he takes her in and teaches her to be a busker. Then, after persuading his two busker chums that it would be more profitable to form an ensemble ("the individual is washed up and cooperating is the thing, today," he tells them), he and Libby join Arthur and Gentry to rehearse a new street act. The quartet become a successful queue team, but Libby has ambitions for a stage career. An opportunity arrives with her association with a popular songwriter; Charlie, expressing his jealousy and love for her, proposes to Libby, but she rebuffs his offer and makes fun of him. He reacts by running out and disappears for a time. "Libby" becomes a successful West-End performer, while Charlie has been periodically in trouble, occasionally being arrested for creating disruptions and behaving in an unruly manner. Eventually, Libby discovers him masquerading as a blind beggar in Piccadilly; sorry for what has happened, she arranges for him to audition. However, "as he recites Kipling's 'If,' he realizes his proper place, rushes out of the theatre, and returns to entertaining theatre queues." [39]

The realism of the film was painstakingly crafted by the production crew; as Higham has noted, the producers "decided to use London locations as a living background for the story, shooting in the West End, and using queueing theatre goers as extras"; as a result the film had "a striking and vivid immediacy, a feeling of London itself as a living ingredient of the drama." [40]

The producers extensively publicized this quality of the film in an attempt to attract moviegoers; one fan magazine with an elaborate article on the making of the feature concentrated on this aspect of the production, noting that "half the Buskers of the West End were there in person" while the film was being made. [41] But in spite of the excellent production values, the box-office attractiveness of the stars and the publicity effort, the film was a major "commercial failure." [42] In part, this disappointing lack of success for an otherwise well mounted production again may have been related to the unsatisfying nature of the social elevation occurring in the movie's story-line; if an audience was going to take the time to suspend its sense of reality for a show business "rags-to-riches" romance, it apparently did not want the experience to be generally disappointing.

Two of the more well-known Herbert Wilcox–Anna Neagle screen collaborations were also show-business stories about actresses who rose from impoverished backgrounds through the help of wealthy patrons whom they loved. The first of these, *Nell Gwyn*, an August, 1934 release, concerned the seventeenth-century Cockney orange-seller who became an actress and mistress to Charles II, brilliantly played in this feature by Cedric Hardwicke.

Contemporary reviewers also praised Anna Neagle's spirited performance in the title role; one critic observed that Nell was portrayed as "almost a Gracie Fields type ... an attractive vulgarian, whose hearty laugh and honest outspokenness give her a considerable advantage over the stuck-up ladies of Charles's court." [43]

Moviegoers flocked to the film, breaking box-office records in many communities. [44] *Film Weekly*'s fan poll rated the film the third best of the year, (behind Hitchcock's *The 39 Steps* and the Korda production of *The Scarlet Pimpernel*, and just ahead of Hitchcock's *The Man Who Knew Too Much*) and Anna Neagle's performance was cited as the fourth best film performance of the year. [45] Part of the attraction for the film aside from the performances and Anna Neagle's beauty was clearly the story-line, with the idea of a King becoming infatuated with a brash, Cockney girl apparently quite appealing. The author of a letter to *Film Weekly*, for instance, praised the movie's depiction of "real people," observing about the genuineness of the portrayal of Nell and the other common people in the film that "one felt they were real ... [people] who, if alive to-day, might be found at any football match on a Saturday afternoon." [46]

Another filmgoer writing in the same magazine a few weeks later argued that the reason *Nell Gwyn* succeeded was because it was "honest" with its story of the "King who loved the orange-girl" theme "[making] you feel you are glimpsing reality with all good nature and vivacious vulgarity"; the writer added that the good feeling the film engendered was best illustrated in the "scene in the Drury Lane Theatre where the whole audience and ultimately the King join in [singing] Nellie's song" as if in a music hall, a sequence which invariably "set the modern audience singing inside" the cinema. [47] The filmgoer concluded:

> History and its protagonists have this peculiar fascination for the mass of people who without perhaps knowing or caring very much about accuracy of detail, like to feel that history is being recreated before their eyes – not gibed at, or illuminated, but brought to life. [In *Nell Gwyn*] you feel that you have been lucky enough to look for a moment across time into another age. [48]

Wilcox and Neagle were equally successful with a similar story a year later in their film *Peg of Old Drury* about the colorful Irish actress Peg Woffington who rose from humble origins as an Irish bricklayer's daughter to become a great Shakespearean actress; though somewhat romanticized, the film centered on the young woman's love for the great actor David Garrick, again played by Cedric Hardwicke, upon her arrival in London in the 1740s, and his tutoring of her to make her an actress and to bring her into society. Interestingly in the feature, Peg's ambition and belief in London as a city "where the streets are paved with gold, they tell me" were contrasted with the views of her practical, worldly-wise washer-woman mother who disdained material success and regarded London as a "misbegotten, foreign, heathen conglomeration of wickedness"; again success was seen as being not always completely beneficial.[49]

Reviewers noted the similarity of the film to its predecessor, one suggesting the film was "almost a redoing of *Nell Gwyn*" and its story of "another . . . who also had risen from the gutter" to love a famous wealthy man.[50] Although the critical response to the feature was not as favorable as the earlier production, moviegoers nevertheless continued to support the Wilcox–Neagle screen collaboration, and again *Film Weekly* readers placed the production third in rankings of best pictures of the year (behind Rene Clair's *The Ghost Goes West* and the Robert Stevenson production of *Tudor Rose*), rating Miss Neagle's performance as the third best (behind Nova Pilbeam's Lady Jane Grey in *Tudor Rose* and Robert Donat's comic portrayal in *The Ghost Goes West*).[51] The success of these historical biographies and Miss Neagle's remarkable versatility subsequently inspired Wilcox to cast her twice in the highly regarded filmed biographies of Queen Victoria later in the decade.[52]

COMPLICATIONS IN INTER-CLASS ROMANCE

But not all features with a romance between a working-class character and an upper- or middle-class character portrayed the love affair as trouble free or even desirable. For example, in one of Laurence Olivier's early features, *Potiphar's Wife*, released in the spring of 1931 and based on a play by Edgar Middleton, Olivier plays Straker, the chauffeur for Lord and Lady Bromford, played by Norman McKinnel and Nora Swinburne, respectively. In this familiar story, when the rich, attractive, but bored, woman's efforts to seduce the chauffeur are resisted, the angry lady charges him with assault and has him arrested. The assumption in such a plot was that one should be wary of the attentions of amoral upper-class idlers.

In *Dance Pretty Lady*, a February, 1932 release directed by Anthony Asquith and based on Compton Mackenzie's novel *Carnival*, Ann Cassar is Jenny Pearl, a ballet dancer in the Edwardian era, who has risen from a working-class, Cockney background to a promising dance career; she soon falls in love with an aristocratic artist named Maurice Avery, played by Carl Harbord, but his suggestion that she should become his mistress because he does not believe in the institution of marriage is rebuffed. Her unhappiness and his departure overseas leads her to believe that he has deserted her, and in her loneliness, she allows herself to become the mistress of his friend Danby (Norman Claridge), a submission she deeply regrets. Eventually Maurice returns and, stricken with remorse after realizing his departure had precipitated the unhappy affair, he finds Jenny, comforting and forgiving her. Again the image of amoral upper-class philanderers was suggested in this somewhat melodramatic romance.

Sometimes a relationship between an upper- or middle-class character and a working-class protagonist was portrayed as being unpleasant and unhappy in contrast to the more natural and more desirable relationship of two people from the same class. In the March, 1933 romance, *The Golden Cage*, Anne Grey plays Venetia Doxford, a girl who marries a rich man, but who still loves and longs for an impoverished hotel clerk, and in *Mannequin*, a feature released in December of the same year, Harold French is boxer Peter Tattersall who deserts his sweetheart, Heather Trent (portrayed by Judy Kelly) for a wealthy society aristocrat, Lady Diana Savage (Diana Beaumont), before ultimately coming to his senses and returning to his true love.

In the February, 1937 musical *Kathleen Mavourneen*, Sally O'Neil in the title role is an Irish waitress working in the dock area of Liverpool to try to support herself and her younger brother and sister; she is in love with Mike Rooney, a stevedore who also happens to be a singer, played by Tom Burke. When Mike buys her tickets home for a visit to her aunt (Sara Allgood), her happiness at the farm in Ireland seems to be assured; but on the farm she is the object of the affections of a rich local landowner named Denis O'Dwyer, portrayed by Jack Daly. Torn between the security the landowner's wealth would provide, especially for her brother and sister who are threatened with an orphanage, and her love for the stevedore, she ultimately rejects the rich man for Mike.

Another Irish setting was to be found in the June, 1938 musical *Mountains O' Mourne* in which Niall MacGinnis is Paddy Kelly, the young singing son of a tenant farmer, who is in love with Mary Macree, played by Rene Ray, the daughter of another tenant farmer. The landlord of both farms has a nephew named Errol Finnegan who also loves Mary. When a bad growing season leaves the farmers in debt for their rent, the hard-hearted landlord has both families evicted, and both the Macrees and the Kellys go to Dublin to find work. In an effort to help the family, Paddy secures an audition from a BBC talent scout, but when he reaches London, he immediately becomes a victim of a pickpocket named "Dip" Evans, played by comic Jerry Verno, who takes all his money. But an old village friend named Peter O'Laughlin (Kaye Seely) working as a London policeman comes to Paddy's aid; identifying the perpetrator as "Dip" Evans, he forces the streetwise pickpocket to return the money and to reform by helping the innocent Irish farmhand. After Paddy's triumphant audition, O'Laughlin agrees to become his manager, and Dip promises to serve as his valet. At this point, the relationship between Mary and her now successful boyfriend is complicated when Paddy is persuaded to obtain the services of a woman named Violet Mayfair, played by Betty Ann Davies, whose society background enables her to teach the inexperienced young singer how to behave properly in society. Finding herself captivated by the young ex-farmhand, Violet tries to derail Paddy's romance with Mary by intercepting their correspondence, though Dip tries to thwart her sabotage.

At New Year, Paddy is performing in Dublin, and he tries to locate Mary, who has now become a cafe hostess. Mary's affections are still being sought by Errol who has learned of a secret will which will make Mary a wealthy woman. Mary and Paddy reunite and discover that Violet's treachery had caused the break in their communication with one another. Paddy's performance turns out to be a great success; Dip manages to wrest the will revealing Mary's fortune from the conniving Errol, and "all ends well with the return of the two families to their respective farms."[53] Although the *Monthly Film Bulletin*, in its review of the film, noted that the "theme of local boy making good and returning to his village and his childhood love affair after falling in and out of the wiles of the society vamp" was "hackneyed," it nevertheless found the feature to be "fresh and amusing" within the framework of its plot conventions.[54]

In such movies, although the plot devices were often artificial and contrived, a relationship between people from the same class background nevertheless was presented as being clearly somehow preferable to one between people of different classes. Sometimes, however, the problems created when this kind of inter-class love affair occurred in a film story were more than a little far-fetched. For instance, in the May, 1935 crime film, *Brides to Be*, crooks frame an innocent shop girl for a theft in order to spoil her romance with a millionaire. In *Mr What's His Name*, an April, 1935 farce comedy written by screenwriter Frank Launder early in his career, Seymour Hicks plays Alfred Henfield, a successful married businessman who develops amnesia and takes on a new identity, in the process marrying a lowly beautician. After starting another business, he "eventually, by an accident, finds himself in the house of his original wife who, thinking him dead, has married again"; gradually, his memory of his earlier life returns, and "he is left with no recollection of the years between," leading to problems for his second wife.[55] Ultimately, according to a contemporary review of what was termed "a really first class . . . comedy," a "neat solution" is devised.[56]

But by far the most interesting films which observed problems in romances between members of different classes were those which reflected, however subtly or artificially, the difficulties arising from class consciousness and social elitism. One of the earliest British features to have a sound sequence with dialogue was Victor Saville's popular early 1929 film *Kitty*, based on the novel by Warwick Deeping, which was released originally as a silent but which subsequently had a talking section added. The story of the film, which was set in 1914, concerns Kitty Greenwood, portrayed by Estelle Brody, a hard-working shop girl in a gift and teashop where many soldiers home on leave stop for tea; in the movie, Kitty falls in love with a young soldier named Alec St George, played by John Stuart, who turns out to be the last son of a wealthy family of aristocrats. His mother, Mrs St George (Dorothy Cumming), disapproves of the relationship because she dislikes the thought of her son with a lowly shop girl; but Alex marries the kind-hearted young girl

136

in spite of his mother's upper-class snobbery and leaves for the war. His mother, however, attempts to subvert the "unsuitable" marriage by writing to her son that Kitty is being unfaithful to him. Affected by the news, Alec is badly injured, losing the use of his legs; when he returns in a wheelchair, paralyzed and suffering from amnesia, Kitty proves her faithfulness and flees with him away from the interference of the mother. This love story, with its class-conscious overtones was one of the most popular films of the year; *Film Weekly* readers rated it the third best feature of 1929.[57]

A similar plot was to be found in the 1930 filmed version of the old T.W. Robertson comic play *Caste*. Also set in 1914, the movie's story centers on the daughter of a Cockney drunk who marries the soldier son of a Marquis who is missing in action and is presumed to be dead. Interestingly, a number of these features dealt with wartime situations, and it was perhaps not coincidental that the First World War traditionally has been considered by historians and sociologists to have been a key period in the beginning of a blending of the British class structure. With the war effort bridging classes and bringing people of different backgrounds together for the first time in a unified activity, social barriers were penetrated as never before, and such story-lines in later features seem to have reflected a subtle awareness of this social phenomenon.

Although not the central focus of the story, a similar wartime, inter-class relationship figured in the plot of the October, 1934 dramatic release, *My Old Dutch*, a story which had been filmed once before in the silent era. Starring Betty Balfour and Gordon Harker, the film was characterized by more than one reviewer "as a Cockney 'Cavalcade'"; as the *Monthly Film Bulletin* observed, "[the movie] reflects the joys and sorrows, the occupations and relaxations of the typical London working man," against a background of the wartime years, "depicting" with "an excellent sense of proportion and emphasis, the daily life of a London family, father and mother, children, uncles and aunts and all . . . sensations of air-raids [and] the fun of Hampstead Heath, . . . [with] just the right amount of sentiment and pathos."[58] The *Film Weekly* review made the comparison to *Cavalcade* even more explicit, noting that "though [it was] not on the same scale, and one wouldn't expect it to be . . . it employs the same idea of covering forty years in the life of one family, with background references to the major political and national events of the period."[59]

Significantly, however, even in a film about a "typical London working man's family," in *My Old Dutch*, a working-class character, in this case the son, again falls in love with the daughter of a wealthy industrialist and weds her, though she is expelled from the family for marrying beneath her station.[60] The story of this "low-life *Cavalcade*" concerns a Cockney couple named Lil and Bert, played by Miss Balfour and Michael Hogar, "who get engaged on 'Ampstead 'Eath, marry, have a son, sacrifice everything to make him a 'gent' and lose him in the war."[61] The son's wife, Valerie

Paraday (Glennis Lorimer), is the daughter of an industrial magnate, portrayed by Peter Gawthorne; Valerie is pregnant when the news of her husband's death arrives, and she subsequently dies giving birth to a baby boy who is named Jim. Lil endeavors to obtain legal custody of her infant grandson in a dispute with his maternal grandfather who had objected to his daughter's runaway marriage. At the time of the Great Strike, Jim, played by Mickey Brantford, is put in danger when agitators set fire to a petrol station, and he finds himself trapped until he is rescued by Bert. But the rescue exacts a great price as Bert is crippled and is not released from the hospital for a year. Realizing she cannot support her grandson properly, Lil gives in and relinquishes custody to the child's rich relations, and the film ends as Bert and Lil celebrate their fortieth anniversary secure "in their knowledge that their grandson is well provided for and somebody thinks of them."[62] The reviewer in *Picturegoer Weekly* commented that the "atmosphere" was "most convincing" with "the various landmarks of their lives – such as the Great War, its aftermath, and the Strike ... introduced in a natural and unpretentious, but wholly effective manner," adding that "it is a typically English picture – English in its sentiment ... humour and ... attitude to life and simplicity of theme."[63]

In publicizing *My Old Dutch*, the appeal naturally was made directly to an older audience among the working classes, and publicity stunts reflected this conception of which moviegoers would be most attracted to the film. Special showings were arranged in the larger cities for elderly patrons with special prizes for those who had been married forty years or more; at the Surrey County Cinema in Sutton, the manager:

> arranged a very pleasant tea party for workhouse inmates, who were brought to and from his theatre in coaches provided free. The Mayor of Sutton presented gifts of cigarettes and sweets to the old couples, who certainly had the time of their lives.[64]

Similar events took place in a number of other cities, especially in industrial areas. Often processions of costers were used to promote the film on city streets, and in some of the bigger cinemas, elaborate prologues were produced concerning the lives of Cockneys, with several of these short stage shows centering around the famed Albert Chevalier song which provided the inspiration for the movie's title.[65]

Class consciousness in films in which the working-class characters romanced upper- or middle-class characters was depicted sometimes comically and sometimes seriously. For example, Adrian Brunel's *While Parents Sleep*, a "frothy light-hearted comedy with a strong farcical element" released in September, 1935 poked fun at elitist attitudes; based on Anthony Kimmins's play, the film had a theme centering on the clash between members of different grades of society with their different codes of manners."[66] In the movie, Neville Hammond, played by Romilly Lunge, plays an officer in the guards who is the elder son of a society couple, Colonel and Mrs Hammond (Athole Stewart and Ellis Jeffreys); Neville is infatuated with the wife of his commanding officer, Lady Cattering, portrayed by Enid Stamp-Taylor. Meanwhile, Neville's somewhat irresponsible younger brother Jerry (Mackenzie Ward) is a naval officer who is also something of a woman-izer; he meets a shop girl named Bubbles Thompson (Jean Gillie) at a fair and he quickly falls in love with her. Everyone gathers for supper at a dinner party hosted by the Hammonds, and in the course of the event Lady Cattering makes fun of Bubbles. The next evening, Neville "brings Lady Cattering to stay with his parents"; but later that night, Bubbles and Jerry discover Neville and Lady Cattering in a "compromising situation." Though Bubbles now has an opportunity to get even for the embarrassment of the previous evening, she chooses not to take revenge; consequently, "Neville realises his folly, and Bubbles' heart of gold is recognised by her snobbish future mother-in-law, and so all ends happily."[67]

Another light, if slightly melodramatic, entertainment was the musical *Father O'Flynn* a late 1935 release. In this feature, Jean Adrienne is an Irish girl who is adopted by the village priest, played by Tom Burke; the girl is "loved by the squire's son." Unfortunately the squire objects to the marriage because her father has been involved in illegal activities. When the father shows up, he entices her to go away with him; in England, he uses her money to open a gambling den. Father O'Flynn and the squire's son arrive just in time and rescue her after a major fight takes place. The squire then reconsiders his objection and "agrees to the marriage of the young couple."[68]

By contrast with the comedy of *While Parents Sleep* and the naivety of *Father O'Flynn*, the October, 1931 release *Hindle Wakes* based on the famous 1912 British play by Stanley Houghton, was a grim, almost cynical, reminder of the class divisions in British society. Directed by Victor Saville, this film was the third of four times the play has appeared in a screen version. Set during the annual mill workers holiday (which coincided with an ancient Anglo-Saxon religious festival), the story of the movie concerns a Lancashire mill girl who enjoys the company of the mill owner's son during a weekend fling at the time of the wakes but then refuses the urgings of her family to participate in a forced marriage with him. As *Picturegoer Weekly* observed, the film was "delicately handled and thoroughly convincing drawing a vivid picture of the independent spirit of the mill girl [played by Belle Chrystall] in her fight against a conventional marriage which could only have led to unhappiness."[69] The review in *Film Weekly* suggested that the feature actually had a degree of social commentary by showing the background of "Lancashire, with its black brooding factories, its drab, uniform streets, its clog-shod and shawl-wrapped women" and by taking the "laughter and the tragedy in the lives of its people" to be "brilliantly blended into entertain-ment which appeals straight to the heart"; the film's plot "has the strength of simplicity," with its "independent-minded mill-girl" whose "strength of character is contrasted dramatically with the anger of her parents who consider that she has been wronged." [70]

But rather than emphasizing the potential critique of the class divisions in British society that would be inherent in such a plot, publicity for the film took a different approach. For instance, the official house magazine of the chain of Paramount Astoria Cinemas, the *Astorian*, heralded the coming feature as "the story of a girl who defied convention" and noted that the plot:

> turns on modern feminine independence in sexual affairs, put over in brilliantly alternated scenes of humble mill life, breezy Blackpool gaieties, parental devotion, and poignant drama . . . alternating amid the grime and smoke of Lancashire's mill district, and the hectic gaieties of Lancashire's pleasure ground, Blackpool. [71]

While the heroine was determined and practical, the factor that motivated her refusal to marry was a realization of the pressures that would result from an inter-class romance. She learns that her lover will be cut off from his inheritance, and in spite of his noble protestations that he will be happy to work for her, she is honest and sensible enough to understand what obstacles such a marriage would face immediately.

Especially well received in Northern industrial areas, the film was mostly promoted as a story of provincial life, and rather than centering any publicity on either the drab living conditions of industrial workers, the cinemas, by contrast, were gaily decorated in festive colors, almost making the film a pageant of regional lifestyles. For example, in Birmingham, the cinema manager:

> very effectively decorated his attendants with the insignia of the mill towns of the north, namely clogs and shawls, and further added to the alternativeness of the occasion by securing the services of a local band, which played appropriate musical offerings to the delighted audience prior to the presentation of the picture . . . . At Newcastle, the manager . . . adopted pretty much the same methods. [72]

At some cinemas, in an almost regionally patriotic manner, the lobby would be filled with a display of merchandise and goods produced by the mills, and ushers would be dressed in clogs and shawls. [73] The impression generated of the film was thus emphatically not that of a social critique, and in this way any socially inflammatory aspects of the movie were de-emphasized. Yet the movie was popular, ranking in the top six of the *Film Weekly* poll. [74]

Occasionally in these features, opposition to a working-class character's romance with a member of the wealthy or elite of society would not only come from above, but also from the working-class characters themselves.

Usually, a feature of this type would have a humorous format. For example, in the obscure March, 1933 comedy release, *Going Straight*, the servants of Lady Peckham are reformed criminals. Their loyalty to their employer causes them to worry about the developing relationship between Lady Peckham's novelist son and his secretary whom they suspect of dishonest intentions; accordingly, in this short comedy, they oppose the developing romance and try to "save" him from the office worker.

In another light musical comedy, the March, 1936 feature *King of Hearts*, the plot involved a "simple story of the love of a middle-class boy for a working-class girl."[75] Based on Matthew Boulton's play, "The Corduroy Diplomat," the plot centers on the efforts of the snobbish Mrs Ponsonby, played by Amy Veness, to spoil the love affair and prevent the marriage between her son Jack (Richard Dolman) and the working-class girl May Saunders (Gwenllian Gill). At first Mrs Ponsonby tries to get May fired from her job as a waitress in the local pub. When this effort fails, she goes to May's father Bill, a docker, portrayed memorably by Will Fyffe, to try to bribe him into spoiling the relationship. At first he is receptive to her appeal, for he, too, has his doubts about the wisdom and prospects for success of such an alliance. But ultimately convinced of the sincerity of the two lovers, the old worker outwits the mother, and the wedding takes place after all. Though largely forgotten today, *King of Hearts* was apparently popular enough in its time to earn a re-release within four years.

In a few rare instances in features of this type in the thirties, the comic situation of the romance between lovers of different social backgrounds was used for a slight amount of political satire, both on the right and on the left. In *Tilly of Bloomsbury*, a May, 1931 release, the emphasis was more on the comic than on the satire. Starring comedian Syd Howard, the film concerns the aristocratic Lady Marion Mainwaring, played by Ellis Jeffreys, who is the wife of Abel Mainwaring, a Member of Parliament. Their son, Dick Mainwaring, is in love with Tilly Welwyn (Phyllis Konstam). Mrs Mainwaring considers this romance to be inappropriate because Tilly is merely the daughter of a humble boardinghouse keeper named Percy Welwyn (Edward Chapman) and his wife Amelia (Ena Grossmith). In this movie, based on Ian Hay's play, Syd Howard as Samuel Stillbottle helps the lovers keep the affair going in spite of the family opposition. The mild satire in the film came from the impression it gave of the elitist attitudes from a woman so close to parliamentary influence. But at best, the satire was heavily muffled, if it could be said to have existed at all. In fact, the film was more an escapist enterprise, and it resisted making any significant social statements, for the most part. That it was amusing and fun to see a stuffy Member of Parliament's wife made to seem ridiculous was apparent. One writer observed in *Film Weekly* that *Tilly of Bloomsbury* was a perfect film to "appeal to the average working girl," and he added that "more such films were needed."[76]

But much more effective satire was to be found in the 1934 quota film,

141

Hyde Park, starring George Carney. In this amusing little feature, Carney is Joe Smith, a "soap box orator" and Socialist, "who spends his Sunday mornings in the Park running down the capitalists"; Joe's daughter Mary (Eva Lister) is "knocked down accidentally" by the son of Lord Lenbridge, a young man named Bill (Barry Clifton), and the little mishap initiates an unlikely romance between the two. But Joe will not permit any thought of his daughter's marrying an aristocrat. Ultimately, the problem is resolved when "Bill hits on the idea of presenting [Joe] with one thousand pounds which he makes him believe is a legacy from an aunt . . . [which] changes Joe's political outlook and leads to wedding bells."[77] The implied criticisms of Socialist values was attacked by some reviewers; the critic in *Picturegoer Weekly* called the film "naive and artless," and he especially disliked the film's "attempt to be witty at the expense of the alleged insincerity of Socialists."[78]

Though *Hyde Park* was somewhat predictably more pointed in its satirizing of the political left than *Tilly of Bloomsbury* was in its mild lampooning of elitism and class consciousness among politicians, both films were in the tradition of the depictions of class contrasts in film romances. In most of these cases, whenever and wherever the relationship occurred, the tendency was to blur the distinctions for those involved in the romance; correspondingly, the differences in the social standing of the parents or the associates of the protagonists usually was exaggerated. That is, the distinctions between the lovers in speech patterns, apparel, grammar, and other external characteristics ordinarily tended to be minimized, while the contrast between those attempting to hamper the relationship would be made more extreme. The effect of this practice was to make a more dramatic contrast in the film plot; admittedly in a curious way, this custom reflected the way actual social class distinctions tended to break down, that is, with the younger generations feeling more equalized and more adaptable to change.

STATISTICAL OVERVIEW

In this chapter, then, the portrayal of class relationships in a variety of different types of films made in Britain during this period has been surveyed. The assumption that British movies dealt exclusively with upper- or middle-class characters has been shown to be false. In fact, as Table 6.4 reveals, the over whelming majority of British features each year involved some kind of interaction between working-class characters and middle- or upper-class characters; in most years, at least two out of every three films had some kind of interaction in this way.

Not many of these features, however, in any way attempted to address the concept of elitism or class consciousness, as Table 6.5 demonstrates. Of those films which did include class consciousness as a theme, a large proportion were comedies or escapist films; few cinematic treatments of this topic could be considered serious studies.

Table 6.4 Films in which there is a clear interaction in
the plot between working-class characters and
middle- or upper-class characters

Year	Proportion of the films released	%
1929	57 of 86	66.3
1930	69 of 99	69.7
1931	80 of 134	59.7
1932	119 of 150	79.3
1933	122 of 181	67.4
1934	141 of 183	77.0
1935	127 of 185	68.6
1936	153 of 219	69.9
1937	158 of 211	74.9
1938	109 of 158	69.0
1939	69 of 98	70.4

Table 6.5 Films dealing with class consciousness and
elitism as a theme

Year	Proportion of the films released	%
1929	10 of 86	11.6
1930	10 of 99	10.1
1931	21 of 134	15.7
1932	32 of 150	21.3
1933	26 of 181	14.4
1934	37 of 183	20.2
1935	24 of 185	13.0
1936	24 of 219	11.0
1937	16 of 211	7.6
1938	16 of 158	10.1
1939	11 of 98	11.2

The relationships between the different classes was also remarkably
consistent. Tables 6.6 and 6.7 reveal that the percentages of British movies
released in which working-class characters were taken advantage of by upper-
or middle-class characters, and, correspondingly, the percentages of films in
which working-class characters took advantage of upper- or middle-class
characters were remarkably similar.

By contrast, however, films in which-working class characters helped
upper- or middle-class characters far outnumbered movies in which upper- or
middle-class characters helped working-class characters, as Tables 6.8 and 6.9
show.

Perhaps the argument can be made that such figures reflected a continuing
attitude of deference and service, even in the midst of a period of social

Table 6.6 Films in which working-class characters are
victimized or in some way exploited by middle- or
upper-class characters

Year	Proportion of the films released	%
1929	23 of 86	26.7
1930	19 of 99	19.2
1931	16 of 134	11.9
1932	25 of 150	16.7
1933	25 of 181	13.8
1934	36 of 183	19.7
1935	41 of 185	22.2
1936	43 of 219	19.6
1937	38 of 211	18.0
1938	20 of 158	12.7
1939	18 of 98	18.4

Table 6.7 Films in which middle- or upper-class
characters are victimized or are in some way exploited
by working-class characters

Year	Proportion of the films released	%
1929	11 of 86	12.8
1930	17 of 99	17.2
1931	18 of 134	13.4
1932	26 of 150	17.3
1933	27 of 181	14.9
1934	30 of 183	16.4
1935	31 of 185	16.8
1936	21 of 219	9.6
1937	24 of 211	11.4
1938	16 of 158	10.1
1939	15 of 98	15.3

dislocation, which would again suggest that British cinema during this period
reinforced traditional values and beliefs.

Tables 6.10 and 6.11 reveal, the criminals in British films more frequently
were of upper- or middle-class origin. In speculating on this contrast, several
possible explanations might be offered. One is that by having criminals of
upper- or middle-class origin, studios avoided the danger of establishing role
models among the working classes. On the other hand, these figures may
simply reflect the fictional or dramatic origins of the properties made into
films and may simply be coincidental.

Table 6.8 Films in which working-class characters are helped in some way by middle-class and/or upper-class characters

Year	Proportion of the films released	%
1929	10 of 86	11.6
1930	17 of 99	17.2
1931	23 of 134	17.2
1932	37 of 150	24.7
1933	38 of 181	21.0
1934	44 of 183	24.0
1935	39 of 185	21.1
1936	55 of 219	25.1
1937	38 of 211	18.0
1938	32 of 158	20.3
1939	17 of 98	17.3

Table 6.9 Films in which working-class characters help or serve in some way middle- or upper-class characters

Year	Proportion of the films released	%
1929	32 of 86	37.2
1930	39 of 99	39.4
1931	52 of 134	38.8
1932	65 of 150	43.3
1933	70 of 181	38.7
1934	84 of 183	45.9
1935	72 of 185	38.9
1936	80 of 219	36.5
1937	95 of 211	45.0
1938	64 of 158	40.5
1939	42 of 98	42.9

One must note that descriptions and reviews of films are never as reliable as first hand viewing. However, accepting these limitations, the figures are revealing of a general point of view in British cinema which avoided any major questioning of challenging of either the social structure of the society or of its political and economic components. That is not to say that such a radical emphasis was to be expected in an essentially entertaining and escapist medium. But, at the same time, without any such controversy, the cinema in Britain can be seen as a reinforcing institution which strengthens rather than questions assumptions at the foundation of society.

Table 6.10 Films in which criminals are identifiable as
middle- or upper-class

Year	Proportion of the films released	%
1929	26 of 86	30.2
1930	27 of 99	27.3
1931	43 of 134	32.1
1932	51 of 150	34.0
1933	59 of 181	32.6
1934	61 of 183	33.3
1935	59 of 185	31.9
1936	87 of 219	39.7
1937	63 of 211	29.9
1938	38 of 158	24.1
1939	38 of 98	38.8

Table 6.11 Films in which criminals are identifiable as
working-class

Year	Proportion of the films released	%
1929	21 of 86	24.4
1930	11 of 99	11.1
1931	27 of 134	20.1
1932	34 of 150	22.7
1933	32 of 181	17.7
1934	37 of 183	20.2
1935	36 of 185	19.5
1936	41 of 219	18.7
1937	37 of 211	17.5
1938	27 of 158	17.1
1939	17 of 98	17.3

In this manner, then, the content of the British cinema in its portrayal of
the class structure can be seen as a medium for maintaining the *status quo*.
This conservative orientation can be seen also in examinations of film
genre, subjects, and personalities which will be considered in the next
chapter.

7

THEMES IN BRITISH FILMS
The downside of success

The optimistic attitude and escapist outlook of British features in the thirties were readily apparent even for those who never went to the cinema. Even without any knowledge of the content of British movies, an observer, noting the various film titles would find certain philosophical viewpoints and pre-occupations repeated. These titles may have provided subliminal messages that could have had an effect on even the non-moviegoer.

For instance, titles from Depression era films in Britain often carried expressions of joy, hopefulness, and happiness, urging an enjoyment of life in spite of adversity. Table 7.1 provides a listing of some of these film titles that consisted of positive, optimistic, uplifting little messages of good cheer.

Admittedly, the psychological impact of these titles might be impossible to measure; but a pedestrian walking along a street and seeing, maybe even without consciously reading, expressions like "Things Are Looking Up," "Happy Days Are here Again," or "Keep Smiling" on a cinema marquee probably would be affected in a positive way, as if they had noticed inspirational messages. In other words, some degree of subliminal psychological impact, however small, would seem to have been a likelihood. Accordingly, the possibility that seeing such titles might have helped public spirits in general during troubled times would not seem to be an unreasonable or remote assumption.

Other film titles carried other messages. For example, numerous feature titles demonstrated expressions of confidence or support as seen in films like *Leave it to Me* (1930), *Help Yourself* (1932), *Forging Ahead* (1933), *A Cup of Kindness* (1934), *A Real Bloke* (1935), *It's in the Bag* (1936), *Where There's a Will* (1936), *Keep Fit* (1937), *Well Done Henry* (1937), *The Show Goes On* (1937), *Miracles Do Happen* (1938), *Come on, George* (1939), and *Let's Be Famous* (1939). Some movie titles conveyed a sense of faithfulness and devotion; examples would include *I'll Stick to You* (1933), *The Pride of the Force* (1933), *Loyalties* (1933), *Servants All* (1935), *Faithful* (1935), *Our Fighting Navy* (1937), *For Valour* (1937), and *The Lion Has Wings* (1939). Obviously, many titles of this kind imperceptibly suggested a sense of national loyalty. Other titles implied a nostalgia for revered traditions [*Lest We Forget* (1934),

147

Table 7.1 Some film titles from the 1930s expressing optimism, joy and happiness and urging an enjoyment of life

1931	Let's Love and Laugh	The Happy Ending
1932	Looking on the Bright Side	Happy Ever After
	Smilin' Along	Say it With Music
1933	Letting in the Sunshine	As Good as New
1934	Love, Life, and Laughter	Love-Mirth-Melody
	By-Pass to Happiness	My Song Goes Round the World
	Happy	Sing As We Go
1935	Things Are Looking Up	We've Got to Have Love
	Look Up and Laugh	
1936	Sunshine Ahead	Everybody Dance
	On Top of the World	The Happy Family
	Full Speed Ahead	Happy Days Are Here Again
	Cheer Up	This'll Make You Whistle
1937	The Sky's the Limit	Sing as You Swing
	Let's Make a Night of It	It's a Grand Old World
	Jump for Glory	It's Never Too Late to Mend
	Wake Up Famous	
1938	Simply Terrific	Oh Boy!
	Climbing High	Save a Little Sunshine
	Keep Smiling	
1939	Cheer Boys Cheer	Full Speed Ahead
	Happy Event	

Those Were the Days (1934), Sixty Glorious Years (1938), and The Good Old Days (1939)] or a hopefulness for a Utopian future [Taxi to Paradise (1933), A Glimpse of Paradise (1934), Anything Might Happen (1934), and Tomorrow We Live (1936)].

But escapist, wish-fulfillment fantasies were also represented in these film titles. Dozens of features had titles with gambling, wishing, or most prominently, luck figuring in the names of movies; Table 7.2 demonstrates this preoccupation which might have related to the public's desire for better luck and happier circumstances.

Many film titles were humorous in nature; puns and parody titles were very prominent. Table 7.3 lists some examples of films with titles that were puns, and 7.4 illustrates some parody film titles.

Such jokes, wordplays, and witty remarks maintained the sense of a cinema as a place of mirth and enjoyment, a haven against the grim reality outside, where a sense of humor did not seem out of place.

These titles, then, effectively provided a blatant public announcement of the uplifting, confidence building, escapist function these movies seemed to be

Table 7.2 Some film titles from the 1930s in which wishing, gambling or luck figured

1930	Children of Chance		
1931	Third Time Lucky	The Sport of Kings	The Chance of a Night Time
1932	A Lucky Sweep A Game of Chance	Lucky Ladies Lucky Girl	The Last Coupon Born Lucky
1933	Hundred to One Double Bluff The Lucky Number My Lucky Star	Just My Luck Lucky Blaze Heads We Go	The Wishbone Up for the Derby Friday the Thirteenth
1934	Lucky Loser Wishes	How's Chances	The Luck of a Sailor
1935	It's a Bet Car of Dreams	Some Day Lucky Days	A Little Bit of Bluff The Luck of the Irish
1936	Once in a Million If I Were Rich Irish for Luck	Pot Luck Unlucky Jim Dreams	Wednesday's Luck Luck of the Turf
1937	Take a Chance Lancashire Luck The Last Chance	The Penny Pool Spring Handicap	Lucky Jade Racing Romance
1938	Double or Quits Luck of the Navy	Follow Your Star	Darts Are Trumps
1939	Lucky to Me	The Stars Look Down	

performing in society. But these messages were not only seen in the cinema foyers; the themes that repeatedly appeared in the films themselves also projected these attitudes.

DEPICTIONS OF DISAPPOINTMENT IN SHOW BUSINESS SUCCESS

A basic concept in numerous British features was the goal of achieving success, either in the form of fame or wealth. Judging by titles alone, the pre-occupation of numerous films centered on an escapist fantasy of large amounts of money; dozens of movies had titles that dealt with cash, fortune, or wealth. Such concerns reflected undoubtedly a desire for financial stability and economic improvement. Table 7.5 lists some of these film titles.

But, interestingly, many of the films that contained stories of wealth and success portrayed such fortunes as being shallow, empty, and unsatisfying. Often the outcome of a rags-to-riches rise for a character in a feature was an unhappy experience in which he or she would realize how much happier circumstances had been prior to the financial gain. The effect of this kind of plot outcome was to suggest to audiences that people were better off with

149

Table 7.3 Some film titles from the 1930s which contained puns

1929	Auntie's Antics	
1930	A Sister to Assist 'Er	
1931	Hot Heir	
1933	Night of the Garter Falling for You [involves mountain-climbing]	I'll Stick to You [concerns a glue inventor]
1934	The King of Whales	Give Her a Ring [about a telephonist]
1936	Apron Fools	
1937	Knights for a Day	
1938	I See Ice Thank Evans	Lighting Conductor [about a bus conductor] Many Tanks, Mr Atkins
1939	Hospital Hospitality	

Table 7.4 Some film titles from the 1930s containing parodies and wordplays

1930	Not So Quiet on the Western Front [*All Quiet on the Western Front*]
1931	Who Killed Doc Robin? [*Who Killed Cock Robin?*]
1932	The Bad Companions [*The Good Companions*]; Mr Bill the Conqueror
1933	Send 'Em Back Half-Dead [Frank Buck's *Bring 'Em Back Alive*] My Old Duchess [*My Old Dutch*]
1935	The Public Life of Henry the Ninth [*The Private Life of Henry VIII*]
1936	Windbag the Sailor [*Sindbad the Sailor*]; Dishonour Bright
1937	Beauty and the Barge [*Beauty and the Beast*]

what they had, and, implicitly, that wishing for riches and fame or even an improvement in one's economic situation was folly.

One type of success frequently used in such rags-to-riches story-lines involved the film industry itself. Perhaps because the lifestyles of movie stars and movie producers were so visible and well publicized, audiences could make this type of success story the object of their fantasies and dreams; accordingly the features that filmgoers saw often provided plenty of opportunity for them to experience the transformation vicariously.

For instance, a melodrama entitled *Lucky Jade* released in March, 1937, had a maid attempting to portray herself as an actress seeking a screen career and getting into trouble as a result. In the film, Mr Marsden, a crusty old collector of jade, decides to give his three servants notice and then has an accident, falling down the stairs after which he is hospitalized with concussion. Betsy Bunn, his parlormaid (Betty Ann Davies), wants a film career

Table 7.5 Some film titles from the 1930s in which money, riches, and cash figure prominently

1930	The Price of Things	Big Business	The Road to Fortune
1931	Tons of Money	Bill's Legacy	Rich and Strange
1932	Money for Nothing	Above Rubies	Money Means Nothing
	Account Rendered	Money Talks	
1933	Money for Speed	Cash	Purse Strings
	High Finance	The Jewel	Strike It Rich
1934	Rolling in Money	Money Mad	Easy Money
	Borrow a Million	Too Many Millions	
1935	Brewster's Millions	Windfall	The Price of Wisdom
	The Price of a Song	Off the Dole	Say It With Diamonds
1936	Millions	Fame	If I were Rich
	Digging for Gold		
1937	The Price of Folly	The £5 Man	The Man Who Made Diamonds
	Fifty Shilling Boxer	Feather Your Nest	
	Change for a Sovereign		
1938	Easy Riches	Penny Paradise	We're Going to Be Rich
	The Villiers Diamond		
1939	The Midas Touch		

and decides to use the opportunity afforded by the temporarily vacant house. She holds a party at which she presents herself as an actress to some theatrical agents she has invited. Marsden's nephew, John, played by John Warwick, and his pal Bob Grant, portrayed by Derek Gorst, who have just returned from Australia, show up at the gathering. Also present are two thieves eager to rob Marsden of the jade and who see in the event an opportunity not only to have access to the stones but also to frame the maid for the theft. When the jade is discovered to be missing the next day, Betsy, who is under suspicion sets out to follow them; at the same time, she is followed by Marsden's nephew and his buddy. The chase that results provides the parlormaid Betsy with far more adventure than she had anticipated, and the underlying message is that she would have been better to have been satisfied as a maid.

One of the more celebrated, if nonsensical, examples of this plot-line was *Okay for Sound*, the first film of the famed sextet of comedians known as the "Crazy Gang," consisting of the teams of Bud Flanagan and Chesney Allen, Jimmy Nervo and Teddy Knox, and Charlie Naughton and Jimmy Gold. The "Crazy Gang" had been so named after a series of successful annual "Hellzapoppin'"-like stage appearances at the London Palladium, which came to be known as "Crazy Week." When the popular revue was translated to the movie screen, a slight framing plot was incorporated. In the story-line the six comedians are "work-shy" street musicians who are given an extra job by a movie producer who needs city types for a movie he is making. But while in costume, the "Crazy Gang" are incorrectly identified as a syndicate of financiers who were to arrive at the studio at approximately the same time; as a result, they are given complete control of the studio, with calamitous results. The film, released in April, 1937, was interspersed with what the *Monthly Film Bulletin* called "cleverly introduced interludes by other music hall experts, such as Lucienne and Ashour, the Robinis, the Radio Three and the J. Sherman Fisher Girls."[1] To imply a serious content to *Okay for Sound*, thus, undoubtedly would be to distort the intent of the film. Naturally, the emphasis in the feature was on humor and farce, in the broad music hall tradition; but the implicit message was that executive positions were not intended for the working classes and that disorder would result if the working classes were put in charge.

The general perception that the wealth and fame of a career in show business carried with it mixed blessings and, often, heartbreak or disappointment was reinforced in several popular features. For example, the summer, 1936 release *One Good Turn* starred Leslie Fuller as Bill Parsons, a kindhearted coffee stall keeper, and Georgie Harris as his assistant, Georgie, and concerns the efforts on behalf of the two stars to keep a stage-struck girl from being cheated by a fraudulent producer. The girl, Dolly Pearson, played by Molly Fisher, is the daughter of Bill's landlady, portrayed by Clarissa Selwyn, to whom the financially troubled coffee-vendor is in debt. In spite of Bill's doubts, the landlady agrees to invest her savings in a stage show so that Dolly can be the star. Bill and Georgie attempt to save her money, become involved improbably with a band of Chinese gangsters, and ultimately help to make the stage performance a success. The image of the swindling producer is a reminder of the disreputable nature of some show-business figures, and a suggestion that the transformation to becoming a success is fraught with perils for unsuspecting, unprepared show-business innocents from the working classes.

This message is much more clearly emphasized in numerous other features, most of which have nothing to do with show business. The theme that good luck or material fortune often brings unhappiness or troubles appears not only in films about the working classes but also in movies about middle-class characters, aristocrats, and even monarchs; it suggests that one should be satisfied with one's lot in life and that success sometimes results in unpleasant changes not only in an individual's circumstances but also in his personality.

A classic example of this film is the musical *Britannia of Billingsgate*, one of the most popular films made in England to be released in 1933; the story concerns the talented wife of a Cockney fishmonger who becomes a film star and whose family is thereby unnaturally disrupted. Based on a play by Christine Jope-Slade and Sewell Stoke, the plot of the film was summarized in four successive issues of *Film Weekly* in the late spring of 1933 prior to the general release of the film in July. The details of the movie's plot are worth discussion because of the attitudes it conveys about success.

In the feature, Violet Loraine plays Bessie "Britannia" Bolton who runs a fried fish stand and whose husband, played by Gordon Harker, is a fish-monger at Billingsgate. The arrival of a movie crew at the fish-market is cause for great excitement, especially to Bessie's daughter, Pearl, portrayed by Kay Hammond, who is a devoted film fan and who reads the fan magazines devoutly. Most of the onlookers strain to catch glimpses of the popular film star Harold Hogarth (Walter Sondes) or the Italian director Garibaldi, depicted by Anthony Holles possibly as a caricature of the popular con-temporary Italian comedy director, Monty Banks. But while everyone else crowds around the shooting location, Bessie, who is uninterested in such foolishness, stays away, singing to herself. A switch in the sound truck is inadvertently thrown when Bessie's bumbling husband climbs aboard the vehicle in an effort to get a better view of the movie crew; a recording is then made in such a way that Bessie's voice is picked up and preserved, unknown to anyone. When the film-makers later hear her voice, they rush back to Billingsgate to find out who sang so beautifully; as a result, when her identity is discovered she is signed to a lucrative film contract and is made a movie star.

Bessie and her family now have far more money than they have ever had before. With the cash, family members are able to indulge themselves by purchasing various long-desired extravagances, not all of which are good for them to have; while Pearl for example, goes on a spree buying fashionable clothes, her brother Fred, played by the young John Mills, obtains a motor-bike for dirt-track racing, in spite of the fact that a leg injury he had sustained prevents any serious competition or prolonged riding. No supervision is pro-vided by Bessie's boastful and cocky husband Bert who obtains a job as an organizer which quickly goes to his head. As well as his newly acquired white spats, striped trousers, and an artificial "superior" accent, he now has all the beer he wants.

Bessie, in the meantime, must be absent from her family because she must stay near the studio; although she is homesick and already recognizes prob-lems with her new success because no one is at home to care for her family, a visit to them convinces her that they all want her to proceed and be a success. Reluctantly, she goes back to work, and the family quickly becomes involved in all sorts of problems.[2]

For example, Pearl, who is infatuated with film star Hogarth, manages to steal his house key. On the night of the premiere of Bessie's movie, Pearl, acting on a fantasy she had read once in a screen magazine, sneaks into Hogarth's lodgings and awaits his return from the premiere. Informed of Pearl's intentions at the premiere by her friend, Mrs Wigglesworth, played by Drusilla Wills, Bessie immediately departs to rescue her daughter, before she can receive the applause of the filmgoers. In the meantime, Hogarth has returned home, and finding Pearl in his bed, is attempting to eject her when Bessie arrives. When Hogarth protests his innocence, Bessie, knowing her daughter's obsession with movie stars, believes him and starts spanking Pearl.

She then learns that Fred is racing his motorbike in spite of the danger of far more serious leg damage. Concerned not only about Fred's safety, but also about her husband's tendency to wager and drink excessively at such events, Bessie hurries off to the racetrack.[3] When she arrives, the race is already underway; Bessie is arguing with her son's girlfriend when Fred's knee, as predicted, gives out, and he has to leave the race. But before anyone can stop him, Fred's inebriated father, thinking he must keep up the family name, takes over the motorbike, and in spite of his inexperience, heads out onto the racetrack.[4] His comic driving and the chase that ensues is climaxed when he goes head over heels into a nearby pond. The Italian director Garibaldi, who has finally caught up with the star of his picture, seeing this performance is so amused that he instantly offers a contract as a comedian to the uninjured but waterlogged Bert; but the fishmonger rejects the offer saying, "I've 'ad all the riot I want. It's me for a good long rest. Work? I'd sooner go back to me fish."[5]

Britannia of Billingsgate was highly publicized at the time of its release as a response to those who had been requesting more films about ordinary people. Though the film hardly could be labelled "realistic" much publicity was circulated about the authenticity of its opening sequence at the fish-market. An article appearing in *Picturegoer Weekly* in March emphasized the film's realism, at least in the opening scenes, noting that, as in the film, a real unit had been sent to the locations to get atmosphere, and real porters had been hired to provide local color as extras. The producers were "nervous" because they feared "that some of the picturesque profanity of the neighborhood would be recorded," though "in practice" the "language was found to be so respectable – though perhaps forceful – that they recorded it without qualms." The article noted that thirty porters were hired to do studio work for a few days though they balked at being made up which they considered to be unmanly; instead they consented to appear "in their scaly overalls and their celebrated iron millinery – those felt hats on which they balance an odd hundred weight or so – preserving their natural untouched complexions." The set design on one of the largest studio floors at Shepherd's Bush studios was a "wonderful full size reproduction of Lower Thames Street with St Mary-at-Hill trailing up into cunning perspective," and it included real borrowed "pair-horse railway vans," crates, and "boxes redolent of the odor of dead sea fruit." The extras, the magazine reported, had an enjoyable time cheering the actors, though they "roused a sarcastic welcome to an actor dressed as a city police-constable who was chaffed unmercifully with local and domestic wisecracks."[6]

The *Gaumont–British News*, the in-house publication for the studio and its exhibitors, sent word to cinema managers while the film was being made in February that this authenticity angle could and should be exploited when the film was to be distributed during the coming summer months as it referred to the

> remarkable replica of the entrance to the market . . . [the] railway carts piled high with fish boxes . . . [and] better than this . . . a company of thirty real porters in all the splendour of their historic leather hats, under which is stored so much rich Cockney humour [and] . . . traditional . . . language.[7]

Indeed, managers followed up this suggestion with imaginative ideas. For example, reinforcing the idea that the film portrayed a slice of working-class life, it publicized the fact that during the run of the film, pictures would be taken of the patrons as they left the theater, and forty pictures would be chosen and displayed subsequently in the vestibule for a prize; the publicity generated by the idea was credited with helping to make the movie even more of a hit than expected.[8] The idea was that, in this way, audience members could in reality, feel what it was like to be a celebrity. Responding to the publicity campaign, the fan magazines gave the feature a favorable buildup. *Film Weekly* told its readers that the film "should be a success" because "it does what critics have been praying for, and filmgoers crying for" by taking "a story of ordinary London people" and telling it "against familiar London backgrounds"; the magazine said that in *Britannia of Billingsgate*, the film-goer "can almost smell the fish in Billingsgate Market," can "get a camera's eye view of London's newest and most elaborate film studios in action," can witness "a free show in a big London cinema," and can observe "all the thrills of a dirt-track."[9] Reviewers, on the other hand, were somewhat disappointed that the movie did not sustain its early scenes of life among working-class street people; many agreed with the comment made in a December issue of the same publication that observed "At the beginning of *Britannia of Billingsgate*, we saw the true comedy of humanity," but asked "why need it have developed into a conventional 'newly rich' comedy?"[10]

The real theme of the film, however, conventional, is the way in which success has an unpleasant impact on the traditional lifestyle of these supposedly "ordinary" English people. The fact that Bessie is also known, perhaps symbolically, as "Britannia" and that her husband is portrayed by the British screen's most recognizable Cockney, Gordon Harker, suggests that the family is to be regarded by the audience as essentially representative of all working-class families. This apparent symbolism makes the family's rejection of success much more potent a message. The dialogue and the actions show why this point must be made.

Bessie's success allows Pearl to put her seemingly harmless fancies into a potentially tragic reality. Without Bessie's screen career, Pearl would have been able to dream of meeting and perhaps offering herself to a movie star, but the likelihood of her actually having the opportunity to compromise herself in this way was remote. With her mother making movies, and unable to supervise her actions, Pearl almost "lost her virtue."

Similarly, where Pearl could have sustained moral or spiritual damage, Fred, being able to acquire his long-desired motorbike, now had the means to suffer physical damage. The implication that Bessie was able to keep Bert in line under normal circumstances was made by his rapid transformation from an essentially harmless, good-humored, if thickheaded, fishmonger to a pompous, unpleasant braggart after she had to leave her family.

Publicity centered on this theme; the studio apparently supplied pre-release stills on the film which were published in an April issue of *Film Weekly* and the text observed that the film's story dealt with a "family threatened with demoralization" because of "the effects of too much prosperity." [11] Clearly the message of the film in the midst of a national economic crisis was that unlimited success did not necessarily mean unlimited happiness. In this case at least, it had meant the disruption of the family and the distortion and even over-turning of some very traditional values.

The rejection of prosperity by Bessie is made fairly clear and is at least implied in the case of the more childish father. When Bessie is finally made aware, by Mrs Wigglesworth, of the disruptions in her family she unhesitatingly abandons her new responsibilities to return to her more traditional duties. When the spotlight at the premier is focused on her seat, she is gone. Later, when Garibaldi runs up to tell her that the premiere was a great success, she responds, "Rats, I've business to attend to"; when he persists in his effort to have her consider contract offers, she dismisses him, risking her career, with the comment, "I don't care; they'll have to wait." [12] Bessie has a very clear picture, in spite of her success, of what aspects of life are most important; she admits that when she was forced to be apart from her family, she was unhappy, worrying about them and how they were taking care of themselves, and when her fears are realized she is swift to abandon her film career. Even Bert seems to be sobered by his experiences, turning down the potential for another film career in the family. The plot may be unrealistic, the motivation may be suspect, and the story-line conventional but the message is clear. The same point is made in dozens of features throughout the decade.

The kind of disappointment possible as a result of the success sought in show business was demonstrated effectively in another variation of this plot, a March, 1936 comedy release entitled *Fame*. In this film, described perhaps inappropriately by one reviewer as a "light-hearted story," Syd Howard plays a screen-struck Yorkshireman named Oswald Bertwhistle, "an inefficient shopwalker with histrionic aspirations who wins a 'Film Face' newspaper competition which entitles him to play the part of Oliver Cromwell in a film"; following a farewell from the entire community, Oswald departs for London.

After the journey, during which he has difficulties with an escapee from jail and problems establishing his identity at his hotel, he appears at the Studio and "proceeds to be the most complete and unmitigated failure as an actor," though "he, alone, is unable to realise this." Assuming that he is "an immense success," he telegrams home about his triumph, and the whole town gathers to greet him; meanwhile, he discovers the reality of his failure, and when he arrives, his old mother, portrayed by Muriel Aked, who has figured out the truth of his experience, "sends him home to make a cup of tea while she explains the situation to the Mayor," who is played by H.F. Maltby.[13] Perhaps missing the basic poignancy of the story the reviewer merely praised Howard's "individual type of humour" observing that "in the opening scenes as the inefficient shopwalker quoting Shakespeare at astonished and indignant customers, he is extremely funny, and his burlesque attempts to portray Cromwell are no less amusing."[14] But the reviewer in *Film Weekly* commented on the "pathos" of the feature with Bertwhistle's being fired from his job and then ultimately learning that he has "just been used as a publicity stunt."[15]

Of course, the film industry often accentuated its star-making ability and appealed to movie fans' dreams of fame and success. In short stories, in fan magazines, and in popular fiction, tales of working-class characters getting a "break" in the movies were common.[16] Throughout the decade, articles told how amateur writers could submit stories to the film studios and become screenplay authors, or, more frequently, how various people could be discovered and become film performers.[17] Similarly, biographical articles intended to publicize British stars often emphasized their humble, ordinary backgrounds. The fan magazines were filled with stories about the working-class backgrounds of various actors and actresses which undoubtedly provided material for many aspiring stars' fantasies. For instance, a publicity sketch in a January, 1938 issue of *Film Weekly* accentuated the point that Barry K. Barnes, the star of *The Return of the Scarlet Pimpernel*, had begun as a lorry-driver and as a clerk, while a similar biographical article in the same publication five years earlier had centered its discussion on the fact that the film star it was describing, the comic Albert Burdon, had risen from a past in the industrial community of South Shields where he had worked as a boilermaker and clerk.[18]

Likewise, the humble, working-class pasts of directors also were considered in publicity articles; *Film Weekly* observed in a late 1930 article that Britain's prominent director, Alfred Hitchcock, had started as a mere clerk, and, the same year, an item in the *Stoll Herald* noted that director Harry Lochman had begun his working life as a newsboy.[19]

Often contests and publicity efforts were geared around the dream of nonprofessional actors and actresses to be "in the movies." Alexander Korda for example arranged for one such talent search in conjunction with the enormous Deutsch Odeon circuit of cinemas in 1937 when he had unknowns appear in short subjects and then gave moviegoers the opportunity to vote on their performances.[20] Similarly, a stunt in 1930 involved a public search for a leading lady to appear in a major British production; this publicity effort occurred eight years before the better known public relations master stroke of David Selznick to find a Scarlet O'Hara for his production of *Gone with the Wind*.[21] Another article published in conjunction with a 1931 film release entitled *Black Diamonds* about coal miners devoted much of the discussion about the feature to the fact that the film would star a young colliery worker and a Yorkshire girl.[22] In fact, an article in *Picturegoer Weekly* in 1932 reassured the public that the film industry was constantly attempting to find new stars in all walks of life.[23]

Probably the most visible evidence of such "attempts to find new stars," though, was a local phenomenon. Throughout much of the decade of the 1930s, neighborhood cinemas would hold regularly scheduled talent nights that came to be known as "Do As You Please" nights; these events invariably proved to be "very successful," and, as one official in the Gaumont–British Film Corporation reported, "resulted in greatly improved business wherever they were run."[24] Dignitaries and public officials received the idea of such contests, with their implications for wish-fulfillment, favorably. For instance, at the "small manufacturing town" of Luton, when such a competition was held at the Palace Theatre, the manager reported to the *Gaumont–British News* that the "Mayor and Mayoress visited the theatre at the invitation of the management and gave the prizes away," at the same time making "a lengthy speech of the excellent idea of the competition."[25]

The types of acts that would appear at such an amateur event rarely displayed the kind of talent needed for feature films. For example, the program at one such competition at the Hippodrome in Wolverhampton consisted of nine acts lasting a total of about forty minutes prior to the film showing; wrote the manager, the performers "were very carefully selected from a large number of entries," and the result was "a good variety program consisting of two singers, one toe dancer, a banjo and piano act, one red-nosed comedian in song and patter, a double twin (man and girl), one whistler (lady), a piano–accordion act, and an eccentric dancer." In fact it was "this latter 'turn'" that "went over very big" and accordingly "was selected as No. 1 for the finale."[26] Other such competitions, such as beauty contests, sometimes even promising a film try-out, also took place on a regular basis at the cinema, and these events were reportedly especially popular in working-class districts like the London East End.[27] But whether or not film careers were really likely to result from such competitions seems to have been unimportant to the aspirants because, as one manager noted, just the dream of such a try-out enabling a person to "maybe win fame and fortune" was sufficient; accordingly, these talent contests "have improved business considerably wherever staged."[28]

Clearly, the implicit assumption in such articles and in such publicity efforts was that the average man on the street could achieve stardom in the film industry if he had talent, and if he worked hard to utilize his abilities effectively; a spring, 1931 article in one fan magazine made precisely this point when it noted that "lorry drivers, engineers, railroadmen, chauffeurs, store clerks, pugilists, artists and dock jumpers have climbed from sweaty servitude to the glory and independence of stardom." The piece concluded that screen performers "it would seem, are merely working men (and girls) in luck," adding that the "majority of the screen's great personalities were cradled in mean streets and back alleys" with "very few blue-blooded aristocrats among the stellar fortunes." [29]

But, if the film industry, in various ways, emphasized its fantasy qualities, just as much publicity was directed at the difficulty and problems involved in becoming an actor or actress. In an article in *Picturegoer Weekly* entitled "How to Get in the Talkies – If You Must," writer E.G. Cousins wrote of the prospects one faced in trying to become a screen performer. Cousins said that he knew "scores of people who have tried to break into the movies" but that "most of them are starving because there is not enough extra work in British studios to give more than a handful of them a bare living"; he added that while some of them are "quite as handsome as any star on the screen," truthfully "the lucky ones – have gone back to their jobs" because they have realized that the "odds are about the same as those against your becoming a cabinet minister." [30] An interviewing secretary at one of the film studios noted in one fan magazine how painful it was to have to disappoint so many movie hopefuls; she was quoted as saying in reference to the would-be stars, "some of them look so downcast and miserable when I tell them that they cannot have an interview that I can hardly bring myself to turn them away." [31]

And even when an aspirant found his or her way onto a movie set, the fan magazines noted that the pay was hardly likely to result in a fortune. In the summer of 1933, an extra seeking to work his or her way into the film industry could expect to earn a guinea for eight hours of work and a half-crown for six hours of overtime; as one publication observed, this one pound sixteen shillings for a day's work "might be the first [employment] of the year." [32] P.C. Mannock was more specific in a January, 1930 article telling readers that if "they contemplate breaking into pictures" they should realize that their names "will be put on a list of thousands of names, most of whom . . . will naturally be [preferable]" because of their previous experience. Even if "in a month or so," they may be chosen, the experience might not prove to be particularly rewarding. For instance, they might be told to wear "an evening dress" which the extra is required to provide and to "catch an early morning train" for which they might have to "pay a three shilling fare." Then they must purchase their own meals, assuming "there is time," and then "hang about all day in sudden and extreme changes of temperature in very mixed company" only to "get shoved and herded, loiter or dance looking bright and gay, until 7:30 or later." Finally, they "then [must] wait a long time in a queue for the magnificent sum of a guinea, out of which all . . . expenses have to be met – including two shillings commission to an agent." Because of the uncertainty, the call may be "next day, or next week, or in two months time, tramping up and down agents' stairs hopelessly." Even for those "with influence," Cousins warns that "one shilling for a 'test' . . . is almost out of the question." Even more discouragingly, Cousins concludes, when a "big crowd [is] wanted" in order "to save money" the production firm will hire "at five shillings a day some of the unemployed from the local exchange."[33]

Studio executives also seemed to have been painfully aware of the disappointment and suffering experienced by real life Oswald Bertwhistles whose "ambition outstrips [their] cinematic fitness"; as one industry spokesman wrote, "there is a pathetic side to this desire to win fame by way of the screen which aspirants altogether fail to realise."[34] One studio executive whose "instructions" were "to turn away 'hopeless' cases" commented that, while his observations were "brutal," he felt "that ninety-nine percent of the gushing aspirants who do apply for film work ought never to have left home"; he observed that the "most pathetic of all" was "the 'village beauty' up from the country" whose "contours usually bear comparison with a cottage loaf" whose "face is plain" but who "will have the nerve to tell you that everyone 'back home' thinks she's the spit of Greta Garbo." The executive noted that "whether they are country girls, town girls, factory girls, or the elegant, *refeened* type," they all believe themselves to be "wonderful" for movies, "even those with sticking-out teeth." And such hopeful vanity was not confined to females. For instance, one "male applicant" had "once said to me: 'Seriously, don't you think I'm dashed handsome, what?'" thereby showing that men are just as self-deceived. The executive explained that this particular man was a "down and out" who had no experience but who was "hard-up" and "urgently in need of a guinea"; he concluded that the would-be film actor was "under the false impression that he looked like Lewis Stone."[35] Such stories were funny, but they also were pathetic. The same executive added that sometimes letters came from hopefuls with enclosed snapshots, and he said he "couldn't help feeling sorry" for a girl from the industrial North who had sent a letter which read that she had "always been told" she would "make a hit" on the screen. Though her boy had indicated to her that she has "the loveliest hair he's ever seen," the photograph she supplied did not show her hair properly. Even more pathetically, the executive quotes her as writing "Don't take any notice of the lumps on my legs because they're varicose veins" but adding "they won't show if I wear a long dress."[36]

Another studio official, responding to a column in the *Daily Express* calling for more native English actresses from "amongst the ranks of the everyday working girl," observed that even when the improbable happened, that is, when someone was discovered and made a film in a featured role, there was a "grim side to the story"; if she was unsuccessful, there were few options "when she is 'dropped.'" Much of her life will consist of "seeking jobs in the various agencies that abound" or of "hanging around studios in the hope of being remembered and 'spotted.'" Too often, "the thrill of the glittering lights in her blood" will dim the "loss of the really comfortable office job" she "once held"; unless she has the luxury of a good home and comfortably fixed parents behind her, "if she is dependent upon her earnings" her life may never be stable. The executive concludes that since "positions in the business world are not too easily obtained," an individual "should think well before giving it up for exclusive romance in Shadowland."[37]

The "Do As You Please" competitions were no less brutal; the music hall antecedents of these pre-film entertainments were apparent in the audience participation in the judging of the amateur performers. One cinema manager from the Empire Theatre in Mile End reported that "the enjoyment of the whole affair is not complete without . . . [allowing] the audience full license to show their keen dislike of any particular competitor";

> In this district the nature of the "bird" takes many forms, and they are certainly very hearty in character (perhaps "fruity" would be a better term) and add to the enjoyment of all concerned. Among many incidents that caused great enjoyment, was the case of one entrant, Miss Emily White, who at first interview, said she would sing "O.K. Baby" and she was "going to paralyse 'em, Guvnor" . . . Emily, with costume and silk hat complete, managed to scrape through six bars of her song, when the audience nearly "paralysed" her. Another gentlemen who considers that Al Jolson never knew how to put over a song, attempted to render "There's a rainbow round my shoulder," with the result that even when a water bladder (from the "gods") hit him full in the face, and he was "blacked-out," he was still attempting to finish the first verse.[38]

The manager conceded that the "entrants . . . must be imbued with a keen desire to win, at the time of entry, and during the course of the competition," but he did not seem to care what happened to their feelings.[39]

But publicity about the stars emphasized that many of them had experienced much adversity and many setbacks. For example, a discussion of the career of Flora Robson in *Film Weekly* underscored the fact that she had "lived several lives" filled with "poverty, illness, disappointment and uncertainty," all of which "she has had her share of."[40] Many stories of this nature promoted the idea of persistence of effort as the key to some stars' success; for instance, a career article on Aileen Marson observed that she had failed repeatedly, but "kept trying" and, in the process, "had become a success," and another story, about Annette Benson, highlighted the fact that she had struggled and had been unemployed for a long time, but eventually had become a star because she did not give up.[41] Even the effervescent Cicely Courtneidge was depicted in at least one article as a star who had "triumphed over self doubts and adversity."[42]

This attitude valuing perseverance apparently was not lost on the film-going public; one letter-writer from a working-class area in London observed in a note to *Film Weekly* in the spring of 1933:

> Filmgoers can learn a valuable lesson from the stars. We continually read that these glamorous beings of the screen are really quite ordinary folk, and that scarcely one in a hundred has succeeded without a hard fight. We, too, can imitate them and refuse to be discouraged by set backs, but continue to give our best to the task in hand.[43]

So the anecdotes not only enabled working-class moviegoers in a curious way to identify with persons working in the motion picture industry, but also provided them with an understanding of the suffering necessary in aspiring to the glamor and fame of a film career. On the one hand, these articles suggested that success of this kind in show business was achievable only rarely and only at an enormous and often painful cost. At the same time, they provided a glimpse beneath the glittering, make-believe surface of the film business, allowing the movie-going public to feel closer to those exalted figures of envy and admiration in discovering that they too had had to overcome adversity in their lives.

THE SCREEN PROBLEMS OF ROYALTY, WEALTH, AND POWER

Show business was not the only form of success shown to be troublesome. Other instances of good fortune were portrayed as equally unsatisfactory in a variety of different movies.

For instance, if a filmgoer thought it would be desirable to be a member of royalty, a movie like the May, 1936 historical release *Tudor Rose* might have convinced him otherwise. Directed by Robert Stevenson, the film featured British child star Nova Pilbeam as the ill-fated Lady Jane Grey and concerned the political machinations during the reign of Edward VI that led to the attempt to make her queen after his death. Reviewers praised the production, noting that "the direction is sensitive, sympathetic, and intelligent, and the subject is treated with dignity and restraint"; the acting in the film was said to be "excellent" with Nova Pilbeam "delicate and appealing" as the tragic heroine, and Cedric Hardwicke "arresting" in his portrayal of the "ruthless, scheming" Earl of Warwick.[44] Graham Greene, in his review for the *Spectator* however, objected to the characterizations in the scenario, particularly that of the three child protagonists; he disliked the portrayal of Edward VI as a "preparatory schoolboy who wants to get out in the garden and play with a gun," the depiction of the "weakling Lord Guildford Dudley" as a "tender and romantic 'boy husband,'" and especially the notion of Lady Jane Grey "herself, perhaps that nearest approach to a saint the Anglican Church has produced" and also "a scholar of the finest promise" herein "transformed into an immature child" who is "glad to be released from tiresome lessons."[45]

But it was precisely these elements which transformed the film into a dramatic and, as one commentator has written, "most moving" tragedy; according to Ivan Butler, the essence of *Tudor Rose* was "the loneliness and pathos of royal pawns, used merely to further the schemes of unscrupulous power-seekers" with the fundamental tragedy that of "the young Nova Pilbeam as the pathetically vulnerable political puppet."[46]

Indeed, the advertising for the film emphasized the child's naivety and innocence; as one theater promoted the movie, *Tudor Rose* was the story of "Lady Jane Grey who died for England and knew not why."[47] Had the child characters been portrayed as less innocent, their victimization as a result of the political scheming would not have seemed as ruthless and tragic. The implicit effect of the story, and especially of the ultimate execution of the girl, was to demonstrate again that royal figures did not necessarily have carefree, desirable lives. While the historical portrayal of Lady Jane Grey as a school-girl tired of her studies or of Edward as a schoolboy wanting to escape the pomp and circumstance of the position he must endure by going out to play may have been questionable, the result was to provide audiences with an opportunity to identify with otherwise remote royal figures. Remarkably popular, *Tudor Rose* was subsequently reissued and was voted the second most popular film of 1936 in the *Film Weekly* poll; Nova Pilbeam's perform-ance was also honored by fans in the same poll as being the best of 1936.[48]

Similarly, the far more famous Alexander Korda production of *The Private Life of Henry VIII* made the historical Henry a real person, incarnated in the figure of Charles Laughton who won the Academy Award for his perform-ance. The overwhelming and somewhat surprising success of this relatively low budgeted feature has been discussed by numerous authors, but the basic idea of portraying the monarch in what John Grierson has referred to as the "tradition . . . of the native vitality and vulgarity of the English music hall" must be given at least partial credit.[49]

At least one frequently told story about Korda's inspiration for the film suggested that he was influenced by the working classes in his selection of a film topic; the story suggested that upon the director's arrival in England in 1931, he overheard a taxi driver singing the famed music hall tune by Harry Champion, "I'm 'Enery the Eighth, I am," and immediately decided to make a film about the king. According to the director's nephew, whether true or not, "this story was much beloved in England, and Alex repeated it so often that it became part of his legend"; even "Winston Churchill used to tell it to people with glee."[50] However, Korda continued, "if the music hall song had any significance for him, it lay in the fact that the English had already trans-formed Henry into a comic figure of folk legend"; since the recently pub-lished, best selling biography of the monarch by Francis Hackett had made Henry a current subject of attention, Korda naturally was attracted to the historical figure.[51]

The working classes could identify with the sixteenth-century king as he was depicted in the movie, in spite of his being a remote figure obscured in myth and legend. As Korda's biographer Karol Kulik has written, "Laughton's puffed-up monarch . . . alternately vulgar, morose, forceful, and vulnerable" essentially "was a sympathetic character."[52] More specifically, Kulik suggested that the film was "an exploration of Henry's humanity" in which the direction replaces the "stereotyped image" of the Tudor monarch as some kind of a "Bluebeard" with an "equally stereotyped characterization of a 'vulnerable man'"; Kulik asserts that while the film's protagonist "is tender and sentimental as well as blustering and vulgar, the emphasis is always on Henry as 'victim' of manipulating women." To clarify this concept, "the two wives who don't comfortably fit into the image . . . Catherine of Aragon and Jane Seymour . . . are both disposed of as quickly as possible."[53] After the death of Jane Seymour, Henry no longer seems "in control of his life," and "at the film's close Henry has become just another hen-pecked spouse whose wife, Katherine Parr, natters away at him about watching his diet and keeping warm."[54] Henry's displeasure at the arranged marriage with the unattractive Anne of Cleeves also contributed, as Michael Korda has noted, to the sympathetic portrayal; when the King heads to the bridal chamber, he "turns to his advisors (who persuaded him to undertake this dynastic match) and the audience, and exclaims, 'The things I do for England!'"[55] Clearly, he would have been happier without his monarchical responsibilities.

This point was made repeatedly throughout the feature; for example, after Edward is born, the king leans over his crib at the grinning infant and says softly, "Smile while you may. You'll find the throne of England no laughing matter." His inability to enjoy privacy, even when sneaking off for a liaison with one of his ladies in waiting, is a particularly frustrating royal disadvantage for the monarch, and his irritation at having to marry Anne of Cleeves for purposes of state underscores his unhappiness. This displeasure is expressed more dramatically when, at one point, prior to his marriage to Catherine Howard, while attending a state dinner, Henry appears morose. One of his advisors comments "Your Grace is sad tonight; what can we do to cheer your Grace?" The King asks, "What could you do to cheer my loneliness?" The advisor answers, "Your Grace is lonely; that is the penalty of greatness, sire." The King replies, "Greatness. I would exchange it all to be my lowest groom who sleeps above the stable with a wife who loves him." Even a stableboy was more fortunate in this sense than the monarch.

In a variety of ways, *The Private Life of Henry VIII* suggested a parallel relationship between the King's unhappiness and the daily problems of the working classes; that is, the monarch's private life was no more successful than that of his subjects. The opening section of the movie showed how the troubled King, with his new wife, Jane Seymour, experiences the same kind of daily marital annoyances that any husband might have encountered. For instance, at one point, the exuberant girl breaks into a state meeting and

164

interrupts the session to show off her new dress; barely restraining his anger, the King mutters, "Softly, sweetheart, we have affairs of state here," to which she cloyingly and annoyingly whines, "Henry, you haven't said a word about my dress." As if to underscore the point, the scene then shifts to shortly after the execution of Anne Boleyn; an obviously working-class couple are discussing the death of the Queen. The conversation between the two characters demonstrates that the King is not the only one to have marital irritations. The husband observes that "one must admit, she died like a queen," and the wife agrees, adding "Wasn't that frock so divine?" When the husband responds, "Was it? I didn't notice," the wife indignantly replies "You wouldn't notice," adding that she hasn't "had a new dress in a year." The husband then tells her sarcastically, "Alright, you shall have one for your execution," to which the wife answers by slapping him. Michael Korda noted that the quality in the story of Henry VIII that "appealed" to Alexander Korda was precisely "the paradox of Henry's being henpecked by his wives like any ordinary husband," and it was this aspect of the production which was underscored in the advertising; for example, one cinema billed the film as "The Amazing and Amusing story of Bluff King Hal's Loves and Wives until he became a henpecked husband – Henry VIII's jest – Life was just 'one d— wife after another.'"[56]

The dialogue in the film emphasized that the working classes were to pity the King's predicaments; for example, in one section, the kitchen staff discussed the monarch's marital problems. The exchanges are intercut cleverly as the staff make comparisons between food and the king's marriage difficulties. For instance, the pastry cook notes that "marriage is like pastry – one must be born to it." Another cook thinks that the institution is more like "these French stews" which are a problem because "you never know what you're getting until it's too late!" The gossip continues with one cook astonished that the King's advisors would be "trying to make him marry again," and another, referring to Anne of Cleves, adding "I'd like to see them, after that German business." The sympathy expressed in the kitchen workers' scene clearly is for the King. Says one woman, "After all, you can't say he hasn't *tried*!" and another adds "Tried too often, if you ask me, to say nothing of the side dishes – a little bit of this and a little bit of that!"; she concludes knowingly "What a man wants is regular meals" which provides the cook an opportunity to chime in, "Yes, but not the same joint every night!" Puns abound in the latter part of the scene when the cook observes "A man loses his appetite after *four courses*"; the monarch "got into the soup with Catherine of Aragon, cried stinking fish with Anne Boleyn, cooked Jane Seymour's goose, and gave Anne of Cleves the cold shoulder!" to which another kitchen worker remarks, "God save him! It's no wonder he suffers in the legs."[57]

Likewise, the ending of the movie, with the aged King sneaking bites of a chicken leg against the wishes of his wife, similarly suggests a relationship between the monarch and the filmgoers in which "Laughton establishes a certain roguish complicity between himself and the audience as if asking [them] . . . to overlook his previous . . . transgressions because of his age and infirmities." [58]

Charles Higham, in his biography of Laughton, attributed the film's success in making the King a pitiable character to Laughton's superb performance. Higham argues that Laughton depicted the monarch as "grandiose, vainglorious, and pathetically dependent on women"; he contends that the feature's most effective sequence and Laughton's "finest moment" occurs "when he breaks down upon hearing of Catherine's adultery with his favorite, Thomas Culpepper." Higham observes that Laughton depicts the monarch "clasping his beringed fingers to his face," and then after "[weeping] copious tears . . . looking suddenly resolute as we know that he will have both of them sent to the block." By contrast with earlier in the film, Higham remarks that in the final scene Laughton's portrait of the monarch is that of "a fond, foolish man, feebly plucking at a capon which in his youth he would have torn apart with his bare hands"; now "henpecked by a hatchet-faced Catherine Parr," he addresses "the audience with a sad, ironical farewell." [59]

Laughton's wife, Elsa Lanchester, has observed that her husband researched extensively for the role to give his performance legitimacy.[60] Kurt Singer in his biography of the actor cited a specific example of how Laughton's research and especially his empathy contributed to the pitiable character of the historical figure he portrayed. Singer comments that the "greatest scene" in the film was the sequence in which Henry aged fifty-one, tries "to impress his new, young and sexy wife, Catherine Howard" with his continuing vigor and manliness by entering a wrestling match. After triumphing over England's best wrestler, he demonstrates "that he is still in the prime of his life . . . only to collapse afterward"; now "weak and sick," he attempts to avoid his bride, fearing "that she will see him 'old and defeated,'" which, of course, gives her the opportunity to meet with her former lover. Singer describes the wrestling scene as "marvelous," noting that Laughton had even sought instructions from a professional wrestler; but he contends that "in the scene that followed," Laughton "really surpassed himself" with the "greatest bit of acting he had ever done." Laughton "could enter into it fully" because "he knew what it was like to fear rejection on physical grounds" having "gone through many such experiences in his younger days"; Singer concludes that if indeed Laughton was so believable in this feature, "it was because in many a scene he played himself." [61]

Not unexpectedly, Korda's film and especially Laughton's performance received uniformly enthusiastic praise from the British public. *Film Weekly* honored Laughton's Oscar-winning performance by rating it the best of the year, and fans voted the film second best of the year.[62] But most impressive was the film's financial impact; reissued frequently, it was one of the most successful in the history of the British film. Costing about £58,000 to make, the film earned over a half million pounds in its first year of distribution and as late as 1964 was still bringing in ten thousand pounds a year in revivals.

The movie's immediate impact was to persuade financiers that British films could succeed internationally and could compete on the world market. It thus signalled an increase in film investment and production in Great Britain. New studios were financed, and with new facilities came new jobs. Korda himself developed a mystique of success and even the national government is reported to have been instrumental in encouraging the Prudential Assurance company, which became his primary backer, to build Korda new studios at Denham at a cost of more than a million pounds.[63] While these new studios were being constructed, Korda continued using Elstree Studios for his films, some of which he directed and some of which he produced. Korda developed lofty intentions with his new agreement with United Artists as a statement at that time indicates:

> The aim of the new organization will be . . . to bring back to England any great English artistes who have not heretofore produced in this country . . . and other artists of world wide importance, although not of British origin will be invited to join and to produce their pictures here.[64]

Thus, according to Ernest Betts, Korda's Henry VIII and its legendary profits have usually been credited with "having launched the boom in the mid thirties"; certainly the film's reception in Britain and the United States "made it easy for other producers to raise money for production," though it also facilitated the process by which a number of "get rich quick promoters, some from the continent" were able to combine ventures "with City underwriters in wild cat production schemes." As Betts concludes, in this way, Korda "with a single picture, may be said to have achieved what the 1927 Films Act was designed to do but failed to do"; that is, by his example, Korda "increased production in British studios on a considerable scale."[65] It has been argued that in the end, the boom (or as British film-maker Basil Wright called it, "the filmic South Seas Bubble") may have back-fired in that its lack of stability scared some investors; but most film authorities agree with the conclusion reached by Ian Dalrymple who, writing on behalf of the British Film Academy, hailed the Korda Henry VIII feature as "the key film in the history of British Cinematography."[66]

If in British films royalty or the nobility sometimes found fortune and success to be mixed blessings, other, less aristocratic, characters also encountered a variety of difficulties when they gained wealth or other advantages. Indeed, an improvement in their fortunes often led characters to unpleasant alterations of their value systems. For instance, in the spring, 1936 release *First Offence*, the son of a wealthy Parisian medical man becomes spoiled by his riches and becomes involved in a car theft gang; starring the young John Mills as Johnnie Penrose, the son of Dr Penrose, played by

H.G. Stoher, the film also features Lilli Palmer as Jeanette, Johnnie's pretty girlfriend. When Johnnie's father refuses to allow his extravagant son to have the new luxury car that has been obtained for him, as a lesson to teach him that he must stay out of debt, the young man, who has just made a date with the beautiful Jeanette, decides to "steal his own car from the new owner [to whom the car had been sold by his father] in order to be at his rendezvous on time"; this action leads him into trouble when other criminals witness his theft and thereby induce him to become a member of their gang. When Jeanette's own financial distress impels her to participate by becoming a decoy for the thefts, the two young lovers find themselves caught up in a web of criminal activity. Ultimately, the couple are hunted by the police after attempting to take a stolen vehicle with forged documents to Marseilles. When the car is wrecked, Johnnie urges that the two seek a new beginning. He goes back to Paris to find Jeanette's brother Michael, but the police raid the gang's hideout and Michael is shot. Johnnie is able to get away only through a fortunate meeting with his wealthy father and a recognition that he has learned a valuable lesson; he returns to Jeanette, and the couple board a ship for a voyage to a new beginning. Reviewers objected to the uneven quality of the picture and the fact that the "tone of the film changes from Paris in springtime to an intricate and sordid story of car thieves"; the fact that Johnnie enters a life of crime "of his own volition weakens our interest in him, and not even his love affair with Jeanette, whom poverty has forced [into desperation] . . . can justify his sudden plunge into a life of crime."[67]

One of comic Leslie Fuller's film vehicles, though in a lighter vein, contained the same basic concept, that is, the idea of riches can alter one's values, not necessarily for the better. In *The Last Coupon*, a summer, 1932 release, Fuller is a coal-miner named Bill Carter who thinks he has won twenty thousand pounds on the football pools. As a result of the expected money, Bill's normally frugal lifestyle suddenly changes, and his wife Polly played by Mary Jerrold has to try to keep Bill from wasting his prize. Ultimately Bill discovers, after treating all his friends, that he had absent-mindedly neglected to mail the coupon, thereby invalidating his prize. One of the writers on the film, Frank Launder, has observed that while the feature was "based on a corny but . . . successful North of England play," by Ernest Bryan, it nevertheless proved to be "a corny box-office success."[68] The reviewer in *Picturegoer Weekly* praised the movie, noting the way the expected fortune affected both protagonists. The critic characterized the feature as being "typically British humour of a domestic order which, if you like broad music hall methods, will give you all the laughs you could want"; the review went on to observe that Leslie Fuller had gained a "wide following with his own particular type of robust humour" which merited the reception he receives and that in the role of his wife, Polly, Mary Jerrold was "excellent." In particular, the review praised "a dream sequence in which she imagines she and Bill are trying to break into society" and a boxing match "which Bill – thinking he is now wealthy – helps to promote"; overall, *Picturegoer Weekly* concluded "the mixture of slapstick and satire is judiciously blended to please the popular taste, and it will not fail." [69]

The film's popularity prompted a re-make, *Spring Handicap*, about five years later, directed by veteran film-maker Herbert Brenon with Will Fyffe featured as the miner now named Jack Clayton who experiences similar problems after, this time, inheriting a substantial legacy. Much better known but with a very similar plot was Carol Reed's October, 1938 release, *Penny Paradise*, which was recirculated in subsequent years. Set in Liverpool, the story concerns a tug-captain named Joe Higgins, played by Edmund Gwenn; with his daughter Betty (Betty Driver), Joe has "two ambitions" in life: he wants "to become skipper of the *Mersey Queen*, the newest tug on the river," and he hopes "to win a football pool." One Saturday evening, he believes he has accomplished his second goal when he checks on the results of the games. In order to celebrate, he provides a festive party at a local pub, but problems develop when he bickers with the widow he has been courting portrayed by Marie O'Neill, and when Betty is romanced by a young fellow who is interested in her because of the money. Joe also finds himself at odds with Aunt Agnes, played by Ethel Coleridge, who believes that she is entitled to a portion of the prize. The question becomes irrelevant when Joe's mate, Pat (Jimmy O'Dea), reveals that he neglected to post the coupon. But Joe's clever daughter manages to provide good news when she arranges to have Joe's bosses assign him to the position he has always wanted, as captain of the *Mersey Queen*.[70] Reviewers were taken with the film; said the *Monthly Film Bulletin*, "the human and homely story" is performed "with disarming simplicity, and in a friendly atmosphere" by a "group of completely ordinary North Country people" who "react in characteristic fashion to what is a daydream to thousands of their fellows – the winning of a football pool." The review praised the "good character drawing," the "unaffected and telling dialogue," and the "many clever directoral touches" by Carol Reed which "help to make up the total excellent effect." [71]

Occasionally in a film of this nature it was political values that were altered by new-found success. Another Herbert Brenon directed production, *Yellow Sands*, released in the summer of 1938 and based on the play by Eden and Adelaide Philpotts, was a rural comedy in which Marie Tempest plays Jennifer Varwell, an elderly woman trying to decide how to distribute her four thousand pounds of savings among a group of grasping relatives. Set in Cornwall, the story revolves around a group of communist fishermen led by her nephew to whom she decides to leave her money. The *Monthly Film Bulletin* found the film to be "an enjoyable picture and a pleasant holiday from the stereotyped" in spite of the fact that "there is as marked a social difference between Jennifer and her relatives as between her over floral cottage and the austere stone dwellings of the fishing hamlet which form part of the excellent landscape photography." [72]

169

One of Alfred Hitchcock's less characteristic features, the December, 1931 release *Rich and Strange* had a similar theme which was developed by Hitchcock himself; as John Russell Taylor has summarized the essence of the story, "the basic notion is that an ordinary suburban couple" receive "a lot of money from a rich uncle which changes their life, mostly for the worse, as they set off, two innocents abroad, to go round the world on a cruise."[73] At the outset of the film, the husband and wife, Fred and Emily Hill, played by Henry Kendall and Joan Barry, are essentially bored with life. But with their unexpected fortune they are able to associate with a somewhat wealthier group of people on the cruise. Accordingly, as Taylor put it, "soon they are not so innocent," exhibiting a "snobbery" that "leads both of them into trying to appear much grander than they are"; Fred, is "particularly" affected when he "becomes enamoured of an obviously bogus princess." Taylor concludes that "much of the comedy on shipboard turns on social humiliation of various kinds," so it does "not come as a complete surprise when things take a nasty turn."[74]

Additionally, though Hitchcock was an effective "critic and satirist" of "the drab home life Fred and Emily left," as Donald Spoto has observed, Hitchcock was "perhaps most critical of those who invite chaos by an inordinate yearning for excitement"; noting that the "exotic ports of call, glamorous Paris, the mysterious East, and the fabric of life aboard ship provide the Hills with little final fulfillment," Spoto explains that Hitchcock has demonstrated how "their adventures only show them how worthless riches can be."[75] Contemporary fan magazines were cognizant of this implication of the story of *Rich and Strange*; *Picturegoer Weekly*, for instance, noting that the film concerned "two ordinary people and the effect of money on them" told its readers that after they saw the film "you will think twice [about wanting to win the Irish Sweepstakes]."[76]

But probably the best known example of a film where success altered the protagonist's value system was the Victor Saville production of A.J. Cronin's novel, *The Citadel*. In this celebrated late 1938 release directed by King Vidor, and re-released in subsequent years, Robert Donat plays the idealistic and enthusiastic Dr Andrew Manson who begins his first assignment in "dire financial straits" in a Welsh mining town.[77] But his enthusiasm quickly turns to disillusionment when he learns of the unsanitary conditions which the local bureaucracy tolerate. In time, however, after saving a seemingly stillborn infant and after laboring through a typhoid epidemic, he proves his dedication; late one night, with an equally dedicated, though perennially inebriated colleague, named Dr Denny (Ralph Richardson), who has become his best friend, he blows up the offending drains in a gesture of radical defiance forcing an end to the constant struggle with typhus. Soon, Dr Manson takes a position with the Miner's Medical Aid Society and marries the local schoolteacher, played by Rosalind Russell. Though successful in saving several workmen in a mine disaster, his constant poverty and a running conflict with a corrupt union official lead to dissatisfaction. But when superstitious miners, aroused by the corrupt union leader, destroy his laboratory, and with it considerable promising tuberculosis research he had been conducting, the doctor and his wife leave the community, to try practise in London. There after a year-long struggle to make ends meet by serving the poor, he encounters an old student chum named Freddie Lawford, portrayed by Rex Harrison, who is a society doctor catering to hysterical, wealthy, hypochondriatic matrons. Freddie encourages him to give up his service to the poor and take on a society practise.

Gradually, Dr Manson is seduced into this fashionable Harley Street lifestyle, and "his idealism fades before the line of easy money obtained from wealthy women with imaginary complaints." [78] His loss of ideals is demonstrated when he turns down a proposal from Dr Denny who has come to London to suggest that he and Manson form a clinic for humanitarian and scientific purposes. Distraught by his friend's now apparent corruption, Denny gets drunk and is seriously injured in a traffic accident. When an incompetent society physician named Dr Emery (played by Cecil Parker) bungles the operation on his friend, killing him, Dr Manson, realizing that Denny was right and that he has betrayed his profession, denounces the surgeon. Manson risks his career further by removing one of Emery's patients against his wishes and by taking the child to a researcher specializing in the child's disorder who is disliked by the medical community. Brought before the medical board for possible suspension of his license, Dr Manson delivers a stirring speech, and ultimately he and his wife return to a mining community to continue their research on silicosis.

In *The Citadel*, the pernicious effect of wealth on the protagonists' value system was all the more pronounced for its social implications. Raymond Durgnat has suggested that

> the film is something of a link between two genres, or rather cycles: Warners' biographies about medical idealists (notably Doctors Pasteur and Ehrlich . . .), and two other Welsh-mining films: Ford's *How Green Was My Valley* and Carol Reed's *The Stars Look Down*, both of which it anticipates.[79]

Whatever the antecedents of *The Citadel* were, or whatever were its connections to other movies, there can be little question that the film was seen as an attempt to bring a motion picture with a social content to British screens; Vidor himself told interviewer J. Danvers Williams in a December, 1938 issue of *Film Weekly* that he saw the film as "the *Potemkin* of the thirties." [80] However overstated his comment may have been, back in 1938, the film was perceived as a potent feature, loaded with social commentary. For instance, the *Monthly Film Bulletin* referred to the film as "a forceful – although at times intensely emotional – attack on certain abuses which, it is claimed, exist in medical life today." [81] In fact, the social content was thought to be so strong at the time of the film's release that in order to avoid any libel suits, a disclaimer had to be added by the producers at the outset of the film saying that the conditions depicted in the movie no longer existed.[82]

Part of the reason for the film's effectiveness, in this sense, was the realistic atmosphere of the movie. Vidor used real miners and shot part of the film on location which, as John Baxter has noted, made, especially "the first half [of the feature] . . . rich and precise."[83] This quality of *The Citadel* was especially praised at the time of the picture's release. For instance, in an editorial, one of the fan magazines applauded the movie as breaking new ground in British film production. *Film Weekly* emphasized that one feature of the production "which will strike British filmgoers keenly [is] the realistic view in the early scenes of poverty in a mining district in Wales"; as Dr Manson visits the poorhouses and as the miners respond to him, audiences will "have the impression of seeing a new aspect of England on the screen." The article emphasized the film's reality and commented that "it seems about the first time that we have been shown the rows of box-like houses, their humble but often cheerful and independent occupants, naturally and without undue comic or dramatic emphasis"; it concluded that since "*Film Weekly* readers have so often and so angrily complained that British films only show working-class people as figures of fun," audiences seeing *The Citadel* accordingly "will eagerly welcome the slice of British life" portrayed in this production.[84]

Certainly, the authenticity of the movie's settings were highly praised at the time of the film's release. In *Film Weekly*, the reviewer of the feature commented that "the first half of the picture, with its graphically captured Welsh mining town atmosphere is the most impressive part of the film."[85] The *Monthly Film Bulletin* added that "some of the passages, notably when Manson is fighting for the life of a new-born child in the Welsh village, and the last scene before the council of doctors, are probably among the most moving which have yet been seen on the screen"; the review praised "the settings, particularly those of Welsh life and scenery," as being particularly "convincing," and it applauded the film's director for "skillfully [maintaining] a balance between the pitfalls of a too obvious emotionalism on the one hand and dry-as-dust propaganda on the other."[86]

This realistic quality made what Ivan Butler called "the theme of idealism eroded by success" all the more effective in the movie.[87] But additionally, Robert Donat's performance, which earned him an Academy Award nomination, also must be credited, and indeed, it has been called "magical" and "one of his finest"; to make believable the previously idealistic Dr Manson's corruption, as in "the marvelous sequence where, [as] a successful doctor, he concentrates on ordering an *hors d'oeuvre*, only half hearing a distressed mother who is telling him about her daughter's serious illness," was essential for the film to work dramatically and to be as convincing as it was.[88] Whether or not *The Citadel* was an overt social statement or just an effective, realistically mounted melodrama, its portrayal of success as an influence that corrupts personal values is undeniable.[89]

Changed values were not the only unpleasant by-product of riches. Often in these films, wealth brings unwanted involvement with crooks and other undesirables. For instance, in several early comedies, specifically working-class characters, find that fortunes they have obtained recently attract the attentions of criminals. In *Hotel Splendide*, a March, 1932 Jerry Verno comedy directed by Michael Powell, a clerk inherits a resort hotel built on a field where an ex-convict buried his money, and the inevitable encounters with criminals trying to recover the fortune lead to humorous mayhem. In another feature with a similar plot-line, *The Innocents of Chicago*, the protagonist inherits a dairy in Chicago which is used by gangsters as a front for a bootlegging operation; directed by Lupino Lane, this April, 1932 release was based on the Reginald Simpson – J.W. Drawbell play, "The Milky Way." A Gordon Harker comic vehicle, *This is the Life*, released in September, 1933 concerned teashop owners who inherit money but find themselves harassed by gangsters from Chicago. An amusing variation of the plot was the May, 1936 release *Not So Dusty* in which veteran music hall comics Wally Patch and Gus McNaughton portray Dusty Gray and Nobby Clark, a pair of Cockney dustmen who are given an antique book which is discovered to be valuable, as a reward for finding a brooch; but the good fortune is soon complicated when an unscrupulous book collector subsequently hires a gang of thieves to recover the priceless volume, and the "misadventures" that follow, according to the *Monthly Film Bulletin* provided "good light entertainment of an unsophisticated type . . . in the [comic] music hall tradition . . . [with] the Cockney atmosphere . . . well and consistently carried out."[90]

In another farcical comedy, the June, 1937 feature, *The Penny Pool*, just the prospect of winning a fortune leads a factory girl into trouble, in this case resulting in her being fired temporarily from her job. In this "musical comedy extravaganza," popular music hall entertainer Duggie Wakefield and his gang (Billy Nelson, Chuck O'Neil, and Jack Butler) appeared as a group of crazy "down and outs" who help the victim recover her prize-winning football coupon from a "wicked foreman" who, after "unjustly" accusing her of filling out the coupon during "working hours," had fired her and then taken the ticket for his own; when the ticket "wins first prize . . . Douglas and his gang unmask the villain, and see that the heroine gets her rights."[91] The reviewer from the *Monthly Film Bulletin* concluded that in associating the film's topic to the "Penny Pool," a subject both "topical" and "popular," the "producers have run no risks" because "they have given the public in abundance what the public has shown it likes." The review also praised the comedy as being "of the homely down-to-earth slapstick variety, with plenty of burlesque and knockabout fun" particularly in sequences where Wakefield and his gang can "reproduce their well-known garage scene, and in addition obtain work in a factory, join the local defence corps, and [be] medically examined"; the reviewer concludes that "the film is music hall entertainment at its brightest and funniest, and as such should have a wide popular appeal."[92]

Sometimes, however, the criminals who victimized characters that had won fortunes produced grimmer consequences. In *Dead Men Tell No Tales*, the colorfully titled March, 1938 melodrama based on Francis Beeding's novel *The Norwich Victims*, a middle-aged matron named Miss Haslett (Christine Silver) works at a preparatory school run by the supercilious young Dr Robert Headlam, played by Emlyn Williams. When Miss Haslett finds that she has won a jackpot in a French lottery, she travels to Paris to receive her prize. In London, she encounters a peculiar hunchbacked Frenchman with a beard named Louis Friedberg who makes his living as a moneylender. He murders her and has his secretary pretend to be Miss Haslett in order to obtain the cash prize. A police inspector named Martin, portrayed by Hugh Williams, is assigned to the case; he is also the fiancée of Elizabeth, Headlam's cousin (Leslie Brook). When a clue is discovered at the school, the young master who accidently found it is subsequently discovered having been hanged in the garage. The disappearance of Friedberg is thought to be related to the burned out remains of a car with a body inside until Elizabeth notices that a satchel found nearby is the property of Headlam, who then abducts her in his auto. Inspector Martin gives chase, and Headlam is pursued to the school garage where he commits suicide. Clearly, the film implies that the lottery prize had brought with it death and madness; in this suspenseful production, reviewers praised Emlyn Williams's "remarkable performance" in the "dual role [which] . . . dominates the whole [production]."[93]

Equally frightening was the January, 1937 release *Love from a Stranger*, directed by Rowland V. Lee and based on an Agatha Christie novel and a Frank Vosper theatrical adaptation. In this thriller, Carol Howard, played by Ann Harding, similarly, is the winner of a lottery. She argues with her fiancé and ends up marrying a suave gentleman named Gerald Lovell, portrayed by Basil Rathbone who had simply come "to view her flat." While "her dreams of luxury and travel are realised," when she arrives home with the intention of acquiring a cottage in the country, her acquaintances realize that "something is wrong." Ultimately the audience learns that Gerald has a history of murdering wealthy women, a fact explained to Carol by her former fiancé Ronald Bruce (Bruce Seton). When Gerald wants her to sign some papers which he claims to be a mortgage transfer, Carol finds out that the document, in truth, would turn over her entire fortune to him. A cat and mouse game ensues between the two with Gerald attempting to murder her, and Carol ultimately causing Gerald to have a heart attack after she convinces him she "too has committed . . . murder" and has poisoned his coffee.[94] Again the implication was that those who won fortunes ought to prepare themselves for consequences not totally desirable.

Occasionally in a lighter comic vein, what seemed to be a vast improvement in a character's situation through an inheritance or legacy turned out to be an onerous burden as a result of a condition of a will. In *Boys Will Be Girls*, a Leslie Fuller summer, 1937 comic release, Fuller's character, Bill Jenkins, will inherit a fortune if he can quit smoking and drinking; his endeavors to accomplish these goals prove to be almost more complicated than the inheritance is worth. Another farce comedy released in February, 1938, *Make it Three*, involved an even more troublesome condition of inheritance. A bank clerk named Percy (played by Hugh Wakefield) finds that he has been named beneficiary of a fortune on the condition that he must serve a three-month term in prison. The term cannot last longer than three months nor can it be less than three months. Seeking the assistance of an ex-convict who is planning a bank heist, Percy becomes involved in a bungled burglary and is caught and sent to jail. However, his demanding fiancée, played by Diana Beaumont, now insists that unless he marries her in three months, the engagement will be broken off. Percy's cell-mate Big Ed, portrayed by Edmund Willard, also creates a problem for him by insisting he participate in a jailbreak. Outside prison, he uses the opportunity to marry his girlfriend, thereby meeting her obligations before returning to prison with "both [of his] difficulties . . . of course, finally overcome." [95]

Another unlikely plot occurred in the first film of the long-running and extremely popular "Old Mother Riley" series which lasted over fifteen years with veteran music hall comic Arthur Lucan portraying his stage character, the old washer-woman, Old Mother Riley. With his wife, Kitty McShane, playing the old woman's long-suffering daughter, the series lasted well into the fifties with more than fifteen films made during that time. However, the first feature, perhaps not surprisingly, introduced the character, almost tangentially. In this first film, a rich match manufacturer named William Briggs places a provision in his will that he will leave his fortune to his widow and son on the one condition that they make a houseguest of the first individual selling his product that is encountered on the street, and that they allow the person to remain for no less than six months. If the guest chooses to depart for any reason whatever, the inheritance will go to the Briggs's sister and her husband. Of course, the first match-seller they meet is Old Mother Riley who agrees to accept the invitation as long as she can bring her daughter with her. This conflict results in "strange and embarrassing incidents," but the widow is all the more determined to keep Old Mother Riley from leaving, much to the irritation of her sister-in-law and her husband, who "conspire with the butler to stage a fake robbery" and then "make it look as if the old match-seller was the thief." In court, Old Mother Riley expresses dissatisfaction with the conduct of her defense, so she "takes the law into her own hands, and with considerable shrewdness shows up the conspiracy"; the film's ending is made all the happier with "an improbable romance between her daughter and the son "of the match king." [96] Though reviewers did not think much of *Old*

Mother Riley audiences loved it; the film was re-released continually over the next ten years.

In some features, wealth was accompanied in the plot by unwanted pests. Occasionally the object of this harassment was matrimonial in nature. For instance in the February, 1932 comedy, *Lord Babs*, based on Keble Howard's 1928 stage farce and directed by Walter Forde, Bobby Howes plays a ship's steward who inherits an earldom, but as a consequence, finds himself unhappily engaged to the daughter of a pork-pie merchant; to discourage the relationship, he pretends to revert to childhood. In a similar story, *Her Imaginary Lover*, a November, 1933 comedy release based on A.E.W. Mason's novel *Green Stockings*, Laura La Plante is Celia, an heiress who creates an imaginary fiancé to discourage fortune hunters.

In *Get Off My Foot*, a late 1935 comedy release, Max Miller "the cheeky chappie" plays Herbert Cronk, a Smithfield meat porter, who gets into trouble after a fistfight with his pal, Joe, played by Reginald Purdell. In the midst of the conflict over the barmaid, Matilda, portrayed by Vera Bogetti, Joe falls from the riverside footpath into the water. Herbert jumps in after him to save him but is unable to locate his friend. His fears that he might inadvertently have caused his friend's death are fed by Matilda who insists that Joe will be wanted for murder. However, Matilda is secretly working with Joe in an attempt to blackmail Herbert. To prevent the arrest he fears, Herbert runs away and becomes a tramp; for a while he works chopping wood and doing odd jobs. Eventually he becomes a butler on the estate of the impoverished Sussex family of Major Rawlingcourt (Morland Graham). Herbert falls in love with Marie, the family maid, portrayed by Chili Bouchier. But when the Major learns that his butler is really an heir to a half-million pound legacy from an Australian uncle, he tries to marry his daughter Helen, played by Jane Carr, to Herbert to gain his fortune. The balance of the film, written in part by Frank Launder, concerns Herbert's efforts to repel Helen and thwart that relationship with her and to develop his love affair with Marie. One reviewer commented that one of the best qualities of the film was its satirical approach, specifically the "opportunities . . . for a few digs at the hunting and riding crowd."[97]

Swindlers and annoying relatives often seemed to be attracted by the newly obtained inheritances of some film protagonists. In the May, 1937 comedy *Merry Comes to Town*, Zasu Pitts is Winnie Oatfield, a middle-aged spinster who is troubled by greedy relatives who think her small legacy is actually much larger than it is. Another comedy, a June, 1935 release, *Hello Sweetheart*, which was based on a George M. Cohan play, "The Butler and Egg Man," concerned a young poultry farmer, Henry Pennyfeather, played by Claude Hulbert, who gains a small inheritance. The money attracts a group of unscrupulous American businessmen led by Gregory Ratoff who are seeking a victim and who think they have found him in the naive Mr Pennyfeather. Gradually, the farmer "is flattered and inveigled into financing a film production; he attempts to interfere in the direction, is swindled, and left in the lurch," though he "eventually manages to turn the tables on his former associates."[98] Usually in these films, in spite of the difficulties, the protagonist would prevail.

But some films showed that fortune could bring special problems. For instance in *A Lucky Sweep*, a March, 1932 comedy, the title proves to be ironic. Diana Beaumont is Polly, a maid, who decides to buy an Irish Sweepstake ticket for her fiancé, Bill Higgins, played by John Longden, even though she knows that he is opposed to all forms of gambling; but when the ticket wins, Bill's beliefs cause others to think he has stolen the ticket, and much explaining must take place before the subsequent complications are cleared.

In one of Anthony Asquith's early features, the summer, 1933 release, *The Lucky Number*, the effort to gain a fortune proved to be worthless. In the plot, Clifford Mollison portrays Percy Gibbs, a professional football player whose girlfriend has "jilted" him, which inspires him to take a break and have a holiday. After returning to London from Paris, he attends a funfair where he encounters Winnie, a sideshow worker played by Joan Wyndham to whom he is attracted. When the two of them go to a pub for a drink, Percy discovers his wallet which was full of his money is now gone. The pub's proprietor, depicted by Gordon Harker, agrees to take in payment a lottery ticket Percy had purchased in France. The next day, to his consternation, Percy finds it was the winning ticket, and he and Winnie attempt all sorts of subterfuge to retrieve the ticket from the publican. When they succeed, Percy hurries to Paris – only to learn that the promoter of the lottery has stolen all of the money. Percy returns to playing football and marries Winnie.[99]

To give the film a sense of authenticity, Asquith used members of the Arsenal Football Club and shot many of the scenes on location at a football match or outside a real pub. Contemporary reviewers praised the film for precisely these qualities. The reviewer in *Film Weekly* observed that *The Lucky Number* had a believable understanding of ordinary people "reminiscent of René Clair."[100] The documentary filmmaker, Basil Wright, added in *Cinema Quarterly*, that he noticed a "firmness of touch about the main sequences" and he recommended "for special attention the pub scenes" that are "witty, authentic and beautifully directed and cut". He praised Gordon Harker, observing he "has never been in better hands" and especially cited "in the best sequence in the film," with excellent use of "natural sound," the scene in which a "superb Yorkshireman (Frank Pettingell) whom Asquith, in incredibly few feet, gets blindly, disgustingly, obscenely, but above all gorgeously, drunk."[101] This sense of believability provided the movie with a feeling that the characters were real; this truthful tone meant that the implicit message about the trouble involved in pursuing riches was all the more effectively portrayed.

In a few films, the problems resulting from success or good fortune were somewhat bizarre. An eerie, fantastic quality could be found in the December, 1933 Sound City release, *Eyes of Fate*; in this film, Allan Jeayes is a book-maker named Knocker, who through some unknown circumstance comes to possess a copy of tomorrow's newspaper, and uses it to win a fortune at the races. But in the end, in the newspaper, he reads of his own death.

Much better known, however, was Alexander's Korda's production of the H.G. Wells short story, *The Man Who Could Work Miracles*, about the humble little draper's assistant, George McWhirter Fotheringay, played by Roland Young, who "suddenly finds he has the power to work miracles". The film was described perhaps incorrectly by the *Monthly Film Bulletin* as a "sociological comedy," and was in some respects a summation of this theme in British movies in the 1930s.[102] The opening of the feature, as effectively described by Graham Greene in his review of the film in the September 4, 1936 *Spectator*, suggested the one-in-a-million chance of success for the ordinary working man. Greene describes "a dark handsome colossus [brooding] obscurely through a starry night"; he is "Our Brother, the Giver of Power," and after discussing the inadequacies of the planet Earth and its pathetic creatures with his two celestial brothers, the audience is shown a Kentish inn and a floor-walker at the local drapery "whom the Giver of Power has decided to endow with miraculous gifts, so that he may learn what really lies in the heart of a small mortal creature."[103] Extending through the sky an enormous hand with outstretched finger, the Giver of Power says "I will choose anyone . . . this little man for instance" and the little man selected is the meek Fotheringay.

Initially, Fotheringay has no idea what to do with his gifts, and the "mir-acles" he does perform "are hardly above the level of conjuring tricks" such as "the automatic tidying up of the draper's shop or removing a girl's freckles."[104] But Fotheringay is dissatisfied. Because he is a "decent little fellow at heart" he is eager to "benefit mankind," but he soon realizes that "it is impossible to help one section of the community without hurting another." Suggestions come from many associates. His supervisor at work and a local banker endeavor to use his powers for financial profit. A minister at a local church suggests idealistically that he use the powers for the creation of a modern Utopia, but the plans are impractical. As an example, he urges Foth-eringay to reform a tough-minded old colonel by changing his supply of whisky to something "non-alcoholic" and "unpleasant" and "by converting his sword and rifles into ploughshares and other agricultural implements." When this effort is rewarded by the angry colonel attempting to shoot him, Fotheringay comes to understand that it is impossible to "please all the people all the time"; accordingly he creates a huge castle from which he will try to prepare "a better world for that neglected being 'the man in the street.'"[105] Thus, the humble working man, in his frustration, has symbolic-ally rejected the existing world; as Graham Greene wrote, "badgered by busi-ness, by conservatism, by religion to make *their* world," the "little man" represented by Fotheringay "rebels" and announces he "will make his own [world]"; summoning "before him all the great men, soldiers, politicans, and lawyers," he "gives them till day to form a plan for a peaceful society."[106]

But even the "world's greatest minds, past and present" insist that devising "a blueprint for a harmonious and peaceful society" is not an easy task, and Fotheringay in his frustration has given them only until the morning to formulate their plan.[107] "When the Reverend Mr Maydig (Ernest Thesiger) protests that the time is too short, that the sun is already setting," Fotheringay becomes outraged.[108] Somewhat foolishly, "to demonstrate his own power" to them, the clerk ". . . orders the world to stop rotating"; naturally, "universal chaos ensues."[109] With the earth literally coming apart around him, the terrified Fotheringay suddenly realizes the inadequacy of his wisdom to deal with his gift; understanding that power and wealth, for all one's good intentions, can have horrible consequences, he cries out, "Let everything be as it was before," and suddenly, the chaos comes to an end. As the reviewer in *Picturegoer Weekly* observed, the clerk "surrenders [his power] for good and all – and very glad he is to do so."[110]

No clearer statement of the implicit messages in these films could be found than in *The Man Who Could Work Miracles*. George McWhirter Fotheringay, the typical ordinary man, when granted success in god-like proportions could only misuse his ability. The suggestion the film carried was inevitably weighted toward the *status quo*. "Let everything be as it was before," Fotheringay shouts both to the gods that granted him the power and to the audience that wished it possessed the power, and all will be well. Reviewers generally rejected this very overt philosophizing as well as the philosophy. Said *Picturegoer Weekly*, the frequency with which characters "expound Wellsian philosophy" was so great "that one is left regretting that there is so little of the jam of entertainment value to so much of the powder of sociological diatribe, especially as the author's doctrine seems to be one of despair."[111] The *Monthly Film Bulletin*, though gentler in its criticism, still felt the film consisted of far too much message; commenting that in its "original form," the *Man Who Could Work Miracles* was "an arousing little tale, subtly but lightly treated"; however with the "large propagandist element" that has been "superimposed" on the film, the story becomes "heavier and at the same time less convincing." The comic element which was "spontaneous and effective" in the original story has been "pressed too far into the background by the propaganda"; the review suggests that the film should have paid "less attention to the crudities of propaganda" and "more to the niceties of construction" which "would have made this a smoother unity" though it concedes that "some of the propaganda undoubtedly has its own value."[112]

But by far the film's most savage critic was the leftward-leaning Graham Greene. Criticizing what he referred to as "a sea of abstractions, couched in Mr Wells's embarrassing poetic diction," Greene called the film "pretentious" and described the Wellsian philosophy as "muddle, a rather too

Wellsian muddle"; he concluded that with Wells's "childish love of fancy dress" exhibited by the "little man as dictator of the world [going] most improbably Tudor," and with a "touch of sexual vulgarity" represented by "a beauty chorus of Kentish concubines suspiciously reminiscent of Mr Korda's idea of Henry VIII's wives" the result is an "entertainment, sometimes fake poetry, sometimes unsuccessful comedy, sometimes farce, sometimes sociological discussion," but "without a spark of creative talent or a trace of film ability." [113] But if critically the film and its not-so-implicit theme was rejected, commercially the feature did not do badly, particularly in the United States of America, though, it must be conceded that many filmgoers undoubtedly went to see the spectacle. However, critically unacceptable the film proved to be, *The Man Who Could Work Miracles* was popular enough to earn a reissue some years later; but more importantly, the film was the clearest and certainly most spectacular expression of a constant and continual theme of British cinema in the decade.

In this section, then, the variations on the cinematic theme of "the bitter fruits of success" have been considered. From success in movies, societal success, political success, and material success to the infinite power of George McWhirter Fotheringay, the sometimes pernicious impact of these seeming benefits were explored in dozens of British features in the 1930s. Table 7.6 reveals the frequency of this theme.

Table 7.6 Films in which success or good fortune produces problems or unhappiness

Year	Proportion of the films released	%
1929	31 of 86	36.0
1930	26 of 99	26.3
1931	42 of 134	31.3
1932	39 of 150	26.0
1933	44 of 181	24.3
1934	45 of 183	24.6
1935	38 of 185	20.5
1936	86 of 219	39.3
1937	70 of 211	33.2
1938	66 of 158	41.8
1939	40 of 98	40.8

The figures are impressive. In three years, (1929, 1931, and 1937) one of every three movies made in England related this theme in some variation, and in four other years, (1930, 1932, 1933, and 1934), the ratio was one of every four features released. In 1936, 1938, and 1939, almost two of every five films released suggested this concept; only in 1935 did the figure drop as low as one in five productions.

Table 7.7 Films in which success or good fortune
produces happiness

Year	Proportion of the films released	%
1929	13 of 86	15.1
1930	17 of 99	17.2
1931	16 of 134	11.9
1932	19 of 159	12.7
1933	33 of 181	18.2
1934	36 of 183	19.7
1935	30 of 185	16.2
1936	42 of 219	19.2
1937	39 of 211	18.5
1938	41 of 158	25.9
1939	42 of 98	42.9

These figures are not to suggest that success and fortune were never viewed as producing unqualified happiness. But the figures in Table 7.7 are substantially smaller. Thus, as a rule, British films suggested to their audiences that good fortune should be regarded warily and with caution; time and again, these feature demonstrated that filmgoers who were not well situated in society did not really need to envy those who were more successful.

8

THE EMPHASIS ON COOPERATION AND SELF-SACRIFICE

Cooperation and self-sacrifice were greatly admired and valued in British features during the Depression era. These characteristics repeatedly could be found as themes in British film, as Tables 8.1 and 8.2 demonstrate; in all but two years approximately one of every three movies in the decade involved working-class characters banding together to help one another, and, though the fluctuation was substantially greater, self-sacrifice as a theme figured in an equally large number of features. In three of the years, the total topped the two in five mark, and in one year, though admittedly an unusual year, the total approached one in two.

The numerous variations producers developed from these ideas and the frequency with which such concepts appeared in movies suggested, again, that an implicit message was being delivered to moviegoers. Whether intentional or not, the point seemed to be that in dealing with a crisis or problem, if people banded together to help one another and if they made sacrifices for one another, whatever difficulty they encountered could be overcome. Such a philosophy had implications then as a proper approach to a more extensive emergency such as a nation-wide economic Depression.

Cooperation, especially among working-class characters, was expressed in films in a variety of ways. The diversity of features with this theme might best be approached by examining the work of two prominent individuals in the film industry, one a director and the other a performer, whose films usually exhibited this quality.

JOHN BAXTER AND THE THEME OF COOPERATION

A director whose work has been neglected for too long, and who seems to have been especially devoted to this theme was John Baxter. His movies almost invariably provided vivid examples of what could be accomplished when working-class characters got together to help one another. Having directed almost fifty motion pictures, the best known of which probably was the 1941 filmed version of the stage play *Love on the Dole* starring Deborah Kerr, Baxter was nevertheless a forgotten figure by the time of his death in 1975 at

Table 8.1 Films in which working-class characters
band together to help one another

Year	Proportion of the films released	%
1929	31 of 86	36.0
1930	30 of 99	30.3
1931	26 of 134	19.4
1932	35 of 150	23.3
1933	57 of 181	31.5
1934	61 of 183	33.3
1935	70 of 185	37.8
1936	75 of 219	34.2
1937	73 of 211	34.6
1938	55 of 158	34.8
1939	37 of 98	37.8

Table 8.2 Films in which self-sacrifice figures as
theme

Year	Proportion of the films released	%
1929	42 of 86	48.8
1930	24 of 99	24.2
1931	31 of 134	23.1
1932	42 of 150	28.0
1933	40 of 181	22.1
1934	74 of 183	40.4
1935	57 of 185	30.8
1936	69 of 219	31.5
1937	85 of 211	40.3
1938	50 of 158	31.6
1939	36 of 98	36.7

the age of 79. Film historian Jeffrey Richards has argued eloquently and convincingly in a short retrospective review of two of Baxter's productions that the director's career should be re-examined by film scholars; Geoffrey Brown and Anthony Aldgate have taken an excellent first step in this direction with their 1989 study of Baxter's films which centers around the theme of what they quite appropriately refer to as Baxter's "common touch."[1] But another useful approach, and perhaps a more workable one for discussing Baxter's films is to examine the general theme of cooperation.

A good illustration of Baxter's work was an early 1934 feature entitled *Say It With Flowers*. The film had an essentially simple plot. As the review in *Picturegoer Weekly* observed, *Say It With Flowers* was "of the same 'family' as *Doss House*," (also directed, significantly, by Baxter); that is, the film was "a slice of London's market life and of those folks who earn their living in the market."[2] Specifically, the story concerned Kate Bishop, a flower vendor, played by Mary Clare, who is the "uncrowned queen of the market" and her husband of forty years, Joe (Ben Field) "who makes his daily journey [with a donkey] to Covent Garden to buy the flowers." When Kate is absent one day because of an illness which the doctor "insists" must be treated with a "seaside convalescence," she and her husband face a serious dilemma because they have no money; Joe must sell his donkey and speaks to his friend Bill, who runs the fish and chip shop, about his problem. Bill and the other market people plan a fund-raising event for Kate and Joe with a concert involving music hall stars such as Florrie Forde, Marie Kendall, and Charles Coburn, and the "evening is a bumper success."[3] The reviewer concluded that the story notwithstanding, "the enjoyment of the picture depends ... on the characterization," and he added that "there is more entertainment in this unambitious film ... than in many alleged super-productions," provided that the audience has no objection to "Cockney humour."[4] The *Monthly Film Bulletin* added that "the many characters are well drawn ... [in this] very human and well handled ... study of coster life ... and each contributes his quota of Cockney wit and humour."[5] In commenting on this "plotless" style of Baxter's features, Richards has observed that "structurally the films eschew the conventional linear narrative completely" with plots that are "no more than slender threads, woven into a colourful pattern of incidents, bits of business, snatches of dialogue" and with a "style" that is "anecdotal" but whose "effect is a sympathetically recreated panorama of everyday life" with "extensive details of working-class life" and of "the people's entertainment, the music hall."[6]

But while the setting of the film with its lovingly recreated street market and the friendly exchanges between the realistic characters provided a potent and effective picture of working-class life, to put such a simple interpretation on the feature would be understating the point. *Say It With Flowers* had the subtitle, "A Human Story," after all, and even the "modes of speech, topics of conversation and authentic-sounding catch phrases" which Richards contends were used to establish atmosphere, at the same time related to the theme. At the outset, Kate demonstrated her deference to the gentry and stage performers by observing "in my opinion, the higher they are, the nicer they are"; but later, after the onset of her illness, she despaired that no help could be expected from them, commenting, "I wonder if those folks who is high up in the world realise what a few pounds means to people like us."[7] Even politicians received gentle criticism from her; as she pointed out to an unemployed worker, "It don't seem to make much difference who's in and who's out; they do nothing except draw their £400 and try to look intelligent."[8] Richards cites such quotes as atmosphere, rather, they seemed to underscore the need for community effort.

This kind of story, then, about simple people joining together in some kind of decent human endeavor, was a common theme in Baxter's films; in a curious way, the methods he used to film his productions oddly mirrored the philosophy such movies implicitly set forth. In *Say It With Flowers*, Kate's friends organize their concert plans secretly to prevent her pride from being damaged, and decide to ask old music hall stars for help because, as one stall-keeper observes, "they have always looked after our class." As Richards has noted correctly, the "almost tangible rapport" that the music hall performers "establish with the audiences" is derived "partly [from] the songs which, with their memorable tunes and simple sentiments, constitute a folk memory" of "past joys and sorrow shared"; but he observes that the rapport also comes from their own identities which are "themselves, embodiments of a tradition, comforting reminders of a continuity, comradeship and common humanity." [9]

Baxter's knowledge of the music hall and its stars was first-hand: a former theatrical manager, Baxter had worked for years with touring shows before gaining a cinema name with his work on two, early, low budget productions, *Reunion* and *Doss House*, both of which have been discussed elsewhere. Baxter immediately displayed a unique fascination for what other directors might have dismissed as the "dregs of humanity." But Baxter was interested in what John Montgomery referred to as "the men of the streets and the gutter, who might seem to the casual observer to be men of yesterday with no future, but who were in fact down, but not out"; with compassion, warmth and "rich sentiment," Baxter's visual approach was to focus on the people he saw in real life, evoking their humor, explaining their problems, and reminding filmgoers that these were the individuals and characters from society who should not be forgotten. Employing music hall veterans and street performers, photographing them with little make-up, and making certain that their clothing was authentic, Baxter endeavored to create a realistic vision of "humanity crowding together for warmth and comfort" and using "the "humour of the down-and-out," their "only protection against a society which had little use" for them. Montgomery characterized Baxter's cinematic style by noting that "in his innocence of film methods," he concentrated on "[moving] his camera freely up and down the lines of faces, in and out among the players, in their rags and newspapers, their sacks and tatters." [10]

When these atypical directorial tastes were exhibited for the first time in *Doss House*, his "semi-documentary" style resulted in a favorable public response, and "the film made a handsome profit." [11] With subsequent successes, Baxter attracted a degree of attention. Given a "free hand" by producer Julius Hagen, in announcing his plans for *Say It With Flowers*, Baxter observed that his chief goal was "realism" and in this film, he wanted to do a Cockney story; accordingly, he said, he had "wandered about the East End," and "picked up ideas and atmosphere" for his production, a practice he continued throughout his career.[12] And, significantly, in the same publicity statement, Baxter said his new film would have "No Stars." [13]

There was a reason for this practice; Baxter delighted in hiring out-of-work ex-music hall performers, many of whom were nearly destitute, to appear in his films. As one commentator in *Picturegoer Weekly* observed in 1934 about his hiring practices, Baxter's "chief peculiarity" is his knack of "[conjuring] up film actors out of the empty air, as it were," referring specifically to "stage veterans whom no one in the studios has even heard of before"; his "secret" is that he once had been a "variety agent," and consequently "knows practically everyone in the music hall world" so that "when he conceives a character he has (from long practice) an immediate inspiration as to who will best fit the part ... even if he or she has never done a day's film work before." [14] In a sense, like Frank Capra or John Ford in America, this English director assembled something of a repertory company for his films out of this group. Perennials like George Carney, Nellie Brown, Edgar Driver, Johnnie Schofield, Mark Haley, Harry Terry, Vi Kaley, and countless other music hall artists were seldom out of work when Baxter was shooting a film in the mid thirties. As one grateful veteran stage performer reminisced,

> All these people ... and all of us have good reason to thank John Baxter for his constant employment and encouragement over the years. It was a fact that if you stood in the queue outside the Baxter and Barter casting office at 91 Regent Street in those far-off middle thirties years, either J.B. or Arthur Woof [his casting assistant] would come along and do their best to fit you into one of the films being made at Shepperton on Twickenham .... And every Christmas, J.B. sent out hampers of food to the fifty or more extras, the crowd artists who were at the bottom of his employment list – the ones he hadn't been able to engage – who lived in and around the buildings ... behind the old Shaftsbury Theatre and the fire-station. Few producers and directors had his particular common touch, or cared so much for out-of-work variety artists and minor players during the days of the Depression. And it is no coincidence that some of the titles of his films reflected his sympathy for the neglected – *The Common Touch*, *Lest We Forget*, *Doss House*, *Men of Yesterday* ... and *Music Hall*.[15]

Like the story-line of his *Say It With Flowers*, Baxter's actions demonstrated a belief that a solution to problems of poverty could be found with such concerted efforts, and the loyalty he inspired among his group of regulars, at least on a theatrical level, did nothing to contradict this attitude. During the making of *Say It With Flowers*, touching reports circulated about how on visiting the sound stage during production, "the first thing you would have heard was the whole caboodle of old time music hall artistes," "veterans fighting hard to restrain their emotions" at being able to "hear cheering again." [16]

But aside from his creation of a virtual stock company, other numerous parallels suggest that John Baxter was a sort of English Frank Capra (though without the fame). It was said in fact that Baxter preferred Capra's films, when he himself needed entertainment.[17] Like Capra, Baxter's philosophy was "that humour was the best way of making a serious point, and he also felt that Depression audiences did not want humourless tracts lecturing them on a state of affairs they knew only too well."[18] At one point, he was quoted as saying, "if you can make them laugh, you can make them think." Writer John Montgomery observed an effective illustration of this approach, noting that in one feature, Baxter wanted to depict children playing their games in the "cobbled streets" of an industrial neighborhood. In the scene, he was trying to underscore the need for recreation and playing fields in the major cities of Britain, where youngsters had no recreational areas and must accordingly find their fun dodging traffic in the dangerous streets. Despite the seriousness of the issue, Montgomery observes, "Baxter knew that the best way to put over this [idea] was by means of a comedy 'gag,'" so he began the scene with a cricket game under way in a yard with the wickets painted on a wall and "the group of working lads enjoying their lunch-hour game"; the bowler delivers the ball, the batsman hits, and the "ball soars away out of the picture." Freezing at the sight, "the players stand still and wait silently" until "suddenly there comes a crash, followed by the tinkle of broken glass." Immediately, the game "is abandoned, as all the players [scatter] in different directions."[19]

Capra's self-stated concern for the "small man" was even echoed in the title of one of Baxter's films, a spring, 1935 release entitled *The Small Man*, of which unfortunately, no print seems to exist. Accounts in contemporary publications suggest that this feature shared the general theme of community cooperation. In the story a group of tradesmen in a town in the country find themselves "gradually being squeezed out by the advent of chain stores"; when "an offer from a big concern" to purchase the site occupied by the small shops finally arrives, all but one of the interested parties are ready to capitulate, "but Mrs Roberts, the draper, holds out in spite of all arguments."[20] Ultimately encouraging her colleagues to stand together against the chain store, "her obstinancy proves to be a blessing."[21]

Like that of a typical Capra hero, Mrs Roberts's individual integrity inevitably served to mobilize the group; and the "villains" in Baxter's film, like so many of Capra's classic stock opponents, as typified usually by character actor Edward Arnold, were pompous, de-humanized corporate figures of authority who mindlessly seemed to ignore their responsibilities to their fellow man. For instance, one scene from *The Small Man* easily might have been Capra's. In the sequence, the shopkeepers unite and travel to London in order to discuss their situations with the arrogant business executives who are endangering their small stores. Impressed by London, the shopkeepers initially find themselves somewhat overwhelmed by the size of the edifice in which their appointment is to take place. Montgomery notes, "Baxter made his little group ... walk along imposing passages into an immense hall" where "the woman with the general store, the fish-shop proprietor, the baker, and the man who ran the hardware shop looked insignificant in the entrance to the magnificent offices"; however, "once inside the boardroom their courage and sense of humour returned, and they were able to win a tough fight."[22] Through Mrs Roberts's efforts, "they are offered far better terms than they were originally projected," and the big-city chain is forced to capitulate.[23] Here again, as in Capra, was the theme of country decency, honesty, and strength opposed to city cynicism and sophistication.

Again, reviewers praised Baxter's portraits of real people. In a favorable account of the film, *Picturegoer Weekly* observed that "it is the individual characterizations which form the main source of interest" particularly praising "Walter Amner, as a fishmonger's assistant," and Edgar Driver as the fishmonger, and also noting that "as David, the ironmonger, a Welshman Roddy Hughes is excellent, while George Carney is in great form as a Cockney barger"; the review concludes that the film's "humour is induced naturally and is unforced, and the human touch all through makes the atmosphere particularly pleasing."[24]

Another typical Baxter production was the summer, 1937 release, *Talking Feet*, about a working-class little girl's efforts to raise funds and save a hospital in her neighborhood by organizing a concert at the local Hippodrome. Child dancing star Hazel Ascot portrays the daughter of a fishmonger from London's East End. The girl's name is Hazel, and at the outset of the film, she is headed to a rehearsal of a pantomime when her dog Patch is injured in a street accident. The tearful little girl brings the dog to the hospital where the kindly Dr Hood played by John Stuart agrees to try to heal the animal and to Hazel's eternal gratitude, he succeeds. When word spreads throughout the neighborhood that Dr Hood's hospital may have to close because of lease problems, the whole area is mobilized to try to keep it open, and the resourceful Hazel commits herself to doing whatever she can for the man who saved her dog. She urges that the community approach Mr Shirley, the manager of the local Hippodrome, to try to obtain use of his theater for one night for a fund-raising event. With her theatrical sense, the talented youngster's efforts are successful, and the second part of the feature consists of individual performances from music hall entertainers. Of course, the effort to rescue the hospital is a triumph, and the money obtained keeps Dr Hood's facility open. As the *Monthly Film Bulletin* observed, "the story is sentimental but human, and the atmosphere is genuine."[25]

In *Song of the Plough*, a December, 1933 release which was reissued later in the thirties, Baxter focused his attention on a tithe sale. In this feature, a yeoman farmer in Sussex named Freeland, played by Stewart Rome, is suffering through various financial reverses and is faced with a tithe sale. In the prerelease publicity for the film, the custom of friends in such sales who would "often . . . pitch in, buy it, and give it back" was discussed, but the item which appeared in *Film Weekly* several months prior to the movie's release observed that in the plot for this feature, the practice would be subverted by the villain who would "keep bidding it up." [26] Though the film subsequently hinged on a sheepdog race, the fact that Baxter again focused attention on a cooperative venture among ordinary people to overcome a problem was significant.

Even one of Baxter's feebler efforts a late, 1934 release, *Flood Tide*, centered on the mutual friendship and cooperation between a barge captain and a lock-keeper's family. Filmed on location around the Thames Estuary, the story concerns lock-keeper Ben Salter and his wife (played by Wilson Coleman and Minnie Rayner) who have served for thirty years along the river and who are now about to retire. The Salters want their son Ted (Leslie Hatton) who is in the Navy to marry Betty (Janice Adair), the daughter of their old friend Captain Bill Buckett; Captain Buckett (the venerable performer George Carney) is a bargee who arranges for the Salters to run a public house in their retirement. The retiring couple are happy because their pub still will be within a short distance of the river they love. But the problem is that Ted currently is infatuated with Mabel, a disreputable barmaid played by Peggy Novak who works in a waterside saloon. Ultimately the barmaid bypasses Ted to marry a rich rival, and after the young Salter leaves to make one final, unsuccessful appeal to Mabel, he returns to find that he is in serious trouble because his ship has departed. Captain Buckett saves the day for the sailor who now has decided he wants to marry Betty after all when he transports the young man to his ship in the nick of time. Captain Buckett also completes his triumph by "winning the cup at the Barges' Regatta." *Picturegoer Weekly* was impressed by the fact that "there are some impressive shots of the Thames" but it regretted that "the real atmosphere of the river and the drama of its people are never quite able to penetrate the general artificialities – and superficialities – of the drama." [27]

Another unsuccessful, but no less interesting example, the summer, 1934 release, *Music Hall* might almost be seen as a metaphor for British society. Again, the plot is a relatively familiar one, conforming to Baxter's typical format. *Music Hall* concerns the drab and deteriorating old Empire Theatre in Workhampton. The theater has long since ceased to be a profitable endeavor and has been suffering financial losses so severely that now the manager intends to close it, which would result in the loss of many jobs. George Carney this time is the stage manager, Bill, who believes that the facility has been failing because it has been operated under old-fashioned methods; accordingly, he convinces the previous operator of the theater, Mr Davis, who had been in show business for many years, to preserve the theater. Davis renovates the structure, redecorating the interior, and prepares a gigantic program which seems to provide the public with good, traditional entertainment; the result is a great success with many veteran performers doing their acts. Jeffrey Richards quotes Davis expressing his philosophy as "fashions change but human nature is about the same," a sentiment with which Baxter clearly agrees. [28] The theater might be seen in microcosm as a little society in itself; this society which is obviously in trouble turns to traditional values in order to return to prosperity. This microcosmic analogy was underscored by the theme of the stage show which saved the theater: "Music Hall's Answer to the Depression." Even when events were at their darkest, and the staff were faced with dismissal, the box-office girl pointed out, "Let's do what thousands of others are trying to do – keep smiling," thereby re-emphasizing the parallel between British society and the group of people involved in the theater.[29]

Baxter further indicated in another of his films, *Hearts of Humanity*, that in cooperation was a kind of redemption. In this fall, 1936, release, the Reverend John Maitland (Wilfrid Walter) is the Rector of Rexhaven, a small rural community. Malicious gossip initiated by the family of Jack Clinton, played by British screen heavy Eric Portman, forces Maitland to resign. Ultimately Clinton discovers that the scandalous information was incorrect; to atone for his error and to inform the churchman that his reputation has been exonerated, he sends his son Mike (Bransby Williams) to find Maitland in London where he is working with the unemployed in the various "haunts of the down-and-outs" and in the "riverside underworld."[30] The *Monthly Film Bulletin* was particularly impressed that the feature showed real scenes of London noting that "in the search we are taken to St Martin's Crypt, the embankment, the Arches, and the dosshouses."[31] The young man locates Maitland, who is endeavoring to halt the exploitation of down-and-outs and wanted men by disreputable shipowners, who send deteriorating vessels out with crews of such men, and then scuttle the ships without regard for the men in order to collect the insurance. Clinton agrees to assist the reverend, and the two of them gather the proof and ultimately arrange for the arrest of the shipping criminals. By cooperating with the churchman and helping him, Mike, representing his father, succeeds in redeeming himself and his family.

The only major problem, aside from the film's obvious emotional naivety was Baxter's customary devotion to his music hall friends; predictably, Maitland in his missionary work, also runs a "talent-spotting" contest at a deserted music hall, and with this superfluous addition, the film ends with the down-and-outs being given "a good time" at the contest.[32] The *Monthly Film Bulletin* thought it to be a rather effective film, in spite of such flaws, calling the story a "moving one"; praising the camera work, the "excellent" action, and the sympathetic portrayal of "the existence of the down-and-outs," the publication observed that "the humour of the outcasts has been caught in the dialogue and in many of the situations." The reviewer found a "minor blemish" only in the notion "that the poor are represented as somewhat pious – they listen to wireless sermons and church music, while the wealthy dance to hot jazz in a big hotel."[33] The film earned several reissues in subsequent years.

But the boldest evocation of Baxter's theme occurred in a May, 1936 release entitled *Men of Yesterday* which he both produced and directed. In this film, the director even went so far as to suggest that his theme of cooperation among individuals could settle international disputes; that is, if ordinary men were able to meet without the attentions of diplomats and governments, peace efforts in the world could be attempted with more effective prospects. This belief was daringly elaborated in what *Film Weekly* called an "earnest and unpretentious appeal for peace through the reunion of ex-soldiers of all nations."[34] The poignant production acknowledges the phenomenon which was described in the *Monthly Film Bulletin* as occurring "in Britain and in almost every nation that took part" in the first World War of "ex-servicemen . . . [organizing] themselves . . . [by forming] . . . Associations, Leagues, and Legions to keep alive the spirit of comradeship that was the only thing of value in that holocaust."[35] The plot centers on Major Radford, a middle-aged former officer (Stewart Rome), who uses his spare time to assist and see to the concerns of former servicemen. Major Radford's newest effort is to reunite veterans who are members of one of these national associations, not only from countries like England and France but also from Germany. Unfortunately, before his efforts can be achieved, a new supervisor at work, believing that Radford is becoming too old, asks for his resignation, informing him that the cause is his age and the fact that his business ideas are too "old-fashioned." The effect on the ex-Major is devastating; he begins to doubt himself, and not only finds his enthusiasm for the reunion gone, but is also so disappointed that he considers suicide. After flashbacks inspired by the recollections of the men whom he commanded, (showing the leadership abilities that caused him to be admired by both his superiors and by those who served under him) his ex-batman played by Sam Livesey induces him to overcome his Depression, and he accomplishes his goal of an international gathering. Here, an individual again attempted to bring together ordinary people to cooperate in a joint effort to find international harmony.

In spite of the potentially controversial nature of the topic, the *Monthly Film Bulletin* reviewer felt that in his opinion the proposal was not an attempt to be politically controversial. Explaining that Baxter was not "fishing in the troubled waters of political theory," the reviewer observed that the "suggestion offered, that the fraternization of old soldiers can make a special contribution to world peace – is put forward as one that is intensely practical and that can be accepted by all shades of opinion"; the reviewer added that "Baxter's direction, though stressing the emotional passages rather unnecessarily, shows a rare regard for authentic atmosphere" and praised Stewart Rome for providing "a finely etched, if sentimental, performance as the Major." The review also singled out George Robey, Ella Shields, and Will Fyffe for their appearances, but observed that "it is on the scores of men appearing as, presumably, themselves that the film depends so successfully for its broad effects"; the reviewer concluded that "for detail," *Men of Yesterday* "depends on genuine people with genuine feelings."[36]

However, praise for the film was not universal. For instance, *Film Weekly* argued that the film had a clear "propaganda purpose" which it conceded "would have been better served" by centering the story on the "international work of ex-servicemen in the cause of peace, without the introduction of a personal and domestic story"; the reviewer contended that whenever the plot "is concerned with Major Radford's efforts to found a league of ex-servicemen with the goodwill of the men themselves, or even with the flash-back reconstruction of the . . . atmosphere in France, their sincerity gives" the story a "certain simple vitality." By contrast when the plot "wallows through the sentimentalities of the Major's private life," the film becomes "hopelessly artificial." [37]

The *Monthly Film Bulletin*, perhaps reflecting a leftward orientation was more favorable, praising the screenplay of Gerald Elliot and Jack Francis. The reviewer called "the script . . . a fine piece of writing that preserves its integrity even when inclined to be over-sentimental"; objecting only to "an opening sequence that is made more prominent than its importance warrants," the reviewer concluded that the "various elements of humour and tragedy of person and nation, of youth and middle-age, are wrought with understanding and brought together with skill." [38]

Though improbable and naive, the film clearly was an evocative work again centering on cooperation; though not by any means radical in nature, Baxter's philosophy, then, as it was expressed to working men in his films, again suggested forbearance, patience, and understanding through a sense of cooperation as a solution to problems. His films were all the more meaningful because of the attention they paid to the working classes; if a message were to be interpreted from his features, as in so many other British films, it would be another inducement to maintain the *status quo*.

In the mid thirties, Baxter's attention to unusual film topics earned him a rather prominent reputation. E.G. Cousins, the well known film commentator, observed about him that while "British producers [only] once in awhile try to do *English* films, but usually turn back to more reliably imitating Hollywood," John Baxter, by contrast, "seems to appreciate the possibilities of our country"; in the process, he had "quietly dug himself in at Twickenham Studios and is there proceeding to turn out a series of pictures in which he is inserting large chunks of British life unadorned." [39] Publicity about the director noted his common qualities; said one story in one fan magazine, Baxter "has the simplest of tastes," enjoying "nothing . . . better than sausages and fried onions for his midday meal." It went on to explain that he is "apt to disappear between pictures, collecting local colour for the next one" and adding for instance that "what he doesn't know about doss houses isn't worth knowing" and that "he must have walked up and down London's markets for *Say It With Flowers*." [40] Letters to fan magazines from filmgoers showed that audiences were reacting favorably to Baxter's productions and admired his work. [41]

Yet, sadly, Baxter's career has been almost forgotten today and except for the noble efforts of Brown and Aldgate is much overdue for rediscovery. His interests were especially significant in that they so directly contradict the assumption that the British film industry ignored the working classes as subject matter in their movies. Baxter's preoccupation with community efforts and banding together to help one another also should be considered in the light of its sociological significance during the Depression years.

GRACIE FIELDS AND THE THEME OF SELF-SACRIFICE

In contrast to that of John Baxter, the name of Gracie Fields was so well known, that it now has an almost legendary reputation. As Graves and Hodge suggested in *The Long Week-End*, Gracie Fields, with her "Lancashire accent and humorous, long-suffering but optimistic sentiment . . . truly represented contemporary England."[42]

Where "Who's Afraid of the Big Bad Wolf" in the United States was said to have been America's anthem against the Depression, the title song of Gracie Fields's 1934 hit film, *Sing as We Go*, written by songwriter Harry Parr-Davies, served Great Britain in a similar capacity. Because the song was so identified both with Fields and with contemporary Britain during these difficult years, it was worth examining in some detail.

Significantly, the song's verse melodically begins with a minor downward scale suggesting an unsettled mood and a dark, somber atmosphere; correspondingly, the words address a personification of depressed spirits as they ask "Blues, where are you now?" and add, "You ought to know that I've no use for you." The words then turn inward, as if seeking to inspire one's own psyche; "Frown, get off my brow," the tune goes on, "It's plain to see that from now on we're through." The minor chord now shifts to a major chord suggesting resolution, and the verse then leads into the marching refrain by commenting optimistically, "I see a better day coming in sight."

The phrase "sing as we go" now melodically becomes an upward major scale, suggesting a positive progression. Indeed, the chorus of the tune depicts an attitude unconcerned not only with the anxieties about tomorrow but also even with the problems of today. If we are to be out of work, the song suggests, then, as preposterous as it may be, we should become unemployed with vigor, enthusiasm, and confidence. We should "sing as we go and let the world go by," and in the process we will "say goodbye to sorrow," because we can console ourselves remembering that "there's always tomorrow to think of today."

Finally, the lyrics urge that this confidence and positive attitude should be exhibited throughout all levels of society. "Although the skies are grey," regardless of whether one is a "Beggar or king, you've got to sing a gay tune." Indeed, this optimism is what makes it worth going on in the face of adversity; that is, "a song and a smile, making life worthwhile, so sing as we go along." Fields punctuates the last phrase "So sing as we go along" by imitating a trumpet call after the word "Sing," thus emphasizing that the tune is attempting to wake up the spirit of the people hearing the words.

The song's context in a film in which Gracie indeed loses her job, becomes unemployed, and nonetheless keeps her cheerfulness in the face of adversity made the tune even more evocative. Both the song Gracie sings and the example she sets represent an approach to hardship that is remarkably powerful. The fact that her public image during this period seemed so genuine, approachable, and open and the way in which she was able to create a persona with which filmgoers could identify made her a potent figure in an era when traditional values and beliefs could have been easily shaken or overturned. Like the other rousing optimistic songs she introduced, "Sing As We Go" conveyed a "forget-your-troubles" attitude; but unlike other escapist tunes sung by other Depression-era performers, Gracie Fields's song suggested a community attitude of good cheer as a way to overcome any "slump," whether economic or spiritual. Her native, infectious, Lancashire sense of humor and working-class wisdom prompted Sam Eckman, the British chief of Metro Goldwyn Mayer, in 1936 to describe her as a British "female counterpart of the late Will Rogers."[43] Accordingly, her popularity among the working classes was unsurpassed.

Various attempts have been made to analyze the enduring and endearing charm of Gracie Fields. In a perceptive retrospective on her career film historian Jeffrey Richards eloquently assessed her talent. Noting the combination of "a phenomenal singing voice, a natural comic talent and an inexhaustible vitality," Richards referred to the "remarkable . . . range" of her voice with its "power, purity, and tonal shadings, enabling her to sing anything and everything" from "opera, ballads, [and] hymns" to "comic songs," and he commented on the "bubbling sense of fun which she harnessed to impeccable comic timing, exuberance". Citing her "inability to resist sending up the pompous or pretentious," Richards wrote that "above all she was natural and real, with none of the stilted artificiality, cultivated poise and cut glass accents of her English female acting contemporaries."[44] But her extraordinary talent was only a small part of the incredible appeal she had for ordinary British working class moviegoers. At least as important, if not more significant, was an extremely widely publicized personality contributing to an image that suggested she was honest and down-to-earth, that she was in fact still one of the people.

Her appearance was a part of this persona; Miss Fields's common looks made her seem all the more real and lovable to working-class filmgoers. One letter writer in *Film Weekly* described her appearance as a "pleasing plainness" and actually worried that with her new contract with America's Twentieth Century Fox Company, she might be made too glamorous.[45] The implication was that if she became fashionable she would no longer be one of the people. Another letter-writer contrasted the "hard-working" actors and actresses like Gracie Fields who must "really *work* [sometimes in] smaller parts battling through mud and rain . . . [being] pushed about in a mob, shrieking, or crawling about on hands and knees" with those glamorous stars with more "glory" who only "have . . . to lounge about in beautiful clothes, speak in longing tones, and kiss"; he added, "who ever saw Greta Garbo being kicked downstairs in a film, or . . . scrubbing a floor [like Gracie]?" [46]

This quality by which Gracie Fields maintained her identity with the working classes was the key to her overwhelming popularity. A moviegoer wrote *Picturegoer Weekly* in 1933 that she liked "Gracie" because "she does not pretend to be what she ain't! Once kinema stars try to emulate the aristocracy it leaves me cold." [47] Accordingly, Miss Fields's well known preference for a simple lifestyle was well publicized. For example, an item in a 1934 issue of *Film Pictorial* observed that "there's no swank about Gracie . . .; when the all-electric kitchen gets too much for her, she seizes an old frying pan and a pound of sausage and cooks them on the sitting-room fire." [48] A character sketch in the same publication two weeks later attributed her "appeal to the masses" to the fact that she possessed "no social ambitions" because she was "Lancashire to the core and as straight as they make 'em up here"; the sketch observed that "if she doesn't like a thing she says so and that's that," and she doesn't care whether you "take her or leave her." But the author observed "you seldom leave her" because "in fact, Gracie is rather like the Cinderella of legend," having "no use for pretension . . . and . . . [being] proud of Rochdale and the mother who encouraged her as a child to climb up the slippery ladder of fame." [49]

Her manager, Bert Aza, often related that in "her stubborn refusal to become sophisticated," she had kept "her tastes . . . always . . . simple and homely," and that as an example of this down-to-earth quality, even when she was extremely wealthy, "when she comes to my office and we have tea, it is Gracie who bustles around and collects the cups and carries them outside." [50] And the producer of several of her features, Basil Dean, told readers in a September, 1933 issue of a fan magazine that, in spite of her fame, "she lives in the simplest possible way" in "just a simple flat with a serviceable unostentatious car"; he reported that on her travels she wanted "no meals in glittering fashionable hotels, among luxury suites and society's darlings," but instead preferred to "[return] to the comfortable theatrical 'diggings' that she knew in her days of struggle." During the summer of 1933, Dean emphasized that she had toured the North country in a caravan, preferring "the quiet, simple life which this affords her" rather than "being waited upon hand and foot at big hotels in the towns"; Dean concluded that aside from her "supreme qualities as an artiste," Gracie Fields exhibited "a kindness and modesty about her that endears her to all whom she meets in the studio." [51] Such stories clearly helped emphasize her image as a woman of the people.

With the incredible success of her films Miss Fields became quite wealthy; however, a danger that she might lose popularity with fans because of her riches never developed because of the well-publicized amount of charity work which she undertook. In fact, her generosity was also a crucial part of her public image. Dozens, even hundreds of stories, circulated about her acts of charity which became almost as well known as she; indeed her agent observed that "her generosity is, of course, a by-word," and added that "she would give the coat off her back to a deserving case." [52] Basil Dean, in the article cited above, noted that in spite of her high-paying contracts, "money doesn't mean all that much to Gracie" except that it had afforded her with opportunities she had "always craved," specifically "the power to make other people happy;" Dean speculated that "there must be many thousands of poor players and chance acquaintances whom she has met on Life's journey, who bless her name" because "her charity and kindness have taken a thousand forms." He cited, as an example, that when she heard that the football team from her home town of Rochdale was short of funds and would have "to cancel an important match" she "telegraphed immediately to the manager asking him to accept the money required for the engagement." Dean went on to point out that her reputation for charity was "widespread" to the point that "none . . . of the thousands of letters asking for help which reach her . . . goes unread." Of course the Gracie Fields Orphanage, which she endowed, was her "dearest" charity. [53] Such publicity made her generosity common knowledge to the public that adored her.

From time to time Miss Fields would donate all manner of items, from articles of clothing to film props to the various charities she supported, all of which would be described in detail by fan magazines. One of the more unusual instances of her kindness is cited in Bert Aza's reminiscence of Miss Fields, where a picture caption noted that in September, 1935, "Gracie performed one of those kindly acts for which she is so famous"; after learning "that a horse belonging to a young greengrocer had been killed in a road accident" and that he "couldn't afford another" which meant that "his livelihood was lost," Miss Fields "bought him a new pony and one night, after the theatre, she gave it to him." [54] The actress worked tirelessly to raise money, especially for orphanages; for instance one fan magazine reported that her efforts had earned four thousand pounds for the Peacehaven Children's Orphanage in Sussex, and the magazine encouraged filmgoers to help Gracie earn the additional twenty thousand pounds the orphanage needed. [55] This publicity and her efforts endeared her to the public.

Her reputation was never weakened in the thirties by the suggestion that these actions were artificial and contrived. In fact, her film colleagues and co-workers strengthened her image by their public comments. Moviegoers read plenty of evidence in publicity stories that suggested that this down-to-earth, charitable quality was not a pretense and that her likability was recognized by her colleagues in the film industry. Her rather wooden co-star in several films, John Loder, wrote in an April, 1934 article in *Film Weekly* titled "What I Think of Gracie" that "everybody from the gate-keeper to the studio manager loves her" and that she was "untouched by back-biting"; said Loder, "unlike others she *is* modest and unassuming off-screen" and it "never occurs to her that she is famous." [56] He added that "she gives herself no airs or graces, was not pretentious, [and] wants only to be sincere and genuine" and noted that when filmgoers come to her movies, she was genuinely "afraid . . . people won't get their money's worth"; finally, he concluded, everyone admired her as a hard worker, always the "first on the set and the last to leave."[57] Filmgoers were told in fan magazines that she regarded others in her production crew as members of a team, and that unlike other stars, at the end of a production she would get together to party with the workmen on the crew and "thank her fellow workers."[58] Her acts of charity also had their parallel within the film industry; *Picturegoer Weekly* had a feature in a 1936 issue dealing with the help "Gracie" gave "struggling film makers," one example of which involved her co-producing a later 1935 version of the J.M. Synge play, "Riders to the Sea."[59]

To British cinema audiences, then, Gracie Fields became "Our Gracie," an expression that at once demonstrated the affection they felt for her and the success with which she had been able to retain her working-class identity; she was not simply Gracie Fields, the "Lancashire Lassie" who started from humble origins, but she was "*Our* Gracie." As one writer in a 1934 issue of *Film Pictorial* expressed the point, the singer–actress had earned the nickname "Our Gracie" mainly "because she belongs *to* the people, is *of* the people, and *for* the people."[60]

Film fans apparently digested all of the information and publicity about her; a letter-writer to *Screen Pictorial* magazine in June, 1938, wrote:

> Film stars . . . can take a lesson from Gracie Fields in the art of spending wisely their enormous salaries . . . . There are few film stars who would devote a whole performance to charity, but Gracie Fields is an exception. We have only to look at her orphanage for verification of this fact. "Our Gracie" never forgets her mill companions or her home town, Rochdale, either. Whenever that town is mentioned it is always associated with her name.[61]

Another letter was even more expressive; the moviegoer wrote of his admiration for Gracie Fields, saying "I want to shake her hand, pat her heartily on the back and shout at the top of my voice: 'Well done, Gracie! Well done!',", because "even in the hardest times Gracie Fields still keeps us 'Looking on the Bright Side.'"[62] Probably the most overt demonstration of the public's affection for Miss Fields was the simple fact that she could never go anywhere without attracting a massive crowd of well-wishers; traffic jams inevitably accompanied her personal appearances, and even the mere rumor that she would be passing the gates at Gainsborough studios one day during the spring of 1933 resulted in a crowd of citizens waiting to see her.[63] These manifestations of her popularity continued throughout the decade.

Richards has suggested another factor in Miss Fields's popularity aside from her "magical rapport with her audience," arguing that along "with her defiantly working-class image and her undiluted Northern vitality," the fact that she rose "from poverty to stardom via natural talent and hard work," was especially appealing to filmgoers; indeed it was a story "that would have delighted the heart of Samuel Smiles . . . whose ideas still carried weight in the thirties."[64] Working-class people could take pride in her success. Thus, with "her undisguised . . . pure Lancashire . . . origins and naturalness," and with the fact that she never went "posh" and never lost her accent, Richards rightly asserts that "Gracie became a symbol for the nation in the Thirties" with a " 'never say die' spirit" and a "repeated set of injunctions to eschew despair or apathy, anger or revolution"; Miss Fields thus delivered a "message of courage, hope, cheerfulness," that came not from "a politician or statesman" but from "one of their own, who knew what they were enduring and whose advice could be trusted." In "rejecting maudlin self-pity" she provided "an answer to the Depression [that emphasized] a robust and optimistic self-reliance, of which her own career was a paradigm"; Richards concludes that "Gracie had become Britannia, the spirit of the nation" embodying "the best of British character" and representing "what Britain would ideally like to seem."[65]

With her standing throughout much of the decade as "the most popular actress on the stage, screen, or radio in Britain" Gracie Fields could command attention from her audiences.[66] If her spirit was not apparent from her films, in several contributions to fan publications, she specifically expressed her philosophy of how to deal with adversity. For example, in an October, 1933 article in *Film Weekly*, she pointed out that her optimism was not that of a "pollyanna." Conceding that "Life provides all the laughs I want," Miss Fields observed that she was "not one of these goody-goody people who preach that life is always funny if only you look at it with a smile" because she was aware that events could be very "hard at times"; adding that "even the cheeriest person cannot face all life's trials with a grin," she admitted that "there have been times when I couldn't see anything funny in life at all."[67]

In another article in one film fan publication's annual two years later, she elaborated on this attitude in a predictably colloquial, almost conversational, style. In the article Miss Fields observed that "Life's all very well when things are going smoothly," but "for most of us . . . there is usually a time of unhappiness or suffering beforehand" because "there's such a lot of sorrow in the world." She added that she was "glad" she had learned "to look on the funny side of things" when she was a youngster because she came to realize "there always *is* a funny side if you take the trouble to find it." She went on to explain being able to recognize the ironies generated by the dramatic shifts and turns a person's future can take. Miss Fields wrote that life can drive you to the "last ditch of despair, [getting] you almost down and out," before "something quite unexpected happens"; asking her readers, "haven't you ever felt as though you were right at the bottom of a big black well, with a great dark cloud pressing down on you from above," she commented that just "when you feel you can't stand it one more minute doesn't the cloud invariably shift off and let a ray of sunshine stab away down to the heart of your well of misery?" She concluded that the "awkward thing" about "being human" is that "we generally forget life has played the same joke on us before" and that "life turns around and laughs at us"; if that is the case, then "the great thing is to laugh back, laugh louder, and show Fate that we're not beaten."[68] Such homespun philosophy was comparable to that given the American people by the equally beloved Will Rogers.

These almost inspirational messages, Miss Fields explained, were ideas and beliefs that she derived "from the raw material of human nature and from the everyday things of this workaday world . . . things which we have all at some time experienced"; she added that her attitudes were reflected in her films and that she had learned to make people laugh from her dealings with ordinary, working people, "through the highways and byways . . . of England." Miss Fields recalled that she had "lived . . . in little streets, travelled on the roofs of trams, walked in public parks . . . and heard women in the street markets summarize the day's news in a few, terse, caustic sentences"; as a result she knows "what makes a Durham miner laugh, and what makes a Liverpool sailor grin, or a hard-headed but warm-hearted . . . housewife chuckle for I've met them all."[69]

These sentiments were evoked most clearly and most emphatically in the cheerful songs that were chosen to be sung in her movies. Many of the tunes, most of which were written by her longtime, song writing collaborator Harry Parr-Davies, were bright, infectious melodies which Miss Fields's distinct and forceful voice projected nicely; the tunes were easily whistled and were effectively developed for the moviegoer to be able to remember. The emphasis in the lyrics usually centered on positive thoughts; bad days were to be forgotten and only good days were ahead. One of the best of these tunes, with its gentle melody and lovely bouncy refrain, was Parr-Davies's "My Lucky Day" from *This Week of Grace*. In the verse of the tune she explains that when she "awoke today," she "missed those skies of grey"; now that they were gone, "good luck has come my way," and "I don't know what to say" because "I'm so excited to think I'm through with blue days." The chorus that follows is a lovely, lilting melody in which she delights in the fact that she's "simply walking on air," without a "wary old care" because "this is just my lucky day." The song explains that she has been confident of such a turn of events; "I knew that someday this was bound to be," but now "my lucky star has been faithful to me." So, the tune concludes "I'm dressed in my Sunday best shoes," and she's "said goodbye to the blues" on this "lucky day." From the same film, another Parr-Davies song, "Happy Ending," implied in the verse that evil or "Satan" had brought unhappiness to the world, but that in time, conditions would be (and actually were) improving. Therefore, the lyrics suggested "Let's have a happy ending, look at the sun trying to drive those shadows away." The words go on to express similar positive developments that will be coming soon; indeed, "the longest lane will soon be bending, flowers will bloom, spreading the good news." The singer rejoices in the fact that "Hallelujah, I'm myself again" so "let us be gay, and all the clouds will roll away"; in other words, if we overcome our despair, and if we are true to ourselves, whatever problems that affect us will disappear.

Another emphasis in these songs was on those constant qualities of life that had no price and were unaffected by social conditions. In *Sing As We Go*, in a beautifully evocative sequence in which the lights of the Blackpool amusements are extinguished, Miss Fields, who plays an unemployed factory worker, quietly sings the hauntingly lovely Parr-Davies lullaby, "Love is Everywhere," while the camera focuses on various working-class lovers and married couples holding hands or embracing. The song's verse observes that "In this hurried life of ours, we find time to gather flowers" because "Sentiment is something heaven sent to bring us pleasure"; therefore "in the language of each heart, one part ideally stands apart," and "Love is king of every little thing, our life's way to treasure." This "measure," the lyrics suggest, is available to everyone regardless of their circumstances; indeed, "like a melody without an ending, to its strains a million hearts are blending, love is everywhere." Accordingly, Gracie wistfully notes, "If by a stroke of chance, my heart shall find romance, I'll do my best to make it stay"; therefore, "I hope some day maybe, this love will come to me, whatever fate may send my way." The obvious suggestion was that in spite of unemployment or "whatever fate may send" a person could be happy if he or she was loved.

Even in her comic songs, Miss Fields dealt with traditional virtues. For instance, in *This Week of Grace*, she performed her amusing "Heaven Will Protect an Honest Girl" written by Weston and Lee; though obviously played for laughs, the song, about a naive North-country village girl who goes to London to make her living, nevertheless reflected attitudes about the dangers and corruption in the city. The sketch, hilariously sung and acted by Miss Fields, has the mother advising the daughter to beware of rich playboys in the city. She reminds her, "remember when in London, though you're just a servant 'gell,' you're a blonde, the sort that gentleman ensnare"; therefore "with your youth and fatal beauty, when you get to Waterloo, there'll be crowds of dukes and millionaires, all waiting there for you." After singing the chorus which affirms that "heaven will protect an honest girl," the song nonetheless advises that "When these rich men tempt you, Nellie, with their sparkling moselle," she should "say, 'Nay, Nay,' and do be very 'care fu-ell.'" But if such entreaties fail, and if heaven is not all that successful in protecting an honest girl, then the mother has more practical advice; she melodically suggests that "if some old bloated, blasé, roué, swell" threatens to kiss her, then "Breathe a prayer he shall not do it, and then biff him with the cruet," and in this way "Heaven will protect an honest girl." The performance goes on for numerous verses with Gracie assuming various characters and doing the lines in a North Country dialect; but underneath the humor was still a fundamental reinforcement of traditional values and beliefs, however humorously portrayed.

Gracie Fields's movies emphasized not merely optimism, good humor, and the traditional virtues, but also the theme of cooperation. Time and again in her features, the character Miss Fields portrayed would serve as a motivator for unified, joint action requiring cooperation among the characters to solve a problem. Even audiences came to expect such elements in Miss Fields's films; one letter writer characterized the typical role played by Miss Fields as being that of a "working girl who meanders through dismal scenes cheering others with songs, sentimental and gay." [70]

In her first film, *Sally in Our Alley*, based on Charles McEvon's old North country play, *The Likes of 'Er*, and directed by Maurice Elvey, Miss Fields plays Sally Winch, who works as a waitress in a working-class coffee shop in a tenement area in the East End of London. The plot revolves in part around Sally helping a mistreated juvenile delinquent named Florrie, played by Florence Desmond, who has become a liar and thief as a result of her miserable homelife; dreaming of escape from her dismal slum existence, the girl wastes all her time reading film magazines and imagining herself as a movie star. Using sympathy and understanding, Sally reforms the girl, in the process allowing her to ruin her flat in a tantrum. The other feature of the plot concerns Sally's love for her ex-soldier boyfriend George, portrayed by Ian Hunter, from whom she has been separated. George, who has been made lame in the war, refuses to rejoin Sally, because his pride will not allow him to approach her in a crippled state. In the end, Sally is reunited with her boyfriend through the combined efforts of the now-reformed Florrie and other working-class friends.

The film also features an interesting and somewhat unusual emphasis on class divisions which suggested that cooperation was more easily accomplished among the people of the working classes. Jeffrey Richards has written about what he calls the film's "bitter class conflict" which culminates in Sally being invited "by an upper-class lady out slumming" to a party where she apparently thinks it would be "amusing to have a working-class girl perform"; after Sally is "looked down on because of her clothes" and subsequently is "[glamorized] . . . as part of a class putdown," the "awkward and embarrassed" girl nonetheless effectively performs "Fred Fanakapan" to warm applause and then to subsequent indifference as the upper-class partygoers "then pointedly [ignore her]." She is paid, given a cheque, emphasizing her status as hired entertainment, rather than a guest. Stunned, she eventually leaves the party alone and unnoticed. As Richards eloquently puts it, *Sally in Our Alley* and especially this sequence "[reveal] hermetically sealed class divisions and a patronizing attitude to the working class with a sharp critical edge which leaves the audience . . . angry and uncomfortable." [71]

Although the cooperation theme was not overt in *Sally in Our Alley*, it was implicit. Clearly, without Sally's help, Florrie would continue to lie and cheat her way possibly into a life of crime; likewise, without Florrie's intervention leading George into the cafe, Sally and the ex-soldier would not have been reunited. The songs that Miss Fields sang also suggested a "community spirit." For example, the song that was to become Gracie Field's trademark, "Sally," written by Bill Haines, Harry Leon, and Leo Towers, and originally intended to be sung by a man, urged "Sally" never to "wander" from her "alley" (or community) because her presence served as a guarantee against "grey [skies]," or unhappiness. The song observes that "when skies are blue, you're beguiling," but "when they're grey, you're still smiling"; perhaps for that reason "You're more than the whole world to me."

Similarly, the somewhat nonsensical "Fall in and follow the band," by Haines and Leon, in which Sally leads a group of street urchins in a little procession, also evoked the image of the working classes as a cooperative group. The song urges listeners to "come and hear the cutest little band, in the land"; since "everyday they're marching down our streets," she suggests we all "fall in and follow the band." In mentioning items familiar to the working classes, the connection between "the band" and objects such as "tin cans" or "ash pans" was implied. Interestingly, this song was sometimes used in advertising campaigns for the film, with processions of working-class children through tenement districts paid to follow around a large poster with Gracie Fields's face, the name of the movie, and the cinema where it was playing.[72] Even in the comic song "*Fred Fanakapan*," the ritual of courting was seen as a cooperative venture where "all our family turned up to see what she had found."[73] Modestly budgeted, *Sally in Our Alley* became an instant hit when it was released in July, 1931 and in reissues throughout the thirties, and was "one of the biggest money-spinners ever turned out of the British studios."[74]

In her second film, *Looking on the Bright Side*, released in September, 1932, Miss Fields is Gracie, a manicurist living in an East-End tenement who is in love with a song-writing hairdresser named Laurie, played by Richard Dolman. Laurie derives much of his inspiration from Gracie and from the neighborhood in which they live, and the songs he writes are good. In the plot, Gracie helps Laurie sell his tunes to a show business producer who really wants to sign Gracie for his show; but when she refuses, he agrees to hire the songwriter anyway. Laurie becomes infatuated with Josie, a society stage star, portrayed by Wyn Richmond; as a result, he stops working and with his inspiration gone, he finds himself unable to write and is fired. In order to help Laurie, the jilted Gracie agrees to perform his music on the stage and following a successful debut, the two are reunited during a party given for Gracie at the tenement. Again, a sense of interdependency was suggested in *Looking on the Bright Side*; when Laurie and Gracie worked together, success was achievable, but when they separated and worked apart, not only did Laurie find that his inspiration was gone, but the disheartened Gracie could not keep a job. Another success, the film, as Basil Dean has observed, "played to enormous business in every part of Great Britain and the Commonwealth, except the West End of London."[75] Dean's comment reflected an important qualification to Gracie Fields's appeal. By and large, while her films were immensely successful, that triumph, particularly in the early part of her film career, was not reflected in the West End of London where a different audience from that of ordinary cinemas could be found. Ironically, the West End audience was usually the group from which the influential critics were derived; it is therefore perhaps not surprising that those people who wrote about film would believe that the British cinema ignored the working classes, for those films that were directed to the working classes rarely, if ever, played the West End.

Where these early Gracie Fields vehicles reflected the theme of cooperation on a personal, individual basis, some of her later films extended this theme to a broader level. Probably Miss Fields's best film was the September, 1934 release *Sing As We Go*. Ivan Butler has written that "coming in the middle of the Depression ... the film has an all-pull-together-now and keep-on-keeping-cheerful atmosphere about it that stimulated rather than irritated contemporary audiences." [76] Although the *Monthly Film Bulletin* dismissed the feature as "typical Lancashire humour" with "Gracie Fields as herself," in fact the movie represented something of a departure not only for Gracie Fields, but also for the British film industry. [77] For the first time in a Gracie Fields film, a high quality screenplay had been prepared, in this instance by the noted author J.B. Priestley; Miss Fields had insisted on final approval of the screenplay, particularly after some of her fans had complained in fan magazines about the poor quality of the scripts in her movies following the release of *Love, Life and Laughter*. [78] Also, with most of the film shot on location in Blackpool, the film escaped the studio-bound quality of other contemporary British productions.

The story-line also was timely. In the film, the cotton mill in which Gracie Platt works is closing down, and a deputation of the workers encourages her to go talk with the sympathetic Hugh Phillips, the young son of the plant supervisor, played by John Loder, to see if anything can be done to keep the mills open; when he tells her that only new equipment can make the plant workable, though saddened by the prospect of her own unemployment in the midst of hard times, Gracie realizes her co-workers need to be cheered up. Telling them that if the mills must close, then it would be best to try to approach the problem in a positive manner; "if we can't spin, we can still sing," she tells them, and she leads the now out-of-work laborers out of the factory, marching to the upbeat tune "*Sing As We Go*." After discussing the situation with her uncle Murgatroyd, Gracie chooses to obtain seasonal employment in Blackpool, travelling to the city by bicycle to save money, in a lively and amusing sequence. At first she obtains employment as a servant in a boarding house. But the job soon disintegrates when the star boarder becomes too familiar with her: Gracie crowns him with a dish of rhubarb and quits. At a fortune teller's house she meets Phyllis, a girl who has travelled from London to enter a beauty contest; Phyllis, portrayed by Dorothy Hyson, offers to share her accommodation with Gracie who accepts the proposal while she hunts for other employment. Among the jobs Gracie tries, with varying degrees of success are "song plugging for a music publisher," assisting a "palmist," and "selling toffee and acting as the 'vanishing lady' for an illusionist"; she is substantially more successful in helping Phyllis, proving "instrumental" in "saving [her] from making a fool of herself after she has won the beauty contest."[79] At the same time, she serves as Cupid for the romance between her friend and Hugh, whom Gracie secretly loves. In the end, the mill is reopened when Phillips finds new capital and a new synthetic silk process, and Gracie is given a position as welfare officer at the factory; as the film closes amid superimposed Union Jacks and billboard signs that read "Prosperity" and "More Men at Work," Gracie leads the workers back into the factory again to the lyrics of "Sing As We Go."

The whole experience of unemployment was thus treated almost as a vacation, and the implicit assumption was that by staying cheerful and resourceful, Gracie had shown the way by which workers could survive the crisis until management could get the machines running again. The tone of the film, in spite of the graphic depiction of the fears of unemployment, was anything but bitter, and the basic idea was that management was concerned and wanted to help its employees; thus workers should cooperate, find temporary work, and all would be well.

The film was remarkable in its realistic setting, if not in its realistic plot. As Basil Dean has written, "one unanticipated by-product" of the location shooting "among the Blackpool crowds was the information that the film now provides for the social historian on the life and times of holiday makers" in the early 1930s by showing "the shops and shoppers, their dresses and general demeanour, and, most noticeably, the friendly relations between the public and the police."[80]

When the film was revived in the 1970s at the National Film Theatre in London, the program notes were even more emphatic about the film's historical value, observing that "it remains today the only cinematic record we still have of the industrial North" because " no documentary survives to give us the feel for the place and the times"; conceding that "most of the domestic scenes – Gracie's home, the boarding house, the fortune teller's establishment – are broad caricatures," the notes maintain that the sequences "do sketch their models fairly and shrewdly," adding that "the boarding house scenes, in particular, give . . . the feel and the smell and the atmosphere of the place." The notes concluded that in the well-known scene with Gracie "leading the crowd of singing workers out of the factory," the film provides "a real, if momentary, sense of the whole situation – the marches and the misery and the fortitude it took to combat them."[81]

In the next film, Look Up and Laugh, released in the summer of 1935, though the heroine Grace Pearson may be more lower middle-class than working class, the emphasis in the story shifted even more dramatically to cooperative effort in solving a seemingly hopeless problem.[82] In this feature, also made from a J.B. Priestley screenplay, Gracie is a music hall performer who returns home for a visit to her father, a small merchant in the village market. She arrives singing the title song, with its upbeat lyrics ('though we've to strive/It's good to be alive/So laugh your troubles away"; "happiness is around the corner"; "the best in life is free"), but she quickly discovers that a crisis is taking place. The owner of the rival local department store, Mr Belfer, played by Alfred Drayton, is endeavoring to tear down the market, putting all the stall-holders out of work. Belfer, who wants to build a new branch of his store on the site, argues that the market is old-fashioned. But Gracie's father, who is leading the fight against Belfer, maintains that it is still used by the people, and is fighting the move at a meeting when he collapses. Though in the process Gracie gives up a chance of a West-End stage job, the heroine immediately takes over for her father in rallying the other stall-holders, most of whom, significantly, are played by veteran music hall comics. Gracie leads a price war against the department store, and at one point, sabotages Belfer's establishment; but eventually Belfer succeeds in getting his crony, the mayor to shut off the market's utilities, and the stall-holders, led by Gracie, respond by staging what amounts to a sit-in inside the market. Only Gracie's resourcefulness and a last-minute discovery of a royal charter result in victory for the small merchants in the market (most of whom speak in a distinctly working-class rather than *bourgeois* manner).[83] By uniting and motivating the stall-keepers, Gracie preserves their market. A subplot in which Belfer's daughter and Gracie's brother are revealed to be lovers, though implausible, underscored the cooperation theme, and suggested that long-range agreement between the two sides, at least in a symbolic sense, is inevitable. The film is also interesting at the metaphorical level, supporting both the *status quo* and the monarchy: in *Look Up And Laugh*, tradition is seen as protecting the people in the form of King Edward III's charter which overcomes the tyrannical businessmen.

In other films, cooperation was a key element in the implicit message of the movie. Although the show business atmosphere became more prominent in Miss Fields's later films of the thirties, the emphasis in such features as *Queen of Hearts* or *The Show Goes On* continued to be on the cooperation theme. The idea that a stage troupe was a little company in which cooperation was essential appeared in both films. Particularly in *The Show Goes On*, the pain of theatrical life with the periodic unemployment and uncertainty, the crude boarding houses, the crowded third-class travelling conditions, and life in the provinces suggested an interesting parallel to the misery and uncertainty of working-class lifestyles. One of the last of her English films, *Keep Smiling*, released in late 1938, made the point more emphatically with Miss Fields appearing as Gracie Gray, a music hall performer who assembles a collection of unemployed variety artistes to form a travelling show. Constantly plagued by financial problems and the danger of a greedy rival producer, the company triumph in the end because of their loyalty to each other and their ability to persevere.

Even in those Gracie Fields features that were not specifically related to this theme, similar elements do make an appearance. For instance, her third film, *This Week of Grace*, a summer, 1933 release, was characterized accurately by *Picturegoer Weekly* as a "Cinderella in Modern Dress" like so many other movies of the period; but cooperation was again at least an implicit theme in one sequence.[84] The highly contrived plot concerned Miss Fields as Grace Milroy, a factory girl who has a good sense of humor which she shares with her beer-loving father and her brother Joe, played by music hall performers Frank Pettingell and Duggie Wakefield respectively. When she is put out of work, a chance meeting with the eccentric Duchess of Swinford (Nina Boucicault) results in Gracie being placed in charge of her estate, Swinford Castle. Arriving with her family at the estate, to the consternation of the staff, Gracie succeeds with clever and gentle management practices in putting the estate in order, in the process falling in love with Clive (the nephew of the Duchess), who is played by Henry Kendall. Ultimately they are married, and after minor problems, he opens a garage, and they live happily ever after. In one sequence, however, Gracie helps the people of the nearby village stage a concert to help the vicar; in the scene she urges cooperation, asking the villagers to work together.[85]

In another production, *Love, Life, and Laughter* released in March, 1934 which was even more of a formula film, Miss Fields is Nellie Gwyn, a barmaid from Chelsea, who is discovered by a talent scout and is urged to make a film about the life of Nell Gwyn, her namesake. At the same time, she meets and falls in love with a prince of the Ruritanian country of Granau, played by John Loder. Eventually realizing she would be depriving the country of his talents if she married him and forced him to renounce his throne, she breaks off the relationship and encourages him to marry the more acceptable Princess Grapfel. Even in this typical and cliché'-ridden plot, the theme of cooperation for dealing with problems reappears, as the primary focus of Nellie's life is to raise money for a children's hospital; in her pub at the outset of the movie, she constantly urges regulars to contribute pennies to help the hospital, and even at the end of the film, after sacrificing her relationship with the prince, she asks only for a contribution to her charity.

Gracie Fields's last British film, *Shipyard Sally*, probably summarized this theme in her features most effectively. Released, interestingly just before the outbreak of war, the film is an almost blatant patriotic appeal for all British citizens to work together. Just as "Sing As We Go" became the anthem of the response to the Depression, the popular "Wish Me Luck As You Wave Me Goodbye," again by Harry Parr-Davies, was to become symbolic of British soldiers going off to war, as it adds to the exhortation to that the send-off should be "with a cheer, not a tear, make it gay!" The song asks for a positive memory until there can be a reunion as the lyrics continue, "Give me a smile I can keep all the while, in my heart while I'm away"; the poignancy of the words, as sung by Miss Fields, was not lost on a generation that had come to love her and that now faced an impending war. Though the war-time facet of the song's lyrics was not overtly a part of the film, it certainly represented an unstated but palpable undercurrent.

In the plot, Sally Fitzgerald and her father, the major, played respectively by Miss Fields and veteran comedian Syd Howard, are unsuccessful music hall performers who decide to retire and open a pub near the shipyards. But the closing of the plants caused by the slump quickly brings problems. Though Sally continues to serve the penniless workers who are unable to pay their tabs, in time, the pub is threatened with bankruptcy. Sally encourages the men to join together and put through a petition, pointing out that "Britain owes you a lot; demand work." Learning that a commission will convene in London to consider the problem, Sally is dispatched to meet with Lord Randal and to show him a petition signed by all the workers. Unfortunately, Sally's efforts to gain an appointment with the official are not very successful, particularly when her father demonstrates "his card-sharping propensities." Forced to resort to "distinctly unorthodox" and comic "methods," Sally "[impersonates] a 'hot' American singer," gaining access to a party, and then being invited for a week-end. What appears to be a disaster when the "real [singer] . . . indignantly turns up" ultimately becomes a "triumph" as Sally's "sincere plea for the workers makes the commission review its findings." [86] Unaware that the petition has succeeded, Sally and her father find people cheering them when they return to Clydebank, and the film ends with everyone returning to work.

Richards has observed the "staunchly patriotic . . . framework" of the film. He noted that the feature begins with the launching of the "Queen Mary" as "Rule Britannia" is played, and it concludes with Miss Fields singing "Land of Hope and Glory" while the workers return to their jobs amidst a "montage of ships being launched and Union Jacks waved." Richards adds that even the songs she sings are selected to provide a sense of unity, since she "contrives to sing 'Annie Laurie' and 'Danny Boy' too, to keep the other parts of the United Kingdom happy." [87] But in addition to this element of patriotism, Richards added that the film portrayed the "solution to unemployment" as "an appeal to the good nature of the government, and not any revolutionary act," pointing out that a "communist chauffeur appears in the film, denouncing the ruling class, but he is gently mocked and his solution is clearly disavowed by the film." [88]

But if communism was denounced in the film, combining in a unified effort was not. By encouraging the workers to organize and let their opinion be known, Sally led and came to represent in a specific way in this film the spirit of cooperation. In the philosophy of *Shipyard Sally*, the uniting was necessary so that the government and management could know what the people wanted and how they proposed to deal with the problem; then they could help them and return the cooperation.

207

COOPERATION AND SELF-SACRIFICE IN OTHER FILMS

Of course, the general theme of cooperation to overcome a problem by no means was confined to the social comedies of John Baxter and the escapist, working-class musicals of Gracie Fields. Literally dozens of features throughout the decade, some of them serious, centered on this concept. For instance, when Gracie Fields's sister, Betty Fields, attempted her first film, an early 1936 release entitled *On Top of the World*, the cooperation theme was extended to suggest the necessity not only of the workers cooperating and helping one another, but also of cooperating with management. The story begins with the passing of Old Schofield who has made a great success as a trainer of greyhounds in the village of Millford; his daughter, Betty, a mill worker played by Betty Fields, tries to assume his responsibilities, in which capacity she makes the acquaintance of Mr Preston, the local mill owner portrayed by Charles Sewell, who also has an interest in the dogs. Meanwhile labor problems ensue at the mill with agitators arousing the workers; when a strike is called, Betty dedicates herself to the wives and children of the strikers. Although Betty must sell most of the greyhounds she inherited to meet her expenses, she does keep the best dog, "Our Betty," and enters her in the Greyhound Derby at White City; "Our Betty" wins the final, and Betty gives her money to the relief fund to start a food kitchen for the wives and children of the strikers. Meanwhile, the agitators continue to influence the workers who now decide to set fire to Preston's home; but "Betty reasons with them and persuades them to dismiss the agitators," and the mill owner then "agrees to consider their terms . . . [so that] everything ends happily."[89] The film was atmospheric, and it had the virtue of the presence of veteran performers like Frank Pettingell and Wally Patch.

Here the simple "let's-stick-together-and-cheer-up" message of Gracie Fields was taken one step further; the heroine, though ostensibly demonstrating her loyalty to the working classes and her desire to help them by aiding the wives and children of the strikers, and even by selling her favorite greyhound "Our Betty" to raise money for them, nevertheless sympathizes with the mill's management. Her sense of cooperation, then, was a cooperation between the workers and management. The reviewer in the *Monthly Film Bulletin* noted the artificiality of this plot and observed that the whole concept was "very naive" with "an unpleasant atmosphere of snobbery"; commenting that "the political theme plays a big part in the story and is more than a little inconsistent," the review objected to the depiction of the owner "as doing his utmost for the men . . . running the mill for their sakes." When "finally he yields," the agitators "who could logically take credit for this are chased out of the village by the men"; indeed, the reviewer remarked, the "agitator is a ridiculous figure who would be laughed off any soap box."[90]

Whether audiences felt the cooperation theme had been taken too far was another question; interestingly, though Betty Fields's career did not develop in any way approximating that of her sister, the film did achieve at least a minimal degree of success, to the extent that it earned subsequent reissues. Indeed, a reviewer in a fan publication that was somewhat more popular than the *Monthly Film Bulletin* made no allusion to the questionable politics of the film, concluding that, in the film, "through the wit and sympathy of a woman is harmony and prosperity restored."[91]

Several films with the cooperation theme were overtly comic and saw cooperation and the process of helping one another in a humorous light. For instance, in the March, 1933 social comedy, *The Wishbone*, veteran variety artiste Nellie Wallace plays Mrs Beasley, a charlady who gains a modest inheritance of fifty pounds and decides for once in her life to be extravagant and just enjoy herself; but in the end, she decides to use the money to help a busker who is down on his luck. In a more farce-orientated comedy released in the spring of 1938, entitled *On Velvet*, veteran character comic Wally Patch is a Cockney bookie named Harry Higgs; he and his friend Sam Cohen (Joe Hayman) lose heavily at the races, but their wives, played by Vi Kaley and Mildred Franklin, insist that they do something to recover the lost money. Now virtually broke, the two agree to pool all of their extra money to set up a television advertising company, and in the end, they are successful. In spite of a low budget and very poor reviews, the film was popular enough to be reissued a few years later.

One of the most popular farce comedies with this theme was one of the better "Old Mother Riley" features entitled *Old Mother Riley, MP*. In this well received August, 1939 member of the series, which earned frequent reissues, Mrs Riley's neighbors in her tenement complex support her in a combined campaign to oppose the efforts of a villainous landlord to demolish their flats, and ultimately their work results in a political career for the washer-woman. The *Monthly Film Bulletin* observed that the plot was "fantastic" but the reviewer called it "good honest music hall of the robust type."[92] In the film, Mrs Riley is a washer-woman who is fired by her employer who also happens to be her landlord. Old Mother Riley becomes further annoyed when she and her friends learn that the uncaring landlord also plans to tear down her cottage and the tenements of her neighbors in order to build luxury apartments. Since he is also seeking to be elected to Parliament, Old Mother Riley is induced by her friends to oppose him. A hectic campaign follows, and to her astonishment, the washer-woman is elected. Once in the House of Commons, she delivers a somewhat unusual but nonetheless impassioned speech on behalf of her friends. As a result of her eccentricities, she is made a member of the Cabinet, being appointed Minister of Strange Affairs. To everyone's surprise, she manage to induce the Emperor of the Ruritanian country of Rocavia and others to pay a fifty-million-pound debt to Great Britain.

But more dramatic, and sometimes much more serious, features showed cooperation in daily life in more realistic settings with ordinary people. For instance, in a summer, 1937 quota release entitled *Night Ride*, fired truck drivers unite to set up their own company; the climax of the film concerns their efforts to help rescue a group of trapped miners. Most notably, the success of Robert Flaherty's March, 1934 release, *Man of Aran*, which in a semi-documentary style concerned the struggles of the Aran islanders to survive and make a living, inspired several more fictional features that nevertheless showed the interdependence of other remote provincial communities.

By far the most famous of these real-life stories, *Man of Aran*, took three years to make and was the subject of intense publicity when it finally was released.[93] As Ivan Butler has written, the film "tells of the life of the lonely islanders off the West coast of Ireland," and it movingly describes "their struggle to wring from an increasingly hostile environment the bare necessities of existence, their fortitude, their stubbornness, but above all their common humanity."[94]

Publicity for the film emphasized the necessity of cooperation among the islanders for survival. In an advance publicity release distributed by the studio long before the film premiered, the feature was characterized as being a "real-life drama of human existence on an island where a living has literally to be wrested from a barren land"; the item added that "the islanders"

> have to create a means of cultivation. In a small plot of field bounded by walls built of loose rock the men of the household pound the limestone outcrop with sledgehammers into some semblance of a level. From the shore the women and children collect seaweed and sand, also precious handsful of real soil to be found in the crevices between the rocks on the higher slopes of the islands .... [A]fter months of unrelenting toil, they are able to raise crops, principally potatoes, although sometimes the land reclaimed in this way is turned into pasture for rearing cattle. But not surprisingly, the islanders inevitably turn to the sea to augment their means of existence. In this sphere their courage and daring are demonstrated [when] ... a curragh team of three oarsmen [manoeuvre] their frail craft built of laths and cowhide in the tumbling Atlantic breakers round the island's rocky fringe.[95]

Lobby displays and publicity stunts in connection with the film's release also suggested these jointly conducted survival endeavors. In Newcastle, for example, the manager of one cinema arranged a display from the Hancock Museum of Natural History of materials needed for survival in a remote seaside village, and the Prior of St Dominics Church in Newcastle, who was invited to the press showing, delivered a sermon on the film entitled "Courage and Contentment."[96] School children were shown the film in Saturday morning special matinees and then were encouraged to write essays on what they saw.[97] Allied Fisheries arranged for eighty grocers' shops to have "display cards emphasizing the 'Search for Food' motif" of the film.[98] Though some of the intellectual critics were upset that much of the film, particularly the shark hunt had been staged, surprisingly the public loved the film; even in the usually difficult summer months, a division manager in the Gaumont–British chain reported that the film "was a box office success at every hall." [99]

One of the features prompted by *Man of Aran* was *Turn of the Tide*, a November, 1935 release directed by Norman Walker, starring Geraldine Fitzgerald, and based on the novel *Three Fevers* by Leo Walmsley. The review in *Film Weekly* described the film as "a simple story of the everyday lives of fisher folk" with "a vivid glimpse of life in a North of England fishing village" that has all the authenticity of a "documentary." [100] The story concerned a confrontation between two families, the Fosdycks and the Lunns, in a Yorkshire coastal community and was supposedly based on an actual village feud in the North of England. [101] But, as Ivan Butler has suggested, the real "antagonism" lies "between the adherents of older, traditional methods of fishing and the newcomers with more up-to-date equipment," a conflict "paralleled by the rivalry between youth and age – the younger members of each family combining to try out the modern age together." [102]

In the story, the Fosdyck family has fished the area for over four hundred years, and Old Uncle Isaac Fosdyck, played by J. Fisher White, seriously expresses indignation at the "intrusion of these upstart 'furriners,' the Lunns," who have a modern motorboat. By contrast, the Lunn family contend peacefully that the fish in the ocean are abundant, and more than enough can be harvested for both families. Old Isaac is not persuaded, however, and a "struggle for supremacy" follows – "though each camp – with the exception of Isaac – has a sneaking regard for the other." The common ground between them is facilitated by the romance between Ruth Fosdyck (Geraldine Fitzgerald) and John Lunn (Niall MacGinnis). Eventually, the younger Fosdycks decide to join with the Lunns to invest in a bigger boat that can be used for deep sea fishing; to pacify Isaac they make him a senior partner in the new firm. *Picturegoer Weekly* concluded that "through calm and storm, fog and sun, prosperity and hardship, [and] ... distress and discord, ... the story bowls bravely along on an even keel before a stiff breeze of human interest." [103]

Critics were pleased with the realism of the characters and the settings. *Film Weekly* observed that *Turn of the Tide* had succeeded in spite of the fact that it contained no battles, murder, or sudden death. The movie "instead ... shows incidents common in the lives of fishermen"; the audience goes "with them to sea in open boats," and goes "into their homes and workshops." The movie permits filmgoers to "see them courting in a tongue-tied fashion ... [and] hear the wives give the husbands the rough side of their tongues"; it provides an opportunity to "see them dressed in their strange and uncomfortable Sunday-best." [104] By concentrating on the common activities, and by having the younger members of the feuding families want to cooperate with one another, the film again emphasized the theme of harmony and united efforts as the way to overcome difficulties.

Publicity for the movie attempted to portray it as a "thoroughly British" or "national" film.[105] Graham Greene, calling it "an unpretentious and truthful film," preferred it to the more widely publicized *Man of Aran*. Writing in the *Spectator*, Greene observed that in its depiction of a "rivalry over the crab-pots . . . of a Yorkshire fishing village" it had become "one of the best English films I have yet seen." He added that while it had been likened to the better known *Man of Aran*, as a film "it is on a quite different plane from Mr Flaherty's bogus and sentimental picture" with its "hopelessly 'literary,'" direction and its over-emphasis on visual beauty. Greene praised Norman Walker's direction stating that it is more "concerned with truth"; Walker doesn't trouble "about silhouettes on skylines, and the beauty his picture catches" is an "exact statement" of "the ordinary life of a fishing village," of the "competition between lifeboat and salvage tug," of the "changing market prices." Accordingly, Walker "doesn't have to *invent* drama as Mr Flaherty does, who painfully reconstructed a type of fishing which the Aran islanders had not practiced in living memory."[106]

The same kind of conflict between divisive older ways and progress, in the sense of community effort, was seen in Michael Powell's summer, 1937 release, *The Edge of the World*, which concerned crofters on a lonely island in the Shetlands. With the islands increasingly barren the younger residents see emigration as logical, while their elders refuse to give up their homes or change their ways. The plot concerns the struggle of crofters on the remote Shetland island of Hirta who try to keep their lives together at a time when peat supplies are dwindling, and food problems are becoming more serious. Young Robbie Manson, played by Eric Berry, favors leaving the island, because he wants to live on the mainland where he can marry. His father, Peter Manson, portrayed by John Laurie, vigorously disagrees, and Andrew Grey (Niall MacGinnis), who is the fiancé of Robbie's sister Ruth (Belle Chrystall) concurs. Robbie and Andrew agree to resolve their dispute on the matter in a traditional way for islanders; they will embark on a daring cliff climb. Unfortunately, a mishap occurs, and Robbie falls to his death. Peter regards Andrew as being at fault, and he breaks his daughter's engagement to the young man. Andrew departs from the island and goes to work on a fishing trawler. In the meantime, Ruth gives birth to their child; but the baby takes ill, and Andrew responds to a message about the situation by returning to take Ruth and the baby to a doctor on the mainland just in time to save the infant's life. Conceding that evacuation is needed, old Peter agrees to arrange for the departure. As the islanders prepare to leave, Peter convinces himself that he must obtain a rare bird's egg in a nest on the cliff; as he climbs to reach it, his rope gives way, and he falls to his death.[107] Here the failure to cooperate and to unite resulted in tragedy.

Praising the "magnificent scenic values" of the picture, with its "storm-swept seas, rugged cliffs, craggy mountain peaks, moors, and old stone cottages," the reviewer in the *Monthly Film Bulletin* nevertheless found the plot to be "feeble and melodramatic"; but, he added, "the normal life on the island in its simplicity and with its hardships is portrayed effectively by the islanders themselves." [108] *Film Weekly*'s review added, the "naturalness" of the islanders "gives the film conviction," and concluded, in contrast to the review in the *Monthly Film Bulletin*, that *The Edge of the World* was "a sound blend of documentary reality and human story." [109]

The film was quite popular; letter writers to fan magazines praised it as a new direction for British cinema, though in fact it really was following along the lines of the earlier *Turn of the Tide*, which did not get a wide distribution. [110] In fact, the film was so well received that not only was it subsequently reissued, but its stay at some theaters on its initial run was as long as three months. [111] The stars of the film were even popular enough to be asked to endorse Ovaltine "for [those who do] vigorous outdoor work, a by-product of success unusual for an independent production." [112]

Similar to cooperation as a theme was the concept of self-sacrifice for the betterment of others. Sometimes the sacrifice was personal, involving only one other character. In fact, the sacrificing of a character's own self interest for the good of either the group or another individual was fairly common in the kinds of story-lines that have just been discussed. For instance, in *Look Up and Laugh*, Gracie Pearson willingly gives up her chance of a West End try-out to help her father and the other stall-holders. Similarly, in *Sing As We Go*, she relinquishes her love for the son of the mill owner so that his relationship with Phyllis can go unimpeded. These more personal sacrifices were paralleled in *Love, Life and Laughter* in which Nellie Gwyn's romance with the prince is terminated by her for the betterment of his Ruritanian country.

But sometimes the sacrifice was central to the plot of the film. For instance, in numerous features, a relative or friend would be willing to accept responsibility for a crime to save another individual from prison. In the early 1929 silent film, *The Last Post*, a British soldier's brother is a revolutionary, and during the General Strike, he shoots another soldier. When he learns what his brother has done, the soldier claims responsibility to protect the brother. This feature released in January of 1929 later had a soundtrack added and was reissued the following year. In *Pal O' Mine*, a March, 1936 release, an old stage doorman and night watchman believes that a safecracking was committed by his son; to protect him, he confesses to the crime, although, in the end, the real culprit is caught. Correspondingly, in *Father and Son*, a September, 1934 crime film directed by Monty Banks and based on Ben Ames Williams's novel *Barker John's Boy*, Edmund Gwenn is John Bolton, a middle-aged ex-convict whose son is a bank teller. When a robbery takes place, the son, thinking his father to be the perpetrator, takes responsibility for committing the crime.

In *Dusty Ermine*, a fall, 1936 release, based on Neil Grant's play, Ronald Squire is Jim Kent, a convicted forger just returning home from his prison term; after a time he is made aware of the fact that counterfeit banknotes are circulating in the area. Although suspicions naturally turn toward Jim, at least his niece Linda, played by Jane Baxter, believes him innocent. Jim then discovers that his nephew Gilbert, portrayed by Arthur Macrae, has fallen in with an international gang of forgers, and the police are on his trail. One of the policemen, Inspector Forsythe (Anthony Bushell) who is in charge of the investigation, has been seeing Linda, and she has become fond of him. In the meantime, Jim has decided to try to free Gilbert from the gang, and he and Linda trail him to Austria, with the police in close pursuit. Ultimately, Gilbert is killed attempting to save Jim who had devised a ploy to rescue his nephew by taking blame for the crime himself. The forgers are captured by the police, and Jim is freed from suspicion. One reviewer said, "the triangular battle of wits between Jim Kent, the forgers, and the police, coupled with the conflict of emotions in Linda and the detective, provide a captivating compound of drama and comedy, the many threads of which are neatly woven together."[113] The fact that Jim is willing to sacrifice himself for his nephew, and that Gilbert gives his own life to save his uncle is an illustration of a familial sacrifice in what is otherwise a straightforward crime film.

This kind of sacrifice was not confined to relatives. In *Old Roses*, a summer, 1935 release, the son of a rich man in a rural village is accused of murder; to save him, an elderly man who is fond of the youth claims to have committed the crime. A much more elaborate plot was the story-line to *Open All Night*, an October, 1934 quota picture directed by George Pearson and based on the play by John Chancellor; in the film, Frank Vosper plays the exiled Russian Grand Duke Anton whose primary delight in life is his job as the night manager of Paragon House, a London night club. In his position, he is able to become involved in various people's lives to help them. As the story progresses, he sees to it that a "free meal [is] given to an out-of-work chorus girl," and "tries to straighten a waiter's love affair"; he also "saves a young man from murder and a typist from making a fool of herself with her unscrupulous boss."[114] He accomplishes these activities by a variety of selfless actions which lead to his having trouble with his employers. Eventually, Anton is summoned by the general manager, who fires him. Remaining courteous and "angelically patient," Anton leaves his job; but because "Paragon House was all that mattered" to him, and because now, without the position he has "nothing further to look forward to," he decides to take his life. While the people about whose lives he has cared "are all still eating and drinking and dancing" he commits suicide, making one last sacrifice by "having carefully left a signed confession concerning the villain's [accidental] death that will clear" one of his young friends "of a charge of murder."[115] Here, an aristocrat who has been deposed once from his native land is deposed a second time, but in the process redeems himself by his help and sacrificial acts. These sacrifices suggested the interdependence of characters' lives and the necessity that people devote themselves to one another no matter what their class or status.

Family obligations, however, were not limited to criminal matters. For instance, in the November, 1933 version of *Sorrell and Son* based on Warwick Deeping's noted novel, H.B. Warner is Stephen Sorrell, an ex-captain and a devoted father, who spends his whole life making sacrifices for his son Kit, played by Hugh Williams, after his wife deserts him; as one cinema billed it, the film was "the moving story of a . . . father who thought no sacrifice too great to protect the future of his son." [116] Filmed more than once, the version made in 1933 was re-released in Britain later in the decade.

A January, 1935 feature entitled *Barnacle Bill* showed another somewhat less saintly but no less devoted father in the title character, played by Archie Pitt; in the film, Bill's first love is the sea but he gives it up to raise his daughter. In the story Barnacle Bill Harris has romanced girls in every port, but he ultimately returns home to marry Mary (Jean Adrienne), the daughter of the landlady of the "Fisherman's Armes," Mrs Bailey, who is portrayed by Minnie Rayner. After a festive marriage, Bill returns to sea before coming home to his wife and the daughter Jill he has fathered. An accident results in the injury and death of Mary, but before she dies, she secures a promise from Bill that he will give up going to sea in order to raise his daughter, a vow he keeps. Jill proves to be a bright young girl and as she grows into a young woman (played by Joan Gardner,) she meets a rich young man who wants her hand in marriage. Bill is skeptical about a marriage that would involve someone "above her station," a concern shared by the young man's aunt. But social barriers between the two lovers ultimately are broken, and "after some misunderstanding" all is resolved happily; "after the wedding Bill decides to return to his first love, the sea." [117]

Sometimes the sacrifice was made either for love or to facilitate love. In the February, 1931 drama, *The Stronger Sex*, starring Colin Clive, for instance, a husband sacrifices himself in a mine disaster to save the man his wife loves. Occasionally kindness provides the motivation for the sacrifice; a good illustration was the December, 1937 release, the *Derelict*. In this film, Tobias "Toby" Meriam, played by Malcolm Morley, is a former Oxford man who took to drink; now middle-aged, he lives on the road with his old pal, Gaspar (Charles Penrose). The two men one day encounter a weary woman leading a donkey cart; her name is Mary (Jane Griffith) and the cart is carrying her crippled son, portrayed by Peter Kernohan. Taking the lead of the cart, Toby learns that the boy could be healed by an operation and that Mary is endeavoring to raise the needed funds by selling pots and pans. To try to assist her, Toby attempts to sell some of his drawings. Eventually, he encounters Sir Benjamin Speake, a wealthy and famous artist played by Frank Strickland who offers to purchase the artwork if a new picture is provided to him on a daily basis for twelve days. Toby agrees and gives Mary the cash he receives. Toby finds himself spending a great deal of time with Sir Benjamin and comes to believe he will eventually be famous, until one day, Gaspar reveals to him a picture in a newspaper that turns out to be a painting by Sir Benjamin called "The Derelict" which clearly is a picture of Toby. Angry at the deception of being used as a model unknowingly, he eventually is calmed when he is told that the boy can now walk, and Mary "persuades him that he still has something to live for."[118] Although *The Derelict* is a very minor film, the theme is one shared by a variety of productions. Most of these features demonstrated self-sacrifice for an individual and, in their moral posture, encouraged people to help themselves and others.

But even more significant were those features in which a character made a sacrifice for a larger group. For instance, the late, 1931 feature, *Men Like These*, concerned the story of a submarine crew trapped underwater when their ship sinks; the film, which was based on a true story, extolls the men for their devotion to duty. Similarly, in *Tell England*, Anthony Asquith's first sound film, the tragedy and sacrifice of the men in the Gallipoli campaign were told movingly; released in the spring of 1931 and based on Ernest Raymond's novel, the plot concerned two boyhood friends, Edgar Doe and Rupert Roy, played by Carl Harbord and Tony Bruce respectively, who enlist in 1914 and become part of the Mediterranean Expeditionary Force. Though Roy rises to captain, Doe is becoming disillusioned with war, particularly after a unit he commanded was viciously cut down by an entrenched Turkish mortar unit. The two friends have a falling out, but Doe regains his confidence after being placed in charge of another assault on the mortar unit. He dies, and his gravestone, along with the markers of his fallen comrades, provides the title for the movie.

> Tell England ye who pass this monument
> We died for her and here we rest content.[119]

Somewhat more contrived, but perhaps more interesting, was *OHMS*, a January, 1937 release, directed by the American film-maker Raoul Walsh. The film was especially curious because it was "undertaken with official assistance, in order to stimulate recruiting" for the British Regular Army.[120] In the story of the film, American character actor Wallace Ford plays Jim Tracey, a petty racketeer from New York who was "involved in a gambling-den murder" and then fled to England, assuming the name of the murdered man. With his new character, he "finds himself committed to enlistment in the British army, whose discipline he does not accept without reluctance." In the army he befriends Bert Dawson, a young lance-corporal (John Mills), and the two of them both pursue the affections of Sally Bridges the Sergeant-Major's daughter (Anna Lee). Ultimately, the regiment departs for China to fight bandits; there finally, Jim becomes a hero by saving the lives of a number of westerners, including Sally, from the bandits, sacrificing himself for his regiment and dying heroically.[121] *OHMS* had a plot-line that seemed very consistent with the American work of Raoul Walsh, which the reviewer in the *Monthly Film Bulletin* seemed to recognize implicitly when he referred to the movie as a "slick application of various well known basic formulas ...

professionally directed ... with excitement, humorous dialogue, and attention to detail in the matter of Army reforms"; even Wallace Ford's "breezy and amusing" performance as the "unruly recruit" Jim Tracey was described as "Cagneyesque." [122] Tracey's sacrifice in the end and his transformation into a hero was similar in nature to James Cagney's role in the later *Fighting Sixty-Ninth*. But as a recruiting film, the *Monthly Film Bulletin* thought *OHMS* was particularly effective: "in making British army life seem desirable, in a style which has hitherto been familiar only in American films." The review noted the amount "of full-dress parading, to the accompaniment of animated military music," and it observed that "barrack-life is otherwise portrayed as a rather jolly affair, interspersed with happy-go-lucky escapades." The review went on to note that "active service" is depicted as "heroic adventure in campaigns against villainous foreigners ... with, apparently, every chance for the individual of using initiative and achieving personal glory." The review concluded that "Army life, in sum, is presented as something broadening and inspiring, which helps the ordinary man to find himself"; with the "film's technical soundness, and vitality" *OHMS* will prove to be "a valuable instrument of propaganda." [123]

OHMS was just one of several features that came out at virtually the same time, all of them in some way either effectively or ineffectively, honoring the sacrifices made by Britain's servicemen. Probably the best of them was *Farewell Again*, released in the summer of 1937, which featured Leslie Banks as the Colonel of a regiment of Lancers from India and Flora Robson as the wife who waits for him at home. The story concerned the men of the regiment who have been waiting for months to get home to their families, but who discover, twenty-four hours from Southampton that their leave has been cut to only six hours. Somewhat episodic, the film dealt with the experiences of several of the soldiers. One reviewer commented on the way *Farewell Again* portrayed the sacrifices of the soldiers which became a "moving tribute" to the dedication of the "men who serve in the British Army"; calling the film "an outstanding achievement," the reviewer praised the scenario which "has been so written that while attention is consecutively concentrated on the personal affairs of a number of individuals each of them contributes to the whole." Likewise, the "climax of the story is reached, not as the ship sails again duty-bound, but with a clear understanding of realities, when the War Office order is received" and the "expectations of a thousand men are dashed." The reviewer concluded that the film was "outstanding" because it dealt "with real people and [presented] something real about England." [124]

A virtually identical plot could be found in the fall, 1936 release *Hail and Farewell*, which, however, achieved far less satisfactory results; similarly, the spring, 1937 production of *Our Fighting Navy*, starring H.B. Warner, though "produced in collaboration with the Navy League" lacked "the grand manner and broad treatment which would give it the requisite depth and emotion," and was accordingly, "neither good entertainment nor effective propaganda." [125] By contrast, both *OHMS* and *Farewell Again* earned repeated reissuances.

Self-sacrifice as a theme also could be found in other genres. For example, in the costume/historical drama, self-sacrifice was almost a tradition. Leslie Howard as Sir Percy Blakeney in the January, 1935 release. *The Scarlet Pimpernel*, risked his life to save aristocrats from the excesses of the French Revolution, as "a personification of the moral compulsion to alleviate human suffering in times of revolution." [126] In Victor Seastrom's summer, 1937 release *Under the Red Robe*, the protagonist is the duelist and gambler Gil de Berault, played by Conrad Veidt, who is in the employ of the sinister Cardinal Richelieu, depicted by Raymond Massey. The Cardinal reprieves Gil from a hanging in order to have him capture the rebel leader, the Duc de Foix. But when Gil arrives at the Duke's castle, he meets and falls in love with the Duke's sister. He captures the Duke, but motivated by his love for the girl, he sets the Duke free again, knowing full well that his actions mean that he has sacrificed his life. But when he returns, the Cardinal considers his action a master-stroke of diplomacy and frees him to enable him to marry the Duke's sister, who had come to plead for his life, knowing that she too was sacrificing her safety in the process. Gil was, at first, a rather ambiguous character, and, interestingly, as in many British historical/costume dramas, the way the movie audience was invited to sympathize with him and to understand that, in the end, he would prove not to be a scoundrel was by his kindness to an obviously impoverished working-class character. In *Under the Red Robe*, at the outset of the film, before Gil was to meet with the Cardinal, he gave money to a street beggar almost unconsciously, suggesting that he made such donations regularly.

One film genre in Britain in which self-sacrifice frequently was seen was in science fiction films. In several films, gigantic public works projects that are the central focus of the plot require unified effort and, accordingly, sacrifice. For instance, Maurice Elvey's film *The Tunnel* (known as *Transatlantic Tunnel* in the USA) starring Richard Dix, Leslie Banks, and Madge Evans fancifully foresaw the day an enormous tunnel would connect the two continents of Europe and North America, a goal which the film vaguely suggested in its triumphant closing scenes with the American President and British Prime Minister would guarantee world peace. To reach this goal, the chief engineer of the project, a man named McAllan, played by Richard Dix, not only surrenders his home life for years, but also in the process, his wife, who, wanting to help, goes to work at the project hospital where she is exposed to a tunnel gas that leaves her blind. "Mac" balks at his son's participation in the project; but he, too, wants to help, particularly after a strike halts the effort, and he is trapped in a mine disaster. Advertising for the feature emphasized the theme of self-sacrifice; for instance, one publicity blurb which noted the wife's blindness and the son's being trapped in the excavation, emphasized. "But the tunnel must go on – a picture of Human Love and Super Human

Effort." [127] The film was extremely popular, earning several reissuances later in the thirties *and* in the forties. [128]

Probably the best known British science fiction film, Alexander Korda's February, 1936 extravaganza, *Things to Come*, starring Raymond Massey, Ralph Richardson, and Cedric Hardwicke also involves self-sacrifice, particularly in the closing sequence when a young couple volunteer for a space mission with no guarantee of survival in order to be the first humans on the moon. The dialogue emphasized the value of their sacrifice; when asked if there is never to be any "rest" from progress, the protagonist Oswald Cabal observes:

> Rest enough for the individual man. Too much and too soon, and we call it death. But for Man, no rest and no ending. He must go on – conquest beyond conquest. First this little planet and its winds and ways, and then all the laws of mind and matter that restrain him. Then the planets about him, and at last, out across the immensity to the stars. And when he has conquered all the deeps of space and all the mysteries of time, still he will be beginning . . . . If we're no more than animals, we must snatch each little scrap of happiness and live and suffer and pass, mattering no more than all the other animals do or have done. Is it this, or that? All the universe or nothingness. Which shall it be?

The implication was that such sacrifice ennobled man and moved him a step closer to God. [129]

In all of these films, then, cooperation and sacrifices were continually subtexts or even the major theme of the production. The lasting message to audiences was that problems could be solved and overcome through such efforts, and that steps could be taken by a person to enable him to transcend his current difficulties. The pervasiveness of these themes makes it probable that a regular moviegoer would have heard this message at the cinema fairly frequently.

9

PATRIOTISM AND CENSORSHIP
Celebrating Britain and limiting social criticism

A persistent motif present in British feature films throughout the decade was the perhaps inevitable reinforcement of patriotic values. Whether the expression of this theme was subtle and implicit or more explicitly overt, a significant portion of Britain's cinematic output was devoted to content that was self-congratulatory in this national sense. Such themes tended to provide an optimistic point of view at a time of national economic crisis. Earlier, the patriotic attitude observable in such films as the Gracie Fields's musicals and in features celebrating the heroism, sacrifices, and military accomplishments of British servicemen was cited. But the prevalence of this "Pro Patria" emphasis in a wide range of different film genres and the occasional appearance of overt celebrations of a kind of national identity make it clear that British filmgoers during this period were very familiar with plots and stories designed to remind them of the glorious islands on which they were fortunate enough to live.

Indeed a substantial portion of the studio product consisted of films in which patriotism was a primary theme of the feature. Table 9.1 identifies those films in which such content reasonably can be seen as the primary focus of the production.

Table 9.1 Films in which patriotism is a major theme

Year	Proportion of the films released	%
1929	5 of 86	5.8
1930	5 of 99	5.1
1931	5 of 134	3.7
1932	9 of 150	6.0
1933	4 of 181	2.2
1934	13 of 183	7.1
1935	16 of 185	8.6
1936	16 of 219	7.3
1937	22 of 211	10.4
1938	14 of 158	8.9
1939	18 of 98	18.4

Throughout the decade, the percentages of movies exhibiting this characteristic tended to remain fairly constant, averaging around 5 percent, though a faint, increase began to develop mid-way through the decade, and the level had risen to about 10 percent in the last few years before the war. The dramatic rise to almost one in five releases in the last year before the war reflected a number of overtly patriotic features apparently rushed into production shortly after the declaration of war in September.

In fact, patriotism had always been associated with the cinema in Britain, even apart from the films shown. The logo of at least one film studio was a personification of Britannia herself, and other logos reminded the audience of qualities that were inherently the objects of British pride. Likewise, virtually every cinema would end its program with a recording of the national anthem and usually a picture of the King. In fact, one letter-writer to a fan magazine was alarmed that the ritual in some cinemas was presented so inadequately; the person wrote,

> Our National Anthem rightly brings the performance of every kinema in the country to a close. But what a dismal, tuneless dirge it is made by the majority of movie theaters . . . . When we come to the conclusion of our screen entertainment, an ancient oft-times cracked slide of the King is projected to the accompaniment of a hollow-sounding gramophone record which wheezes out a half-hearted "God Save the King."[1]

Scratchy records notwithstanding, most cinemas, and certainly the film industry itself, took their role in fostering patriotism and national loyalty seriously. For instance, the *Astorian*, a publication distributed to filmgoers free of charge in the various cinemas of the Astoria chain, told its readers in December, 1931,

> Although . . . we strike rather a bad patch in our national history, I feel somehow or other that the English nation and Astorians will manage to forget our trials during the Christmas season . . . . There can be no doubt that it is the duty of each and everyone of us to foster optimism, and we, in our particular sphere, will continue to endeavor to bring to you, at reasonable prices, health-giving entertainment.[2]

In the same issue, some of the managers of the various cinemas contributed comments, echoing the sentiment, most of them sounding like this manager's statement: "Everyone will join in hoping that we may emerge into the bright sunshine of happiness and contentment with work aplenty for brain and brawn. In Old England's imperishable characteristics, courage, and endeavor, be our brightest hopes."[3]

Frequently, national causes were made part of the displays and publicity efforts in the various cinemas. For example, cinemas throughout the country in the early thirties used displays and promotions to encourage the idea that people should "buy British goods." Display windows, street promotions, and even, in Luton, a "Buy British Ballet," complete with dancing figures representing various British goods and with a finale featuring a "Mr Prosperity," all encouraged cinemagoers with a patriotic appeal to participate in the economic recovery of the nation; managers also utilized the "Buy British" campaign to encourage the viewing of British films, and at least one letter-writer to *Film Weekly* proudly proclaimed that she was doing her part in the "Buy British" campaign by seeing only British movies.[4]

Numerous publicity tie-ins were conducted in conjunction with national events like Royal Weddings, the Royal Jubilee, and the Coronation. In the case of the Jubilee of 1935, many of the cinemas outdid themselves. Displays "with bunting, flags, heraldic designs and banners and cut-out photos of Their Majesties" were common; postcards of "Their Majesties in full regalia" were distributed to lady patrons on special Jubilee nights, and Jubilee Medallions were given to children at the children's shows.[5] Celebrities, both military and political, were invited to cinemas, and merchants often arranged for special window display tie-ins; at a few cinemas, plans were established for special prizes for married couples named George and Mary who had been married for twenty-five years.[6] Replies to telegrams of congratulations to the Royal Couple were posted in cinema lobbies.[7] Of course, such activities were designed not only to encourage a national "feeling of goodwill, confidence, and trust," as one manager expressed it, but also to promote business; however, the interdependence of the two motivations was never lost on the film exhibitors.[8]

The regard in which the film industry held King George V, and correspondingly, the gratitude for the support which it had received from the monarchy were expressed in an editorial eulogy of George V in the January 25, 1936 issue of *Film Weekly*. In the editorial, the point was made that it was under this monarch that the British film industry had developed and, additionally, that it was through the film industry that George V had become so immediately recognizable to all his subjects; in this way, the film industry had both helped and been helped by the monarchy. The writer emphasized that it was "through the medium of the cinema" that "millions of his subjects" came to recognize the monarch, both "as a King and as a man, more intimately than any previous sovereign." Through newsreels, George V was seen as "a familiar and greatly loved figure" during the entire twenty-five years of his reign. *Film Weekly* observed that "the silent screen reflected the kindliness and dignity of his person," and the "talking screen added the magic of his voice – a voice vibrant with humanity"; in this way, "the living image of the man himself" was "brought . . . into the hearts of the people." While mourning him as a "great sovereign," most of his subjects will think of him "as we saw him in those deliberately informal moments, caught by the motion picture camera . . . [moving] among his people and . . . his own family." The editorial concluded that it was "only fitting that this beloved king, whose life was so closely mirrored by the screen" had been "a great and generous patron of the cinema . . . [foreseeing] its importance" and demonstrating "his democratic readiness to assent to the requests of the cameramen on legitimate occasions"; significantly, *Film Weekly* observed, "almost from the outset of his reign" he had been an avid filmgoer, as well, proving to be "intensely interested in *seeing* films, particularly of a national . . . type." [9]

This symbiotic relationship between the film industry and the monarchy was reflected in the content of some of the dramatic films as well as the non-fiction newsreels mentioned in the eulogy. The most potent example was *Royal Cavalcade*, an April, 1935 release which was prepared to be released in conjunction with the Jubilee, apparently after the proposed Winston Churchill screenplay for an Alexander Korda Jubilee film (described by Martin Gilbert in his Churchill biography) had fallen through. [10] Though often confused with the American-made 1933 production of Noel Coward's *Cavalcade* because of its similar name, *Royal Cavalcade* differed in purpose from the Coward work. Rather than concentrating on one family's experiences, the film provided a portrait or panorama of all of the major events involving Britain in the twenty-five years of George V's reign.

With a cast of two hundred and with five separate directors with five distinct units, the

> picture virtually starts with the coronation of King George, and some idea of providing a commentary has been attempted by showing us a newly minted penny which crops up from time to time during the passage of events as it passes from hand to hand. [11]

In *Picturegoer Weekly* producer Walter Mycroft explained how the penny links the sequences. The coin was seen passing over the bar in a pub as "payment for a drink with which to toast the new King's health." The penny then purchases a newspaper whose headline informs of the assassinations at Sarajevo. As a "keepsake," it is taken to the war in France. A soldier retrieves it from the mud of Flanders, and he later gives the penny to his "baby son to keep him from crying during an Air Raid." On Armistice Day, the penny buys a balloon to celebrate the festivities, and later the coin "passes through the pay box at the Wembley Exhibition." The day Princess Mary's wedding is announced, the penny purchases a newspaper headlining the good news, and later the penny is used to buy wire to be used in a "crystal set that brings in one of the first broadcast programmes." [12] In this manner, filmgoers are reminded of the common events and moments they have shared throughout George V's twenty-five years.

The film contained a set of re-enactments to convey a sense of realism and establish a perspective or time frame. Mycroft noted that "Chief amongst these is the tragic suicide of Oates on the ill-fated but glorious Scott expedition to the South Pole." The film also shows Lady Astor "[re-enacting] her entry into the House of Commons as the first woman MP" as well as "other very good topicals" such as "the suffragette's struggle for recognition, the progress of aviation, the Coal lock out, [and] the Great Strike"; these events are "intermingled" with minor vignettes which Mycroft asserted "are interesting in their depiction of changing fashions and modes of life." [13] The film also showed the Titanic, jazz dances that swept the country, and Pavlova's dying swan. Even "George Robey, Harry Tate, and Arthur Prince came down for the reconstruction of the first command performance at which they appeared" in 1912; in addition, the film showed "Florrie Forde . . . in pre- war days trying over a new number called 'Tipperary.' " [14]

This celebration of the reign of George V reinforced a national spirit by showing what the King and his people had survived together; although he himself was not actually present, the King's spirit was shown to be omnipresent, in a curiously tangible way, in the form of the coin bearing his likeness. As John Maxwell, head of the British International Productions explained before the film's release, in an article in *Film Weekly*, this "picture is a great deal more than a 'documentary' record of important events"; the film is literally "the story of the people of Britain as well as of their King and country," revealing "the joys and sorrows they have experienced in the past quarter of a century." Maxwell emphasized that the film was especially effective in its depiction of "the grave period of the King's illness" when the impact "is illustrated not only by the official picture, but also by the human scenes" which reveal the "sympathetic interest and suspense that the millions of the King's subjects felt on his behalf." Thus, the penny in *Royal Cavalcade* is representative of the common experience of Great Britain and her sovereign whose image the coin carries because it "takes us with it to share the lives of the hundreds of people through whose hands it passes." Accordingly, Maxwell proudly concluded, the picture was more than just a pageant or "a record of the lives of King George and his family"; instead "it is the story of King George's People." [15] Predictably, the film did excellent business, and when the coronation of the new King took place a couple of years later, no less than four coronation films with similar patriotic qualities, though none quite as ambitious, were circulated. [16]

Another interesting patriotic feature was an early sound production entitled *One Family* which sought "to show the extent and scope of the British Empire"; in this summer, 1930 production, a little school boy, played by Douglas Beaumont, falls asleep in the middle of a geography lesson and dreams a "vision of Empire conducted by a policeman" portrayed by Sam Livesey. [17] Intended to be "a review of the Empire's markets . . . glorifying the British Empire," according to reviewer Robert Herring, writing in the *Manchester Guardian*, this "most extraordinary picture yet made by a British film" contains "many excellent sequences showing the resources of the Empire and their bearing on the daily life of an ordinary family"; but the film's story said Herring, "is so flimsily whimsical that it nearly negates the very understanding use of the film."[18] In the film, the youngster visits Bucking-ham Palace and "holds a council of the Dominions" which enables the audience to see the variety and extensive range of the countries in the Commonwealth of Nations and in the Empire. The boy travels to South Africa, New Zealand, India, and Scotland for a variety of materials, and he visits the Irish Free State. He also tours Australia where he witnesses the construction of giant dams, the reservoirs that result, and the canals that are then cut to permit the transport of water that irrigates the vast arid lands the audience is shown. Herring observes that "all this, as an expression of man's will, is stirring," and he cites especially "a magnificent sequence" showing Canada's boundless wheat fields which spontaneously "raised a burst of applause from the audience" with whom he saw the film, who seemed to be impressed with the way the scene had been "finely cut and photographed". Praising Walter Creighton's "excellent" use of "serious material," the reviewer asserted that the "portions of the film dealing with men at work express that work with a force and honesty that has never been seen in British films on a large scale, and has rarely been equalled even in Soviet productions."[19] But the sole purpose for the council and the tour turns out to be merely "to collect ingredients for the King's Christmas pudding," and Herring found this justification "hard to swallow."[20] In fact, the metaphor, though strained and childish, of the King as a central figure in this assemblage of peoples and lands was curiously evocative; the variety of the many resources brought to England and the extent of the British influence geographically was an effective reminder of the unifying aspect of imperialism. Additionally, the vivid depiction of the vast wealth of the British Empire would have stirred the heart of any imperialist; and the harmless images of a little schoolboy aided by a standard comic policeman as guides through the Empire made anti-imperialist criticisms of the feature more difficult to express.

But these overtly contemporary patriotic films were far out-numbered by other features that were concerned with historical subjects. Motion pictures like *Fire Over England* and its portrayal of the British defeat of the Spanish Armada, *Rhodes of Africa* with its depiction of the visionary imperialist Cecil Rhodes, *Brown on Resolution* and its story of wartime heroism, and Anna Neagle's two performances as Queen Victoria, *Victoria the Great* and *Sixty Glorious Years*, carried significant nationalistic messages. For instance, one of George Arliss's British productions, *The Iron Duke*, about the Duke of Wellington, was identified at the time of its release as a patriotic feature, particularly at a time when the newspapers were talking about German rearmament.[21] The emphasis in many of these films was on Britain's past triumphs, and the difficulties the nation had to overcome to achieve her successes. Implicitly, the suggestion was that hardship and troublesome times were, in a sense, therapeutic, that they actually led to a strengthening of nation. The logical conclusion was that Britain's current problems were no less difficult than those earlier generations had faced; the notion that this suffering as a result of the Depression would lead to a yet greater tomorrow also was comforting.

Like other themes discussed in earlier chapters, patriotism functioned, then, in British films as a form of reassurance, a motif suggesting that social contentment and loyalty in the face of adversity were the responsibilities of citizens. As a lasting influence in British cinema throughout the decade, the theme of patriotism reminded audiences of the factors that unified society; these factors, the films suggested, had made the nation and the Empire great. The implicit natural inclination resulting from such themes was that people should avoid tampering with the British system because it had survived so many difficulties and had become successful over the years; that is, the impulse resulting from this theme was strongly toward the *status quo*.

The prevalence throughout much of the decade of these themes that urged a maintenance of the *status quo* and that skirted social or political controversy was no accident. Certain factors combined to prevent the popular British film industry from approaching more serious, realistic issues, except in the most cautious way. Only near the end of the decade did British cinema, on a consistent basis, approach social drama somewhat less rigidly.

What is more notable is the fact that for years, especially during the worst of the Depression, some members of the British audiences clamored for the so-called "problem films" that had been prominent (especially at Warner Brothers studios) in American movies since the sound era had begun; at least in the letters to the editor section of the fan magazines, they noticed the absence of such features from British studios. Asked one letter-writer to *Picturegoer Weekly* in 1934:

> Are we not, kinematically speaking, a wee bit too patriotic in this country? . . . England may be a more lawabiding country than America, but I fail to see why filmdom should make it so stodgy and uninteresting. After all, even this country is not perfect – except in films.[22]

Another contributor from Nottingham lamented:

> Shall we never see a film about the unemployed? So far the Depression with its tale of increasing unemployment in every country has lasted four years. Apart from one or two American pictures such as *American Madness*, the screen has made no comment upon the plight of the world and its starving, workless inhabitants. Yet the screen, we are sometimes told, is a mirror of life. Is there no drama in unemployment? Or is the tragedy too bitter to put on the screens of the world?[23]

Likewise, a London filmgoer wanted to know why a movie could not be made "about those persecuted trade unionists, the Tolpuddle Martyrs"; she added "what about the revolt of the hand-loom workers against the new machines?"[24] Another moviegoer from Cheshire observed, in reference to the

American film fantasy *Gabriel Over the White House* about a President who becomes a dictator in order to solve the nation's ills:

Perhaps our producers believe that politics are too sacred to put upon the screen? Yet surely they cannot fail to observe the essential drama inherent in affairs of state? Our present government is fighting the world Depression as earnestly if not as spectacularly as did the mad President impersonated by Walter Huston. Surely there is a film to be made out of that fight?[25]

A letter-writer from South Devon was really frustrated that British productions were so timid; the writer observed that American films tackled all sorts of social issues while British producers avoided such topics, and he commented:

Nearly a century ago, Charles Dickens fearlessly wielding a facile pen in the story of Oliver Twist, exposed the literal hellishness of the poor-law system and brought into being its reform. But injustice, deviation from right, and deplorable conditions did not die with Dickens. Hollywood ever ready to switch the searchlight of the cinema on to her own short-comings gave us gangster films galore – not only to expose that racket but also the initial cause of it – prohibition. Her talkie triumph came in the recent repeal of prohibition. American pictures put the world wise to the revolting horror of chain-gangs; her own reprehensible reformatory system and graft in high places – sparing no one. Britain is by no means immune from condemnatory conditions. Yet Elstree eschews them. Talkies, with acceptable themes, could be trained on the sordidness of our slums – as one of your readers recently suggested. Films could make the unthinking feel the full force of our unemployment figures and the wretchedness they represent. The moral is plain. Propaganda should *not* be set aside where the screen is concerned. It has a definite part on the screen, which should be played by British movies.[26]

Of course, the problem was more complex than simply going out and making a movie, and as has been shown, the question of how many filmgoers were interested in "problem films" was highly uncertain. Because the finances of the British film industry were tighter than in America, fewer risks could be taken. Since audience response to escapist productions had been and continued to be favorable, no reason existed from a financial standpoint for risky ventures in social problem films. But another reason why such films could not be produced in England and also why venturesome producers nevertheless were cautious about making certain kinds of movies related to the Board of Film Censors which reviewed movies in advance. The rather rigid system of censorship to which movies produced in England were subjected muzzled or at least discouraged social criticism and softened even relatively innocuous socio-political commentary.

The details of how British film censorship operated have been explained elsewhere.[27] Basically the British Board of Film Censors was an unofficial organization which, like the Hays office in America, the film industry itself appointed and supported with fees which paid for censoring the films; established in 1912, it was intended to provide voluntary censorship from the industry. Though County Councils held the legal responsibility for films shown in their areas, most of them depended on the Board of Film Censors. A number of eminent persons were appointed to the Board. For example, the President of the Board from 1929 to 1935, Edward Shortt, had been Home Secretary from 1919 to 1922, and several other Board members were MPs. Graham Greene's comments of 1937 about what he called "our absurd censorship" typify the views of those who criticized the system. Remarking that Lord Tyrrell, the President of the Board of Censors, "forbids" the showing of "any controversial subject on the screen," the prominent critic argued that "at the present stage of English culture, a great many serious subjects cannot be treated at all"; citing the Warner Brothers' *I Am a Fugitive from the Chain Gang*, Greene observed that British producers "cannot treat human justice truthfully" in any comparable way, nor could any of the "aged provincial JP's [be held up] to criticism" in a British film. Greene lamented that no British feature could be allowed to "[describe] the conditions in the punishment cells at Maidstone," and he concluded that under the current system at the time he was writing (1937) it simply was not possible "to treat seriously a religious or a political subject" in a British-made film.[28]

The notes from the proceedings of the Board of Film Censors are available in the British Film Institute Library, and they make fascinating reading. Beginning in 1930, the censors permitted film-makers to submit their scenarios in advance; producers and directors welcomed this possibility because, in the long run, it could save them money. If censors objected to a film, the producers simply would not invest the time and effort in making the feature. Where only forty-six films were considered in advance in 1931, by 1937 the figure was up to almost two hundred a year.[29]

Naturally, this prior restraint had a chilling effect on what subjects were to be made. For instance, in 1930 objections were made on "political" grounds to "references to Royal Personages at home and abroad"; on "social" grounds to "pernicious stories of the underworld" and "unrelieved sordid themes"; and on "administration of justice" grounds to "gross travesties of the administration of justice" and "painful prison scenes."[30] In 1931, objections were made to references about the Prince of Wales, "offensive political propaganda, and the presentation of living personages."[31] These objections show the similarity in attitude of the Board to the traditions of theatrical censorship conducted by the Lord Chamberlain's office. These seemingly harmless plot elements made the censors worried and suggested an anti-political bias; the comments in 1936 were fairly explicit.

Politics creeping into films should be avoided. Nothing would be more calculated to arouse the passions of the British public than the introduction on the screen of subjects dealing with religion or political controversy. I believe you are all alive to this danger. You cannot lose sight of one of the first regulations of your licences, which states that no film must be exhibited which is likely to lead to disorder. . . . The Board has been attacked for passing certain innocuous dramatic films which irrational partisans have looked upon as containing insidious propaganda against the state.[32]

The number of exceptions and rejections also increased over the early years of the decade; where 191 exceptions were taken in 1930, by 1935, the figure was up to 526 per year, and the number of films rejected doubled and tripled during the 1930s.[33]

The comments made about specific features also are revealing. For example, in the observations for the period from November, 1930 to December, 1932, the censors made the following statement about an H.F. Maltby stage play called "The Red Light."

The story depicts London on the eve of a Red Revolution, and the attitude of society people to the situation, the seriousness of which none of them realize. A fortnight later, the Revolution is an accomplished fact, a Bolshevist Doctrine's beginning to be enforced against the Rich Capitalist Class. Under no circumstances could a film on these lines receive a certificate.[34]

More intriguing was the assessment of *Tidal Waters*, a projected Gainsborough studio movie about a strike among "watermen" that is, "those who work afloat in barges, tugs, etc."; in the story, "the hero is a foreman of a gang of dockers [who do not go on strike]," and the heroine, who works in a local factory is in sympathy with the watermen.[35]

The author seems to realize the difficulties of handling this subject. He does not propose to stress the differences between capital and labour which led to the strike, and suggests that it might be more of a quarrel between the two sections of workers. Our attitude to the subject has always been very definite. Strikes, or labour unrest, where the scene is laid in England, have never been shown in any detail. It is impossible to show such scenes without taking a definite side either with or against the strikers and this would at once range the film as political propaganda of a type that we have always held to be unsuitable for exhibition in this country. Scenes of sabotage are obviously prohibitive. If therefore the strike is the prominent feature of the story we would consider the subject unsuitable. If the love story is the main feature with a very shadowy reference to the strike in the background, it is possible that the story would be acceptable. In any case, we would suggest that further

229

conversation on the subject and the submission of the full scenario and dialogue sheet would be advisable before incurring expense in the studio.[36]

In relation to a 1933 film, the censors objected to showing a "debate in Parliament," adding "similarly no meeting of the Cabinet should be shown nor should any Cabinet Minister be a portrait or caricature."[37] Another comment in 1933 about a film dealing with Ireland in 1921 observed:

> The whole story is written round the political troubles in Ireland in 1921 and in the opinion of the board, is too recent history to be a suitable subject for a film. It is a very controversial period, and I strongly urge that the sad and unpleasant memories which both sides to the conflict share are best left alone and not raked up through the medium of the screen. No matter how the subject is treated, one side or the other will be angered and much harm result.[38]

A film concerning gang violence leaving London in a "state of terror" was approved "only because ... [the gangs] were so obviously American"; the report added:

> In this country, we do not allow our police to be shown on the screen as incompetent, or accepting bribes from criminals .... Wholesale machine gun murders in the streets of Chicago possibly are deemed to come under the heading of Topicals, but in London, would be quite prohibitive. Nor would we allow a picture of a member of Parliament being murdered on the floor of the House.[39]

About a projected 1934 film entitled *Machines*, concerning " a Manchester steel foreman and his ideas on Capital and Labour relations," the censors wrote:

> I think [it] savours much too strongly of political propaganda to be a suitable subject for the screen. [It is] admitted that the standpoint actually put forward does not belong to any recognized political party in this country, but from whatever angle it is approved, the relations between Capital and Labour will always lead to some controversy.[40]

And one short comment about a 1934 film entitled *Red Square* elicited the memorable statement, "I cannot visualize any deletions which would render it acceptable."[41] Other properties rejected automatically were "anti-Hitler" materials and a proposed biography of Roger Casement.[42] Even films that were approved came in for questioning; for instance, *My Old Dutch* generated "concern" over "street orators working up the people for the strike" in 1926 and over "damage at the petrol depot being done by strikers."[43]

What the Board of Censors did find acceptable was made clear by the general comments prefacing the 1932 reports. In the remarks, the censors observed, "there is an overwhelming majority of the community who desire considerable relaxation and real enjoyment from their visits to the cinema and their attitude is voiced by a judge in the North of England who recently said he thanked God for giving us cinemas"; they cited an ordinary citizen's comment that "cinemas fill a very large part in the everyday life of the working classes, and the tendency of the films is to uplift as well as entertain." [44] In fact, the general attitude of the Board was expressed effectively by T.P. O'Connor, Shortt's predecessor. O'Connor commented that film censorship was based "upon a large body of principles and traditions, which have gradually been built up," that have been designed "to avoid on the one hand, rigidity of view which would exclude . . . any subject that touches human life in any one of its many aspects," and to "prevent" on the other hand "the exhibition of anything which might tend to the demoralization of the mind or morals of the nation"; O'Connor added that the "vigilance" of the censor is "necessitated" because "the kinema has become such a popular institution, reaching more of the people than any other agency whatsoever," thereby making "widespread" any "evil influence permitted to enter it," and because "more than any other form of art or amusement, it has become a domestic institution" appealing to the "whole family." [45]

O'Connor's concern about potentially "disastrous" consequences if this vigilance were to be eased was echoed by others on the Board. At a meeting of film exhibitors in June, 1936 Shortt's successor, Lord Tyrrell, according to Forsyth Hardy, in a 1937 essay, "suggested that cinema needs continued repression of controversy in order to stave off disaster"; Hardy went on to point out that Tyrrell openly expressed satisfaction that the British film industry had released "no film dealing with 'current, burning political questions,'" but that he was concerned that the "thin edge of the wedge" now was being "inserted," and he feared the "lengths" to which "it might go 'unless some check' were put on soon." Clearly, Hardy concluded "the edict [has] gone forth: No controversy." [46] As if to verify this resolve, just two months earlier, the Board had refused a certificate to *Blow Bugles Blow*, a feature made by the Progressive Film Institute. In the feature, the possibility of a General Strike to oppose government activity had played a significant part in the story-line; a collection of unions opposed a war and called for massive resistance to a Prime Minister's call for a declaration of war against France. Such story-lines were clearly too dangerous.

These attitudes, then, naturally kept the character of British films largely in the escapist mode. Protests at the censor's decisions were "relatively rare," according to Forsyth Hardy, because "the trade does not wish to do or say anything which might lead to the abolition of the present form of censorship set up by itself and the substitution of a body under direct government control"; in other words, concluded Hardy, "Wardour Street is scared stiff of the Censor." [47]

But some members of the film industry were not afraid to criticize and suggest an improvement in the censorship process. Actor Edmund Gwenn commented in 1932 on how he thought a censor should "keep abreast of public opinion"; in a piece published in *Film Weekly*, Gwenn observed that in his view the "censor must not be either ahead of or behind public feeling." He went on to explain that if he were to serve on the Censorship Board he would seek to be informed of the public's news "by going myself" and by "sending my staff of examiners among the people." Gwenn reasoned that "by sitting in the midst of crowded audiences, of all sorts and conditions, in the West End of London, and in the East End, in country villages, in manufacturing cities, in University inns," he would be "training [himself] to become sensitive to audience reactions"; in that way, Gwenn argued, as a censor, he would "at least know instinctively what would repel, what disgust, what amuse and what horrify the same majority." Gwenn's contention was that such an approach would guarantee that the censor never would "consider [himself] better qualified to decide what was good for the people of England than they themselves"; Gwenn felt, therefore, that the censor "should trust in the sterling worth of public opinion . . . not endeavour to mould it to [his] ideal." [48]

Where Gwenn rather idealistically proposed reforming the censor himself, Alfred Hitchcock explained that the censor had changed his approach to film making; claiming that he had always been interested in making films that address social issues, Hitchcock lamented, "but I have never been allowed to do so." In a revealing article in *Film Weekly* in 1938, Hitchcock observed that some time after the General Strike of 1926, he had intended to "put the whole thing" on film which he thought would make "a magnificently dynamic motion-picture." But when he "suggested the idea to [his] production chief, he approached the British Board of Film Censors, who immediately vetoed it." Hitchcock added that he would "no doubt, have been allowed to make a wishy-washy picture about the General Strike, but in this form the subject no longer appealed to me." Hitchcock explained that it was his intention "to show fist fights between strikers and undergraduates, pickets and all the authentic drama of the situation." Hitchcock added that he had a similar experience when he wanted essentially to film the siege of Sidney Street in *The Man Who Knew Too Much*. The director wrote that "when the idea was submitted for approval to the Home Office" he was told "that I mustn't show the militia being called out and the house in Sidney Street surrounded by machine guns." Hitchcock went on to complain about all of the story ideas he had proposed only to be restricted in what he could do; "again and again" he wrote "I have been prevented from putting on the screen authentic accounts of incidents in British life" and been told by his production chief after having suggested such "authentic" proposals, "Sorry Hitch, but the censor'd never pass it." Hitchcock remarked that he had only one recourse, which meant avoiding controversial topics and using basically fictional stories. He explained that if he "[implied] 'it can't happen here'" or if he "set [his] story in Central Europe" with foreigners as villians, the censors will not intervene. However "if your picture is too obviously a criticism of the social system, Whitehall shakes its head." Hitchcock concluded that he would like to "weave a film around a pit disaster or an incident of sabotage in the Glasgow dockyards or around the crooked financiers of the city," but he feared that "such subjects, handled as I must inevitably handle them, would have great difficulty getting past the censor"; therefore, he pleaded "do not blame me for ignoring such subjects. . . . blame Whitehall."[49] Aside from providing an interesting possible explanation for the long-standing question in film scholarship of why such a great director as Alfred Hitchcock worked only in the thriller–suspense genre throughout much of this career, Hitchcock's statement shows how drastically the content of British film was altered by censorship.

Clearly, then, this concern on the part of the censor affected the subject matter of British cinema and kept it from being an influence that would in any way incite the public politically. Tables 9.2 and 9.3 show that the number

Table 9.2 Films involving domestic rebellion, upheaval, or disturbance

Year	Proportion of the films released	%
1929	4 of 86	4.7
1930	0 of 99	0.0
1931	0 of 134	0.0
1932	0 of 150	0.0
1933	1 of 181	0.6
1934	2 of 183	1.1
1935	1 of 185	0.5
1936	5 of 219	2.3
1937	3 of 211	1.4
1938	0 of 158	0.0
1939	0 of 98	0.0

of films released in these years which portray, for example, domestic upheavals is very small, and very few British features depicted even foreign rebellions or upheavals.

Obviously, then, the British cinema had gained respect from figures of authority who recognized its uses under the right conditions for promoting domestic peace and tranquillity among the working classes, and its potential dangers under the wrong circumstances for promoting discontent; therefore, it is not surprising that in the 1930s, those same authorities, politicians, and leaders began to make use of films more extensively than they had in the past. For instance, *Film Pictorial* reported in a small item in a late, 1933 issue that the Tory Party had enlisted actor George Arliss to recreate his role as Disraeli for a short "propaganda film for the Conservative party"; the item noted that

Table 9.3 Films involving rebellion, upheaval, or
disturbance outside Great Britain

Year	Proportion of the films released	%
1929	3 of 86	3.5
1930	0 of 99	0.0
1931	5 of 134	3.7
1932	5 of 150	3.3
1933	4 of 181	2.2
1934	10 of 183	5.5
1935	8 of 185	4.3
1936	14 of 219	6.4
1937	10 of 211	4.7
1938	7 of 158	4.4
1939	2 of 98	2.0

"he was made up as Disraeli for this performance as the propaganda film took the great Victorian statesman's ideas as the basis of a stirring message to present-day Britain." [50] Clearly, movies were respected for their potency as a tool of social control.

In this sense, while the content of British popular films in the 1930s served as an informal argument for the *status quo*, the industry-sponsored censorship guaranteed that features challenging the *status quo* were unlikely to be made. Thus, the British cinema in this decade remained highly patriotic as well as escapist and therefore all the more potent in its appeal to the working classes.

10

CONCLUSIONS

That the British film industry, invariably perceived as the "poor cousin" of Hollywood, has been overlooked, would seem to be obvious. Whatever the reason for the neglect, at no time is the lack of attention more obvious than when the period from 1929 to 1939 is considered. Somehow, like an important book on a shelf that loses its prominence when it slips behind the others, becoming hidden from view and forgotten, the British cinema in the thirties has been left relatively unnoticed in the flurry of research recently conducted on motion pictures and on popular culture. This neglect is unfortunate, but it is especially so for the social historian who has so much to learn about contemporary attitudes, perceptions, and values from these motion pictures and from the movie-going experience in general during this decade of economic crisis, uncertainty, and dislocation. Just as in America, during the worst of the Depression, filmgoers in Great Britain flocked to the cinema, no matter how troubled their financial condition. This study has attempted to demonstrate that British features contained rather clear, coherent, philosophic viewpoints that addressed, often implicitly but sometimes explicitly, the various concerns of the people, especially among the working classes, who were living through these troubled times.

Clearly, the glib, oft-repeated, unverified assumptions about British popular films during the thirties must be discarded or at least re-evaluated. The highly influential London West-End critics, from whom so many of the perceptions about the British cinema at this time are derived, were unimpressed by the substantial contribution of the music hall tradition to British movies; they disdained the likes of Gracie Fields, George Formby, and "Old Mother Riley," whom they considered to be crude, vulgar, and cliché-ridden, in spite of the enormous popularity with the working classes of these performers and of their feature films. In fact, these writers, whose views still predominate, really knew very little about the kinds of movies that played more frequently in the provinces and in the working-class neighborhoods; their environment was that of the West-End theater district, the realm of upper- and middle-class audiences, not that of working-class audiences, who obtained their entertainment in the "fleapits" of their neighborhoods.

235

Unfortunately, the judgments about Elstree's productions which have persisted suggest that the British film industry neglected its working-class clientele; but these attitudes were based on inconclusive evidence and more frequently were simply reflective of a point of view that was decidedly contemptuous of traditional working-class entertainers. In fact, the West-End critics, who are more frequently quoted and are more generally accessible fifty years later, were probably among the film commentators least likely to be able to assess accurately working-class tastes. By contrast, reviewers for the fan magazines, whose audiences were the working classes, directed their comments to working-class readers about many films which would never play the West-End cinemas. Accordingly, their analyses are far more revealing about working-class tastes, and they suggest that contrary to the contention that the producers were unresponsive to their working-class patrons, in fact, producers at Elstree were carefully and successfully evaluating the kinds of films the public wanted to see. The usual criticism that most British features were "drawing-room dramas" with snobbish middle- or upper-class protagonists may have been valid for the kinds of films that played the West End, but in other parts of the country, the movies shown were far more diversified with numerous films having a working-class orientation.

Whether or not the West-End perception of the film industry was an accurate critique, the continued box-office performance of the British film among the working classes elsewhere in Great Britain during this decade leads one to conclude that these filmgoers were essentially satisfied with what they were seeing at their movie-houses. Letters to film fan magazines, often from working-class individuals, help confirm these assumptions. At the same time, the profit motive of the administrators in the motion picture producing and exhibiting industries, for the most part, assured that film-makers would continue to address the needs of their audiences. In fact, informal mechanisms such as fan polls, surveys of theater chains, and attention to fan magazine letter-writers, and more formal devices, such as reports of cinema managers and exhibitors, were utilized to respond to filmgoers more directly. Such reports were a good deal more effective than the prejudiced prescriptions of an isolated London critic or intellectual.

While some observers would have wanted British producers to concentrate on social problem films and realism, in most cases, the kinds of movies that were preferred were, as has been shown, essentially escapist films, sometimes with a strong element of wish-fulfillment. Predictably, in such films, the messages that these features conveyed were essentially optimistic concepts; the movies called for hope, cooperation, self-sacrifice, and patriotism, and they centered on traditional, homespun values. The prescription suggested for dealing with adversity was forbearance, not protest or action. Additionally, as has been shown, wealth, status, and power were frequently viewed as being sometimes an unpleasant burden, a reminder that even with hardship, pain, and poverty, sometimes a person could be better off than another who was ostensibly more successful; therefore, envy and frustration with one's lot in life were unnecessary.

The depiction of the class structure was usually uncritical, and though some people objected to the portrayal of the working classes in the music hall tradition, apparently the working classes themselves were those least offended; for the most part, these filmgoers were interested in entertainment, not socio-political commentary, and wanted only an opportunity to laugh or weep, to "lose themselves" from their cares for a few hours of pleasure. That they were being subtly influenced in the process of this escapism to an attitude that was orientated toward the *status quo* probably would have mattered little to them even had they been more aware of it. The films they saw were reassuring and therefore not socially disruptive; but it was precisely that kind of movie, that type of escape, which they apparently enjoyed.

But, perhaps even more important than the films themselves, to this process of escape was the actual experience of going to the movies. Probably no other secular institution provided as much of a haven for the general public in the thirties as the cinema. Dispensing charity as well as relaxation, serving as a baby sitter and as a responsible corporate citizen, the neighborhood cinema especially became a place of escape, where the lowliest person was pampered and looked after as if he or she were a millionaire; here, particularly in the newer, bigger "picture palaces," luxury, comfort, and palatial design were the physical counterparts of the illusions that were being projected on the screen. The cinema managers in this way deliberately sought to create a different environment for their patrons, a refuge from the outside world.

Thus, the statement by Branson and Heinemann in their *Britain in the 1930s,* that British films in this decade were "the heart of a heartless world" carried with it social implications.[1] At the cinema, the working classes escaped their troubled existences into a fantasy world of social as well as material illusions; it was a world at once comfortable, relaxing, sometimes luxurious, and even caring. They were reminded of the continuity in British society in the home-grown films they saw and were able to imagine fantasies, wonderful visions of what their lives would be like if only they could have it a certain way. And yet, the stories they vicariously experienced reinforced values and beliefs that kept them from discontent with their real lives; at least the film industry and individuals responsible for the content of the movies they saw apparently had this idea in mind. Historians looking for reasons why the working classes were not more radical, eager for change, and disruptive during this difficult period may find a partial explanation, then, in the movie-going experience.

But whatever the impact on their political or social views, these implicit values and ideas had, the working classes probably would have had it no other way. The cinemas were the "dream houses," and the luxury of the movies was the "affordable fur" that C. Day Lewis called them in his evocative 1938 poem "Newsreel."[2] The British produced films that insulated them from reality and allowed them to avoid having to concentrate on their own troubles, even if only for a short while.

Gracie Fields, perhaps appropriately, summed up the response of the working classes to the movies in one of her comic songs about a working-class girl on a date at the cinema, and no better description of the enjoyment films provided can be found than this in the musical sketch from her 1938 *Keep Smiling*. In the number, Miss Fields, using her comic North-country accent, personifies a working-class woman telling a friend about the good time that she had at the movies watching a melodrama. In the verse, she explained that "Joe took me to the pictures the other evening" and "it was fine" with "acting [that] was divine"; the character remarked "it's the best film that they've had for years round at the 'ippodrome," and "it's a good job I took me 'ankerchief with me when I left." In the main part of the number, Miss Fields then proceeds to sing about all the problems and travails that befall the heroine of the film, and each line is followed by the weepy expression "Oh I never cried so much in all me life."

The explicit humor in the situation, aside from Miss Fields's hilarious delivery of the material, is that the film she describes sounds so awful; the discussion of the "villain" seizing "the maiden," the lies he tells her to "[entice] her on his yacht" before tying her up "in a proper sailor's knot," and "[facing] the blinding snowstorm" resemble plot elements from a turn-of-the-century melodrama. In fact, if one were to characterize the film simply from the way Miss Fields's persona portrays it, one would use words like "trite," "old-fashioned," "unoriginal," and "worthless," expressions often used in connection with the movies produced by the British film industry in the 1930s. And yet the clearly working-class character Miss Fields personifies says "Oh, it was a luv-ly picture, and I did enjoy it so."

The unstated, somewhat more subtle humor of the sequence is the irony of how the woman responds to what she sees on the screen in contrast to what may, indeed, be going on in her own life. From the accent and comments of the character Miss Fields is portraying, the audience can presume she is clearly of working-class origin. Unless she is an unusual individual, she presumably has experienced what other working-class individuals have lived through in the thirties: unemployment, uncertainty, hunger, and sometimes barely subsistence wages. And yet, her character in referring to the film comments that when she "[thinks] of what that girl went through ... I see her eyes, I hear her voice at night when I'm in bed"; in short, she empathizes with her plight and feels so sorry for the heroine that she "never cried so much in all me life." Reality, to Miss Fields's character, can be forgotten, and instead of being pitied, the filmgoer she portrayed can pity the misfortunes of someone else; she can quite literally escape her own difficulties at the cinema. And it was this function, more than any other, that British films, however aesthetically good or bad, were able to perform in Great Britain in the 1930s.

NOTES

1 INTRODUCTION

1 See, for example, Paul Monaco, *Cinema and Society*, Amsterdam, Elsevier Science Publishing Company, 1976 about France and Germany, though the emphasis in this volume is on the 1920s; Adriano Apra and Patrizia Pistagnesi, *The Fabulous Thirties: Italian Cinema, 1929–1944*, Rome, Electra Publi Gray, 1976; David Stewart Hull, *Film in the Third Reich*, Berkeley, University of California Press, 1969; Erwin Leiser, *Nazi Cinema*, New York, Secker and Warburg, 1974; and especially Siegfried Kracauer, *From Caligari to Hitler*, New York, Princeton University Press, 1947, about films in Weimar Germany. Also see Peter Roffman and Jim Purdy, *The Hollywood Social Problem Film: Madness, Despair, and Politics from the Depression to the Fifties*, Bloomington, Indiana University Press, 1981.

2 George Perry, *The Great British Picture Show*, New York, Hill and Wang, 1974, p. 65.

3 Charles Davy, "Postscript: The Film Marches On," in C. Davy ed. *Footnotes to the Film*, London, Lovat Dickson, 1938, p. 303.

4 The Quota Act has been discussed in many sources, but the best short account is that given in the fourth volume of Rachel Low, *History of the British Film*, London, George Allen and Urwin, 1971. The details and implications of the Act are also discussed in the *Kinematograph Year Book*, London, Kinematograph Publications, published annually in the thirties.

5 Alberto Cavalcanti, "Comedies and Cartoons," in Davy (ed.), *op. cit.*, p. 78.

6 John Fisher, *Funny Way to be a Hero*, London, Frederick Muller, 1973, pp. 14, 21, 22.

7 *Ibid.*, pp. 75–76.

8 *Ibid.*, p. 76.

9 *Ibid.*, pp. 79–80.

10 *Film Weekly*, July 3, 1937, XIX, 455, p. 29.

11 George Arliss, *My Ten Years in the Studios*, Boston, MA Little, Brown and Company, 1940, pp. 9–10.

12 This information can be found, along with other questions relating to film preference in Britain, in George H. Gallup, *The Gallup International Public Opinion Polls: Great Britain, 1937–1975*, Volume I, New York, Random House, 1976, p. 4.

13 Sidney Bernstein, one of the best known figures in the British film industry in the 1930s, owned a chain of Cinemas and periodically conducted a survey among his patrons. As many as 250,000 questionnaires were circulated, of which about fifty percent were returned and used in compiling the data. Accordingly, the surveys

provide a very interesting reference point for assessing certain questions about film-going tastes in the thirties. The questionnaire results are on file in the British Film Institute Library.

14 *Picturegoer Weekly*, April 28, 1934, III, 153, pp. 12–13.

2 MYTHS AND UNSUPPORTED ASSUMPTIONS

1 Alan Wood, *Mr Rank: A Study of J. Arthur Rank and British Films*, London, Hodder and Stoughton, 1952, p. 48.
2 Arthur Knight, *The Liveliest Art: A Panoramic History of the Movies*, New York, Mentor Books, 1979, p. 223.
3 Basil Wright, *The Long View*, New York, Alfred A. Knopf, 1974, p. 103.
4 Gerald Mast, *A Short History of the Movies*, Indianapolis, IN, Bobbs-Merrill, 1976, p. 413.
5 George Perry, *The Great British Picture Show: From the 90s to the 70s*, New York, Hill and Wang, 1974.
6 Jerry Vermilye, *The Great British Films*, Secaucus, NJ, Citadel Press, 1978.
7 During the last ten years, this neglect of the first decade of British sound film production has been mitigated somewhat by several outstanding studies and various isolated monographic publications. Scholars like Anthony Aldgate, Geoff Brown, and Jeffrey Richards have been making significant contributions to an understanding of British film during this and other periods. The contributions of Rachel Low, who completed her monumental multi-volume study of the British film with three volumes on the decade from 1929 to 1939 have provided a comprehensive overview, particularly of the production facet of the industry; see especially, R. Low, *Film Making in 1930s Britain*, London, George Allen and Unwin, 1985. Also see Jeffrey Richards' outstanding overview, *The Age of the Dream Palace: Cinema and Society in Britain, 1930–1939*, London, Routledge and Kegan Paul, 1984. See also Peter Stead's fine study, *Film and the Working Class*, London, Routledge, 1989, and Marcia Landy's ground-breaking *British Genres: Cinema and Society, 1930–1960*, Princeton, NJ, Princeton University Press, 1991.
8 Knight, *op. cit.*, p. 223. See discussion of Quota Act elsewhere. Also see Raymond Durgnat's review of Charles Barr's book *Ealing Studios* in *Film Comment*, July–August, 1978, XIV, 4, pp. 73–76 for a discussion of the politics of British film criticism and the neglect critics in England have for their native cinema of the decades before the 1950s.
9 Wood, *op. cit.*, p. 86.
10 Maurice Kann, "Hollywood and Britain – Three Thousand Miles Apart" in C. Davy ed. *Footnotes to the Film*, London, Lovat Dickson, 1938, pp. 185–202.
11 *Variety*, February 19, 1930, p. 71.
12 *Ibid.* and December 11, 1929, pp. 6, 21.
13 Paul Rotha and Richard Griffith, *The Film Till Now*, London, Spring Books, 1967, pp. 549–550.
14 W. H. Mooring, "What Americans think of British Films," *Film Weekly*, January 15, 1938, XX, 483, p. 9.
15 *Variety*, March 19, 1930, pp. 1, 56.
16 *Variety*, January 29, 1930, p. 26.
17 George Pearson, *Flashback: An Autobiography of a British Film Maker*, London, George Allen and Unwin, 1957, pp. 187–199.
18 Adrian Brunel, *Nice Work: Thirty Years in British Films*, London, Forbes Robertson, 1949, p. 166.
19 Herbert Wolkmann, *Film Preservation: A Report of the Preservation Committee of*

the International Federation of Film Archives, London, National Film Archive, 1965. The rarity of some British films was observed in passing in two articles in two separate issues of *Films in Review* in 1974. In the February issue, film archivist Samuel A. Peeples in his regular column on film preservation and collecting observed that "most of the films made in England in the early '30s are 'lost,' their negatives decomposed and no prints known to have survived" [*Films in Review*, February, 1974, XXV, 2, p. 103.] In the December issue, film historian William K. Everson, in a report on the restoration of a number of films made by Fox studios, after observing the problems of film preservation work, noted that of "the very impressive roster of British films made by Warner Brothers [in England], ... almost all ... were destroyed by Warners in Britain some few years ago. " [p. 605: see William K. Everson, "Film Treasure Trove," *Films in Review*, December, 1974, XXV, 10, pp. 595–610.] See also the recent British Film Institute report on "lost films" which centers on British films in the 1930s: Allen Eyles and David Meeker, eds, *Missing Believed Lost: The Great British Film Search*, London, British Film Institute, 1992.

20 J. Limbacher ed., *Feature Films on 8mm and 16mm: A Directory of Feature Films Available for Rental, Sale, and Lease in the United States and Canada, 5th edition*, New York, R. R. Bowker, 1977.

21 *TV Feature Film Source Book, Part I: Feature Titles*. New York, Broadcast Information Bureau, 1978.

22 Walter Allen, "Mass Entertainment" in John Raymond ed. *The Baldwin Age*, London, Eyre and Spottiswoode, 1960, pp. 225–226.

23 Knight, *op. cit.*, pp. 226, 234–235.

24 Perry, *op. cit.*, p. 65.

25 Alexander Korda, "British Films: To-day and To-morrow," in Davy, ed. *op. cit.*, p. 162.

26 Charles Loch Mowat, *Britain Between the Wars, 1918–1940*, Boston, MA, Beacon Press, 1971, p. 485.

27 George Orwell, *The Road to Wigan Pier*, New York, Penguin Books, 1962, pp. 79–81.

28 *Ibid.*

29 *Film Weekly*, November 3, 1933, IX, 264, p. 26.

30 *Picturegoer Weekly*, December 2, 1933, III, 132, p. 34.

31 *Film Weekly*, July 18, 1931, V, 144, p. 20.

32 *Picturegoer Weekly*, August 3, 1935, V, 219, p. 31.

33 *Film Weekly*, December 20, 1930, IV, 114, p. 20.

34 *Ibid.*

35 *Film Pictorial*, December 17, 1932, II, 43, p. 26.

36 *Screen Pictorial*, January 21, 1933, II, 48, p. 24.

37 *Picturegoer Weekly*, November 7, 1931, I, 24, p. 29.

38 *Film Weekly*, May 26, 1933, IX, 241, p. 3.

39 *Film Weekly*, January 10, 1931, V, 117, p. 17.

40 *Film Pictorial*, December 30, 1933, IV, 97, p. 30.

41 See Andrew Bergman, *We're in the Money*, New York, Harper and Row, 1971; Robert Sklar, *Movie Made America*, New York, Vintage Books, 1975; David Manning White and Richard Averson, *The Celluloid Weapon*, Boston, MA, Beacon Press, 1972; and Peter Roffman and Jim Purdy, *The Hollywood Social Problem Film*, Bloomington, Indiana University Press, 1981.

42 Roy Armes, *A Critical History of British Cinema*, London, Secker and Warburg, 1978, p. 38. Also see Marshall Deutelbaum, "Review of *The British Film Catalogue*", *Film Comment*, May–June, 1974, X, 3, p. 61.

43 See Denis Gifford, *The British Film Catalogue, 1895–1970: A Guide to Entertainment Films*, Newton Abbott, Redwood Press for David and Charles, 1973. See also David Quinlan, *British Sound Films: The Studio Years, 1938–1959*, London, B.T. Batsford, 1984. This subsequent publication with its somewhat longer descriptions of most British features during this period effectively supplements Gifford's information. Gifford also lists a number of films as "revues" which consist of collections of variety acts, often directly from vaudeville or music hall backgrounds.

44 The traditional definition of a feature's length, though somewhat arbitrary, almost uniformly has been approximately thirty minutes, that is three reels, or longer. For example, the Motion Picture Academy of Arts and Sciences, for the purposes of its Academy Awards, has used a length of 3000 feet or just over thirty minutes for its definition of feature length. Film historian William K. Everson of New York University in his excellent December, 1975 article on Jessie Matthews which appeared in the American publication *Films in Review* observed in passing that "the legal definition of a feature [in Britain] was anything over three thousand feet" (see p. 594.) Thus, it was thought best to use the thirty minute figure as a convenient and the most appropriate dividing line in this chapter and succeeding sections. It should be underscored, however, that this figure *is* arbitrary.

45 In this sense, "escapist" films might be defined as films that make no pretense of realism.

46 In America, after the initial craze for musicals in the early sound era had faded, there was a similar leveling or dropping off. See John Kobal's history of film musicals *Gotta Sing, Gotta Dance*, London, Hamlyn, 1970. See also Lee Edward Stern, *The Movie Musical*, New York, Pyramid Books, 1974 and John Springer, *All Talking, All Singing, All Dancing*, New York, Citadel Press, 1969. Richard Barrios' outstanding *A Song In the Dark: The Birth of the Musical Film*, New York, Oxford University Press, 1995, may be the definitive publication on the subject.

47 Carlos Carlens, *Crime Movies*, New York, W.W. Norton, 1980, p. 12.

48 Gifford's categories "act," "chase," and "trick" are not to be found among the features of the decade.

49 These patterns are also observable in the re-releases of short films as well. Of the seventy short films made in the thirties that were reissued, all but one of them (an adventure) were comedies or musicals.

3   DEPICTING THE WORKING CLASSES IN BRITISH FILM IN THE THIRTIES

1 *Film Weekly*, April 23, 1938, XX, 497, p. 11.
2 *Ibid.*
3 *Ibid.*
4 *Ibid.*
5 *Ibid.*
6 *Ibid.*
7 *Ibid.*, May 7, 1938, XX, 499, p. 26.
8 *Ibid.*
9 *Ibid.*
10 *Picturegoer Weekly*, March 25, 1933, II, 97, p. 36.
11 *Film Weekly*, May 29, 1937, XVIII, 450, p. 25.
12 *Picturegoer Weekly*, February 20, 1932, I, 39, p. 30.
13 *Film Pictorial*, December 9, 1933, IV, 94, p. 38.

14 *Film Weekly*, June 22, 1934, XI, 297, p. 28.

15 *Ibid.*, April 10, 1937, XVIII, 443, p. 25.

16 *Ibid.*, October 20, 1933, X, 262, p. 30.

17 *Ibid.*, February 19, 1938, XX, 488, p. 26.

18 *Picturegoer Weekly*, November 5, 1932, II, 76, p. 29.

19 *Ibid.*, May 12, 1934, III, 155, p. 34.

20 *Ibid.*, June 17, 1933, III, 108, p. 33.

21 *Ibid.*

22 *Ibid.*, June 3, 1934, III, 158, p. 34.

23 *Film Weekly*, April 3, 1937, XVIII, 442, p. 23.

24 *Ibid.*, May 19, 1933, IX, 240, p. 29.

25 *Film Pictorial*, December 30, 1933, IV, 97, p. 30.

26 *Film Weekly*, February 27, 1937, XVII, 437, p. 14.

27 *Picturegoer Weekly*, June 3, 1934, III, 158, p. 34.

28 *Film Pictorial*, February 3, 1934, IV, 102, p. 30.

29 *Picturegoer Weekly*, July 30, 1932, II, 62, p. 29.

30 *Ibid.*

31 *Ibid.*, July 18, 1931, I, 8, p.7.

32 *Film Pictorial*, July 22, 1933, III, 74, p. 30.

33 *Film Weekly*, May 7, 1938, XX, 499, p. 26.

34 *Ibid.*, November 12, 1938, XX, 526, p. 24.

35 Philip Slessor, "Edmund Gwenn's Men Are – Real Men," *Film Pictorial*, September 2, 1933, IV, 80, pp. 22–23.

36 "Gordon Harker in Interview with Annette Adams says, 'I Love Cockneys'," *Picturegoer Weekly*, October 13, 1934, IV, 177, pp. 12–13.

37 George Carney, "When Observation Spells Success," *Ibid.*, April 11, 1936, V, 255. p. 17.

38 Robert Stevenson, "Cockneys Come Into Their Own," *Picturegoer*, June, 1930, XIX, 114, pp. 16–17.

39 See, for example, *Film Weekly*, July 24, 1937, XIX, 458, pp. 22, 9–10; *Ibid.*, December 28, 1934, XII, 323, p. 12; *Film Pictorial*, December 9, 1933, IV, 94, p. 22; *Film Weekly*, August 20, 1938, XX, 514, pp. 6–7; and *Picturegoer Weekly*, December 19, 1936, VI, 291, p. 28.

40 See, for example, Alfred Hitchcock's interview with J. Danvers Williams in *Film Weekly*, November 5, 1938, XX, 525, pp. 6–7.

41 J. Danvers Williams, "A.J. Cronin's plans for *The Citadel*," *Film Weekly*, January 29, 1938, XX, 485, p. 12.

42 Norman Loudon, "Put Britain on the Map," *Picturegoer Weekly*, May 6, 1933, II, 102, p. 13.

43 *Ibid.*

44 *Ibid.*

45 *Film Pictorial*, May 26, 1934, V, 118, p. 2.

46 *Film Weekly*, December 7, 1935, XIV, 373, p. 13.

47 *Gaumont–British News*, October, 1931, II, 10, p. 50.

48 *Ibid.*, February, 1934, V, 2, p. 29.

49 *Ibid.*, March, 1935, VI, 3, p. 13.

50 *Stoll Herald*, November 3, 1930, 68, pp. 4–6.

51 *Film Weekly*, October 21, 1932, VIII, 210, p. 22.

52 *Gaumont–British News*, November, 1932, III, 11, p. 29.

53 Lupino Lane, "Should Films Stick to Fantasy," *Picturegoer Weekly*, November 19, 1932, II, 78, p. 20.

54 *Ibid.*

55 Clifford Eccles, "The Films I Should Like to Make," *Film Weekly*, January 2, 1932, VII, 168, p. 7.
56 *Ibid.*
57 *Ibid.*, December 27, 1930, IV, 115, p. 9.
58 J. Danvers Williams, "Confessions of an Epic Maker," *Ibid.*, November 12, 1938, XX, 526, pp. 6–7.
59 Willf Anderson, "Chasing Shadows," September, 1969, p. 13 (privately published).
60 *Ibid.*, December 1969, p. 1.
61 *Ibid.*
62 *Film Weekly*, December 8, 1933, X, 269, p. 26.
63 *Ibid.*
64 The failure to reissue the Renate Muller vehicles was probably not a question of their not being popular but may have been related to the growing Anglo–German international tensions in the latter part of the decade.
65 *Film Weekly*, December 8, 1933, X, 269, p. 26.
66 *Ibid.*, April 29, 1932, VII, 185, p. 22 and *Picturegoer Weekly*, January 2, 1932, I, 32, p. 29.
67 *Picturegoer Weekly*, June 3, 1933, III, 106, p. 32.
68 Albert Burdon, "Humour the Public Wants," *Film Weekly*, January 12, 1934, XI, 274, p. 10.
69 Alan Randall and Ray Seaton, *George Formby*, London, W.H. Allen, 1974, p. 80.
70 Oliver Baldwin, "What Films Do the Public Like," *Picturegoer Weekly*, June 17, 1933, III, 108, p. 13.
71 *Ibid.*
72 *Ibid.*

4   MISTAKEN IDENTITIES

1 *Stoll Herald*, April 3, 1933, VII, 94, n.p. and *Monthly Film Bulletin*, September, 1937, IV, 44, p. 190.
2 *Picturegoer Weekly*, October 12, 1935, V, 229, p. 37. See also George Pearson's *Flashback: An Autobiography of a British Film-maker*, London, George Allen and Unwin, 1957, pp. 196–197, and Anne Edwards, *Vivien Leigh*, New York, Pocket Books, 1977, p. 45.
3 *Film Weekly*, August 27, 1938, XX, 515, p. 28.
4 *Monthly Film Bulletin*, April, 1938, V, 51, pp. 97–98.
5 *Ibid.*, February, 1936, III, 25, p. 24. Character comedian Robertson Hare is perhaps best known as the meek victim of the schemes of Tom Walls and Ralph Lynn in the numerous Aldwych comedies.
6 *Ibid.*
7 *Stoll Herald*, April 6, 1935, XI, 15, n.p.
8 *Ibid.*, October 5, 1935, XI, 41, n.p.
9 *Monthly Film Bulletin*, January, 1938, IV, 48, p. 11.
10 *Ibid.*
11 Maurice Yacowar, *Hitchcock's British Films*, Hamden, CT, Archon Books, 1977, p. 224.
12 *Film Weekly*, May 21, 1938, XX, 501, p. 8.
13 See, for example, the discussion of the film in *Cinegram*, No. 20, 1937.
14 *Monthly Film Weekly*, November, 1937, IV, 46, p. 242.
15 *Ibid.*, May, 1935, II, 16, p. 52.
16 *Ibid.*, June, 1938, V, 53, p. 154.

17 *Ibid.*, October, 1935, II, 21, p. 145.
18 *Stoll Herald*, February 24, 1936, XI, 8.
19 *Film Weekly*, March 27, 1937, XVIII, 441, pp. 32–33.
20 James Dillon White, *Born to Star: The Lupino Lane Story*, London, Heinemann, 1957, p. 282.
21 *Ibid.*, p. 269.
22 *Ibid.*, pp. 251–254.
23 *Ibid.*, pp. 256.
24 *Ibid.*, pp. 266–267.
25 *Ibid.*
26 *Monthly Film Bulletin*, May, 1939, VI, 65, p. 93.
27 White, *op. cit*, pp. 275–276. It is important to remember that the BBC television service was broadcasting a regular schedule of programming to a remarkably large potential audience long before the American television industry began expanding.
28 Parker Tyler, *Classics of the Foreign Film*, New York, Bonanza Books, 1962, pp. 128–129.
29 See R.J. Minney, *'Puffin" Asquith*, London, Leslie Frewin, 1973, p. 73 and Valerie Pascal, *The Disciple and His Devil*, London, Michael Joseph, 1971, pp. 74–75.
30 Pascal, *op. cit*, p. 82.
31 Minney, *op. cit*, pp. 94–95.
32 Pascal, *op. cit*, p. 84.
33 *Ibid.*, p. 83.
34 *Academy Awards: An Ungar Reference Index*, compiled by Richard Shale, New York, Frederick Ungar, 1978, p. 330. Lipscomb, Lewis, and Dalrymple received solace in the form of Academy Awards for adaptation.
35 Pascal, *op. cit*, p. 85.
36 *Ibid.*
37 *Ibid.*
38 *Monthly Film Bulletin*, August, 1938, V, 55, p. 197.
39 *Film Weekly*, June 24, 1939, XXI, 558, p. 5.
40 Bernard Shaw, *Pygmalion*, Baltimore, MD, Penguin Books, 1951, p. 110.
41 *Ibid.*, p. 110.
42 Shaw thought enough of this scene to include it in his 1942 published version of the play with scenes from the movie. It is significant to note here that he did not include the movie's ending in this published form. Shaw, *op. cit*, pp. 38–39.
43 Geoff Brown, *Launder and Gilliat*, London, British Film Institute, 1977, p. 46.
44 Shaw, *op. cit*, p. 37.
45 *Ibid.*, pp. 103–104.
46 *Ibid.*, pp. 21, 28, 31, 81, 36, and 34.
47 *Ibid.*, pp. 35, 34, 81.
48 *Ibid.*, pp. 81, 84.
49 *Ibid.*, pp. 93–94.
50 Roy Armes, *A Critical History of the British Cinema*, London, Secker and Warburg, 1978, p. 103.
51 *Monthly Film Bulletin*, May, 1936, III, 20, p. 81.
52 *Ibid.*, March, 1938, V, 62, p. 66.
53 *Film Weekly*, October 21, 1932, VIII, 210, p. 28.
54 *Picturegoer Weekly*, February 18, 1933, II, 92, p. 22.
55 Graham Greene, *Graham Greene on Film: Collected Film Criticism, 1935–38*, edited by John Russell Taylor, New York, Simon and Schuster, 1972, p. 38.
56 Charles Higham, *Charles Laughton: An Intimate Biography*, New York, Doubleday, 1976, pp. 69, 71.

57 Karol Kulik, *Alexander Korda: The Man Who Could Work Miracles*, London, W.H. Allen, 1975, pp. 154, 158.
58 *Ibid.*
59 Higham, *op. cit*, p. 72.
60 *Film Weekly*, July 2, 1938, XX, 507, p. 5.

5   MISTAKEN IDENTITIES

1 William K. Everson, *The Detective in Film*, Secaucus, NJ: Citadel Press, 1972, p. 188.
2 Perhaps best known for directing the 1941 film version of the famed stage play, *Love on the Dole*, John Baxter has been unfairly neglected. A former theatrical agent whose films invariably centered on ordinary, working-class people or on stories that dealt with music halls, Baxter directed films in the 1930s that are uniformly interesting from a sociological perspective. For that reason, a discussion of many of Baxter's productions can be found in Chapter 8. See also the discussion of the film in Jeffrey Richards, *The Age of the Dream Palace: Cinema and Society in Britain, 1930–1939*, London, Routledge and Kegan Paul, 1984, pp. 299–300. Also see the commentary about the film in the more recent study of Baxter and his work by Geoff Brown and Tony Aldgate, *The Common Touch: The Films of John Baxter*, London, National Film Theatre, 1989, pp. 28–33.
3 *Picturegoer Weekly*, December 9, 1933, III, 133, p. 30.
4 *Film Weekly*, December 8, 1933, IX, 269, p. 32.
5 *Ibid.*, May 12, 1933, IX, 239, pp. 16–17.
6 *Ibid.*
7 *Ibid.*
8 *Ibid.*, December 8, 1933, IX, 269, p. 32
9 *Picturegoer Weekly*, December 9, 1933, III, 133, p. 30.
10 *Ibid.*, December 19, 1936, VI, 291, p. 28.
11 *Film Weekly*, February 6, 1937, XVII, 434, p. 34; and *Monthly Film Bulletin*, December, 1936, III, 35, pp. 213–214.
12 Graham Greene, *Graham Greene on Film: Collected Film Criticism, 1935–38*, edited by John Russell Taylor, New York, Simon and Schuster, 1972, pp. 122–123.
13 John Russell Taylor, *Hitch: The Life and Times of Alfred Hitchcock*, New York, Pantheon Books, 1978, p. 140.
14 Raymond Durgnat, *The Strange Case of Alfred Hitchcock*, Cambridge, MA, MIT Press, 1974, p. 137.
15 Robert A. Harris and Michael S. Lasky, *The Films of Alfred Hitchcock*, Secaucus, NJ, Citadel Press, 1976, p. 61.
16 Maurice Yacowar, *Hitchcock's British Films*, Hamden, CT, Archon Books, 1977, p. 208.
17 Donald Spoto, *The Art of Alfred Hitchcock*, New York, Hopkins and Blake, 1976, p. 64.
18 Durgnat, *op. cit*, p. 139.
19 Yacowar, *op. cit*, p. 212.
20 François Truffaut, *Hitchcock*, New York, Simon and Schuster, 1967, p. 76.
21 Yacowar, *op. cit*, p. 212.
22 Truffaut, *op. cit*, p. 177.
23 Yacowar, *op. cit*, p. 212.
24 *Ibid.*
25 Alfred Hitchcock, in interview with J. Danvers Williams, "The Censor Wouldn't Pass It," *Film Weekly*, November 5, 1938, XX, 525, pp. 6–7.

26 *Ibid.*
27 *Bioscope*, July 20, 1930; quoted in Geoff Brown ed., *Walter Forde*, London, British Film Institute, 1971, pp. 24–25.
28 *Monthly Film Bulletin*, November, 1935, II, 22, p. 167.
29 *Ibid.*, April, 1936, III, 27, p. 62.
30 *Ibid.*, January, 1936, II, 24, p. 7.
31 Greene, *op. cit*, p. 39.
32 *Monthly Film Bulletin*, December, 1935, II, 23, p. 198.
33 *Ibid.*, November, 1936, III, 34, p. 190.
34 *Ibid.*
35 Cited in Donald Deschner, *The Films of Cary Grant*, Secaucus, New Jersey, Citadel Press, 1973, p. 105.
36 Cyril B. Rollins and Robert J. Wareing, *Victor Saville*, London, British Film Institute, 1972, p. 4; and Ivan Butler, *Cinema in Britain: An Illustrated Survey*, London, Tantivy Press, 1973, p. 94.
37 Rollins and Wareing, *op. cit*, p. 15; and John Kobal, *Gotta Sing, Gotta Dance*, London, Hamlyn, 1970, p. 95.
38 *Film Weekly*, April 29, 1932, VII, 185, p. 12.
39 *Gaumont–British News*, December, 1931, II, 12, p. 28.
40 *Ibid.*, May, 1932, III, 5, p. 27; and June, 1932, III, 6, p. 9.
41 *Ibid.*, May, 1932, III, 5, p. 27.
42 *Ibid.*
43 *Ibid.*
44 *Film Weekly*, May 13, 1932, VII, 187, p. 21.
45 *Ibid.*, April 29, 1932, VII, 185, p. 12.
46 *Picturegoer Weekly*, January 2, 1932, I, 32, p. 29.
47 *Gaumont–British News*, April, 1932, III, 4, p. 32.
48 *Ibid.*
49 *Ibid.*, May, 1932, III, 5, p. 4.
50 *Ibid.*, p. 27.
51 Butler, *op. cit*, p. 94.
52 *Gaumont–British News*, December, 1932, II, 12, pp. 28–29.
53 *Ibid.*
54 *Ibid.*, May, 1932, III, 5, pp. 3–4.
55 *Ibid.*
56 *Ibid.*
57 *Ibid.*

6 INTER-CLASS ROMANCE

1 *Monthly Film Bulletin*, December, 1935, II, 23, p. 198.
2 Karol Kulik, *Alexander Korda: The Man Who Could Work Miracles*, London, W.H. Allen, 1975, p. 81.
3 *Picturegoer Weekly*, May 6, 1933, II, 102, p. 13.
4 Peter Noble, *Ivor Novello: Man of the Theatre*, London, Falcon Press, 1951, p. 164.
5 *Ibid.*, p. 165.
6 *Ibid.*, p. 164.
7 *Stoll Herald*, no date, VII, 4, p. 1.
8 Quoted in Noble, *op. cit*, p. 177.
9 W. MacQueen-Pope, *Ivor: The Story of an Achievement*, London, Hutchinson, 1954, p. 142.
10 *Film Weekly*, May 28, 1938, XX, 502, p. 32.

11 This film was reviewed at a showing in London in 1981. See the *Monthly Film Bulletin*, September, 1981, XLVIII, 572, pp. 184–185.

12 *Ibid.*

13 *Ibid.*, p. 185.

14 *Ibid.*

15 *Ibid.*, November, 1936, III, 34, p. 191.

16 *Ibid.*

17 Kulik, *op. cit*, p. 71.

18 John Kobal, *Gotta Sing, Gotta Dance,* London, Hamlyn, 1970, pp. 73–75.

19 James Agate, *Around Cinemas*, Second Series, Amsterdam, Home and Van Thal, 1948, p. 59.

20 *Gaumont–British News*, December, 1931, II, 12, p. 26.

21 *Monthly Film Bulletin*, October, 1935, II, 21, p. 146.

22 Kobal, *op. cit*, p. 103.

23 Michael Marshall, *Top Hat and Tails: The Story of Jack Buchanan*, London, Elm Tree Books, 1978, p. 74. Also see Herbert Wilcox, *Twenty-Five Thousand Sunsets*, New York, A. S. Barnes, 1969, p. 91.

24 *Monthly Film Bulletin*, March, 1937, IV, 38. p. 54.

25 On the back cover of the soundtrack recording of *Everything is Rhythm*, released on the World Records Limited label, Parkbridge House, Little Green, Richmond, Surrey; catalog number SH 197, Peter Orchard provides a detailed synopsis of the film's plot.

26 *Ibid.*

27 *Ibid.*

28 The universality of this escapist, "dance your troubles away attitude" is echoed in the lyrics of one of the film's major production numbers, "The Internationalle." In the song, the lyrics describe a "swaying all around" as if "all of London went to town," and the refrain universalizes the notion that everyone is dancing to the same steps, observing "you will know just what I mean when you've seen Europeans do the Internationalle." Further, the dance bridges all social strata because "Rich man, poor man, King and Solomon . . . fall for its charms."

29 Orchard, record cover, *op. cit*

30 *Ibid.*

31 *Ibid.*

32 *Ibid.*

33 Jeffrey Richards, "Gracie Fields," *Focus on Film*, December, 1979, 34, p. 33.

34 Basil Dean, *Mind's Eye: An Autobiography, 1927–1972,* London, Hutchinson. 1973, p. 210.

35 *Monthly Film Bulletin*, April, 1937, IV, 39, p. 77.

36 *Picturegoer Weekly*, March 2, 1935, IV, 197, p. 34.

37 *Monthly Film Bulletin*, August, 1938, V, 55, p. 198.

38 Charles Higham, *Charles Laughton: An Intimate Biography*, New York, Doubleday, 1976, p. 89.

39 *Monthly Film Bulletin*, August, 1938, V, 55, p. 198.

40 Higham, *op. cit*, p. 88.

41 *Film Weekly*, March 26, 1938, XX, 493, pp. 10–11.

42 Ivan Butler, *Cinema in Britain: An Illustrated Survey*, London, Tantivy Press, 1973, p. 159. See also Kurt Singer, *The Laughton Story*, Philadelphia, PA, John C. Winston, 1954, p. 186.

43 *Film Weekly*, September 21, 1934, XII, 309, p. 33.

44 Butler, *op. cit*, p. 105.

45 *Film Weekly,* May 2, 1936, XV, 394, p. 13.

46 *Ibid.*, October 12, 1934, XII, 313, p. 29.
47 *Ibid.*, January 18, 1935, XIII, 327, p. 10.
48 *Ibid.*
49 Marjory Williams, "Peg of Old Drury," *Picturegoer Weekly*, February 1, 1936, V, 245, pp. 20, 22.
50 *Picturegoer Weekly*, April 20, 1935, IV, 204, p. 26.
51 *Film Weekly*, May 8, 1937, XVIII, 447, p. 11.
52 See Wilcox's autobiography, *op. cit*, and Neagle's memoirs, *Anna Neagle: There's Always Tomorrow*, London, W.H. Allen, 1974.
53 *Monthly Film Bulletin*, June, 1938, V, 65, p. 154.
54 *Ibid.*
55 *Ibid.*, May, 1935, II, 16, p. 56.
56 *Ibid.*
57 *Film Weekly*, July 26, 1930, IV, 93, p. 6.
58 *Monthly Film Bulletin*, October, 1934, I, 8, p. 82.
59 *Film Weekly*, October 12, 1934, XII, 313, pp. 34–35.
60 *Ibid.*
61 *Ibid.*
62 *Picturegoer Weekly*, October 29, 1934, IV, 179, p. 17.
63 *Ibid.*
64 *Gaumont–British News*, January, 1935, VI, 1, p. 9.
65 *Ibid.*, December, 1934, V, 12, p. 9.
66 *Monthly Film Bulletin*, September, 1935, II, 20, p. 131.
67 *Ibid.*
68 *Ibid.*, November, 1935, II, 22, p. 168.
69 *Picturegoer Weekly*, February 27, 1932, I, 40, p. 18.
70 *Film Weekly*, February 27, 1932, VII, 176, p. 23.
71 *Astorian*, February 1, 1932, IV, 6, p. 11.
72 *Gaumont–British News*, October, 1931, II, 10, p. 50.
73 *Ibid.*, May, 1932, III, 5., p. 44.
74 *Film Weekly*, May 26, 1933, IX, 241, p. 7.
75 *Monthly Film Bulletin*, March, 1936, III, 2, p. 42.
76 *Film Weekly*, February 6, 1932, VII, 173, p. 20.
77 *Picturegoer Weekly*, March 16, 1934, IV, 199, p. 25.
78 *Ibid.*

7 THEMES IN BRITISH FILMS

1 *Monthly Film Bulletin*, April, 1937, IV, 39, p. 76. Incidently, Naughton and Gold, in their pre Crazy-Gang years, had appeared separately in an earlier comedy, *My Lucky Star*, which circulated in the summer of 1933 in which Florence Desmond starred as a shopgirl impersonating a film star; in this feature, while posing as the movie star, she falls in love with a porter who coincidentally is posing as an artist. In the end, when the truth is revealed, her happiness is shown to be greater when both characters re-assume their working-class identities. A virtually identical plot occurred in *What's in a Name*, a late 1934 release, which concerned a girl impersonating a film star who is loved by a clerk who also happens to be posing as a foreign composer.
2 *Film Weekly*, May 26, 1933, IX, 241, p. 33.
3 *Ibid.*, June 2, 1933, IX, 242, p. 14.
4 *Ibid.*, June 9, 1933, IX, 243, p. 14.
5 *Ibid.*, June 16, 1933, IX, 244, p. 14.

6 *Picturegoer Weekly*, March 11, 1933, II, 95, p. 30.
7 *Gaumont–British News*, February, 1933, IV, 2, p. 43.
8 *Ibid.*, December, 1933, IV, 12, p. 25.
9 *Film Weekly*, June 30, 1933, IX, 246, p. 30.
10 *Ibid.*, December 8, 1933, X, 269, p. 27.
11 *Ibid.*, April 7, 1933, IX, 234, pp. 18–19.
12 *Ibid.*, June 2, 1933, IX, 242, p. 14.
13 *Monthly Film Bulletin*, March, 1936, III, 26, p. 41.
14 *Ibid.*
15 *Film Weekly*, April 25, 1936, XV, 393, p. 28.
16 See, for example, the short story in *Film Pictorial*, April 15, 1933, III, 60, p. 32. Also see the novels described in *Film Weekly*, May 12, 1933, IX, 239, p. 27, specifically Madeleine Murat's *New Seal*, Putnam's, and Terence Greenridge's *The Magnificent*, The Fortune Press.
17 See *Film Weekly*, April 30, 1938, XX, 498, p. 28; also June 10, 1932, VII, 191, p. 26; and the *Film Weekly Christmas Extra* for 1938, p. 33 about "Your Chance in the Movies." See also *Picturegoer Weekly*, July 11, 1931, I, 7, pp. 23–24. An article in the *Film Weekly Summer Extra* for 1937, p. 55, pointed out that often luck determined what unknowns would get the chance to appear in a film.
18 *Film Weekly*, January 1, 1938, XX, 481, p. 12; also January 20, 1933, VIII, 223, p. 21. Other similar articles can be found throughout the decade. See, for example, the article on Billy Milton in *Picturegoer Weekly*, September 5, 1931, I, 15, p. 7, which emphasized his start as a tie salesman; the discussion of Arlene Whelen in *Film Weekly*, February 11, 1939, XXI, 539, pp. 16–17; the reference to John Longdon's past as a coal miner with the South Wales Coal company in an article in *Film Weekly*, May 17, 1930, III, 83, p. 17; the discussion of Anna Mae Wong's early years working in a laundry, in *Picturegoer Weekly*, October 17, 1931, I, 21, pp. 16–17; the story about how Jessie Matthews' dance partner, Cyril Wells, had been a clerk in Manchester only six years earlier, in *Film Weekly*, December 21, 1935, XIV, 375, p. 22; and the general discussion of the former life of a number of stars in *Picturegoer Weekly*, May 30, 1931, I, 1, pp. 8–9. Also see the autobiographical article by Stanley Lupino, "My Awful Past," as told to Philip Slesser, in *Film Pictorial*, March 25, 1933, III, 57, pp. 6–7.
19 *Film Weekly*, October 25, 1930, IV, 106, p. 26; and *Stoll Herald*, August 25, 1930, 58, p. 5.
20 *Film Weekly*, July 3, 1937, XIX, 455, p. 7.
21 *Ibid.*, December 13, 1930, IV, 113, p. 10.
22 *Ibid.*, February 28, 1931, V, 124, p. 6.
23 *Picturegoer Weekly*, September 10, 1932, II, 68, p. 5.
24 *Gaumont–British News*, January, 1933, IV, 1, p. 25.
25 *Ibid.*, February, 1933, IV, 2, p. 20. See also the characterization by a manager of his working-class clientele in the same publications, September, 1931, II, 9, p. 15.
26 *Ibid.*, March, 1933, IV, 3, p. 15.
27 *Ibid.*, July, 1933, IV, 7, p. 13; see also, August, 1933, IV, 8, p. 15 and January 1933, IV, 7, pp. 31–35, in the same publication.
28 *Ibid.*, December, 1931, II, 12, p. 14. During the period of the music hall, the antecedents of the "Do As You Please" nights were the notorious "Trial Turn Matinees" which apparently and curiously were not well received by audiences.
29 *Film Weekly*, March 21, 1931, V, 127, p. 10.
30 E. G. Cousins, "How to Get in the Talkies – if You Must," *Picturegoer Weekly*, February 27, 1932, I, 40, p. 12.
31 *Film Weekly*, January 16, 1932, VII, 170, p. 8.

32 *Ibid.*, July 14, 1933, X, 248, pp. 8–9.

33 P.C. Mannock, "What Film Work Means," *Picturegoer*, January, 1930, XIX, 109, p. 15.

34 *Gaumont–British News*, July, 1932, III, 7, p. 28.

35 *Ibid.*, May, 1933, IV, 5, p. 33.

36 *Ibid.*, p. 34.

37 *Ibid.*, July, 1933, III, 7, p. 43.

38 *Ibid.*, June, 1931, II, 6, p. 4.

39 *Ibid.*

40 *Film Weekly*, September 25, 1937, XIX, 467, pp. 11–12.

41 *Ibid.*, November 23, 1934, XII, 319, p. 13; also, May 31, 1930, III, 85, p. 8.

42 *Picturegoer Weekly*, June 3, 1933, II, 106, pp. 12–13.

43 *Film Weekly*, March 31, 1933, IX, 233, p. 29.

44 *Monthly Film Bulletin*, May, 1936, III, 28, p. 84.

45 Graham Greene, *Graham Greene on Film: Collected Film Criticism, 1935–38*, edited by John Russell Taylor, New York, Simon and Schuster, 1972, p. 73.

46 Ivan Butler, *Cinema in Britain; An Illustrated Survey*, London, A.S. Barnes, 1973, p. 117.

47 *Stoll Herald*, August 17, 1936, XI, 34, no page.

48 *Film Weekly*, May 8, 1937, XVIII, 447, p. 11.

49 Quoted in Karol Kulik, *Alexander Korda: The Man Who Could Work Miracles*, London, W.H. Allen, 1975, p. 93.

50 Michael Korda, *Charmed Lives*, New York, Random House, 1979, p. 73.

51 *Ibid.*, p. 99. Kulik suggests that at least two other explanations for the movie's inspiration are plausible. In one of them, "during a meeting, a statue of Henry VIII in the room caused Laughton's agent to remark on the resemblance between Charles and the monarch," and in the other, during a "meeting in Paris, . . . the idea simply came up in a discussion between Alex and Laughton about possible film roles suited to the actor's talents"; but the "first story was Korda's own favourite, and he seemed to delight in leading journalists to believe that he had known nothing about Henry VIII until he came to London." In fact, twelve years earlier, Korda had made a film with Henry VIII as a character (Kulik, *op. cit.*, p. 85.)

52 Kulik, *op. cit.*, p. 73.

53 *Ibid.*, p. 90.

54 *Ibid.*, pp. 90–91.

55 Korda, *op. cit.*, p. 102.

56 *Ibid.*, p. 73; and *Stoll Herald*, no date or page, IX, 7.

57 Quoted in Kulik, *op. cit.*, p. 92.

58 Korda, *op. cit.*, p. 102.

59 Charles Higham, *Charles Laughton: An Intimate Biography*, New York: Doubleday and Company, 1976, p. 44.

60 Elsa Lanchester, *Charles Laughton and I*, New York, Harcourt Brace, 1938, p. 112.

61 Kurt Singer, *The Laughton Story: An Intimate Story of Charles Laughton*, Philadelphia, John C. Winston, 1954, pp. 118–119.

62 *Film Weekly*, April 5, 1935, XIII, 338, p. 7.

63 Kulik, *op. cit.*, p. 119.

64 *Ibid.*, p. 88.

65 Ernest Betts, *The Film Business*, New York, Pitman, 1973, p. 102.

66 Charles Oakley, *Where We Came In*, London, George Allen and Unwin, 1974, p. 135.

67 *Monthly Film Bulletin*, February, 1936, III, 25, p. 24.

68 Geoff Brown, *Launder and Gilliat*, London, British Film Institute, 1977, p. 46.
69 *Picturegoer Weekly*, December 3, 1932, II, 80, p. 22.
70 *Monthly Film Bulletin*, September, 1938, V, 56, p. 288.
71 *Ibid.*
72 *Ibid.*, July, 1938, V, 54, p. 181.
73 John Russell Taylor, *Hitch: The Life and Times of Alfred Hitchcock*, New York, Pantheon Books, 1978, p. 110.
74 *Ibid.*, p. 113.
75 Donald Spoto, *The Art of Alfred Hitchcock*, New York, Hopkinson and Blake, 1976, p. 31.
76 *Picturegoer Weekly*, August 1, 1931, I, 10, p. 22.
77 Clive Denton, "King Vidor," in *The Hollywood Professionals*, Volume V., New York, A.S. Barnes, 1976, p. 17.
78 *Monthly Film Bulletin*, December, 1938, V, 59, p. 276.
79 Raymond Durgnat, "King Vidor," *Film Comment*, July–August, 1973, IX, 4, p. 40.
80 King Vidor, "How I Made *The Citadel*," interview J. Danvers Williams, *Film Weekly*, December 24, 1938, XX, 532, pp. 6–7.
81 *Monthly Film Bulletin*, December, 1938, V, 59, p. 276.
82 Butler, *op. cit.*, p. 129.
83 John Baxter, *King Vidor*, New York, Monarch Press, 1976, p. 57.
84 *Film Weekly*, December 24, 1938, XX, 532, p. 3.
85 *Ibid.*, p. 21.
86 *Monthly Film Bulletin*, December, 1938, V, 59, p. 276.
87 Butler, *op. cit.*, p. 129.
88 Jeffrey Richards, "A Star Without Armour: Robert Donat," *Focus on Film*, 8, p. 20.
89 Raymond Durgnat's discussion of the film's ideology in his career article on director King Vidor (*op. cit.*) is interesting. Durgnat argues that rather than being a left-wing statement, *The Citadel* "veers to the right." Conceding that "the film remains faithful to the book's attack on the mercenary spirit of the medical profession," Durgnat maintains that the picture portrays the primary barriers to the miner's health as being "bureaucracy," and the miners themselves "as a superstitious mob," rather than the "healthy capitalistic instincts of the mine-owners." Durgnat goes on to argue that "the idea of a doctor's cooperative as a solution to the problem of medicine for the poor isn't simply a paraphrase of the idea of a National Health Service (introduced in Britain seven years later)" but rather is "primarily an alternative to it – a demonstration that Socialism would be unnecessary if only an 'inspirationalist' change of heart were to be followed through by the medical profession itself." Durgnat contends that because the "miners' mob is . . . more destructive," the film's vision of "progress would seem to lie, not in mass movements of any kind, but in a technical medical breakthrough by a dedicated individual" (p. 40.)
90 *Monthly Film Bulletin*, May, 1936, III, 28, p. 82.
91 *Ibid.*, June, 1937, IV, 41, p. 124.
92 *Ibid.*
93 *Ibid.*, February, 1938, V, 49. p. 34.
94 *Ibid.*, January, 1937, III, 36, p. 10.
95 *Ibid.*, February, 1938, V, 49, p. 35.
96 *Ibid.*, August, 1937, IV, 43, pp. 166–167.
97 *Ibid.*, November, 1935, II, 22, p. 170;
98 *Ibid.*, December, 1935, II, 17, p. 70.
99 R. J. Minney, *"Puffin" Asquith*, London, Leslie Frewin, 1973, p. 238.

100 *Film Weekly*, August 25, 1933, X, 254, p. 22.
101 Quoted in Minney, *op. cit.*, p. 79.
102 *Monthly Film Bulletin*, September, 1936, III, 32, p. 148.
103 Greene, *op. cit.*, p. 97.
104 *Monthly Film Bulletin*, September, 1936, III, 32, p. 148.
105 *Picturegoer Weekly*, September 12, 1936, VI, 227, p. 26.
106 Greene, *op. cit.*, p. 98.
107 Kulik, *op. cit.*, p. 185.
108 Greene, *op. cit.*, p. 98.
109 *Picturegoer Weekly*, September 12, 1936, VI, 277, p. 26.
110 *Ibid.*
111 *Ibid.*
112 *Monthly Film Bulletin*, September, 1936, III, 32, p. 149.
113 Greene, *op. cit.*, pp. 97–98.

8   THE EMPHASIS ON COOPERATION AND SELF-SACRIFICE

1 Jeffrey Richards, "On 16 mm," *Focus on Film*, 30, pp. 48–50. See also Brown and Aldgate, *The Common Touch: The Films of John Baxter*, London, National Film Theatre, 1989.
2 *Picturegoer Weekly*, January 27, 1934, III, 140, p. 6.
3 *Ibid.*
4 *Ibid.*
5 *Monthly Film Bulletin*, April, 1934, I, 3, p. 22.
6 Richards, *op. cit.*, p. 48.
7 *Ibid.*
8 *Ibid.*
9 *Ibid.*
10 John Montgomery, *Comedy Films, 1894–1954*, London, George Allen and Unwin, 1968, pp. 189–190.
11 *Ibid.*
12 *Film Weekly*, November 17, 1933, X, 266, p. 25.
13 *Ibid.*
14 *Picturegoer Weekly*, April 14, 1934, III, 151, p. 33.
15 Comments from information file on John Baxter at the British Film Institute Library. Taken from an obituary in the *Stage*, March 6, 1975.
16 *Picturegoer Weekly*, December 9, 1933, III, 33, p. 34.
17 Montgomery, *op. cit.*, p. 194.
18 Richards, *op. cit.*, p. 49.
19 Montgomery, *op. cit.*, p. 194.
20 *Picturegoer Weekly*, April 13, 1935, IV, 203, p. 22.
21 *Ibid.*
22 Montgomery, *op. cit.*, p. 199.
23 *Picturegoer Weekly*, April 13, 1935, IV, 203, p. 22.
24 *Ibid.*
25 *Monthly Film Bulletin*, July, 1937, IV, 42, p. 143.
26 *Film Weekly*, August 11, 1933, X, 252, p. 25.
27 See *Picturegoer Weekly*, December 15, 1934, IV, 186, p. 19.
28 Richards, *op. cit.*, p. 49.
29 *Ibid.*, p. 48.
30 *Film Weekly*, May 22, 1973, XVIII, 449, p. 33.

31 *Monthly Film Bulletin*, November, 1936, III, 34, p. 191.
32 *Film Weekly*, May 22, 1937, XVIII, 449, p. 33
33 *Monthly Film Bulletin*, November, 1936, III, 34, p. 191
34 *Film Weekly*, January 2, 1937, XVII, 429, p. 28.
35 *Monthly Film Bulletin*, May, 1936, III, 28, p. 82.
36 *Ibid.*
37 *Film Weekly*, January 2, 1937, XVII, 429, p. 28.
38 *Monthly Film Bulletin*, May, 1936, III, 28, p. 82.
39 *Picturegoer Weekly*, June 23, 1934, IV, 161, p. 28.
40 *Film Pictorial*, January 27, 1934, IV, 101, p. 14.
41 See, for example, letters in *Ibid.*, December 30, 1933, IV, 97, p. 30.
42 Robert Graves and Alan Hodge, *The Long Weekend: A Social History of Great Britain, 1918–1940*, New York, W. W. Norton, 1963, p. 297.
43 *Picturegoer Weekly*, January 18, 1936, V, 243, pp. 10–11.
44 Jeffrey Richards, "Gracie Fields: The Lancashire Britannia," *Focus on Film*, 33, p. 27. A more recent and equally perceptive analysis of Fields's screen persona can be found in Marcia Landy, *British Genres: Cinema and Society, 1930–1960*, Princeton, NJ, Princeton University Press, 1991, pp. 334–341.
45 *Film Weekly*, November, 20, 1937, XIX, 475, p. 24.
46 *Film Pictorial*, January 28, 1933, II, 49, pp. 26–27.
47 *Picturegoer Weekly*, April 8, 1933, II, 99, p. 33.
48 *Film Pictorial*, April 7, 1934, III, 111, p. 4.
49 Maud Miller, "Why Not Give Gracie Fields a Real Chance," *Ibid.*, April 21, 1934, III, 113, p. 12.
50 Bert Aza, *Our Gracie: The Story of Gracie Fields*, no publication information, p. 8.
51 Basil Dean, "Is Gracie Fields Worth £2 a Minute?," in *Film Pictorial*, September 30, 1933, IV, 84, p. 20.
52 Aza, *op. cit.*, p. 18.
53 Dean, *op. cit.*, p. 20.
54 Aza, *op. cit.*, p. 6.
55 *Film Pictorial*, November 12, 1932, II, 37, p. 10.
56 John Loder, "What I Think of Gracie," *Film Weekly*, April 20, 1934, XI, 288, p. 13.
57 *Ibid.*
58 *Film Weekly*, January 1, 1938, XX, 481, p. 20.
59 *Picturegoer Weekly*, February 29, 1936, V, 249, p. 10.
60 Herbert Harris, "Robey was Right," *Film Pictorial*, July 28, 1934, IV, 127, p. 26.
61 *Screen Pictorial*, June, 1938, p. 61.
62 *Film Pictorial*, April 8, 1933, III, 59, p. 32.
63 *Picturegoer Weekly*, May 27, 1933, III, 105, p. 29.
64 Richards, "Gracie Fields," *op. cit.*, pp. 28–29.
65 *Ibid.*
66 Montgomery, *op. cit.*, p. 179.
67 Gracie Fields, "How I Get My Film Laughs," *Film Weekly*, October 13, 1933, X, 261, p. 7.
68 Gracie Fields, "Love, Life and Laughter," *Film Pictorial Annual*, 1935, pp. 24–25.
69 Fields, "Film Laughs," *op. cit.*, p. 7.
70 *Film Weekly*, November 20, 1937, XIX, 475, p. 24.
71 See Jeffrey Richards, "Gracie Fields: The Lancashire Britannia – Part II," *Focus on Film*, n.d., 34, p. 25.
72 *Gaumont–British News*, August, 1932, III, 8, p. 7.

73 The lyrics of the song describe in satirical fashion a fairly common experience for working-class families, the courtship ritual of meeting the family. With lines like "The family then all questioned Fred as fast as they could speak. How much he got in bank book, how much he earned a week," Miss Fields played all the roles and gently satirized this universal experience.

74 *Picturegoer Weekly*, April 21, 1934, III, 152, supplement.

75 Basil Dean, *Mind's Eye, An Autobiography, 1927–1972*, London, Hutchinson, 1973, p. 166.

76 Ivan Butler, *Cinema in Britain: An Illustrated Survey*, London, A. S. Barnes, 1973, p. 107.

77 *Monthly Film Bulletin*, September, 1934, I, 6, p. 70.

78 *Film Weekly*, March 23, 1934, XI, 284, p. 3.

79 *Picturegoer Weekly*, October 6, 1934, IV, 176, p. 16.

80 Dean, *Mind's Eye, op. cit.*, p. 206.

81 Program notes to showing of *Sing As We Go*, National Film Theatre, London, August 15, 1978.

82 Jeffrey Richards argues that as Gracie Fields's film career developed, her *persona* shifted from working class to middle class or show business character. Though technically correct, the fact of the matter is that there is no fundamental alteration to her accent or spirit in the films. Her surroundings did slightly improve in some of her films, but the character she portrayed was still a very lovable "Gracie" who had not really changed. Richards's argument that she was becoming more a symbol of the nation and therefore had to represent all classes is an ingenious, but not completely convincing, one. For a later analysis of Gracie Fields and her films see Jeffrey Richards's discussion in his *The Age of the Dream Palace: Cinema and Society in Britain 1930–1939*, London, Routledge and Kegan Paul, 1984, pp. 169–190.

83 The fact that most of these supposedly *petit-bourgeois* characters who are rallied by Gracie are so recognizably the same actors who portray working-class characters in other films also undercuts the argument that the audience was to view Gracie as a middle-class character in this film.

84 *Picturegoer Weekly*, June 3, 1933, III, 106, p. 32.

85 *Film Weekly*, September 22, 1933, X, 258, pp. 20–21.

86 *Monthly Film Bulletin*, August, 1939, VI, 78, p. 156.

87 Richards, "Gracie Fields – II," *op. cit.*, p. 35.

88 *Ibid.*

89 *Monthly Film Bulletin*, February, 1936, III, 25, p. 24.

90 *Ibid.*

91 *Picturegoer Weekly*, July 25, 1936, VI, 270, p. 26.

92 *Monthly Film Bulletin*, August, 1939, VI, 78, p. 156.

93 For the most detailed account of the making of the film, see Arthur Calder-Marshall's excellent study of Flaherty, *The Innocent Eye*, Baltimore, MD, Penguin Books, 1967.

94 Butler, *op. cit.*, p. 108.

95 *Gaumont–British News*, April, 1933, IV, 4, p. 46

96 *Ibid.*, June, 1934, V, 6, p. 39.

97 *Ibid.*, September, 1934, V, 9, p. 3.

98 *Ibid.*

99 *Ibid.* The program notes for the film when it was screened at the National Film Theatre some years ago give some indication of the negative, or at least chilly, reception the so-called intellectual critics gave the film when it was released. John Minchinton wrote:

What is extraordinary is the manner in which the film was received by some thirties critics and documentary purists ... who were offended because Flaherty had the islanders relearn the art of shark fishing for the film. Alistair Cooke: "I had the good luck, or misfortune, to see this film with two men straight from Aran. Although they had never before seen a moving picture, they still behaved in a remarkable way. When they weren't howling with laughter, they mumbled in protest. Afterwards they swore that this was not Aran, that no boat would come through that storm, that Aran is not nearly as bare as you gather, that the natives haven't worn caps like that for seventy years." C. A. Lejeune: "It is safe to surmise that Flaherty intended all these incidents to be illustrative of a central theme, but he is himself so familiar with the theme that he has come to believe that the bare statement of circumstances is enough to suggest it. When Flaherty sees a woman walking along the shore with a basket of seaweed on her back, it is for him exciting and dramatic, because he knows by experience the struggle for existence that the load represents. But when the audience sees the same picture, they see only the woman and the seaweed. *Man of Aran* is a sealed document, the key to which is still in Flaherty's own mind. My official tip for the week is *Man of Aran*. My unofficial tip is *It Happened One Night*. I know that this statement will bring down upon me the bitter contempt of film societies, film groups, and film theorists, generally, but we all have our weaknesses, and mine happens to be a preference to story over seaweed, however patiently gathered and sufficiently displayed.

Quoted from *The British Film Institute Presents the Thirties: Britain*, May 26, 1964 to July 12, 1964, National Film Theatre.

100 *Film Weekly*, April 18, 1936, XV, 392, p. 34.
101 *Ibid.*
102 Butler, *op. cit.*, p. 112.
103 *Picturegoer Weekly*, November 16, 1935, V, 234, p. 19.
104 *Film Weekly*, April 18, 1936, XV, 392, p. 34.
105 *Ibid.*, December 7, 1935, XIV, 373, p. 13.
106 Graham Greene, *Graham Greene on Film: Collected Film Criticism, 1935–38*, edited by John Russell Taylor, New York, Simon and Schuster, 1972, pp. 29–30.
107 *Monthly Film Bulletin*, July, 1937, IV, 42, p. 141.
108 *Ibid.*
109 *Film Weekly*, July 17, 1937, XVIII, 457, pp. 9–10. To distribute the film, Powell, who had worked on the film for three years, assembled a cooperative of six to seven hundred independent theaters.
110 *Ibid.*, January 22, 1938, XX, 484, p. 14. In fact, it is said that because *Turn of the Tide* was not widely circulated, J. Arthur Rank became interested in promoting moral movies, as Butler points out, *op. cit.*, p. 112.
111 *Film Weekly*, October 9, 1937, XIX, 469, p. 9.
112 *Ibid.*, November 6, 1937, XIX, 473, pp. 28–29.
113 *Monthly Film Bulletin*, July, 1936, III, 30, p. 147.
114 *Film Weekly*, April 5, 1935, XIII, 338, p. 76.
115 *Monthly Film Bulletin*, November, 1934, I, 10, p. 93.
116 *Stoll Herald*, April 23, 1934, VIII, 17, no page.
117 *Monthly Film Bulletin*, January, 1935, I, 12, pp. 112–113.
118 *Ibid.*, December, 1937, IV, 47, p. 268.
119 R. J. Minney, *"Puffin" Asquith*, London, Leslie Frewin, 1973, p. 65.

120 *Monthly Film Bulletin*, January, 1937, III, 36, p. 10.
121 *Ibid.*, pp. 10–11.
122 *Ibid.*, p. 11.
123 *Ibid.*
124 *Ibid.*, August, 1937, IV, 43, p. 165.
125 *Ibid.*, April, 1937, IV, 39, p. 76.
126 *Ibid.*, January, 1935, I, 12, p. 119.
127 *Stoll Herald*, March 10, 1935, XI, 8, no page.
128 *Gaumont–British News*, December, 1935, VI, 12, p. 39.
129 Extended discussions of these films can be found in several books on science fiction pictures. See especially John Baxter, *Science Fiction in the Cinema*, New York, A. S. Barnes, 1970, and John Brosnan, *Future Tense: The Cinema of Science Fiction*, New York, St Martin's Press, 1978.

9   PATRIOTISM AND CENSORSHIP

1 *Picturegoer Weekly*, August 13, 1932, II, 64, p. 32.
2 *Astorian*, December 21, 1931, IV, 3, p. 3.
3 *Ibid.*
4 *Gaumont–British News*, February, 1932, III, 2, p. 4; and *Film Weekly*, October 17, 1931, VI, 157, p. 20.
5 *Gaumont–British News*, April, 1935, VI, 4, p. 5.
6 *Ibid.*
7 *Ibid.*
8 *Ibid.*, January, 1935, VI, 1, p. 7.
9 *Film Weekly*, January 25, 1936, XV, 380, p. 3.
10 See Martin Gilbert's discussion of the proposed film in *Winston Churchill, V. 1922–1939*, London, Heinemann, 1976, pp. 561–563; 589–590.
11 *Picturegoer Weekly*, April 27, 1935, IV, 205, pp. 18–19.
12 Walter Mycroft, "The Inside Story of Cavalcade," in *Ibid.*, May 4, 1935, IV, 206, p. 26.
13 *Picturegoer Weekly*, April 27, 1935, IV, 205, p. 19.
14 Mycroft, *op. cit.*, p. 26.
15 *Film Weekly*, March 22, 1935, XIII, 336, pp. 4–5.
16 *Film Weekly*, May 8, 1937, XVIII, 447, p. 46.
17 *Picturegoer*, September, 1930, XIX, 121, p. 52.
18 Robert Herring, "One Family," in Alistair Cooke ed., *Garbo and the Night Watchmen*, London, Secker and Warburg, 1971, pp. 36–38.
19 *Ibid.*, p. 38.
20 *Ibid.*
21 *Gaumont–British News*, May, 1935, VI, 5, p. 13.
22 *Picturegoer Weekly*, November 17, 1934, IV, 182, p. 34.
23 *Ibid.*, July 29, 1933, III, 114, p. 30.
24 *Film Weekly*, June 4, 1938, XX, 503, p. 28.
25 *Film Pictorial*, December 23, 1933, IV, 96, p. 38.
26 *Ibid.*, February 3, 1934, IV, 102, p. 30.
27 Much has been written about British Film Censorship. Neville Hunnings March's *Film Censors and the Law*, London, Allen and Unwin, 1967, is generally regarded as one of the better such studies available. See also articles by Jeffrey Richards, *Historical Journal of Film Radio and TV*, 1981, I, 1 and 2.
28 Graham Greene, "Subjects and Stories," in C. L. Davy (ed.), *Footnotes to the Film*, London, Lovat Dickson, Ltd., 1937, pp. 66–67.

29 Great Britain, British Board of Film Censors, "Annual Reports." These unpublished documents are arranged in a loosely chronological order with no regular page headings. They are to be found in the British Film Institute Library.
30 *Ibid.*, 1930.
31 *Ibid.*, 1931.
32 *Ibid.*, 1936.
33 *Ibid.*, 1930; and 1936.
34 *Ibid.*, 1931.
35 *Ibid.*, 1932.
36 *Ibid.*
37 *Ibid.*, 1933.
38 *Ibid.*
39 *Ibid.*
40 *Ibid.*, 1934.
41 *Ibid.*
42 *Ibid.*
43 *Ibid.*
44 *Ibid.*, 1932.
45 Quoted in Low Warren, *The Film Game*, London, Werner Laurie, 1937, p. 143.
46 Forsythe Hardy, "Censorship and Film Societies," in Davy, (ed.), *op. cit.*, pp. 264–265.
47 *Ibid.*
48 *Film Weekly*, March 5, 1932, VII, 177, p. 28.
49 *Ibid.*, November 5, 1938, XX, 525, pp. 6–7.
50 *Film Pictorial*, November 4, 1933, IV, 89, p. 20.

10   CONCLUSIONS

1 N. Branson and M. Heinemann. *Britain in the 1930s*, New York, Praeger, 1971, pp. 246–248.
2 Robin Skelton ed.. *Poetry of the Thirties*, Harmondsworth, Penguin Books, 1971, pp. 69–70.

REFERENCES

PRIMARY SOURCES

Unpublished

Bernstein, Sidney. "A Memorandum on the Scarcity of the Film Supply Together With a Scheme to Assist British Film Production." MS.

—— 'Cinema Questionnaire Results, 1934 and 1937." MS.

British Board of Film Censors. "Annual Reports."

British Film Institute Library. Screenplay Collection and Director File.

Cinematograph Exhibitors' Association of Great Britain and Ireland. "Annual Reports."

Roditi, Edouard. "Problems of the British Film Industry." Pamphlet, London, 1936–37.

Rowson, Simon. "British Influence through the Films." Address to the Royal Empire Society, London, March 20, 1933.

—— 'The Social and Political Aspects of Films." Paper read to British Kinematograph Society, London, no date given.

Published

Periodicals from the 1930s.

Astorian
Bioscope
British Film Studio Mirror
Cinegram
Commercial Film
Commercial Film Review
Fanfare
Film Daily Yearbook of Motion Pictures
Film Lover's Annual
Film Pictorial
Film Weekly
Gaumont–British News
Gebescope News
International Motion Picture Almanac
Kinematograph Yearbook
Kino News
The Listener

Monthly Film Bulletin
Movie Fan: The National Screen Magazine
Movie Owner
Nash's Pall Mall Magazine
New Cinema
Picturegoer
Picturegoer Weekly
Pictureshow Annual
Screen Pictorial
Sight and Sound
Socialist Review
Stoll Herald
The Times
Variety

Memoirs, autobiographies, collections of reviews.

Agate, James. *Around Cinemas*. Second Series. Amsterdam: Home and Van Thal, 1948.
Aherne, Brian. *A Proper Job*. Boston, MA: Houghton Miflin, 1969.
Anon. *British Film by an Englishman*. Worthing: E. D. Laine Private Printing, 1938.
Arliss, George. *My Ten Years in the Studios*. Boston, MA: Little, Brown and Company, 1940.
Aza, Bert. *Our Gracie: The Story of Gracie Fields*. London. [Published by the author, no date.]
Brunel, Adrian. *Nice Work: Thirty Years in British Films* London: Forbes Robertson, 1949.
Burdidge, Claude. *Scruffy: The Adventures of a Mongrel in Movieland*. London: Hurst and Blackett, 1937.
Cooke, Alistair, ed. *Garbo and the Night Watchmen*. London: Secker and Warburg, 1971.
Dean, Basil. *Mind's Eye: An Autobiography, 1927–1972*. London: Hutchinson, 1973.
Desmond, Florence. *By Herself*. London: George Harrap, 1953.
Field, Audrey. *Picture Palace*. London: Gentry Books, 1974.
Fields, Gracie. *Sing As We Go*. London: Frederick Muller, 1960.
Flanagan, Bud. *My Crazy Life*. London: Frederick Muller, 1961.
Fox, Roy. *Hollywood, Mayfair, and All That Jazz*. London: Leslie Frewin, 1975.
Gielgud, John. *Distinguished Company*. Garden City, NY: Doubleday, 1973.
—— *Early Stages*. London: Falcon Press, 1939.
Greene, Graham. *Graham Greene on Film: Collected Film Criticism 1935–38*. Edited by John Russell Taylor. New York: Simon and Schuster, 1972.
Grierson, John. *Grierson on Documentary*. Edited by Forsythe Hardy. London: Faber, 1979.
Hardwicke, Cedric. *A Victorian in Orbit*. London: Methuen, 1961.
Hare, Robertson. *Yours, Indubitably*. London: Robert Hale, 1956.
Harrison, Rex. *Rex: An Autobiography*. New York: William Morrow, 1975.
Hepworth, Cecil. *Came the Dawn*. London: Phoenix House, 1951.
Hulbert, Jack. *The Little Woman's Always Right*. London: W. H. Allen, 1975.
Lanchester, Elsa. *Charles Laughton and I*. New York: Harcourt Brace, 1938.
Lawrence, Gertrude. *A Star Danced*. New York: Doubleday, 1955.
Lejeune, C. A. *Thank You For Having Me*. London: Hutchinson, 1964.

Lockwood, Margaret. *Lucky Star: The Autobiography of Margaret Lockwood*. London: Odhams Press, 1955.
Maltby, H. F. *Ring Up the Curtain*. London: Hutchinson, 1950.
Matthews, A. E. *"Matty."* London: Hutchinson, 1952.
Matthews, Jessie. *Over My Shoulder*. London: W. H. Allen, 1976.
Neagle, Anna. *Anna Neagle: There's Always Tomorrow*. London: W. H. Allen, 1974.
Pascal, Valerie. *The Disciple and His Devil*. London: Michael Joseph, 1971.
Pearson, George. *Flashback: An Autobiography of a British Filmmaker*. London: George Allen and Unwin, 1957.
Powell, Michael. *Million-Dollar Movie*. New York: Random House, 1992.
Robey, George. *Looking Back on Life*. London: Constable and Company, 1933.
Rotha, Paul. *Documentary Diary*. New York: Hill and Wang, 1973.
Talents, Sir Stephen. *The Projection of England*. London: Faber and Faber, 1932.
Travers, Ben. *Vale of Laughter*. London: Geoffrey Bles, 1957.
Wilcox, Herbert. *Twenty-five Thousand Sunsets*. New York: A. S. Barnes, 1967.

Others

Anderson, Willf. "Chasing Shadows" and "The Battle of Hollywood." *Home Movie Wonderland Catalogs*.[Privately published]
Anon: *The Film in National Life*. London: George Allen and Unwin, 1932.
Davy, Charles, ed. *Footnotes to the Film*. London: Lovat Dickson, 1937.
Gallup, George H. *The Gallup International Public Opinion Polls: Great Britain, 1937–1975*, New York: Random House, 1976.
Griffith, Hubert. "Films and the British Public." *Nineteenth Century and After*. (August, 1932), pp. 190–200.
Klingender, E. G. and Legg, Stuart. *Money Behind the Screen: A Report on Behalf of the Film Council*. London: Lawrence and Wishart, 1937.
Knowles, Dorothy. *The Censor, the Drama, and the Film, 1900–1934*. London: George Allen and Unwin, 1934.
Warren, Low. *The Film Game*. London: T. Werner Laurie, 1937.

SECONDARY SOURCES
Biographies

Beveridge, James. *John Grierson: Film Master*. New York: Macmillan, 1978.
Connell, Brian. *Knight Errant: A Biography of Douglas Fairbanks, Jr.* New York: Doubleday, 1955.
Druxman, Michael. *Basil Rathbone: His Life and Films*. New York: A. S. Barnes, 1973.
East, John. *Max Miller: The Cheeky Chappie*. London: W. H. Allen, 1977.
Edwards, Anne. *Vivien Leigh*. New York: Pocket Books, 1977.
Findlater, Richard. *Michael Redgrave: Actor*. London: Heinemann, 1956.
Fisher, John. *Funny Way to Be a Hero*. London: Frederick Muller, 1973.
—— *George Formby*. London: Woburn-Futura, 1975.
Glyn, Anthony. *Elinor Glyn*. Garden City: Doubleday, 1955.
Hamilton, Virginia. *Paul Robeson*. New York: Harper and Row, 1974.
Hayman, Ronald. *John Gielgud*. New York: Random House, 1971.
Higham, Charles. *Charles Laughton: An Intimate Biography*. New York: Doubleday, 1976.
Howard, Leslie Ruth. *A Quite Remarkable Father*. New York: Harcourt, Brace and Jovanovich, 1959.

Korda, Michael. *Charmed Lives*. New York: Random House, 1979.

Kulik, Karol. *Alexander Korda: The Man Who Could Work Miracles*. London: W. H. Allen, 1975.

Lane, Margaret. *Edgar Wallace*. New York: Book League of America, 1936.

Lasky, Jesse. *Love Scene: The Story of Laurence Olivier and Vivien Leigh*. New York: Thomas Crowell, 1978.

MacQueen-Pope, W. *Ivor: The Story of an Achievement*. London: Hutchinson, 1954.

Marshall, Michael. *Top Hat and Tails: The Story of Jack Buchanan*. London: Elm Tree Books, 1978.

Noble, Peter. *Anthony Asquith*. London: British Film Institute, 1951.

—— *Ivor Novello: Man of the Theatre*. London: Falcon Press, 1951.

Randall, Alan and Seaton, Ray. *George Formby*. London: W. H. Allen, 1974.

Robyns, Gwen. *Vivien Leigh: Light of a Star*. New York: A. S. Barnes, 1974.

Seaton, Ray and Martin, Roy. *Good Morning Boys: Will Hay*. London: Barrie and Jenkins, 1978.

Seton, Marie. *Paul Robeson*. London: Dennis Dobson Books, 1936.

Shipman, David. *The Great Movie Stars: The Golden Years*. New York: Crown Publishing Company, 1970.

Singer, Kurt. *The Laughton Story: An Intimate Story of Charles Laughton*. Philadelphia, PA: John C. Winston, 1954.

Taylor, John Russell. *Hitch: The Life and Times of Alfred Hitchcock*. New York: Pantheon Books, 1978.

Thornton, Michael. *Jessie Matthews*. London: Mayflower Books, 1975.

Trewin, J. C. *Robert Donat: A Biography*. London: Heinemann, 1968.

White, James Dillon. *Born to Star: The Lupino Lane Story*. London: Heinemann, 1957.

Wood, Alan. *Mr Rank: A Study of J. Arthur Rank and British Films*. London: Hodder and Stoughton, 1952.

Film history

Anon: *The Elstree Story: Twenty-one Years of Film Making*. London: Clarke and Cockeran, 1949.

Anstey, Edgar. "The Regional Life of Britain as Seen Through British Films." In *The Year's Work in the Film: 1950*. edited by Roger Manvell, London: The British Council by Longmans and Green, 1950.

Barr, Charles. *Ealing Studios*. London: Cameron and Tayleur, 1977.

Bidwell, Dennis. "Fifty Years of Cinema in Ampthill." *Bedfordshire Magazine*. XVI, 127 (Winter, 1978), p. 294.

Chanon, Michael. *Labour Power in the British Film Industry*. London: British Film Institute, 1976.

Fielding, Raymond. *The March of Time, 1935–1951*. New York: Oxford University Press, 1979.

Grenfell, David. "An Outline of British Film History: 1896–1962." London, 1962 [Privately published pamphlet.]

Harley, John Eugene. *World-Wide Influence of the Cinema*. Los Angeles: University of Southern California Press, 1940.

Hunnings March, Neville. *Film Censors and the Law*. London: George Allen and Unwin, 1967.

Huntley, John. *British Technicolor Films*. London: Skelton Robinson, 1947.

Jarvie, I. C. *Movies and Society*. New York: Basic Books, 1970.

Koenigil, Mark. *Movies in Society*. New York: Robert Speller and Sons, 1963.

REFERENCES

Mayer, J. P. *British Cinemas and Their Audiences: Sociological Studies.* London: Dennis Dobson, 1948.

Minchinton, John. "The British Film Institute Presents: The Thirties – Programme Notes." London: British Film Institute, 1964.

Monaco, Paul. *Cinema and Society.* New York: Elsevier Scientific Press, 1976.

Montgomery, John. *Comedy Films, 1894–1954.* London: George Allen and Unwin, 1968.

Perry, George. *Movies from the Mansion: A History of Pinewood Studios.* London: Elm Tree Press, 1976.

Phelps, Gary. *Film Censorship.* London: Victor Gollancz, 1975.

Pronay, Nicholas. "British Newsreels in the 1930s." *History.* LVI, 188 (1971), pp. 411–418, and LVII, 189 (1972), pp. 63–72.

Smith, Paul. *The Historian and Film.* Cambridge: Cambridge University Press, 1976.

Trevelyan, John. *What the Censor Saw.* London: Michael Joseph, 1973.

White, David Manning and Averson, R. *The Celluloid Weapon.* Boston: Beacon Press, 1972.

Film studies

Aldgate, Anthony. *Cinema and History: British Newsreels and the Spanish Civil War.* London: Scholar Press, 1979.

Balio, Tino. *United Artists.* Madison: University of Wisconsin Press, 1974.

Brown, Geoff. *Launder and Gilliat.* London: British Film Institute, 1977.

—— ed. *Walter Forde.* London: British Film Institute, 1977.

—— and Aldgate, Tony. *The Common Touch: The Films of John Baxter.* London: National Film Theatre, 1989.

Butler, Ivan. *Cinema in Britain: An Illustrated Survey.* London: A. S. Barnes, 1973.

Costello, Donald P. *The Serpent's Eye: Shaw and the Cinema.* London: University of Notre Dame Press, 1965.

Durgnat, Raymond. *The Strange Case of Alfred Hitchcock.* Cambridge, MA: MIT Press, 1974.

Gough-Yates, Kevin. *Michael Powell.* London: British Film Institute, 1971.

Landy, Marcia. *British Genres: Cinema and Society, 1930–1960.* Princeton, NJ: Princeton University Press, 1991.

MacPherson, Don. *Traditions of Independence.* London: British Film Institute, 1980.

Manvell, Roger. *The Film and the Public.* Harmondsworth: Penguin Books, 1955.

—— and Baxter, R. K. N. *The Cinema,* 1952. Harmondsworth: Penguin Books, 1952.

Minney, R. J. *The Films of Anthony Asquith.* New York: A. S. Barnes, 1976.

Petley, Julian. *Capital and Culture: German Cinema, 1933–45.* London: British Film Institute, 1979.

Richards, Jeffrey. *Swordsmen of the Screen.* London: Routledge and Kegan Paul, 1977.

—— *Visions of Yesterday.* London: Routledge and Kegan Paul, 1973.

Rohmer, Eric and Chabrol, Claude. *Hitchcock: The First Forty-four Films.* New York: Frederick Ungar, 1979.

Rollins, Cyril B. and Wareing, Robert Jo *Victor Saville.* London: British Film Institute, 1972.

Spoto, Donald. *The Art of Alfred Hitchcock.* New York: Hopkinson and Blake, 1976.

Stead, Peter. *Film and the Working Class.* London: Routledge, 1989.

Truffaut, François. *Hitchcock.* New York: Simon and Schuster, 1966.

Vermilye, Jerry. *The Great British Films.* Secaucus, NJ: Citadel Press, 1978.

Yacowar, Maurice. *Hitchcock's British Films.* Hamden, CT: Archon Books, 1977.

REFERENCES

General film history and the history of the British film.

Armes, Roy. *A Critical History of British Cinema*. London: Secker and Warburg, 1978.

Barnes, John. *The Beginnings of the Cinema in England*. New York: Barnes and Noble, 1976.

Betts, Ernest. *The Film Business*. New York: Pitman, 1973.

Cowie, Peter. *A Concise History of the Cinema, Volume I: Before 1940*. New York: A. S. Barnes, 1971.

Dickinson, Thorold. *A Discovery of Cinema*. London: Oxford University Press, 1973.

Durgnat, Raymond. *A Mirror for England: British Movies from Austerity to Affluence*. New York: Praeger Books, 1971.

Eyles, Allen and Meeker, David, eds. *Missing Believed Lost: The Great British Film Search*. London: British Film Institute, 1992.

Knight, Arthur. *The Liveliest Art: A Panoramic History of the Movies*. New York: Mentor Books, 1979.

Low, Rachel. *The History of the British Film, 1918–1929*. London: Allen and Unwin, 1971. [The previous three volumes of this multi-volume history deal with the periods 1896–1906 (written with Roger Manvell), 1906–1914, and 1914–1918.]

—— *The History of the British Film, 1929–1939: Documentary and Educational Films of the 1930s*. London: Allen and Unwin, 1979.

—— *The History of the British Film, 1929–1939: Films of Comment and Persuasion of the 1930s*. London: Allen and Unwin, 1979.

—— *The History of the British Film, 1929–1939: Film Making in 1930s Britain*. London: George Allen and Unwin, 1985.

Mast, Gerald. *A Short History of the Movies*. Indianapolis, IN: Bobbs–Merrill, 1976.

Oakley, Charles. *Where We Came In*. London: George Allen and Unwin, 1974.

Perry, George. *The Great British Picture Show: From the 90s to the 70s*. New York: Hill and Wang, 1974.

Rhode, Erik. *A History of the Cinema*. New York: Hill and Wang, 1976.

Richards, Jeffrey. *The Age of the Dream Palace: Cinema and Society in Britain 1930–1939*. London: Routledge and Kegan Paul, 1984.

Robinson, David. *The History of World Cinema*. New York: Stein and Day, 1973.

Short, K.R.M., ed. *Feature Films as History*. London: Croom Helm, 1981.

Sussex, Elizabeth. *The Rise of the British Documentary Movement*. Berkeley: University of California Press, 1971.

Wood, Leslie. *The Miracle of the Movies*. London: Burke Publishing, 1947.

Wright, Basil. *The Long View*. New York: Alfred A. Knopf, 1974.

Reference works

Enser, A. G. S. *Filmed Books and Plays*. London: Andre Deutsch, 1971.

Gifford, Denis. *British Cinema*. New York: A. S. Barnes, 1970.

—— *The British Film Catalogue, 1859–1970*. London: David and Charles, 1973.

McCarty, Clifford. *Published Screenplays*. Kent, OH: Kent State University Press, 1976.

Miscellaneous

General

Bedarida, F. *A Social History of England, 1851–1975*. London: Methuen, 1976.

Branson, N. and Heinemann, M. *Britain in the 1930s*. New York: Praeger, 1971.

REFERENCES

Harris, John S. *Government Patronage of the Arts in Great Britain*. Chicago, IL: University of Chicago Press, 1970.

Houri, Peter. *Working the Halls*. London: Sussex House, 1973.

Mills, Gordon. *Hamlet's Castle: The Study of Literature as Social Experience*. Austin: University of Texas Press, 1976.

Minihan, Janet. *The Nationalization of Culture: The Development of State Subsidies to the Arts in Great Britain*. New York: New York University Press, 1977.

Pearsall, Ronald. *Popular Music of the Twenties*. Totowa, NJ: Rowman and Littlefield, 1976.

Peterson, Theodore; Jensen, Jay and Rivers, William. *The Mass Media and Modern Society*. New York: Holt, Rinehart, and Winston, 1969.

Roebuck, Janet. *The Making of Modern English Society from 1850*. New York: Charles Scribner's Sons, 1973.

Skelton, Robin, ed. *Poetry of the Thirties*. Harmondsworth: Penguin Books, 1971.

Discography

"Bands on Film: Harry Roy and His Famous Band in *Everything is Rhythm*." World Records, SH 197.

"Cicely Courtneidge and Jack Hulbert." World Records, SH 113.

"Focus on: Gracie Fields." Decca, FOS 27/8.

"George Formby: The Man With the Ukulele," World Records, SH 126.

"George Formby: Music for Pleasure." MFP 50335.

"Gracie Fields: Stage and Screen" World Records, SH 170.

"Jack Buchanan." World Records, SH 283.

"Jessie Matthews: Over My Shoulder." Decca Eclipse, ECM 2168.

"London Screenscene: Jack Buchanan and Jessie Matthews – the Thirties." Decca – Ace of Clubs, ACL 1140.

"Movie Star Memories." World Records, SH 217.

"Presenting George Formby and His Ukulele." World Records, SH 151.

"We'll Smile Again: Flanagan and Allen." Ace of Clubs Treasury Series, ACC 1196.

INDEX

266

www.ingramcontent.com/pod-product-compliance
Ingram Content Group UK Ltd.
Pitfield, Milton Keynes, MK11 3LW, UK
UKHW020859280225
455677UK00006B/98